Chad Carter

Microsoft® XNA™

UNLEASHED

Graphics and Game
Programming for
Xbox 360 and Windows

 SAMS | 800 East 96th Street, Indianapolis, Indiana 46240 USA

Microsoft® XNA™ Unleashed: Graphics and Game Programming for Xbox 360 and Windows

ISBN-13: 978-0-672-32964-7

ISBN-10: 0-672-32964-6

Library of Congress Cataloging-in-Publication Data

Carter, Chad.
  Microsoft XNA unleashed : graphics and game programming for Xbox 360 and Windows / Chad Carter. — 1st ed.
    p. cm.
  ISBN 0-672-32964-6
  1. Microsoft XNA (Computer file) 2. Computer games—Programming. 3. Video games. I. Title.
  QA76.76.C672C383 2007
  794.8'1526—dc22

                          2007025607

Printed in the United States of America
First Printing July 2007
10 09 08 07   8 7 6 5 4 3 2

Trademarks

Warning and Disclaimer

Bulk Sales

Pearson offers excellent discounts on this book when ordered in quantity for bulk purchases or special sales. For more information, please contact:

U.S. Corporate and Government Sales
1-800-382-3419
corpsales@pearsontechgroup.com

For sales outside of the U.S., please contact:

International Sales
international@pearsontechgroup.com

Editor-in-Chief
Karen Gettman

Acquisitions Editor
Neil Rowe

Development Editor
Mark Renfrow

Managing Editor
Gina Kanouse

Project Editor
Andy Beaster

Copy Editor
Teresa Horton

Indexer
Erika Millen

Proofreader
Eileen Clark

Technical Editor
Shawn Hargreaves

Team Coordinator
Cindy Teeters

Media Developer
Dan Scherf

Book Designer
Gary Adair

Composition
Fastpages

The Safari® Enabled icon on the cover of your favorite technology book means the book is available through Safari Bookshelf. When you buy this book, you get free access to the online edition for 45 days. Safari Bookshelf is an electronic reference library that lets you easily search thousands of technical books, find code samples, download chapters, and access technical information whenever and wherever you need it.

To gain 45-day Safari Enabled access to this book:

- ▶ Go to http://www.samspublishing.com/safarienabled
- ▶ Complete the brief registration form
- ▶ Enter the coupon code **NIMD-6KVM-A2QA-4GMI-2Z7B**

If you have difficulty registering on Safari Bookshelf or accessing the online edition, please e-mail customer-service@safaribooksonline.com.

Contents at a Glance

Table of Contents

Foreword

It's hard to believe that it's been so long since the first version of Managed DirectX was released in 2002. I sit in wonderment at how far we've come in such a short period of time. It wasn't all that long ago when I was just some guy with a crazy idea that games could (and should!) be written in managed code. We released a preview of what would become known as "Managed DirectX" at the Game Developers Conference, and from that point on it's been a non-stop thrill ride. People were excited, and everyone wanted to know if you could get the same kinds of benefits you get from managed code writing games as you do in Windows programming. People were worried about the performance aspects, many people simply didn't believe. As time went on, though, more and more people started to realize the truth. There were a great number of benefits from using managed code, and the performance concerns were overblown.

Everyone began to notice, and soon I was leaving the DirectX team I had been with for so long and moving to a new team that was developing something vaguely called "XNA." Since you have this book, I assume you know what that turned out to be (and if not, keep reading, you will soon enough)! The team had a vision of game development that could change the world. Everything I had hoped to achieve when I started out on this journey so many years ago was achieved and then some. We worked long, hard hours, but we got a release out for people to play with and we did it in record time. Now not only could you develop games that you played on your computer, you could also develop games you could play on your Xbox 360. Nothing like this had ever been done before and I felt honored to be a part of it.

Now, as then, I'm excited for the future of game development. When I see an author write a book like this, I get even more excited, and I hope you do as well. Whether you've never tried to write a game before, or you are simply looking for the "XNA way" of doing things, you'll be pleased with what you find.

For me, I'm anxiously awaiting what the community can develop. I look forward to playing the next generation of amazing games. I get excited as I think of games that break the mold from all the same genres we see today, and do something completely original. I hope you will be the person writing them!

—Tom Miller, Developer
XNA Game Studio Express, Microsoft Corporation

About the Author

Chad Carter is the CTO at Robertson Marketing Group (RMG). RMG services many Fortune 500 companies that utilize the e-commerce system he architected and developed from the ground up for the promotional business sector. He has been creating DirectX applications since 1996 and has developed games using Managed DirectX. Chad created a 3D locomotive simulator for Norfolk Southern that is used to teach children to obey railroad crossing signals. Chad's Web site devoted to the XNA Framework can be found online at www.xnaessentials.com.

Dedication

*To the most beautiful woman in the world, my wife Christy,
and my precious daughter, Caleigh.*

Acknowledgments

There are a host of people responsible for making this book a reality. For starters, my wife was extremely supportive of me writing this book. There were many long hours, late nights, and missing weekends involved in this project and she handled all of the normal duties I typically attend to. There is absolutely no way this book could have been completed if it were not for her support! Christy, I love you. Thank you! I'd also like to thank Caleigh for being patient with her daddy when he had to stop playing and "work on the book."

Next, I want to give praise to my Lord, God Almighty, who sustained me during these past few months to actually complete this book. I also need to thank the prayer partners and the Joshua's Men group for their prayers for me as I took on this task.

Brian Wilson, a coworker and a friend, deserves a big thank you for helping me keep to the goals I set. Those Thursday meetings really motivated and inspired me! I look forward to reading your book, Brian!

Next, I'd like to thank Neil Rowe, the acquisitions editor at Sams Publishing. He agreed to work with me on this project and was my main point of contact at Sams. Although the original deadline was not met (partially due to the refresh version of the XNA Framework being released), there was never any major pressure from Neil. I'd like to also thank the rest of the Sams team that I had direct contact with on this project including Mark Renfrow, Cindy Teeters, Teresa Horton, Andrew Beaster, and Mary Sudul. I'd also like to thank the rest of the Sams team that I did not have any communication with but were behind the scenes making this book a reality. I'm looking forward to seeing those names on the first page of this book.

A big thank you goes out to Shawn Hargreaves, an XNA Framework developer at Microsoft, who was the technical editor of this book. The book is definitely better because of his expertise! His blog can be found at http://blogs.msdn.com/shawnhar/. Even before he was the technical editor of this book, his blog and his forum answers helped me tremendously in learning this technology. I'm very thankful that Shawn was the technical editor of this book.

I'd like to thank all of the XNA Framework developers and Microsoft in general for making this great technology!

I'd like to thank the XNA community in general for all of the excellent tutorials and sample code that were produced in such a short amount of time. With a community like this, we really could be on the verge of YouTube for games!

I'd also like to thank my parents, John and Sandra Carter, for providing me with a good education and instilling a good work ethic in me. Their support means the world to me. I'd also like to thank my wife's mom and dad, Wilson and Vicki Newsome, for helping our family with many of the duties that I normally handle, but abandoned to write this book.

My brother, Joshua Carter, recently joined the Army and is in boot camp as I write this. Having a brother serve our country brings me great joy and a tremendous amount of pride. Thank you and all of our troops for helping keep this country free.

Finally, I'd like to thank you for picking up this book. I hope that it serves it purpose and brings insight into some of the mysteries of writing games. This book does no good if it is not read, so thank you and happy programming!

We Want to Hear From You!

As the reader of this book, you are our most important critic and commentator. We value your opinion and want to know what we're doing right, what we could do better, what areas you'd like to see us publish in, and any other words of wisdom you're willing to pass our way.

As a senior acquisitions editor for Sams, I welcome your comments. You can fax, email, or write me directly to let me know what you did or didn't like about this book[md]as well as what we can do to make our books stronger.

Please note that I cannot help you with technical problems related to the topic of this book, and that due to the high volume of mail I receive, I might not be able to reply to every message.

When you write, please be sure to include this book's title and author as well as your name and phone or fax number. I will carefully review your comments and share them with the author and editors who worked on the book.

Email: feedback@samspublishing.com

Fax: 317-428-3310

Mail: Neil Rowe, Senior Acquisitions Editor
            Sams Publishing
            800 East 96th Street
            Indianapolis, IN 46240 USA

Introduction

Many developers became interested in programming because they saw a video game and thought, "How did they do that?" This book helps demystify what is required to make video games. Being able to write games on a next-generation console like the Xbox 360 has never been an option for the masses before. Now with the XNA Framework, games can be written for the console.

By the end of the book, readers will have created two complete games and many demos along the way. This book takes a serious look at performance-related issues when writing games using XNA for Windows and the Xbox 360. It devotes two chapters to the High Level Shader Language (HLSL), which is a necessity for writing great games. It covers physics and artificial intelligence (AI). It also covers special effects, including explosions, transitions, and how to create a 3D particle system. It also demonstrates how to create a sound project using the Microsoft Cross-Platform Audio Tool (XACT) and how to integrate the sound into the game. Saving and loading a high score list and creating full menu system are also taught in this book. In general, this book contains a great foundation for many topics that need to be learned to create a full game.

Who Should Read This Book?

This book was written for developers. The reader should have a good understanding of programming in general. The book uses C#, but if the reader knows any modern language like C++, Java, or VB.NET he or she will have no problem understanding the code in this book. The book assumes some understanding of the Microsoft .NET Framework, as that is what the XNA Framework runs on. Without prior experience writing code using the .NET Framework, the reader might have to do a little research now and then, but should not have trouble reading this book.

This book was written with a few different audiences in mind. Business application developers who want to use their programming skill set to write computer games are one audience. Graphics and game developers who have been around the OpenGL and DirectX block should also find useful information in this book—especially in seeing how things are done "the XNA way." The book also targets readers who have some programming experience but have not done anything formal. The book teaches by example. It is written in such a way that if readers are not in front of their computers, they can still get valuable information from the book because the code is listed in the book as it is being discussed.

Hardware and Software Requirements

The code in this book is compiled against the XNA Framework 1.0 Refresh. In order to complete the games and demos in this book the requirements that follow must be met.

Supported Operating Systems

The following operating systems are supported:

- Windows XP Home Edition
- Windows XP Professional Edition
- Windows XP Media Center Edition
- Windows XP Tablet Edition
- Windows Vista Home Basic Edition
- Windows Vista Home Premium Edition
- Windows Vista Business Edition
- Windows Vista Enterprise Edition
- Windows Vista Ultimate Edition

Windows XP requires Service Pack 2 or later.

Hardware Requirements

When running XNA Framework games on Windows, a graphics card that supports Shader Model 1.1 is required. This book has samples that use Shader Model 2.0 and a couple that use Shader Model 3.0. To get the most from this book, a graphics card that supports Shader Model 3.0 is required. The graphics card should have the most up-to-date drivers. Updated drivers can be found on the graphics card's hardware vendor Web sites.

When running XNA Framework games on the Xbox 360 console, a hard drive must be connected to the console.

Software Requirements

All of the software required to utilize the XNA Framework on Windows is free:

Microsoft Visual C# 2005 Express Edition

Microsoft XNA Game Studio Express

DirectX 9.0c

Instructions on installing the software can be found in Chapter 1, "Introducing the XNA Framework and XNA Game Studio Express."

Code Examples

The source code for examples in this book can be found on the accompanying CD. Any updates to the code can be downloaded via www.samspublishing.com or www.xnaessentials.com/unleashed.

PART I

Get Up and Running with XNA on Your PC and Xbox 360

IN THIS PART

Introducing the XNA Framework and XNA Game Studio Express

Most developers I know decided to enter the computer field and specifically programming because of computer games. Game development can be one of the most challenging disciplines of software engineering—it can also be the most rewarding!

Never before has it been possible for the masses to create games for a game console, much less a next generation game console. We are coming in on the ground floor of a technology that is going to experience tremendous growth. Microsoft is leading the way into how content will be created for game consoles. Soon other game console manufacturers will be jumping at a way to allow the public to create content for their machines. The great news for the Xbox 360 is that Microsoft has spent so much time over the years creating productive and stable development environments for programmers. We will be installing one of Microsoft's latest integrated development environments (IDEs) in this chapter. Before we get to that, let's take a look at the technology we discuss in this book—XNA.

What Is the XNA Framework?

You have probably heard the statement, "To know where you are going, you need to know where you have been." I am uncertain if that is entirely true, but I do believe it applies here. Before we dig into exactly what XNA is and what it can do for us, let's take a moment to look at DirectX because that is what the XNA Framework is built on.

The Foundation of the XNA Framework

Let's take a journey back to the days of DOS on the PC. When programming games, graphic demos, and the like in DOS, programmers typically had to write low-level code to talk directly to the sound card, graphics cards, and input devices. This was tedious and the resulting code was error prone because different manufacturers would handle different BIOS interrupts, IO ports, and memory banks—well, differently, so the code would work on one system and not another.

Later, Microsoft released the Windows 95 operating system. Many game programmers were skeptical at writing games for Windows—and rightly so—because there was no way to get down to hardware level to do things that required a lot of speed. Windows 95 had a protected memory model that kept developers from directly accessing the low-level interrupts of the hardware.

To solve this problem, Microsoft created a technology called DirectX. It was actually called Windows Game SDK to begin with, but quickly switched names after a reporter poked fun at the API names DirectDraw, DirectSound, and DirectPlay, calling the SDK Direct "X." Microsoft ran with the name and DirectX 1.0 was born a few months after Windows 95 was released. I remember working with DirectDraw for a couple of demos back when this technology first came out.

Because of DirectX, developers had a way to write games with one source that would work on all PCs regardless of their hardware. Hardware vendors were eager to work with Microsoft on standardizing an interface to access their hardware. They created device drivers to which DirectX would map its API, so all of the work that previously had to be done by game programmers was taken care of, and programmers could then spend their time doing what they wanted to—write games! Vendors called this a Hardware Abstraction Layer (HAL). They also developed a Hardware Emulation Layer (HEL), which emulates hardware through software in case hardware isn't present. Of course, this is slower but it allowed certain games to be run on machines with no special hardware.

After a couple of years Microsoft released DirectX 3.0, which ran on Windows NT 4 as well as Windows 95. As part of those upgrades, they introduced Direct3D. This allowed developers to create 3D objects inside of 3D worlds. DirectX 4 was never released, but DirectX 5 was released in 1997 and later had some upgrades to work under Windows 98.

When DirectX 8 came on the scene in 2000, some of the newly available graphics hardware had vertex and pixel shaders. As a result, Microsoft added in a way to pass custom program code to the hardware. Through assembly code, the game developer could manipulate the data the main game passed to the graphics card. This assembly code was consumed directly by the graphics hardware.

When there was no graphics hardware, games were slow, but they were very flexible. Later, as hardware rendering became prominent, the games were faster, but they were not very flexible in that all of the games really started to look the same. Now with shaders, the speed of the hardware is combined with the flexibility for each game to render and light its 3D content differently.

This brings us to present-day DirectX: We are up to DirectX 9 and 10. Before I talk about DirectX 9, I spend some time talking about DirectX 10. DirectX 10 was released at the same time as Microsoft Windows Vista. In fact, DirectX 10 only works on Vista. This is largely due to the fact that Microsoft has made major changes in the driver model for this operating system. DirectX 10 also requires Shader Model 4.0 hardware.

The Xbox 360 runs on DirectX 9 plus some additional partial support for Shader Model 3.0 functionality. DirectX 9 is the foundation for Managed DirectX, an API that exposed the core DirectX functionality to .NET Framework developers. There was a lot of concern about whether this "wrapper" could be as fast as the C++ counterparts. Fortunately, it was almost as fast—about 98 percent was the benchmark touted. I experienced these benchmark speeds firsthand while on the beta team for this technology. I fell in love with Managed DirectX.

The XNA Framework used the lessons learned from Managed DirectX and used that foundation as a launching pad. To be clear, XNA was built from the ground up and was not built on top of Managed DirectX. It didn't use the same namespaces as Managed DirectX and is not simply pointing to the Managed DirectX methods in the background. Although XNA utilizes DirectX 9 in the background, there are no references to DirectX's API like there were in Managed DirectX.

XNA Today

XNA is actually a generic term much like the term .NET. XNA really refers to anything that Microsoft produces that relates to game developers. The XNA Framework is the API we are discussing. The final piece to XNA is the XNA Game Studio Express application, which we discuss in detail later. This is the IDE we use to develop our XNA games.

> **TIP**
>
> In this book, whenever we use the term XNA, we are really referring to the XNA Framework unless otherwise noted.

XNA allows us to do a lot of things. We have easy access to the input devices (keyboard, game pad or controller, mouse). XNA gives us easy access to the graphics hardware. We are able to easily control audio through XNA. XNA provides the ability for us to store information like high scores and even saved games. XNA does not currently have any networking capability. Microsoft wants to use the Xbox Live technology for adding network support to XNA. However, there is more work to be done to make sure Microsoft can provide multiplayer functionality in a secure manner.

To get started using XNA we have to install some software. We need to install the latest version of DirectX 9 as well as have a graphics card that supports DirectX 9.0c and Shader Model 1.1. (You should get a card that supports Shader Model 2.0 as some of the examples, including the starter kit we use in this chapter and the next one, will not run without it.) We also need to install Visual C# Express, the DirectX 9 runtime, and finally XNA Game Studio Express. Fortunately, all of the software is free! If you don't have graphics hardware that can support Shader Model 2.0 you can pick up a card relatively inexpensively for about $35 USD. If possible, you should purchase a graphics card that can support Shader Model 3.0, as a couple of examples at the end of the book require it.

At this point, games cannot be created for commercial use on the Xbox 360 but Microsoft has mentioned they are interested in supporting commercial games in future versions. Fortunately, we can create community games for the Xbox 360 with the Express versions.

XNA Game Studio Express is great for the game hobbyist, a student, or someone just getting started because you do not have to shell out a lot of (any!) money to get up and running. One exception to this is if you actually want to deploy your games on your Xbox 360. To do that, you will need to subscribe to the XNA Creators Club for $99 USD a year (or $49 USD for four months). Remember, writing games for the PC using XNA is totally free!

Oh, in case you are wondering what XNA stands for, XNA's **N**ot **A**cronymed (or so Microsoft says in the XNA FAQ).

Installing Visual C# Express

To get started, we must have the software installed. Let's start by installing Visual C# Express. Visual C# Express is the IDE that is required to run XNA Game Studio Express. XNA requires C# due to how the Content Pipeline is used. There are some people who have successfully created demos using other languages such as VB.NET and even F#. However, this is not supported by Microsoft currently and won't be discussed in this book. This book assumes you have a good understanding of C#. If you know C++, Java, or VB.NET, you should be able to pick up C# pretty quickly.

I am going to be detailed in the steps to make sure that anyone who has not worked with Visual C# Express will be able to get it installed with no issues. Feel free to skip this section if you already have Visual C# Express installed.

To install Visual C# Express, follow these steps:

1. You will need to be connected to the Internet to install the application. The application can be downloaded by browsing to http://msdn.microsoft.com/vstudio/express/downloads/ and clicking the Visual C# Express Go button to download the vcssetup.exe setup program.

2. Optional. On the Welcome to Setup screen select the check box to send data about your setup experience to Microsoft. This way if something goes awry, Microsoft can get the data and try to make the experience better the next time around. This screen is shown in Figure 1.1.

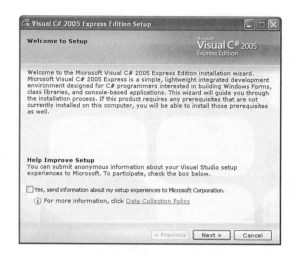

FIGURE 1.1   Select the check box if you want the system to provide feedback to Microsoft about your installation experience.

3. Click Next to continue.

4. The next screen is the End-User License Agreement. If you accept the terms, select the check box and click Next.

5. The following screen, shown in Figure 1.2, has two installation options you can check. Neither of these options is required to utilize XNA.

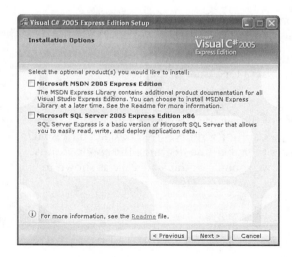

FIGURE 1.2   Neither of these options is required to utilize XNA.

6. Click Next to continue.

7. The next screen, shown in Figure 1.3, asks where we would like to install Visual C#
   Express. It is going to install other required applications including Microsoft .NET
   Framework 2.0. This is required, as C# runs on the .NET Framework. You will also
   notice it requires more than 300MB of space.

8. Click Next to continue.

FIGURE 1.3   Specify which directory you want Visual C# Express to be installed in.

9. Now we are looking at the Installation Progress screen where we will be able to
   monitor the progress of the installation.

10. Finally, on the Setup Complete screen we can see the Windows Update link we can
    click on to get any of the latest service packs for Visual C# Express.

11. Click Exit to complete the installation.

We have successfully installed the first piece of the pie to start creating excellent games
with XNA! Before we continue to the next piece of software, we need to open up Visual
C# Express. It might take a couple of minutes to launch the first time the application is
loaded. Once the Visual C# Express is loaded we should see the Start Page as shown in
Figure 1.4.

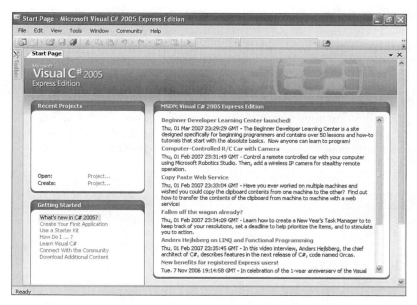

FIGURE 1.4   This is the Start Page inside of Visual C# Express.

The following procedure is optional, but it does ensure that everything is working correctly on our machine.

1. In the Recent Projects section, find Create Project and click the link. You can also create a new project under the File menu.

2. Visual C# Express installed several default templates that we can choose from. Select the Windows Application template as displayed in Figure 1.5.

3. You can leave the name set to WindowsApplication1 as we will just be discarding this project when we are done.

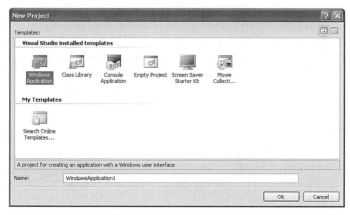

FIGURE 1.5   The New Project dialog box allows you to choose from the default templates to create an application.

   4. Click OK to create the application.

At this point a new project should have been created and we should be looking at a blank Windows Form called Form1.

   5. Press Ctrl+F5 or click Start Without Debugging on the Debug menu.

If everything compiled correctly, the form we just saw in design mode should actually be running. Granted, it doesn't do anything, but it does prove that we can compile and run C# through Visual C# Express. The end result can be seen in Figure 1.6. Let's close down the application we just created as well as Visual C# Express. Feel free to discard the application.

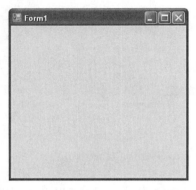

FIGURE 1.6   This is a C# Windows Form application after compiling and running the default template.

Installing the DirectX Runtime

We also need the DirectX 9 runtime if it isn't already on the machine. To get started, follow these steps:

   1. Run the dxwebsetup.exe file from Microsoft's website. This can be found by clicking on the DirectX Runtime Web Installer link at the bottom of the Creator's Club Resources—Essentials web page http://creators.xna.com/Resources/Essentials.aspx. This file contains the redistribution package of the February 2007 DirectX 9. You will need to be connected to the Internet so it can completely install the application.

   2. We are greeted with the End-User License Agreement. Handle with care.

   3. The next screen is a dialog box asking where we would like the installation files to be stored. We can pick any directory we want as long as we remember it so we can actually install the runtime—we are simply extracting the files needed to install the runtime.

   4. Click OK to continue.

5. We will be prompted to create that directory if the directory entered doesn't exist. Click Yes to continue.

6. Wait for the dialog box with the progress bar to finish unpacking the files.

Now we can actually install the runtime by following these steps:

1. Browse to the folder where we installed the files and run the dxsetup.exe file to actually install DirectX 9 onto the machine.

2. The welcome screen we see includes the End-User License Agreement. Select the appropriate radio button to continue.

3. Following the agreement is a screen stating that it will install DirectX—click Next.

4. Once it finishes installing (a progress bar will be visible while it is installing the files) we will be presented with the Installation Complete screen.

5. Simply click Finish to exit the setup.

Now, we can move on to installing XNA Game Studio Express.

Installing XNA Game Studio Express

To use XNA Game Studio Express we must use Visual C# Express. We cannot use Visual Studio .NET Professional nor can we use any other IDE. Although there are people who have successfully been able to run XNA and even get the Content Pipeline (which we talk about in Part III of the book) to work in Visual Studio .NET Professional, it is not officially supported by Microsoft and is not covered in this book.

> **WARNING**
>
> You must run the Visual C# Express IDE at least one time before installing XNA Game Studio Express. If this is not done, not all of the functionality will be installed. If XNA Game Studio Express was installed prematurely, you will need to uninstall XNA Game Studio Express and run Visual C# Express and then exit the IDE. Then you will be able to reinstall XNA Game Studio Express.

To get started complete the following steps:

1. Run the xnagse_setup.msi file from Microsoft's website. The file can be downloaded by clicking on the top link of the Creator's Club Resources—Essentials web site http://creators.xna.com/Resources/Essentials.aspx.

2. Click Next to get past the setup welcome screen.

3. The next screen is the End-User License Agreement. If you accept the terms, select the check box and click Next.

4. This will open up a notification dialog box that explains that the Windows Firewall will have a rule added to it to allow communication between the computer and the Xbox 360. This can be seen in Figure 1.7.

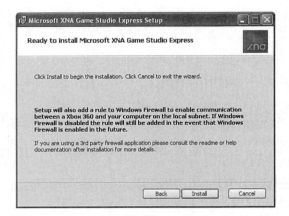

FIGURE 1.7   XNA Game Studio Express modifies the Windows Firewall so an Xbox 360 and the PC can talk to each other.

5. Click Install to continue. The next screen shows the progress of the installation.

6. Once it has completed installing all of the required files we will be presented with the completion dialog box. Simply click Finish to exit the setup.

After we have installed XNA Game Studio Express, we can go to the Start menu and see it added a few more items than those contained in the IDE. Make sure to take time and read through some of the XNA Game Studio Express documentation. There is also a Tools folder that contains a couple of tools we will be looking at later. We will be discussing the XACT tool in Chapter 6, "Loading and Texturing 3D Objects," and the XNA Framework Remote Performance Monitor for Xbox 360 application in Chapter 3, "Performance Considerations." Go ahead and open the IDE by clicking XNA Game Studio Express on the Start menu.

Hmm, this looks identical to the Visual C# Express IDE. There is a good reason for this—it is the same application! When we installed XNA Game Studio Express it added properties to Visual C# Express to allow it to behave differently under certain circumstances. Mainly it added some templates, which we will look at shortly, and it added the ability for Visual C# Express to handle content via the XNA Content Pipeline. It also added a way for us to send data to our Xbox 360, as we will see in the next chapter.

TIP

If you ever uninstall XNA Game Studio Express, you will need to uninstall Visual C# Express first. Otherwise, XNA Game Studio Express will not properly uninstall.

Creating Spacewar Windows Project

With XNA Game Studio Express opened, create a new project and we should see a screen similar to Figure 1.8. Select the Spacewar Windows Starter Kit template and feel free to change the name of the project. Click OK to create the project.

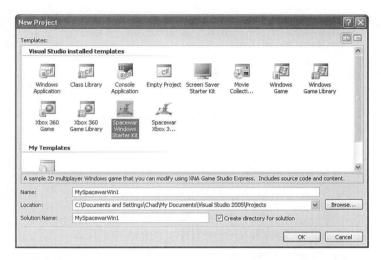

FIGURE 1.8   We can see that installing XNA Game Studio Express added six more templates to Visual C# Express.

Compiling and Running Spacewar

At this point we have our software installed and have even created a starter template that was created by Microsoft that we can take for a spin. We need to make sure we can compile the code. To just compile without running we can press Ctrl+Shift+B or press F6 or click Build Solution on the Build menu. It should have compiled without any issues. You can now press Ctrl+F5 to actually run the game. Have some fun playing the game. Feel free to look around the code and tweak it. Fortunately, you can always re-create the template if something gets really messed up!

Summary

In this chapter we laid the groundwork by getting the all of the software required installed to actually create games on our PC. We even compiled a game and played it. After getting a game session fix, join me in the next chapter where we will get this project up and running on the Xbox 360!

XNA and the Xbox 360

X NA allows us to write games for the Xbox 360, but an Xbox 360 is not required to enjoy XNA. We can write games strictly for the PC. However, if we do want to write games that we can play on our Xbox 360 and share with others to play on their consoles, we need to purchase the XNA Creators Club subscription. Of course, this will also allow us to play other community games (which other developers create) on our Xbox 360 as well.

Creating Spacewar Xbox 360 Project

With XNA Game Studio Express opened, we can follow these steps to create a Spacewar project that can run on the Xbox 360:

1. Create a new project, and we should see a screen similar to Figure 2.1.

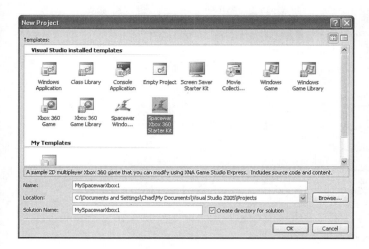

FIGURE 2.1   XNA Game Studio Express provides templates we can use to get up and running quickly.

2. Select the Spacewar Xbox 360 Starter Kit template and change the name of the project if desired.

3. Click OK to create the project.

Buying the XNA Creators Club Subscription

We need an Internet connection because we need to be connected to Xbox Live to deploy our games from our PC to our Xbox 360 console. To purchase the subscription we need to go to the Xbox Live blade in the Xbox 360 dashboard and complete the following steps:

1. Select the Xbox Live Marketplace and then select Games.

2. Go to All Game Downloads and hold down the right trigger to page down to the end of the games.

3. There toward the bottom we see XNA Creators Club. Select this entry as shown in Figure 2.2.

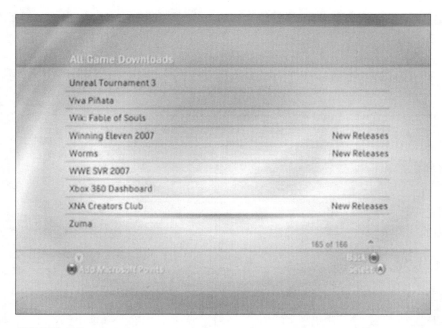

FIGURE 2.2   XNA Creators Club can be purchased through the Xbox Live Marketplace.

CAN'T FIND THE XNA CREATORS CLUB GAME ENTRY?

If you do not see the XNA Creators Club entry it is most likely because of the parental controls that are set up. XNA Creators Club is unrated, which means that we will have to select Allow All Games. Fortunately, we can then change your parental controls to the setting we had before once we have subscribed and downloaded the XNA Game Launcher. Then we will need to enter a valid pass code to actually run the XNA Game Launcher.

2

4. Now select Memberships and pick a plan to purchase.

5. Follow the instructions to enter the appropriate billing information. After entering the billing information, confirm to purchase the plan selected.

6. Under XNA Creators Club, select and download the XNA Game Launcher application.

7. Once the XNA Game Launcher is downloaded, go to Games Blade and click Demos and More as shown in Figure 2.3.

FIGURE 2.3   Demos and More not only allows us to play demos, but it also lets us navigate to the XNA Game Launcher.

8. Select the XNA Game Launcher from the list and finally select Launch to run it.

Connecting the Xbox 360 to the PC

We have the subscription, but we also need to associate the Xbox 360 with the PC. To do this, follow these steps:

1. Go to the XNA Game Launcher's Settings menu and select Generate Connection Key. This will create an encryption key that needs to be entered into XNA Game Studio Express.

2. Choose Accept New Key inside of the XNA Game Launcher.

3. Close the Settings menu and choose Connect to Computer. This screen can be seen in Figure 2.4.

FIGURE 2.4   The XNA Game Launcher allows us to connect to our PC so we can deploy our games.

4. Inside of XNA Game Studio Express, go to Options on the Tools menu. The Options dialog box will open.

5. Select the XNA Game Studio Express Xbox 360 option and click Add.

6. Type the name of the Xbox 360 (this can be anything) and then type the connection key in the spaces provided. An example of this screen is shown in Figure 2.5.

7. Click Test Connection. If everything is successful, XNA Game Studio Express will save the connection key. It is important that the Xbox 360 and the development and deployment PC are on the same subnet. For example, if one is on a wireless router and the other on a wired router, there will be connection issues.

8. Click OK.

9. Click OK to close the Options dialog box.

Now we are ready to deploy to the Xbox 360!

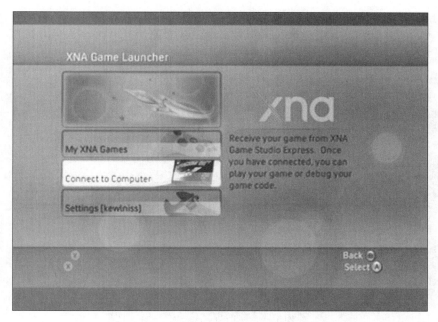

FIGURE 2.5   Associate the Xbox 360 to the PC by entering the connection key generated on the Xbox 360 into XNA Game Studio.

Deploying on the Xbox 360

To deploy on our Xbox 360, we need to perform the following steps:

1. Click Connect to Computer inside of the XNA Game Launcher on the Xbox 360. (If continuing from the previous step then the Xbox 360 is already in this waiting state.)

2. Go back inside of XNA Game Studio Express on the PC and select Deploy Solution from the Debug menu.

3. The Xbox 360 will start receiving the files needed to run the application.

DEPLOYING CONTENT ON THE XBOX 360

Deploying on the Xbox 360 takes a little bit of time, depending on how much content needs to be sent over the wire. The good news is that if content does not change then it does not get sent over again, so we are only waiting on the items we actually changed.

There are a couple of times even after the first deployment that content will be resent to the Xbox 360.

1. While deploying, if an error occurs or if the deployment is stopped for any reason, the next time the project is deployed it will be a complete deployment.

2. If the configuration is different from the last deployment, a complete deployment will occur.

When the files have been fully deployed, the Xbox 360 will revert back to Waiting for computer connection, as seen in Figure 2.6. Also, in XNA Game Studio Express we should see the message Deploy Succeeded in the status bar.

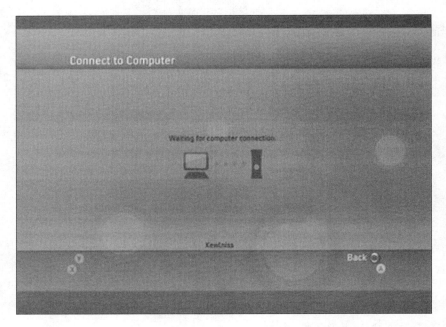

FIGURE 2.6   Before and after deploying a game to the Xbox 360, the XNA Game Launcher shows that it is Waiting for computer connection.

To actually play the game we just deployed on the Xbox 360, simply exit out of the connection screen and then select My XNA Games inside the XNA Game Launcher. We should now see Spacewar as a game that is installed. Select it and then select Play and enjoy the game on the Xbox 360!

STOP THE FIGHTING—QUITTING SPACEWAR

To exit the Spacewar game, go to the main menu by pressing Start and then press the Back button on the game pad.

DISTRIBUTING YOUR GAME

Not only can we deploy our games to our own Xbox 360, we can distribute our game so that others can enjoy our game on their Xbox 360 consoles or their Windows PCs. We can distribute our source code or we can package up our game and content and just distribute the package.

When consumers get the package, they will need an active XNA Creators Club subscription to use the game on their Xbox 360. For Windows, if they do not have XNA

Game Studio Express installed, they will need the XNA Framework as well as certain DirectX 9 files. For more information, please refer to the XNA Game Studio Express documentation. Information can be found in the "Sharing and Distributing Your Game" section under the "Using XNA Game Studio Express" section of the help.

Debugging on the Xbox 360

Without too much pain we were able to get a game running on the Xbox 360. Now comes this question: How hard is it to debug games deployed on the Xbox 360? Well, we will answer that question in this section.

To get started we need to run the XNA Game Launcher and connect to our computer as previously described. Once the console is waiting on a connection, we can press F10 to step into our Spacewar game.

STEPPING THROUGH THE CODE

Make sure you have set the active solution configuration to Debug to step through the code on your Xbox 360.

Follow these steps for this exercise:

1. Open the SpacewarGame.cs file.

2. Put a breakpoint in the first line of code under the constructor.

3. Press F5 to run the application in debug mode.

Visual C# Express will do as expected and stop the code at the appropriate line. We can see that the console has a black screen because it hasn't been told to draw anything yet, as we are holding up the process with our breakpoint. Press F5 to let the game run. When finished with the game, we can close out the Spacewar template.

Creating a Test Demo for the Xbox 360

We are going to create a simple application we can deploy and then debug on the Xbox 360. To get started we need to create another project, but this time we will use the Xbox 360 Game template to start with.

To deploy a game to the Xbox 360, the template created a file called AssemblyInfo.cs. The Windows Game template also creates this file but it holds a little more importance for Xbox 360 games. Once we open this file we can see an attribute called AssemblyTitle. This attribute determines what is displayed under My XNA Games in the XNA Game Launcher on the Xbox 360. Unless overridden by the Windows.Title property through code, this attribute is also used to populate the title of the window in Windows. Overriding Windows.Title has no effect on the Xbox 360.

Not only can we change the title attribute, but we can (and should) also change the description attribute called `AssemblyDescription`. For Windows, this shows up if someone right-clicks the executable and looks at its properties. For the Xbox 360 it shows up in a nice panel carved out just for it inside of the XNA Game Launcher—very cool! There is a 300-character limit on the description. Anything over 300 characters will be truncated and not displayed inside the XNA Game Launcher.

Another thing to note in this code file is the attribute `Guid`. Although the source code comment above this attribute suggests that its only use is for COM, it is actually needed to deploy games to the Xbox 360 as well. Make sure you have a unique globally unique identifier (GUID) for all of the games you create. Fortunately, Visual C# Express does this automatically when it creates the file. As long as our project contains the AssemblyInfo.cs source file we will be able to deploy the application to the Xbox 360.

After changing the assembly title and description we can then press F5 (we need to make sure that the console is waiting for a computer connection) to run the demo on the Xbox 360. On the console we should see a nice blank cornflower blue screen. To exit the demo we only need to press the Back button on the controller. If we did not set the console to be waiting for a computer connection then Visual C# Express will time out trying to deploy the application.

It is easy to just gloss over how simple it was to create a graphics application and deploy it on the Xbox 360. This was not always the case. Just to get this screen up in a Windows environment was challenging in the days before XNA (even with Managed DirectX). We just witnessed how easy it is to get a framework set up, complete with a game loop and that talks to the graphics device.

Our game is now in the XNA Game Launcher's list of games. Simply exit the connection screen and then enter My XNA Games. Now we see a list of the games we have deployed—Spacewar and this demo. In Figure 2.7 we can see that the XNA Game Launcher extracted the title and description from the assembly we deployed.

We talk about Sprite Batches in detail in Part IV of the book where we will discuss 2D in XNA, but to start a debugging exercise we will want to add the following member fields to the top of our class:

```
private SpriteBatch spriteBatch;
private Texture2D spriteTexture;
```

Locate the `LoadGraphicsContent` method and inside of the condition block add the following code:

```
spriteBatch = new SpriteBatch(this.graphics.GraphicsDevice);
spriteTexture = content.Load<Texture2D>("texture");
```

Find an image (.jpg, .bmp, or .tga) and add it into the project. Feel free to use a texture from the Spacewar game folder we created. After the file is added into the project, change the Asset Name in the properties panel to texture. We discuss all of these items in detail in later chapters, so you do not need to worry about any of the details at this point.

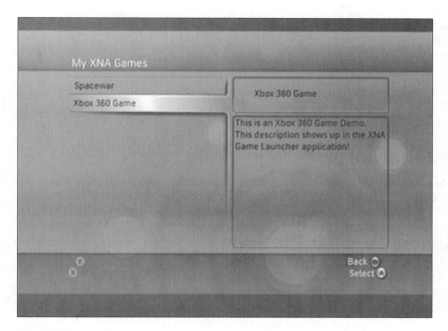

FIGURE 2.7   XNA Game Launcher reads the title and description values entered in the AssemblyInfo.cs file of the XNA applications we deploy.

Finally, add the following code inside of the Draw method under the TODO: Add your drawing code here comment.

```
spriteBatch.Begin();
spriteBatch.Draw(texture, Vector2.Zero, Color.White);
spriteBatch.End();
```

We simply added a texture that will be displayed at the top left corner of our screen. Let's compile and deploy our changes. Once we have completed that task we can put a breakpoint on spriteBatch.Begin() and run the project in debug mode. We need to make sure our Xbox 360 is waiting for a connection before we try to deploy.

When the application is finished deploying we can see the lovely black screen as we haven't let it get into the Draw method. Press F5 to let it process the Draw method once and then take a look at the Xbox 360 screen. We now have our blue screen with the texture we loaded at the top left. We do not need to labor the point of stepping through more code, as we know we will have plenty of opportunity to debug our code as we progress in our game writing journey. We can remove the breakpoint and exit the demo.

The .NET Framework has a System.Diagnostics namespace that is also available on the Xbox 360. This namespace includes a Debug class that includes, among other things, the Write and WriteLine methods. Let's add the following code to the end of the condition inside of the LoadGraphicsContent method:

```
System.Diagnostics.Debug.WriteLine("game content loaded");
```

While we are at it, we should add this line of code inside of the `UnloadGraphicsContent` method:

```
System.Diagnostics.Debug.WriteLine("game content unloaded");
```

That line of code can be put right after the call to unload our content.

We can recompile, deploy, and run the changes on our Xbox 360. We can see inside of the output window of XNA Game Studio the text was printed out! Now we can capture data to our IDE if something is really puzzling us or if we just want to dump data during the game play—a manual log of sorts.

We can set breaks inside of our code and step through pieces of code even while it is running on the console. We can also write information to our output window inside of the IDE while the game is running on the Xbox 360. Wow!

Programming for Dual Platforms

There is something else we need to discuss as we continue our adventure of writing games for the Xbox 360. We need to share as much code as possible for our Xbox 360 game as well as our Windows PC game. Although it is perfectly acceptable to exclusively build applications for one platform or the other, with the XNA Framework it is not that much of a technical jump to use the same code base on both platforms.

With that being said, there are valid reasons why certain developers only target one system or the other. Some developers do not own an Xbox 360 and that is a pretty good reason not to write games for it—it is difficult to debug on a platform without access to it. Some developers require additional components to be present with their game that cannot be installed on the Xbox 360. Some want network support and will roll their own because there is no support for Xbox Live through XNA yet. Some only want to fine tune their game for the Xbox 360 hardware and not worry about the different graphic cards and other PC configurations that their games would need to support.

The goal of this section is to allow us to write one code base that we can easily maintain to work on both platforms. We could start the process by creating a Windows project and then creating an Xbox 360 project that shares the same files. Instead, we will start with the Xbox 360 demo we just created and add a Windows project to the solution. We cannot support both platforms inside of one project but we can support both platforms inside of one solution. We could also create two different solutions and just link the files from one solution to the other—this is what Microsoft currently suggests. However, in this book we will have one solution with two projects that share the same source code location. The idea here is that we can quickly compile our changes in both solutions at the same time. We do this because we want to make sure that we have not added calls to methods that do not exist in the platform we were not actively coding for. We discuss this in more detail in the next section.

Follow these steps to create our Windows Game project inside of our current solution that already contains our Xbox Game project:

1. Right-click the Solution and select Add and New Project from the context menu.
2. Select the Windows Game template and click OK. This will create a subfolder inside the solution with the name of the new project.

3. Close Visual C# Express.

4. Through the file system, move the WindowsGame1.csproj file from the subfolder into the Xbox360Game1 subfolder. Do not move it to the parent folder where the solution file is located.

5. Edit the Xbox360Game1.sln solution file in the parent folder. This can be done through Notepad or another text editor.

6. Find the line toward the top of the file that references the project you just created. Change the line of text so it will reference the new location of the project you just moved. For example, change

```
Project("{FAEA4EC0-301F-11D3-BF4B-00C34F79EFBC}") = "WindowsGame1", "
➥ WindowsGame1\WindowsGame1.csproj", "{F6F0F4BF-D9C6-46DA-8160-C7D5CB702FAE}"
```

to

```
Project("{FAEA4EC0-301F-11D3-BF4B-00C34F79EFBC}") = "WindowsGame1",
➥ "Xbox360Game1\WindowsGame1.csproj", "{F6F0F4BF-D9C6-46DA-8160-C7D5CB702FAE}"
```

7. Save the solution file.

8. Move any Windows-specific files created to the same folder where the project file resides. In this case, we need to move the Game.ico file.

9. Delete the WindowsGame1 subfolder.

10. Open the solution file.

We can see that the solution platforms drop-down list box (located in the Visual C# Express toolbar) now has Mixed Platforms as its selection. This allows us to quickly build, deploy, and run our projects at one time, or we can choose to only work on one platform at a time. Let's set the Windows project as our starting project. This can be done by right-clicking the WindowsGame1 project and selecting Set as StartUp Project. Let's change the solution platform to x86. Currently, XNA does not support 64-bit systems. To make sure we have everything set up properly, we need to run the application. We can do this by pressing F5.

TWO HEADS ARE BETTER THAN ONE: IS THE SAME TRUE ABOUT SOLUTION FILES?

An alternative to having two projects in one solution is creating two individual solutions and linking the files. This is what Microsoft suggests. It is really just a personal preference. The upside to two solutions is that no outside editing in a text editor is required for the solution file. The downside to two solutions is that we would need our machine to use resources to have two Visual C# Express applications loaded for each solution if we wanted to check if changes affected either of the solutions. Regardless if we use one solution or two, when we add files to one project we need to get the other project to recognize them. If we are using two solutions we can add a link to the file as shown in Figure 2.8. If we are using one solution with two projects we can display all files and then right-click and include the file that was recently added in the other project. We could also drag the files from one project to the other inside of the Solution Explorer.

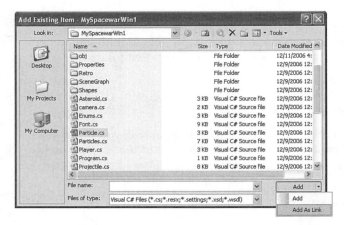

FIGURE 2.8   To add a linked file into a solution we click on the small down arrow beside the Add button in the Add Existing Item dialog box and then click Add As Link.

Visual C# Express compiled and ran the Windows version of the demo and did not bother compiling the Xbox 360 version, which is what we were expecting. Expand the references tree node for both projects. We can see the two XNA references the templates provided us when we set up the projects. If we look at the paths in the properties panel we will see that they are located in two different places. Appropriately, the Windows reference points to \Windows\x86\ and the console reference points to \Xbox360\. This is the reason we need to have two separate projects.

The solution platform drop-down list box tells the Visual C# Express which platforms to compile (and deploy). The project setting Set as StartUp Project tells the IDE which project to run. We cannot run both the executable for Windows and the Xbox 360 at the same time. This really would not be beneficial to us anyway because we could not tell the IDE which application we wanted to break into when debugging. If for some reason we did want to do this then we should go with the two solutions and linked files approach. See the sidebar earlier in this chapter, "Two Heads Are Better Than One: Is the Same True About Solution Files?"

Because the two projects have different references of the XNA Framework we will run into the issue of having functionality in one system and not the other. An example of this is that the Xbox 360 does not have any support for the mouse. Fortunately, we do not have to create and maintain two separate code files for situations like this. Instead we can use a preprocessor directive to tell the compiler to ignore parts of our code if it is compiling for a certain platform. The following code shows an example of compiling functionality specific to Xbox 360:

```
#if XBOX360
    //do Xbox 360 specific code here
#endif
```

The following code shows an example of compiling a Windows-specific functionality:

```
#if !XBOX360
    //do Windows specific code here
#endif
```

This means we can keep our code in one file and put a conditional preprocessor directive around the code we need to handle differently based on a particular platform. Of course, we can opt to create a totally separate file that would be included in one project but not the other. The key is that we have a choice and it will make sense to do it both ways in a larger project. An example would be a large input handler class that might have its own Mouse source file that would be included in the Windows project and excluded from the Xbox 360 project. The main game loop that checks a particular input value might have the condition in place to ignore the mouse information unless it is being compiled for Windows.

The last thing we need to talk about in this section is the difference between PC monitors and television sets. On PC monitors the developers have confidence that any objects they draw on the screen from the top left corner to the bottom right will be seen by the gamer. When developing for a console like the Xbox 360 developers have to account for the fact that not all TVs are created equal. When drawing to a television screen, we need to be aware of two items in particular: aspect ratio and the title safe area. We talk about the aspect ratio in Chapter 4, "Creating 3D Objects." The title safe area is the area of the screen that the user will definitely be able to see. This is the inner 80 percent or 90 percent area of the TV screen. It is beneficial to put any critical text (like a title), game scores, timers, and the like inside of this title safe area while filling all of the screen with our environment. Following is a method taken directly from the XNA Game Studio Express documentation that allows us to easily calculate the title safe area:

```
private Rectangle GetTitleSafeArea(float percent)
{
    Rectangle retval = new Rectangle(graphics.GraphicsDevice.Viewport.X,
        graphics.GraphicsDevice.Viewport.Y,
        graphics.GraphicsDevice.Viewport.Width,
        graphics.GraphicsDevice.Viewport.Height);
#if XBOX360
    // Find Title Safe area of Xbox 360
    float border = (1 - percent) / 2;
    retval.X = (int)(border * retval.Width);
    retval.Y = (int)(border * retval.Height);
    retval.Width = (int)(percent * retval.Width);
    retval.Height = (int)(percent * retval.Height);
    return retval;
#else
    return retval;
#endif
}
```

We can see in this code we use a conditional compilation directive as mentioned earlier. This code simply takes in a percentage—we could pass in either .8 or .9 to let it calculate the title safe area. It only does the calculation if it is compiling for the Xbox 360, other-wise it simply comes back with normal rectangle area.

We can add this method to our demo we created. We can also add the following private member field:

```
private Rectangle titleSafeArea;
```

We can assign a value to this rectangle by adding the following code to the top of the LoadGraphicsContent method:

```
titleSafeArea = GetTitleSafeArea(.80f);
```

By passing in .80 we are stating we want the inner 80 percent of the screen. Now we can edit our code that draws the texture. We do not need to worry about the details of the graphic portion of this code as we will cover it later, but we do want to replace the spriteBatch.Draw line of code with the following line:

```
spriteBatch.Draw(texture, new Vector2(titleSafeArea.X, titleSafeArea.Y),
➥ Color.White);
```

We told the texture to not render at coordinates 0, 0 (top left of the screen) which is what Vector2.Zero told it to do but instead we used the x and y coordinates from the title safe rectangle we retrieved at the beginning of the program. When we run this on Windows, the x and y coordinates will still be 0, but when we run it on the Xbox 360 we will see that it is offset to make up for televisions that do not display all of the screen. We can see an example of this in Figure 2.9.

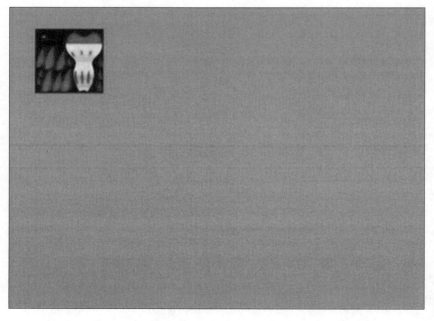

FIGURE 2.9   Displaying a texture in the title safe area of the TV screen.

The .NET Compact Framework on the Xbox 360

We need to discuss another difference between developing for the Xbox 360 and developing for Windows. The difference is the version of the .NET Framework the two platforms are running. Windows runs on the full-blown .NET Framework (2.0 is required for XNA), whereas the Xbox 360 runs on the smaller .NET Compact Framework. The .NET Compact Framework is used in certain Windows CE powered devices such as the Pocket PC, Pocket PC Phone Edition, and Smartphone. As the name implies, it is compact—not only because the devices it typically runs on are compact, but also because the framework itself is a subset of what is available on the desktop. What this means from an Xbox 360 development point of view is that we need to make sure that if we are accessing functionality on the .NET Framework in our code that it also exists in the .NET Compact Framework. Fortunately, the two versions of the XNA Framework each of our projects has a reference to is utilizing the correct .NET Framework, so as long as we keep those references correctly set up, we will get compile errors in our Xbox 360 game if we try to access functionality that is not in the .NET Compact Framework.

The Xbox 360 version of the .NET Compact Framework actually includes items that are not in the other compact devices framework. The console's .NET Compact Framework also includes a few things that the .NET Framework doesn't include. This is mainly due to the type of hardware that is inside of the Xbox 360.

The XNA team at Microsoft worked closely with the Visual Studio team to accomplish the tight integration with Visual C# Express but they also worked very closely with the .NET Compact Framework team to make sure that we could do what we want—make games for the Xbox 360! Without the .NET Compact Framework team, XNA would not work on the Xbox 360.

The .NET Compact Framework team had to add in floating point support as the other hardware the framework previously targeted did not have floating point hardware. They also added support for four of the six hardware threads that map to the Xbox 360's three cores—the other two threads (0 and 2) are reserved. This is something that is not currently available on the desktop, as there are not currently any workstations that have this type of hardware configuration. This book does not cover multithreading but the concepts from typical .NET programming will apply if you choose to tackle that task. In addition, information about the `Thread.SetProcessorAffinity` method will prove to be beneficial.

Summary

This chapter was all about the Xbox 360. We discussed how to buy an XNA Creators Club subscription through Xbox Live. We saw how to download and run the XNA Game Launcher so we could deploy our games on our console.

We created the Spacewar project to run on the Xbox 360. We then deployed and debugged the project on the console. We also created a new Xbox 360 demo starting with the most basic template and discussed important attributes in the AssemblyInfo.cs code file. We saw how to send text to the XNA Game Studio Express output window from inside of the Xbox 360. We also learned about the XBOX360 preprocessor compilation directive and how it can keep the compiler from compiling code for different platforms.

We discussed different ways to set up our projects so we can more easily use the same code base for both our Windows and Xbox 360 projects. Finally, we discussed the .NET Compact Framework that the XNA Framework utilizes on the Xbox 360.

Go play some games and then we can continue our journey into the next chapter, where we discuss ways to make our XNA games perform well in Windows and on the Xbox 360.

CHAPTER 3

Performance Considerations

To be successful at writing games we have to be very aware of the expense of the different tasks we want to perform. Before we write our code we need to have an end goal we are striving to reach. As Stephen Covey stated in his book *The 7 Habits of Highly Effective People,* we need to "Begin with the end in mind." This is crucial for personal growth, but it is also very important when thinking about performance. As software engineers we need to have goals and then continue to measure against those goals as we develop our code. The "end" can change and we need to adjust accordingly.

In this chapter we look at ways to measure how fast our code is running. We discuss key elements to performance tuning when running on the .NET Framework and also on the .NET Compact Framework the Xbox 360 uses.

Measure, Measure, Measure

The title of this section really says it all. In real estate they say what matters is location, location, location. In the performance realm, measuring is what really matters. How else can we know if we are meeting our goals if we do not first take the time to measure along the way?

Before we start writing code we need to take a benchmark measurement. Then we can see as we add functionality whether or not we are adversely affecting our performance goals.

So what is our goal? At the very least our goal should be to have our game run consistently at *n* number of frames per second (fps). Frames per second is the number of times a frame is drawn on the screen per second. The standard for today's games is 60 fps.

A game loop is a loop that updates objects and renders those objects to the screen while processing other elements such as input, sound, artificial intelligence (AI), and physics. Each iteration of the render and draw loop is one frame, so we are stating that our goal is to consistently call the draw loop 60 times each second. XNA provides the game loop for us.

Shortly after Managed DirectX was released, there were several discussions regarding the best method to provide a game loop inside of the Windows environment. Fortunately for us, the XNA team has handled this for us, which most likely came from the discussions started with Managed DirectX. The XNA Framework game loop provides both an `Update` method and a `Draw` method we can override. When we create our game class, we inherit from the `Microsoft.Xna.Framework.Game` class, which provides these and other virtual methods.

The 80–20 Rule

More than 100 years ago, Vilfredo Pareto, an Italian economist, made the statement that 80 percent of Italy's wealth was distributed among only 20 percent of the people. He observed the same thing in other countries' economies as well. This has been called the 80–20 Rule. There have been other variations of this same principle. We have heard things like "20 percent of the people do 80 percent of the work." Successful leaders spend 80 percent of their time cultivating 20 percent of their people. It is hard to know exactly why this principle works, but it does work. The same is true when it comes to performance of our applications: 20 percent of the code will need optimization, as it is the most critical to the overall performance of the application. As 20 percent of our code will do 80 percent of the work, this makes sense.

As we discuss performance measurement in this chapter it is key to keep in mind that we need to be concerned about performance as we write our code, but we should not get bogged down and try to perform micro-optimizations too early. Sir Tony Hoare is famous for the often quoted saying "Premature optimization is the root of all evil." Most of the time when this quote is used, it is suggested that performance measurement is not important. However, it is very important. There is nothing worse than being at the end of a software development cycle and realizing that the application is not performing well.

When we develop any application—even games—we need to make sure we do not fall into the trap of thinking that optimization is the root of all evil. It is not. It is a lot like people quoting the Bible, saying that "money is the root of all evil." Money is not the root of all evil; the *love* of money is the root of all evil. Likewise in software development, it is not optimization that is the root of all evil; rather it is *premature* optimization that is the root of all evil.

So at what point in the development life cycle is it safe to be concerned about performance? There are those at one extreme that say premature is anything before the end of the development cycle. Then there are those that fall into the trap of doing micro-optimizations using micro-benchmark testing (which we discuss at the end of this chapter) before designing their application. Of course, the ideal time to optimize our code is somewhere between these two extremes.

The key to it all really is measurement. We do not know what needs to be optimized unless we measure. There is no reason to try and make a particular method blazing fast if it is only called one time when our application starts. Of course, if our load time is too long, then we would want to take look at what is happening and it might turn out to be that method we were not concerned about to begin with. The point is that we do not assume the method needs optimization until we measure and see it is causing a problem.

As we develop any application we should do performance checks throughout the process just to see how we are doing in relation to our performance goals. If something is taking some time, but we are still within our performance goals, then we can just make a note of it and ignore it for the time being. It might be that there is no need to waste time optimizing that part of the code. If during measuring we do see that we need to make something perform faster, we can make the changes then.

When developing, if we are unsure of what our bottleneck is, we can use profiler tools to help us find the problem areas. I have used the ANTS Profiler from red-gate software (http://www.red-gate.com/products/ants_profiler/index.htm) and have had great success with it. It costs a few hundred dollars, though, and is not in everyone's budget. There is a great open source statistical profiler tool available for windows called NProf, which can be found at http://www.mertner.com/confluence/display/NProf/Home. The tool shows us the amount of time each method in our application took to run, and sums up the total time. So when developing games we need to be aware of times when we are idling in our start menu. There are many resources on the Web that discuss the different tools available and how to use them so we will not dig into it here. The point is that there are tools available for us to find bottlenecks in our code. Using these tools will help us find the 20 percent of our code that needs optimization.

Creating a Benchmark

To get a baseline for our game loop we will start with a new Windows game project. We can call this project PerformanceBenchmark. We will add a frame rate counter and update our window title to show just how many frames per second we are getting "out of the box."

Now we can set the following properties inside of the constructor:

```
//Do not synch our Draw method with the Vertical Retrace of our monitor
graphics.SynchronizeWithVerticalRetrace = false;
//Call our Update method at the default rate of 1/60 of a second.
IsFixedTimeStep = true;
```

The template creates the `GraphicsDeviceManager` for us. We set the `SynchronizeWithVerticalRetrace` property of the manager to false. The default of this property is true. As the name suggests, this property synchronizes the call to the `Draw` method from inside of the XNA Framework's game loop to coincide with the monitor's refresh rate. If the monitor has a refresh rate of 60 Hz, it refreshes every 1/60 seconds or 60 times every second. By default XNA draws to the screen at the same time the monitor refreshes to keep the scene from appearing jerky. This is typically what we want. However,

when measuring the change a piece of code has on our frame rate it is difficult to determine how we are affecting it if we are always drawing 60 fps. We would not know
anything was wrong until we did something that dropped us below that margin keeping
XNA from calling the Draw method fast enough.

We also set the fixed time step property (IsFixedTimeStep) to true. This is the default
value of this property. This property lets XNA know if it should call the Update method
immediately after drawing to the screen (false) or only after a fixed amount of time has
passed (true). This fixed amount of time is 1/60 second and is stored in the property
TargetElapsedTime, which we can change. At this point we do not need the framework
to call Update as often as possible. For this application it does not really matter because
we are not doing anything inside of our Update method.

Let's add the following private member fields to our Game1.cs file:

```
private float fps;
private float updateInterval = 1.0f;
private float timeSinceLastUpdate = 0.0f;
private float framecount = 0;
```

Finally, let's add the frame rate calculation inside of our Draw method.

```
float elapsed = (float)gameTime.ElapsedRealTime.TotalSeconds;
framecount++;
timeSinceLastUpdate += elapsed;
if (timeSinceLastUpdate > updateInterval)
{
    fps = framecount / timeSinceLastUpdate; //mean fps over updateIntrval
    Window.Title = "FPS: " + fps.ToString() + " - RT: " +
        gameTime.ElapsedRealTime.TotalSeconds.ToString() + " - GT: " +
        gameTime.ElapsedGameTime.TotalSeconds.ToString();
    framecount = 0;
    timeSinceLastUpdate -= updateInterval;
}
```

The first thing we are doing with the code is storing the elapsed time since the last time
the Draw method was executed. We then increment our frame count along with the variable that is keeping a running total of the time. We check to see if enough time has passed,
at which point we update our frame rate. We have the updateInterval set at 1 second, but
we can tweak that number if we would like. Once enough time has passed for us to recalculate our frame rate, we do just that by taking the number of frames and dividing it by
the time it took us to get inside of this condition. We then update the title of the window
with our fps. We also write out the ElapsedRealTime along with the ElapsedGameTime. To
calculate our fps we used the real time. Play with the first two properties we set to see the
effect it has on the time. Remember the SynchronizeWithVerticalRetrace property determines how often the Draw method gets called and the IsFixedTimeStep property determines how often the Update method gets called. We can see that the ElapsedRealTime is
associated to the time it took to call our Draw method while the ElapsedGameTime is associated with the time it took to call our Update method.

Finally, we reset our frame count along with the `timeSinceLastUpdate` variable. Let's run the application so we can get our baseline for how our machine is performing.

Now that we have our base number we want to make a note of it. This could be done in an Excel spreadsheet where we can easily track the changes in our performance. We should always try to run our performance tests under the same conditions. Ideally, nothing except the game should be run during all of the benchmark testing.

As an example, let's add the following code inside of the `Draw` method:

```
//bad code that shoud not be replicated
Matrix m = Matrix.Identity;
Vector3 v2;
for (int i = 0; i < 1; i++)
{
    m = Matrix.CreateRotationX(MathHelper.PiOver4);
    m *= Matrix.CreateTranslation(new Vector3(5.0f));

    Vector3 v = m.Translation - Vector3.One;
    v2 = v + Vector3.One;
}
```

It does not do anything other than some 3D math that has absolutely no purpose. The reason we are going through this exercise is to see how our frame rate will drop as we increment the upper limit of our `for` loop. The point is that when we start writing real functionality inside of the `Draw` method we can measure how our frame rate is handling the addition of code. On the included CD, this example is called PerformanceTest1.

Monitoring Performance on the Xbox 360

Measuring performance on the Xbox 360 is relatively easy to do. To begin monitoring how our application is functioning on the Xbox 360 we need to follow these steps:

1. Make sure our Xbox 360 is waiting for a computer connection (and not actually running the game we want to monitor).

2. Open the XNA Framework Remote Performance Monitor for Xbox 360 from the Tools group in the Microsoft XNA Game Studio Express group under All Programs.

3. Select your Xbox 360 console from the Device drop-down list box (it will only show up if step 1 was performed).

4. Tell the tool which game to launch and monitor by entering the name that we stored in the `AssemblyTitle` attribute (discussed in Chapter 2, "XNA and the Xbox 360") into the Application text box. We can enter Spacewar assuming that has been deployed as discussed in Chapter 1, "Introducing the XNA Framework and XNA Game Studio Express."

5. If a game allows any command-line arguments, enter those into the Arguments text box. We can leave it blank for Spacewar.

6. Click Launch so it will start the game on the Xbox 360.

Now that we have the tool running, we can take a moment and look at some of the numbers that are being displayed. Although all are beneficial to watch and we should try to keep the numbers from incrementing too much, the following are some important numbers:

Garbage Collections (GC)

Managed Bytes Allocated

Managed Objects Allocated

Bytes of String Objects Allocated

Managed String Objects Allocated

Objects Not Moved by Compactor

Boxed Value Types

GC Latency Time (ms)

Calls to GC.Collect

A good exercise is to run an empty Xbox 360 game and watch the numbers. Those values will be our baseline. Then as we add functionality we can check the numbers and see if anything is getting out of sorts and act appropriately. Doing this as we go will help us keep our code working in an optimal way and will keep us from having to come back and scour through the code to find out where the bottlenecks are. To determine the amount of time the garbage collector is taking to run, we can take the product of the number of garbage collections that occurred with latency time. This is a key number to be aware of when checking the performance of our garbage collector. We will discuss the garbage collector in detail later in this chapter.

Managing Memory

There are two types of objects in the .NET Framework: reference and value. Examples of value types are enums, integral types (byte, short, int, long), floating types (single, double, float), primitive types (bool, char), and structs. Examples of objects that are reference types are arrays, exceptions, attributes, delegates, and classes. Value types have their data stored on the current thread's stack and the managed heap is where reference types find themselves.

By default, when we pass variables into methods we pass them by value. This means for value types we are actually passing a copy of the data on the stack, so anything we do to that variable inside of the method does not affect the original memory. When we pass in a reference type we are actually passing a copy of the reference to the data. The actual data is not copied, just the address of the memory. Because of this, we should pass large value types by reference instead of by value when appropriate. It is much faster to copy an address of a large value type than its actual data.

We use the ref keyword to pass the objects as reference to our methods. We should not use this keyword on reference types as it will actually slow things down. We should use the keyword on value types (like structs) that have a large amount of data it would need to copy if passed by value.

The other thing to note is that even if we have a reference type and we pass it into a method that takes an object type and we box (implicitly or explicitly), then a copy of the data is actually created as well—not just the address to the original memory. For example, consider a class that takes a general object type (like an ArrayList's Add method). We pass in a reference type, but instead of just the reference being passed across, a copy of the data is created and then a reference to that copy of the data is passed across. This eats up memory and causes the garbage collector to run more often. To avoid this we need to use generics whenever possible.

Understanding the Garbage Collector

A big plus of writing managed code is the fact that we do not need to worry about memory leaks from the sense of losing pointers to referenced memory. We still have "memory leaks" in managed code, but whenever the term is used it is referring to not decommissioning variables in a timely fashion. We would have a memory leak if we kept a handle on a pointer that we should have set to null. It would remain in memory until the game exits.

We should use the using statement. An example of the using statement can be found in the program.cs file that is generated for us by the game template. The entry point of the program uses this using statement to create our game object and then to call its Run method. The using statement effectively puts a try/finally block around the code while putting a call to the object's Dispose method inside of the finally block.

Garbage collection concerns on Windows are not as large as those on the Xbox 360. However, if we optimize our code to run well on the Xbox 360 in regard to garbage collection, the game will also perform well on Windows.

On the .NET Framework (Windows)

As we create objects (when we use the new keyword) they are put into the managed heap. .NET then calculates the needed memory for the object and confirms there is enough memory available on the managed heap. The constructor of the object is called and the executing code returns a reference to that object (a location in the managed heap). Memory is created in a contiguous manner, which means that objects are stored next to each other as they are created.

If memory cannot be allocated on the managed heap, the garbage collector is executed to free up any unused memory. There are assumptions the garbage collector makes to free up memory. One such assumption is that objects that have been just created will only be around for a short while. Another assumption is that objects that have been around for a while will continue to be around for a while. Because of these assumptions the garbage collector has a notion of generations. There are a total of three generations in the .NET Framework. The .NET Compact Framework only has one generation, but we are getting ahead of ourselves, as that is covered in the next section. The first generation (0) stores all the recently added memory, so memory is allocated when variables are created and then memory is "marked" as inactive when the variables go out of scope, get explicitly set to null, and so on. By marking memory as inactive, .NET is actually setting the root (which is just a pointer to the location of memory) to null. At some point in time the memory heap gets full. When this happens the garbage collector runs and sends all objects that are still active (roots are not null) into generation 1, freeing up all of the generation 0 space. If generation 1 gets full, it goes through the same process and pushes up active objects to generation 2. If this last generation is full, a full garbage collection is carried out, which is very expensive. If an object is large enough it will actually skip generation 0 and jump straight into generation 2 so it does not incur the performance hit of putting it into generation 0, maxing out the memory, and repeating the process again in generation 1.

So what does this mean in regard to writing games for Windows? Well, it means we need to be careful of how and when we create objects. We do not want to create very large objects and we want the objects we do create to be short lived so they do not get promoted to generation 1. We need to let go of objects when we are done with them. We need to create objects that are related close together so they can move through the process together. We need to be careful and not associate a short-lived object with a long-lived object, as the long-lived object will keep a reference to it and it will not be collected. Short-lived objects that require little memory do not cause performance issues. Long-lived objects (as long as they are not too large) do not cause performance issues. If the long-lived objects are too big, this will cause the generation 2 memory to become full and full collections will happen more often than we want. We need to keep our objects to a decent size. Objects that are neither short-lived nor long-lived objects are where we run into performance issues. These midlife objects will get promoted to generation 1 and then become inactive. Although this is not a huge problem, it becomes a real concern when the object stays alive and then gets moved into generation 2 and then shortly after dies. By having the object die in generation 2 instead of generation 1 we are paying a very large performance price because when the garbage collector does a full collection (collects data in generation 2) it has to look at each and every object on the managed heap to determine if it is alive or not. While it is inspecting the objects it creates a large load on the CPU that reduces the overall throughput. If there any objects with finalizers, it really hurts the performance of the application. We do not want to generate full collections.

On the .NET Compact Framework (Xbox 360)

The .NET Compact Framework handles garbage collection differently than its desktop counterpart. However, if we try to optimize our code for the .NET Compact Framework, we should also realize the benefits on the desktop version of the .NET Framework. The .NET Compact Framework does not have generations. We can think of it as only having generation 2 actually, in that every collection is a full collection.

The .NET Compact Framework's garbage collector will also compact the memory into a contiguous space when it determines that the memory heap is overly fragmented. If there is not enough memory, the garbage collector will also pitch the code that was compiled just-in-time. The code that is compiled just-in-time is kept in memory to help performance but if memory gets too low the memory will be released.

Finally the garbage collector will go through any objects that are in the finalization queue. This queue also exists in the full .NET Framework and works the same way. As memory is marked as not needed, the garbage collector determines if the object has a finalize method. If it does, the object is actually put into this separate queue before marking the memory on the heap as inactive. Then the next time the garbage collector runs, it loops through the finalization queue and disposes of the objects. This is why it is very important to not utilize the Finalize method unless we are using unmanaged resources. When developing for the Xbox 360 we do not need to worry about unmanaged objects, as we do not have the ability to access them.

Optimization Suggestions

We have discussed how to measure performance and discussed a common performance issue with the garbage collector. Now we are going to look at different optimizations we could make if we determine that a certain piece of code is not performing well. This is considered micro-optimization and should only be done after taking measurements to make sure that the code we are about to optimize really needs it! If we spend our time trying to save CPU cycles on a method that did not need it, then we wasted our time. Worse, we probably made the code less readable. Even worse, we could have introduced bugs during the process that put us even further behind the eight ball.

Although performing micro-optimizations is important, it is really one of the last steps that we do. Great places for this type of optimization are inside of nested loops. For example, our Update and Draw methods are inside of a tight game loop the XNA Framework runs and we will have loops inside of there to update AI logic and check physics and such. Even those could have nested loops. It is at those points that we will be doing most of the micro-optimizations, but we only do this after we have confirmed that a particular section of code is our bottleneck. Measure!

Creating a Micro-Benchmark Framework

When we are trying to make a particular piece of code run faster because we see that it is taking more time compared to everything else in our application, we will need to compare different implementations of completing the same task. This is where micro-benchmark testing can help.

Micro-benchmark testing allows us to take a close look at how fast small bits of code are performing. There are a couple of items to keep in mind as we use micro-benchmark testing, though. The first is that we cannot exactly determine best practices from a micro-benchmark test because it is such an isolated case. The second is that although a piece of code might perform faster in a micro-benchmark test, it might very well take up a lot more memory and therefore cause the garbage collector to collect its garbage more often.

The point here is that although micro-benchmark testing is good and we should do it (which is why we are going to build a framework for it) we need to be careful of any assumptions we make solely on what we find out from our micro-benchmark tests.

XNA Game Studio Express not only lets us create game projects, but also allows us to create library projects. When the library projects are compiled they can be used by other applications—a game, a Windows form, or even a console application.

We are going to create another application, but this time it is going to be a normal Windows Game Library project. This class should be called CheckPerformance. We will be utilizing this library from a console application. The code for the CheckPerformance can be found in Listing 3.1. The purpose of this class is to create methods that perform the same tasks different ways. We will then create a console application that calls the different methods and measure the amount of time it takes to process each method.

LISTING 3.1   The CheckPerformance class has methods that produce the same results through different means.

```
public class CheckPerformance
{
    private Vector3 cameraReference = new Vector3(0, 0, -1.0f);
    private Vector3 cameraPosition = new Vector3(0, 0, 3.0f);
    private Vector3 cameraTarget = Vector3.Zero;
    private Vector3 vectorUp = Vector3.Up;
    private Matrix projection;
    private Matrix view;
    private float cameraYaw = 0.0f;

    public CheckPerformance() { }

    public void TransformVectorByValue()
    {
        Matrix rotationMatrix = Matrix.CreateRotationY(
            MathHelper.ToRadians(45.0f));
        // Create a vector pointing the direction the camera is facing.
        Vector3 transformedReference = Vector3.Transform(cameraReference,
            rotationMatrix);
        // Calculate the position the camera is looking at.
        cameraTarget = cameraPosition + transformedReference;
    }

    public void TransformVectorByReference()
    {
        Matrix rotationMatrix = Matrix.CreateRotationY(
            MathHelper.ToRadians(45.0f));
        // Create a vector pointing the direction the camera is facing.
        Vector3 transformedReference;
```

LISTING 3.1   Continued

```
        Vector3.Transform(ref cameraReference, ref rotationMatrix,
            out transformedReference);
        // Calculate the position the camera is looking at.
        Vector3.Add(ref cameraPosition, ref transformedReference,
            out cameraTarget);
    }

    public void TransformVectorByReferenceAndOut()
    {
        Matrix rotationMatrix = Matrix.CreateRotationY(
            MathHelper.ToRadians(45.0f));
        // Create a vector pointing the direction the camera is facing.
        Vector3 transformedReference;
        Vector3.Transform(ref cameraReference, ref rotationMatrix,
            out transformedReference);
        // Calculate the position the camera is looking at.
        Vector3.Add(ref cameraPosition, ref transformedReference,
            out cameraTarget);
    }

    public void TransformVectorByReferenceAndOutVectorAdd()
    {
        Matrix rotationMatrix;
        Matrix.CreateRotationY(MathHelper.ToRadians(45.0f),
            out rotationMatrix);
        // Create a vector pointing the direction the camera is facing.
        Vector3 transformedReference;
        Vector3.Transform(ref cameraReference, ref rotationMatrix,
            out transformedReference);
        // Calculate the position the camera is looking at.
        Vector3.Add(ref cameraPosition, ref transformedReference,
            out cameraTarget);
    }

    public void InitializeTransformWithCalculation()
    {
        float aspectRatio = (float)640 / (float)480;
        projection = Matrix.CreatePerspectiveFieldOfView(
            MathHelper.ToRadians(45.0f), aspectRatio, 0.0001f, 1000.0f);
        view = Matrix.CreateLookAt(cameraPosition, cameraTarget, Vector3.Up);
    }

    public void InitializeTransformWithConstant()
    {
```

LISTING 3.1   Continued

```
    float aspectRatio = (float)640 / (float)480;
    projection = Matrix.CreatePerspectiveFieldOfView(
        MathHelper.PiOver4, aspectRatio, 0.0001f, 1000.0f);
    view = Matrix.CreateLookAt(cameraPosition, cameraTarget, Vector3.Up);
}

public void InitializeTransformWithDivision()
{
    float aspectRatio = (float)640 / (float)480;
    projection = Matrix.CreatePerspectiveFieldOfView(
        MathHelper.Pi / 4, aspectRatio, 0.0001f, 1000.0f);
    view = Matrix.CreateLookAt(cameraPosition, cameraTarget, Vector3.Up);
}

public void InitializeTransformWithConstantReferenceOut()
{
    float aspectRatio = (float)640 / (float)480;
    Matrix.CreatePerspectiveFieldOfView(
        MathHelper.ToRadians(45.0f), aspectRatio, 0.0001f, 1000.0f,
        out projection);
    Matrix.CreateLookAt(
        ref cameraPosition, ref cameraTarget, ref vectorUp, out view);
}

public void InitializeTransformWithPreDeterminedAspectRatio()
{
    Matrix.CreatePerspectiveFieldOfView(
        MathHelper.ToRadians(45.0f), 1.33333f, 0.0001f, 1000.0f,
        out projection);
    Matrix.CreateLookAt(
        ref cameraPosition, ref cameraTarget, ref vectorUp, out view);
}

public void CreateCameraReferenceWithProperty()
{
    Vector3 cameraReference = Vector3.Forward;
    Matrix rotationMatrix;
    Matrix.CreateRotationY(
        MathHelper.ToRadians(45.0f), out rotationMatrix);
    // Create a vector pointing the direction the camera is facing.
    Vector3 transformedReference;
    Vector3.Transform(ref cameraReference, ref rotationMatrix,
        out transformedReference);
    // Calculate the position the camera is looking at.
```

LISTING 3.1   Continued

```
        cameraTarget = cameraPosition + transformedReference;
    }


    public void CreateCameraReferenceWithValue()
    {
        Vector3 cameraReference = new Vector3(0, 0, -1.0f);
        Matrix rotationMatrix;
        Matrix.CreateRotationY(
            MathHelper.ToRadians(45.0f), out rotationMatrix);
        // Create a vector pointing the direction the camera is facing.
        Vector3 transformedReference;
        Vector3.Transform(ref cameraReference, ref rotationMatrix,
            out transformedReference);
        // Calculate the position the camera is looking at.
        cameraTarget = cameraPosition + transformedReference;
    }

    public void RotateWithoutMod()
    {
        cameraYaw += 2.0f;

        if (cameraYaw > 360)
            cameraYaw -= 360;
        if (cameraYaw < 0)
            cameraYaw += 360;

        float tmp = cameraYaw;
    }

    public void RotateWithMod()
    {
        cameraYaw += 2.0f;

        cameraYaw %= 30;

        float tmp = cameraYaw;
    }

    public void RotateElseIf()
    {
        cameraYaw += 2.0f;

        if (cameraYaw > 360)
            cameraYaw -= 360;
```

3

LISTING 3.1   Continued

```
        else if (cameraYaw < 0)
            cameraYaw += 360;

        float tmp = cameraYaw;
    }
}
```

We do not need to be concerned with the actual contents of the different methods. The main concept we need to understand at this point is we have different groups of methods that do the same task but are executed in different ways. We discuss the details of the Matrix in Chapter 4, "Creating 3D Objects." For now we can take a look at the last three methods in the listing and see they are all doing the same thing. All three methods are adding 2 to a variable cameraYaw and then making sure that the value is between 0 and 360. The idea is that this code would be inside of the game loop reading input from a device and updating the cameraYaw variable appropriately.

Now we can create the console application that will actually call that class. We need to add a new Console Application project to the solution and can call this project XNAPerfStarter. We can name this project XNAPerformanceChecker. The code for Program.cs is given in Listing 3.2.

LISTING 3.2   The program measures the amount of time it takes to execute the different CheckPerformance methods.

```
class Program
{
    static int timesToLoop = 10000;

    static void Main(string[] args)
    {
        while (true)
        {
            XNAPerformanceChecker.CheckPerformance cp =
                new XNAPerformanceChecker.CheckPerformance();

            Stopwatch sw = new Stopwatch();

            //Call all methods once for any JIT-ing that needs to be done
            sw.Start();
            cp.InitializeTransformWithCalculation();
            cp.InitializeTransformWithConstant();
            cp.InitializeTransformWithDivision();
            cp.InitializeTransformWithConstantReferenceOut();
            cp.TransformVectorByReference();
            cp.TransformVectorByValue();
```

LISTING 3.2   Continued

```
            cp.TransformVectorByReferenceAndOut();
            cp.TransformVectorByReferenceAndOutVectorAdd();
            cp.CreateCameraReferenceWithProperty();
            cp.CreateCameraReferenceWithValue();
            sw.Stop();
            sw.Reset();


            int i;
            sw.Start();
            for (i = 0; i < timesToLoop; i++)
                cp.InitializeTransformWithCalculation();
            sw.Stop();

            PrintPerformance("        Calculation", ref sw);
            sw.Reset();

            sw.Start();
            for (i = 0; i < timesToLoop; i++)
                cp.InitializeTransformWithConstant();
            sw.Stop();

            PrintPerformance("           Constant", ref sw);
            sw.Reset();

            sw.Start();
            for (i = 0; i < timesToLoop; i++)
                cp.InitializeTransformWithDivision();
            sw.Stop();

            PrintPerformance("           Division", ref sw);
            sw.Reset();

            sw.Start();
            for (i = 0; i < timesToLoop; i++)
                cp.InitializeTransformWithConstantReferenceOut();
            sw.Stop();

            PrintPerformance("ConstantReferenceOut", ref sw);
            sw.Reset();

            sw.Start();
            for (i = 0; i < timesToLoop; i++)
                cp.InitializeTransformWithPreDeterminedAspectRatio();
            sw.Stop();
```

LISTING 3.2   Continued

```
         PrintPerformance("           AspectRatio", ref sw);
         sw.Reset();

         Console.WriteLine();
         Console.WriteLine("— — — — — — — — — — — — — — — — — — — — — — — —·");
         Console.WriteLine();

         sw.Start();
         for (i = 0; i < timesToLoop; i++)
             cp.TransformVectorByReference();
         sw.Stop();

         PrintPerformance("        Reference", ref sw);
         sw.Reset();

         sw.Start();
         for (i = 0; i < timesToLoop; i++)
             cp.TransformVectorByValue();
         sw.Stop();

         PrintPerformance("            Value", ref sw);
         sw.Reset();

         sw.Start();
         for (i = 0; i < timesToLoop; i++)
             cp.TransformVectorByReferenceAndOut();
         sw.Stop();

         PrintPerformance("ReferenceAndOut", ref sw);
         sw.Reset();

         sw.Start();
         for (i = 0; i < timesToLoop; i++)
             cp.TransformVectorByReferenceAndOutVectorAdd();
         sw.Stop();

         PrintPerformance("RefOutVectorAdd", ref sw);
         sw.Reset();

         Console.WriteLine();
         Console.WriteLine("— — — — — — — — — — — — — — — — — — — — — — — —·");
         Console.WriteLine();

         sw.Start();
```

LISTING 3.2   Continued

```
        for (i = 0; i < timesToLoop; i++)
            cp.CreateCameraReferenceWithProperty();
    sw.Stop();


    PrintPerformance("Property", ref sw);
    sw.Reset();

    sw.Start();
    for (i = 0; i < timesToLoop; i++)
        cp.CreateCameraReferenceWithValue();
    sw.Stop();

    PrintPerformance("   Value", ref sw);
    sw.Reset();

    Console.WriteLine();
    Console.WriteLine("— — — — — — — — — — — — — — — — — — — — — -");
    Console.WriteLine();

    sw.Start();
    for (i = 0; i < timesToLoop; i++)
        cp.RotateWithMod();
    sw.Stop();

    PrintPerformance("   RotateWithMod", ref sw);
    sw.Reset();

    sw.Start();
    for (i = 0; i < timesToLoop; i++)
        cp.RotateWithoutMod();
    sw.Stop();

    PrintPerformance("RotateWithoutMod", ref sw);
    sw.Reset();

    sw.Start();
    for (i = 0; i < timesToLoop; i++)
        cp.RotateElseIf();
    sw.Stop();

    PrintPerformance("   RotateElseIf", ref sw);
    sw.Reset();

    string command = Console.ReadLine();
```

LISTING 3.2   Continued

```
            if (command.ToUpper().StartsWith("E") ||
                command.ToUpper().StartsWith("Q"))
                break;
        }
    }

    static void PrintPerformance(string label, ref Stopwatch sw)
    {
        Console.WriteLine(label + " - Avg: " +
            ((float)((float)(sw.Elapsed.Ticks * 100) /
            (float)timesToLoop)).ToString("F") +
            " Total: " + sw.Elapsed.TotalMilliseconds.ToString());
    }
}
```

We need to also add the following using clause to the top of our Program.cs file:

```
using System.Diagnostics;
```

The System.Diagnostics class gives us access to the Stopwatch we are using to keep track of the time it takes to process the different methods. After starting the timer we then loop 100,000 times and call a method in the CheckPerformance class we created earlier. Once the loop finishes executing the method the specified number of times, we stop the stopwatch and print out our results to the console. When using the Stopwatch object we need to make sure that if we want to start another test that we first call the Reset method. This isn't built into the Stop method in case we just want to pause the timer and start it back up for some reason. We could also use the static StartNew method instead of the instance Start method. The StartNew method effectively resets the timer as it returns a new instance of the Stopwatch.

When we are trying to measure performance on pieces of code that perform very fast (even inside of a large loop) it is important to be able to track exactly how much time it took, even down to the nanosecond level.

Typically timing things in seconds does not give us the granularity we need to see how long something is really taking, so the next unit of time we can measure against is milliseconds. There are 1,000 milliseconds in a second. Next comes the microsecond, and there are 1,000 microseconds in a millisecond. Next is the tick, which is what the TimeSpan object uses. There are 10 ticks in a microsecond. Finally, we come to the nanosecond. There are 100 nanoseconds in each tick. A nanosecond is 1/1,000,000,000 (one billionth) of a second. Table 3.1 shows the relationships between the different measurements of time.

TABLE 3.1   Time Measurement Relationships

Nanoseconds	Ticks	Microseconds	Milliseconds	Seconds
100	1	0.1	0.0001	0.0000001
10,000	100	10.0	0.0100	0.0000100
100,000	1,000	100.0	0.1000	0.0001000
1,000,000	10,000	1,000.0	1.0000	0.0010000
10,000,000	100,000	10,000.0	10.0000	0.0100000
100,000,000	1,000,000	100,000.0	100.0000	0.1000000
1,000,000,000	10,000,000	1,000,000.0	1,000.0000	1.0000000

PrintPerformance, our method to print out the performance measurements, takes in the label that describes what we are measuring along with a reference to Stopwatch object. TimeSpan is the type the .NET Framework uses to measure time. The smallest unit of time measurement this type allows is a tick.

Because we want to measure our time in nanoseconds, we multiply the number of elapsed ticks by 100. Then we take the total number of nanoseconds and divide by the number of times we executed the method. Finally, we display the average number of nanoseconds along with total number of milliseconds the task took to execute.

When we print out our measurements we want the average time it took to execute a method for the number of iterations we told it to loop. The reason we do this instead of just running it once is so that we can easily determine a more accurate number. In fact, we even run an outer loop (that we exit out of by entering text that starts with "E" or "Q") to account for anomalies in performance on the machine in general.

An additional item to note about this code is that we call each method of the CheckPerformance object once before we start measuring execution times. The reason we do this is so the compiler can do any just-in-time compiling for the methods we will be calling so we are not taking that time into account.

Sealing Virtual Methods

Although having virtual methods and virtual classes is extremely beneficial for extensibility and object-oriented design, it also causes a performance hit because virtual methods keep certain runtime performance optimizations from happening. This is because virtual methods require a virtual table lookup to occur. If we are not extending a class or a method then we can actually seal it to help with the performance. This lets the compiler know that no one else will be allowed to override the method and the jitter will generate a direct call to the method instead of the lookup.

Collections

If possible we want to utilize regular arrays instead of collections. Of course, if we need to dynamically add or remove items from our list, then a collection is the way to go.

Regardless of which we use, we always want to have our lists to store a specific type. C# 2.0, which is what Visual C# Express uses as of this writing, has generics that allow us to use strong types so we do not need to box and unbox objects in our lists. If we cannot get by with a regular array of a specific type, then we need to use generics. We should never use a "normal" collection (i.e., one that does not use generics).

Whether we are using normal arrays or a full-fledged collection, we should always set the initial size of our list to be as close as possible to the number of items we expect the list will store. This way the correct amount of memory can be allocated once instead of having to reallocate often due to a growing list.

There is a lot of speculation about foreach loops and the overhead it brings with the garbage collection it causes. When we loop through an array we do not create garbage. When we loop through certain collections we do not create garbage. The key is if the enumerator returns a struct or not. If a struct is returned then the data is put on to the stack and we are in good shape. Looping through a `Collection<T>` will definitely create overhead as the enumerator will box the value and put it on the heap. If we stick with straight arrays when we can, there is nothing to worry about. If we need to work with the list in a dynamic fashion we just need to choose the type of collection we will create— Lists, Stacks, and Queues are all good candidates as their `GetEnumerator` returns a struct and no extra memory is allocated.

Summary

Hopefully we walk away from this chapter with the sense that before any optimization takes place, we need to know what we are going to optimize. To determine what needs a performance boost, we need to measure. Measuring is the key, and it cannot be stressed enough.

We discussed how to measure the real frame per seconds rate at which our game is capable of running. We looked at the remote performance monitoring tool for the Xbox 360 and saw how we could look at critical pieces of information to see how our game performs on the console.

We discussed a typical bottleneck of memory management and how the garbage collector runs.We also created a micro-benchmarking framework that allows us to determine how fast or slow a particular method (or part of a method) is and how it compares to alternative methods to produce the same results.

We really just scratched the surface on performance considerations. Searching the Web for more information on increasing our performance would be extremely helpful. Something that was not even touched on was the fact that knowledge of MSIL can be really beneficial to see what the .NET Framework is really doing with our C# code. We could look at the IL code for any reference of newobj to see when we created an object and look for box to find when we boxed and unboxed items (unknowingly).

The main idea of this chapter is that we must have an end goal. We have to know how well we want our game to perform so we can write our code in such a way to meet those goals. In the real world we have deadlines and writing code fast and writing fast code are often at odds with each other. This is where it is extremely beneficial to know exactly what we are shooting for. We should measure often to determine which piece of new code is causing an adverse affect on performance.

3

PART II

Understanding XNA Basics

IN THIS PART

Creating 3D Objects

In this chapter we examine 3D concepts and how the XNA Framework exposes different types and objects that allow us to easily create 3D worlds. We will create a couple of 3D demos that explain the basics. We will also create 3D objects directly inside of our code. Finally, we will move these objects on the screen.

Vertices

Everything in a 3D game is represented by 3D points. There are a couple of ways to get 3D objects on the screen. We can plot the points ourselves or we can load them from a 3D file (which has all of the points stored already). Later, in Chapter 6, "Loading and Texturing 3D Objects," we will learn how to load 3D files to use in our games. For now, we are going to create the points ourselves.

We defined these points with an x, y, and z coordinate (x, y, z). In XNA we represent a vertex with a vector, which leads us to the next section.

Vectors

XNA provides three different vector structs for us— Vector2, Vector3, and Vector4. Vector2 only has an x and y component. We typically use this 2D vector in 2D games and when using a texture. Vector3 adds in the z component. Not only do we store vertices as a vector, but we also store velocity as a vector. We discuss velocity in Chapter 19, "Physics Basics." The last vector struct that XNA provides for us is a 4D struct appropriately called Vector4. Later examples in this book will use this struct to pass color information around as it has four components.

We can perform different math operations on vectors, which prove to be very helpful. We do not discuss 3D math in detail in this book as there are many texts out there that cover it. Fortunately, XNA allows us to use the built-in helper functions without having to have a deep understanding of the inner workings of the code. With that said, it is extremely beneficial to understand the math behind the different functions.

Matrices

In XNA a matrix is a 4 x 4 table of data. It is a two-dimensional array. An identity matrix, also referred to as a unit matrix, is similar to the number 1 in that if we multiply any other number by 1 we always end up with the number we started out with (5 * 1 = 5). Multiplying a matrix by an identity matrix will produce a matrix with the same value as the original matrix. XNA provides a struct to hold matrix data—not surprisingly, it is called `Matrix`.

Transformations

The data a matrix contains are called transformations. There are three common transformations: translation, scaling, and rotating. These transformations do just that: They transform our 3D objects.

Translation

Translating an object simply means we are moving an object. We translate an object from one point to another point by moving each point inside of the object correctly.

Scaling

Scaling an object will make the object larger or smaller. This is done by actually moving the points in the object closer together or further apart depending on if we are scaling down or scaling up.

Rotation

Rotating an object will turn the object on one or more axes. By moving the points in 3D space we can make our object spin.

Transformations Reloaded

An object can have one transformation applied to it or it can have many transformations applied to it. We might only want to translate (move) an object, so we can update the object's world matrix to move it around in the world. We might just want the object to spin around, so we apply a rotation transformation to the object over and over so it will rotate. We might need an object we created from a 3D editor to be smaller to fit better in our world. In that case we can apply a scaling transformation to the object. Of course, we might need to take this object we loaded in from the 3D editor and scale it down and rotate it 30 degrees to the left so it will face some object and we need to move it closer to the object it is facing. In this case we would actually do all three types of transformations to get the desired results. We might even need to rotate it downward 5 degrees as well, and that is perfectly acceptable.

We can have many different transformations applied to an object. However, there is a catch—there is always a catch, right? The catch is that because we are doing these transformations using matrix math we need to be aware of something very important. We are multiplying our transformation matrices together to get the results we want. Unlike multiplying normal integers, multiplying matrices is not commutative. This means that Matrix A * Matrix B != Matrix B * Matrix A. So in our earlier example where we want to scale our object and rotate it (two different times) and then move it, we will need to be careful in which order we perform those operations. We will see how to do this a little later in the chapter.

Creating a Camera

That is enough theory for a bit. We are going to create a camera so we can view our world. Now we can create a new Windows game project to get started with this section. We can call this project XNADemo. To begin, we will need to create the following private member fields:

```
private Matrix projection;
private Matrix view;
private Matrix world;
```

We will then need to add a call to InitializeCamera in the beginning of our LoadGraphicsContent method. The InitializeCamera method will have no return value. We will begin to populate the method, which can be marked as private, in the next three points.

Projection

The Matrix struct has a lot of helper functions built in that we can utilize. The Matrix.CreatePerspectiveFieldOfView is the method we want to look at now.

```
float aspectRatio = (float)graphics.GraphicsDevice.Viewport.Width /
    (float)graphics.GraphicsDevice.Viewport.Height;
Matrix.CreatePerspectiveFieldOfView(MathHelper.PiOver4, aspectRatio,
    0.0001f, 1000.0f, out projection);
```

First we set up a local variable aspectRatio. This is to store, you guessed it, the aspect ratio of our screen. For the Xbox 360 the aspect ratio of the back buffer will determine how the game is displayed on the gamer's TV. If we develop with a widescreen aspect ratio and the user has a standard TV, the game will have a letterbox look to it. Conversely, if we develop with a standard aspect ratio and the user has a wide screen, the Xbox 360 will stretch the display. To avoid this we should account for both situations and then adjust the value of our aspect ratio variable to the default values of the viewport of the graphics device like in the preceding code. If we needed to query the default value to which the gamer had his or her Xbox 360 set, we can gather that information by querying the DisplayMode property of the graphics device during or after the Initialization method is called by the framework.

However, if we want to force a widescreen aspect ratio on the Xbox 360 we could set the PreferredBackBufferWidth and PreferredBackBufferHeight properties on the graphics object right after creating it. Many gamers do not care for the black bars, so we should use this with caution. To force a widescreen aspect ratio on Windows is a little more complicated, but the XNA Game Studio Express documentation has a great "How to" page explaining how to do it. Once in the documentation, you can find "How to: Restrict Graphics Devices to Widescreen Aspect Ratios in Full Screen" under the Application Model in the Programming Guide.

Second, we create our field of view. The first parameter we pass in is 45 degrees. We could have used MathHelper.ToRadians(45.0f) but there is no need to do the math because the MathHelper class already has the value as a constant. The second parameter is the aspect ratio, which we already calculated. The third and fourth parameters are our near and far clipping planes, respectively. The plane values represent how far the plane is from our camera. It means anything past the far clipping plane will not be drawn onto the screen. It also means anything closer to us than the near clipping plane will not be drawn either. Only the points that fall in between those two planes and are within a 45-degree angle of where we are looking will be drawn on the screen. The last parameter is where we populate our projection matrix. This is an overloaded method. (One version actually returns the projection, but we will utilize the overload that has reference and out parameters, as they are faster because it doesn't have to copy the value of the data.)

View

Now that we have our projection matrix set, we can set up our view matrix. To do this we are going to use another XNA matrix helper method. The Matrix.CreateLookAt method takes three parameters. Let's create and initialize these private member fields now.

```
private Vector3 cameraPosition = new Vector3(0.0f, 0.0f, 3.0f);
private Vector3 cameraTarget = Vector3.Zero;
private Vector3 cameraUpVector = Vector3.Up;
```

Now we can actually call the CreateLookAt method inside of our InitializeCamera method. We should add the following code at the end of the method:

```
Matrix.CreateLookAt(ref cameraPosition, ref cameraTarget,
    ref cameraUpVector, out view);
```

The first parameter we pass in is our camera position. We are passing in the coordinates (0,0,3) for our camera position to start with, so our camera position will remain at the origin of the x and y axis, but it will move backward from the origin 3 units. The second parameter of the CreateLookAt method is the target of where we are aiming the camera. In this example, we are aiming the camera at the origin of the world Vector3.Zero (0,0,0). Finally, we pass in the camera's up vector. For this we use the Up property on Vector3, which means (0,1,0). Notice we actually created a variable for this so we can pass it in by reference. This is also an overloaded method, and because we want this to be fast we will pass the variables in by reference instead of by value. Fortunately, we do not lose much readability with this performance gain.

World

At this point if we compiled and ran the demo we would still see the lovely blank corn-flower blue screen because we have not set up our world matrix or put anything in the world to actually look at. Let's fix that now.

As we saw, the templates provide a lot of methods stubbed out for us. One of these very important methods is the Draw method. Find this method and add this line of code right below the TODO: Add your drawing code here comment:

```
world = Matrix.Identity;
```

This simply sets our world matrix to an identity matrix, which means that there is no scaling, no rotating, and no translating (movement). The identity matrix has a translation of (0,0,0) so this will effectively set our world matrix to the origin of the world.

At this point we have our camera successfully set up but we have not actually drawn anything. We are going to correct that starting with the next section.

Vertex Buffers

3D objects are made up of triangles. Every object is one triangle or more. For example, a sphere is just made up of triangles; the more triangles, the more rounded the sphere is. Take a look at Figure 4.1 to see how this works. Now that we know that every 3D object we render is made up of triangles and that a triangle is simply three vertices in 3D space, we can use vertex buffers to store a list of 3D points. As the name implies, a vertex buffer is simply memory (a buffer) that holds a list of vertices.

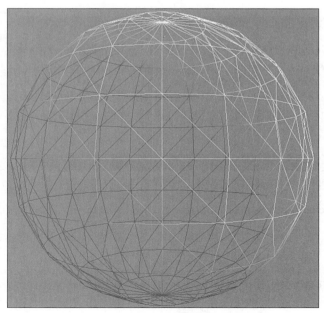

FIGURE 4.1   All 3D objects are made up of triangles.

XNA uses a right-handed coordinate system. This means that the x axis goes from left to right (left being negative and right being positive), the y axis goes up and down (down being negative and up being positive), and z goes forward and backward (forward being negative and backward being positive). We can visualize this by extending our right arm out to our right and positioning our hand like we are holding a gun. Now rotate our wrist so our palm is facing the sky. At this point our pointer finger should be pointing to the right (this is our x axis going in a positive direction to the right). Our thumb should be pointing behind us (this is our z axis going in a positive direction backward). Now, we uncurl our three fingers so they are pointing to the sky (this represents the y axis with a positive direction upward). Take a look at Figure 4.2 to help solidify how the right-handed coordinate system works.

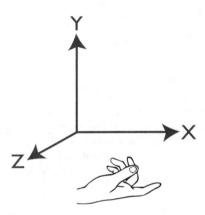

FIGURE 4.2   This demonstrates a right-handed coordinate system.

Now that we know what the positive direction is for each axis we are ready to start plotting our points. XNA uses counterclockwise culling. Culling is a performance measure graphic cards take to keep from rendering objects that are not facing the camera. XNA has three options for culling: `CullClockwiseFace`, `CullCounterClockwiseFace`, and `None`. The default culling mode for XNA is `CullCounterClockwiseFace`, so to see our objects we have to set up our points in the opposite order—clockwise.

TIP

It is helpful to use some graph paper (or regular notebook paper for that matter) to plot out points. Simply put points where we want them and make sure when we put them into the code, we do it in a clockwise order.

Let's plot some points. Ultimately, we want to make a square. We know that all 3D objects can be made with triangles and we can see that a square is made up of two triangles. We will position the first triangle at (-1,1,0); (1,-1,0); (-1,-1,0). That means the first point (-1,1,0) will be positioned on the x axis 1 unit to the left and it will be 1 unit up the y axis and will stay at the origin on the z axis. The code needed to set up these points is as follows:

```
private void InitializeVertices()
{
    Vector3 position;
    Vector2 textureCoordinates;

    vertices = new VertexPositionNormalTexture[3];

    //top left
    position = new Vector3(-1, 1, 0);
    textureCoordinates = new Vector2(0, 0);
    vertices[0] = new VertexPositionNormalTexture(position, Vector3.Forward,
        textureCoordinates);

    //bottom right
    position = new Vector3(1, -1, 0);
    textureCoordinates = new Vector2(1, 1);
    vertices[1] = new VertexPositionNormalTexture(position, Vector3.Forward,
        textureCoordinates);

    //bottom left
    position = new Vector3(-1, -1, 0);
    textureCoordinates = new Vector2(0, 1);
    vertices[2] = new VertexPositionNormalTexture(position, Vector3.Forward,
        textureCoordinates);
}
```

As we look at this function we can see three variables that have been created: `vertex`, `position`, and `textureCoordinates`. The `vertex` variable will store our vertex (point) data. XNA has different structs that describe the type of data a vertex will hold. In most cases for 3D games we will need to store the position, normal, and texture coordinates. We discuss normals later, but for now it is sufficient to know they let the graphics device know how to reflect light off of the face (triangle). The most important part of the vertex variable is the position of the point in 3D space. We saw earlier that XNA allows us to store that information in a `Vector3` struct. We can either set the data in the constructor as we did in this code, or we can explicitly set its X, Y, and Z properties.

We skip over explaining the texture coordinates momentarily, but notice it uses the `Vector2` struct that XNA provides for us. We need to add the following private member field to our class that we have been using to store our vertices:

```
private VertexPositionNormalTexture[] vertices;
```

We need to call this method in our application. The appropriate place to call the `InitializeVertices` method is inside of the `LoadGraphicsContent` method.

If we compile and run our application now we still do not see anything on the screen. This is because we have not actually told the program to *draw* our triangle! We will want to find our Draw method and before the last call to the base class base.Draw(gameTime), we need to add the following code:

```
graphics.GraphicsDevice.VertexDeclaration = new
    VertexDeclaration(graphics.GraphicsDevice,
    VertexPositionNormalTexture.VertexElements);

BasicEffect effect = new BasicEffect(graphics.GraphicsDevice, null);

world = Matrix.Identity;
effect.World = world;
effect.Projection = projection;
effect.View = view;

effect.EnableDefaultLighting();
effect.Begin();

foreach (EffectPass pass in effect.CurrentTechnique.Passes)
{
    pass.Begin();
    graphics.GraphicsDevice.DrawUserPrimitives(
        PrimitiveType.TriangleList, vertices, 0,
        vertices.Length / 3);

    pass.End();
}

effect.End();
```

You might think there is a lot of code here just to draw the points we have created on the screen. Well, there is, but it is all very straightforward and we can plow on through. Before we do, though, let's take a minute and talk about effects.

Effects

Effects are used to get anything in our XNA 3D game to actually show up on the screen. They handle things like lights, textures, and even position of the points. We will talk about effects extensively in Part V, "High Level Shading Language (HLSL)." For now, we can utilize the BasicEffect class that XNA provides. This keeps us from having to actually create an effect file so we can get started quickly.

The first thing to notice is that we create a new variable to hold our effect. We do this by passing in the graphics device as our first parameter and we are passing in null as the effect pool because we are only using one effect and don't need a pool to share among multiple effects. After creating our effect, we want to set some of the properties so we can use it. Notice we set the world, view, and projection matrices for the effect as well as telling the effect to turn on the default lighting. We discuss lighting in detail in the HLSL part of our book, but for now, this will light up the 3D scene so we can see our objects.

TIP

It is a good idea to leave the background color set to `Color.CornflowerBlue` or some other nonblack color. The reason for this is if the lights are not set up correctly, the object will render in black (no light is shining on it). So if the background color is black, we might think that the object didn't render at all.

Now back to our code. Notice that we call the `Begin` method on our effect and we also call the `End` method. Anything we draw on the screen in between these two calls will have that effect applied to them. The next section of code is our `foreach` loop. This loop iterates through all of the passes of our effect. Effects will have one or more techniques. A technique will have one or more passes. For this basic effect, we have only one technique and one pass. We will learn about techniques and passes in more detail in Part V. At this point we have another begin and end pair, but this time it is for the pass of the current (only) technique in our effect. Inside of this pass is where we finally get to draw our triangle onto the screen. This is done using the `DrawUserPrimitives` method in the graphics device object:

```
graphics.GraphicsDevice.DrawUserPrimitives(
    PrimitiveType.TriangleList, vertices, 0, vertices.Length / 3);
```

We are passing in the type of primitive we will be rendering. The primitives we are drawing are triangles so we are going to pass in a triangle list. This is the most common primitive type used in modern games. Refer to Table 4.1 for a list of different primitive types and how they can be used. The second parameter we pass in is the actual vertex data we created in our `InitializeVertices` method. The third parameter is the offset of the point data where we want to start drawing—in our case we want to start with the first point, so that is 0. Finally, we need to pass in the number of triangles we are drawing on the screen. We can calculate this by taking the number of points we have stored and dividing it by 3 (as there are 3 points in a triangle). For our example, this will return one triangle. If we compile and run the code at this point we should see a triangle drawn on our screen. It is not very pretty, as it is a dull shade of gray, but it is a triangle nonetheless. To see a screen shot, refer to Figure 4.3.

FIGURE 4.3   Drawing a triangle as our first demo.

TABLE 4.1   PrimitiveType Enumeration from the XNA documentation.

Member Name	Description
LineList	Renders the vertices as a list of isolated straight-line segments.
LineStrip	Renders the vertices as a single polyline.
PointList	Renders the vertices as a collection of isolated points. This value is unsupported for indexed primitives.
TriangleFan	Renders the vertices as a triangle fan.
TriangleList	Renders the specified vertices as a sequence of isolated triangles. Each group of three vertices defines a separate triangle. Back-face culling is affected by the current winding-order render state.
TriangleStrip	Renders the vertices as a triangle strip. The back-face culling flag is flipped automatically on even-numbered triangles.

Textures

We have a triangle finally drawn on the screen, but it does not look particularly good. We can fix that by adding a texture. Copy the texture from the Chapter4\XNADemo\XNADemo folder (texture.jpg) and paste that into our project. This invokes the XNA Content Pipeline, which we discuss in Part III, "Content Pipeline". For now, we just need to know that it makes it available as loadable content complete with a name by which we can access it. The asset will get the name "texture" (because that is the name of the file). We need to declare a private member field to store our texture:

```
private Texture2D texture;
```

We define our texture as a `Texture2D` object. This is another class that XNA provides for us. `Texture2D` inherits from the `Texture` class, which allows us to manipulate a texture resource. Now we need to actually load our texture into that variable. We do this in the `LoadGraphicsContent` method. Inside of the `loadAllContent` condition, add this line of code:

```
texture = content.Load<Texture2D>("texture");
```

Now we have our texture added to our project and loaded into a variable (with very little code), but we have yet to associate that texture to the effect that we used to draw the triangle. We will do that now by adding the following two lines of code right before our call to `effect.Begin` inside of our `Draw` method:

```
effect.TextureEnabled = true;
effect.Texture = texture;
```

This simply tells the effect we are using that we want to use textures, and then we actually assign the texture to our effect. It is really that simple. Go ahead and compile and run the code to see our nicely textured triangle!

Index Buffers

We have covered a lot of ground so far, but we aren't done yet. We want to create a rectangle on the screen and to do this we need another triangle. So that means we need three more vertices, or do we? Actually, we only need one more vertex to create our square because the second triangle we need to complete the square shares two of our existing points already. Feel free to review a couple of sections earlier where we talked about vertex buffers. We set up three points to make the triangle we just saw. To use the code as is we would need to create another three points, but two of those points are redundant and the amount of data it takes to represent the `VertexPositionNormalTexture` struct is not minimal, so we do not want to duplicate all of that data if we do not need to. Fortunately, we do not. XNA provides us with index buffers. Index buffers simply store indices that correspond to our vertex buffer. So to resolve our current dilemma of not wanting to duplicate our heavy vertex data we will instead duplicate our index data, which is much smaller. Our vertex buffer will only store four points (instead of six) and our index buffer will store six indices that will correspond to our vertices in the order we want them to be drawn. We need to increase our vertex array to hold four values instead of three. Make the following change:

```
vertices = new VertexPositionNormalTexture[4];
```

An index buffer simply describes the order in which we want the vertices in our vertex buffer to be drawn in our scene.

Find the `InitializeVertices` method in our code and add the last point we need for our rectangle. Try to do this before looking at the following code.

```
//top right
position = new Vector3(1, 1, 0);
textureCoordinates = new Vector2(1, 0);
vertices[3] = new VertexPositionNormalTexture(position, Vector3.Forward,
    textureCoordinates);
```

As you were writing the code, I imagine you were wondering about the texture coordinates for the points. We finally talked about textures, but not really how we mapped the texture to the vertices we created. We will take a moment and do that now before we continue our understanding of index buffers.

Texture coordinates start at the top left at (0,0) and end at the bottom right at (1,1). The bottom left texture coordinate is (0,1) and the top right is (1,0). Take a look at Figure 4.4 to see an example.

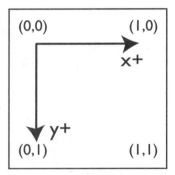

FIGURE 4.4   Texture coordinates start at the top left at (0,0) and end at the bottom right at (1,1).

If we wanted to map a vertex to the bottom center pixel of a texture, what should the values be? The horizontal axis is our x axis and the vertical axis is our y axis. We know we need a 1 in our y coordinate to get to the very bottom of the texture. To get to the middle of that bottom row, we would need to take the value in between 0 and 1, which is 0.5. So if we wanted to map a vertex to the bottom center pixel of a texture, we would map it at (0.5, 1). Back to our demo: Because the vertex we just added was the top right point of the rectangle, the texture coordinate we assigned to it was (1,0).

Now that we have a better understanding of why our texture mapped to our triangle correctly, we can get back to our index buffer. We have added a vertex to our code and now we need to create an index buffer to reference these four points. We need to create another private member field called indices:

```
private short[] indices;
```

Notice that we declared this as an array of short. We could have used int, but short takes up less room and we aren't going to have more than 65,535 indices in this demo. The next thing we need to do is actually create our method that will initialize our indices.

We will name this `InitializeIndices` and we will call this method from inside our `LoadGraphicsContent` method right after we make the call to `InitializeVertices`. Make sure that the vertex was added right before we initialize our vertex buffer and after we created all of the other vertices. This way the code for `InitializeIndices` shown next will work for us. It assumes the latest addition to our list of vertices is at the bottom of the list.

```
private void InitializeIndices()
{
    //6 vertices make up 2 triangles which make up our rectangle
    indices = new short[6];

    //triangle 1 (bottom portion)
    indices[0] = 0; // top left
    indices[1] = 1; // bottom right
    indices[2] = 2; // bottom left

    //triangle 2 (top portion)
    indices[3] = 0; // top left
    indices[4] = 3; // top right
    indices[5] = 1; // bottom right
}
```

In this method we know we are going to create two triangles (with three points each) so we create enough space to hold all six indices. We then populate our indices. We took care to add our vertices in a clockwise order when adding them to the vertex list, so we can simply set our first three indices to 0, 1, and 2. The second triangle, however, needs a little more thought. We know we have to add these in clockwise order, so we can start with any vertex and work our way around. Let us start with the top left vertex (the first vertex we added to our list—index of 0). That means we need to set our next index to be the top right vertex, which is the one we just added to the end of the list. We set that index to 3. Finally, we set the last point to the bottom right vertex, which was added to the vertex buffer second and has the index of 1.

Now we have our vertices created, complete with textured coordinates and position and even normals. We have our indices set up to use the vertex buffer in a way where we did not have to duplicate any of the complex vertex data. We further saved memory by using short instead of int because we will only have a few indices we need to store to represent our 3D object (our rectangle). Also, some older graphic cards do not support 32-bit (int) index buffers. The only thing left for us to do is to actually modify our code that draws the primitive to tell it we are now using an index buffer. To do that, find the Draw method and locate the call to DrawUserPrimitives. We will want to replace that line with the following line:

```
graphics.GraphicsDevice.DrawUserIndexedPrimitives(
    PrimitiveType.TriangleList, vertices, 0, vertices.Length,
    indices, 0, indices.Length / 3);
```

Notice that we changed the method we are calling on the graphics device. We are now passing in both vertex and index data. Let's break down the parameters we are passing in. We still pass in a triangle array as the first parameter and our array of vertices as the second parameter and we are leaving our vertex offset at 0. The next parameter is new and simply needs the number of vertices that is in our vertex array. The fifth parameter is our array of indices (this method has an override that accepts an array of int as well). The sixth parameter is the offset we want for our index buffer. We want to use all of the indices so we passed in 0. The final parameter, primitive count, is the same as the final parameter in the method we just replaced. Because we only have four vertices we needed to change that to our index array. Our indices array has six references to vertices in it and we take that value and divide it by three to get the number of triangles that are in our triangle list. When we compile and run the code we should see a rectangle that was created with our modified vertex buffer and our new index buffer!

As an exercise, modify the points in our vertex to have the rectangle slanted into the screen. This will require modifying a couple of our z values from 0 to something else. Give it a try!

XNA Game Components

Now that we have created this very exciting square, let's take a look at what it did to our performance. In this section we are going to create an XNA `GameComponent`. A game component allows us to separate pieces of logic into their own file that will be called automatically by the XNA Framework. We will take the frame rate code we added in our PerformanceBenchmark project from the last chapter and create a game component out of it. To do this, we need to add another file to our project, which we can call FPS.cs. We need to pick GameComponent as the file type from inside the Add New File dialog box of XNA Game Studio Express.

With a blank fps.cs in front of us we should see the class is inheriting from `Microsoft.Xna.Framework.GameComponent`. This is useful for components where we are only updating the internal data, typically through the `Update` method. For our frame rate calculation, however, we need to have our game component expose the `Draw` method because we want to know how many times a second we can draw our world on the screen. So we first need to change from which class we are inheriting. Instead of inheriting from `GameComponent`, we need to inherit from `DrawableGameComponent` so we can access the `Draw` method. We need to override the `Draw` method and use the same code we used in the PerformanceBenchmark project. To see the definition of the `DrawableGameComponent` to determine what is available for us to override, press F12 while the cursor is inside the `DrawableGameComponent` text.

Listing 4.1 contains the same code we used in the PerformanceBenchmark project. The difference is that it is inside of a drawable game component now. The biggest difference is our constructor so let's take a minute to dissect that now. As we learned in the last chapter, to measure a true frame rate we need to get the screen to draw as many times as it can and not wait on the monitor to do a vertical refresh before updating the screen. We could put this code inside of our main game class but for the projects in this book we typically let the game run a fixed pace and only change it when we are trying to measure our true frame rate. Because of this assumption, the code is set up to take these values in via the constructor of the FPS game component. Typically a game component only requires to pass in a game instance to the constructor but we can require other parameters if we need to. For this game component we are passing the values we initially set at the game level. We have a default constructor that will have the game render as fast as possible. These settings are per game, not per component.

LISTING 4.1   A drawable game component that calculates our FPS

```
#region Using Statements
using System;
using System.Collections.Generic;
using Microsoft.Xna.Framework;
#endregion

namespace XNADemo
{
    /// <summary>
    /// This is a game component that implements IUpdateable.
    /// </summary>
    public sealed partial class FPS
        : Microsoft.Xna.Framework.DrawableGameComponent
    {
        private float fps;
        private float updateInterval = 1.0f;
        private float timeSinceLastUpdate = 0.0f;
        private float framecount = 0;

        public FPS(Game game)
           : this(game, false, false, game.TargetElapsedTime) { }

        public FPS(Game game, bool synchWithVerticalRetrace,
                   bool isFixedTimeStep, TimeSpan targetElapsedTime)
            : base(game)
        {
            GraphicsDeviceManager graphics =
                (GraphicsDeviceManager)Game.Services.GetService(
                typeof(IGraphicsDeviceManager));

            graphics.SynchronizeWithVerticalRetrace = synchWithVerticalRetrace;
            Game.IsFixedTimeStep = isFixedTimeStep;
            Game.TargetElapsedTime = targetElapsedTime;
        }

        /// <summary>
```

LISTING 4.1   Continued

```
    /// Allows the game component to perform any initialization
    /// it needs to before starting to run. This is where it can query for
    /// any required services and load content.
    /// </summary>
    public sealed override void Initialize()
    {
        // TODO: Add your initialization code here
        base.Initialize();
    }


    /// <summary>
    /// Allows the game component to update itself.
    /// </summary>
    /// <param name="gameTime">Provides snapshot of timing values.</param>
    public sealed override void Update(GameTime gameTime)
    {
        // TODO: Add your update code here


        base.Update(gameTime);
    }


    public sealed override void Draw(GameTime gameTime)
    {
        float elapsed = (float)gameTime.ElapsedRealTime.TotalSeconds;
        framecount++;
        timeSinceLastUpdate += elapsed;
        if (timeSinceLastUpdate > updateInterval)
        {
            fps = framecount / timeSinceLastUpdate;

#if XBOX360
            System.Diagnostics.Debug.WriteLine("FPS: " + fps.ToString());
#else
            Game.Window.Title = "FPS: " + fps.ToString();
#endif
            framecount = 0;
            timeSinceLastUpdate -= updateInterval;
        }
        base.Draw(gameTime);
    }
  }
}
```

Now that we have the game component created and added to our project we need to actually use it inside of the demo. To do this we need to create a private member field in our game class as follows:

```
private FPS fps;
```

Then we can add the following code inside of our game constructor after we initialize our graphics and content variables:

```
#if DEBUG
    fps = new FPS(this);
    Components.Add(fps);
#endif
```

We wrapped this with the DEBUG compiler directive but we might want to run in debug mode without rendering the code as fast as possible. We can either change how we are initializing our fps variable by passing in explicit values to the constructor or we can just simply comment out this code. After initializing the fps object we then add the component to our game's component collection. The XNA Framework will then call the component's Update and Draw (and other virtual methods) at the same time it calls the game's methods.

It can be very beneficial to separate logic and items we need to draw to the screen. It provides a nice clean way to separate our code but it does have some overhead. It is definitely not wise to handle all of the objects we want to draw as game components. That is just entirely too many components the framework would need to go through and call Update, Draw, and the other methods for. Instead, if we want to separate our enemies from our player, then it might be beneficial to have our player in its own game component and then have an "enemy manager" as its own game component. The enemy manager could then handle itself which enemies it needed to draw, move, and so on. This way, as enemies came and went, the manager would be handling all of that logic and not the core game class adding and removing a bunch of enemy components. Game components can really help, but we cannot go overboard with it or our performance will suffer.

Checking Performance

Now that we have our fps functionality inside of a game component we can check out if the code we wrote for the demo to display the rectangle is performing well or not. Fortunately, we recorded the frame rate we were getting in the last chapter so we have a baseline from which to work.

We will need to set up an Xbox 360 game project for this solution as we discussed in Chapter 2, "XNA and the Xbox 360." Once we have it set up, we can run our application on our machine and on the Xbox 360 to measure performance.

Machine A ran the benchmark code at about 280 fps. The Xbox 360 ran the same benchmark code at about 5,220 fps. With our new code, Machine A is running at 206 fps. The Xbox 360 is running at only 114 fps—ouch! What did we do wrong? Well, because we tested for performance right away, we know that it has to be an issue with our Draw method, so we should take a look at it again to see what is going on. We can also run the XNA Framework Remote Performance Monitor for the Xbox 360 and see what the garbage collector is doing. If a refresher is needed, information on running this application can be found in Chapter 2.

By launching our demo through the performance monitor tool, we can see that the "Objects Moved by Compactor" value is between 75,000 and 85,000 *every second*. We can see the "Objects not moved by Compactor" value is constantly growing with about 5,000 or more per second. This is obviously not good, and it is why we are thrashing our Xbox 360. Looking in the code we can see that we are creating a new instance of the BasicEffect class on every frame. That has got to be hurting us, so we can make that a member field of the game class because we are never changing it. We can break it out and actually initialize the effect inside our LoadGraphicsContent method as follows:

```
effect = new BasicEffect(graphics.GraphicsDevice, null);
```

Now we can run our application again and look at the frame rate it is spitting out in our debug window. It is much better now, as it is about 2,850 fps. However, that is still a far cry from our 5,220. Checking the frame rate on Machine A reveals that we are running at 207 fps. So although the change really made a difference on the Xbox 360, it did not do much for us on the Windows side of things. Of course, this is expected as the issue we were having was with the garbage collector. Remember, from the last chapter, that each time we were creating a new BasicEffect object in Windows, it was creating it and destroying it all in the same frame and so when the garbage collector ran, it simply removed the dead objects. On the Xbox 360, however, the garbage collector has to go through the entire heap to determine what is dead as it starts to get full. So we have helped our situation on the console, but we are still only running at 53 percent of what we were at the baseline. Let's dig around some more. We also see the following line of code at the top of our Draw method:

```
graphics.GraphicsDevice.VertexDeclaration = new
    VertexDeclaration(graphics.GraphicsDevice,
    VertexPositionNormalTexture.VertexElements);
```

This cannot be doing the garbage collector any favors. Although we need to set our vertex declaration on every frame, we do not need to create it every frame. We can create a private member field to hold our vertex declaration as follows:

```
private VertexDeclaration vertexDeclaration;
```

Now we can actually initialize that variable inside of the LoadGraphicsContent method right after our BasicEffect initialization. The code for this is as follows:

```
vertexDeclaration = new VertexDeclaration(graphics.GraphicsDevice,
    VertexPositionNormalTexture.VertexElements);
```

Finally, we can change the original statement inside of Draw to set graphics device vertex declaration to the variable we just initialized:

```
graphics.GraphicsDevice.VertexDeclaration = vertexDeclaration;
```

Now we are only creating the vertex declaration once and setting it once instead of every frame. This is encouraging, as we are now at about 3,230 fps on the Xbox 360 and the performance is still the same on Machine A at about 207 fps. So just with a little bit of effort we optimized our code from running at a mere 114 fps on the Xbox 360 to a more reasonable 3,230 fps.

What else can we do? Surely just displaying two triangles on the screen should not decrease our frame rate by 39 percent. As we go back to the performance monitoring tool, we can see that our "Objects Moved by Compactor" and "Objects Not Moved by Compactor" values are at a much better number—zero!

If we comment out the DrawUserIndexedPrimitives method we see that our frame rate jumps back up to 5,220 fps. So it means the "problem" exists in this method. Is there anything that can be done with the code we have? As our baseline code did not do anything and this code is actually drawing something (even if it is only two triangles), it might be that this is as good as it gets—after all more than 3,000 fps is not that shabby! However, there has been some debate in regard to if the DrawUser* methods are as fast as their Draw* counterparts. We are going to find out if that is the case.

DrawUserIndexedPrimitives **vs.** DrawIndexedPrimitives

Make a copy of the solution folder we are working on and rename the new folder XNADemo–DIP. We can leave the solution file and everything else the same name. After opening this new project, we need to give it another title in the AssemblyInfo.cs file. We also need to change the GUID value so that when we deploy this it will show up as a new entry in our XNA Game Launcher list. We can just replace any one digit with another digit for this example. This way, we can easily compare this demo with the one we just finished inside of the remote performance monitor for the Xbox 360. Once this has been done, we need to modify our game code by adding the following code to the end of the InitializeIndices method:

```
graphics.GraphicsDevice.Indices = new IndexBuffer(graphics.GraphicsDevice,
    sizeof(short) * indices.Length, ResourceUsage.WriteOnly,
    ResourceManagementMode.Automatic, IndexElementSize.SixteenBits);

graphics.GraphicsDevice.Indices.SetData(indices);
```

We are initializing the index buffer on our graphics device by telling it the size of our indices array as well as setting the ResourceUsage parameter just like we did before. We also tell XNA to handle the memory of this object automatically. Finally we tell it that we have an array of short by setting the IndexElementSize to 16 bits, the size of the short type (System.Int16). The second statement actually sets the array of indices inside of the graphic devices index buffer.

We needed to define our index buffer because the method we are replacing in the Draw method needs to have the data explicitly set on the graphics device. The following is the code we are going to replace our DrawUserIndexedPrimitives inside the Draw method with:

```
graphics.GraphicsDevice.DrawIndexedPrimitives(
    PrimitiveType.TriangleList, 0, 0, vertices.Length, 0, indices.Length / 3);
```

Finally, we need to set the source of our graphic devices vertex buffer. We do that with the following code, which should be placed at the end of the InitializeVertices method:

```
vertexBuffer = new VertexBuffer(graphics.GraphicsDevice,
    VertexPositionNormalTexture.SizeInBytes * vertices.Length,
    ResourceUsage.WriteOnly, ResourceManagementMode.Automatic);
vertexBuffer.SetData(vertices);

graphics.GraphicsDevice.Vertices[0].SetSource(vertexBuffer, 0,
    VertexPositionNormalTexture.SizeInBytes);
```

The first statement is used to populate our vertex buffer with the actual vertices we created. We pass in the graphics device followed by the size of the buffer. The size of the buffer is determined by taking the size of the struct we are using to represent our vertex (in this case it is VertexPositionNormalTexture) and multiplying that by the number of points we have. In this case it is three, but instead of hard-coding three, we grab the length property of our vertex array. The third parameter describes how we plan to use this vertex buffer. We can find all of the different options for this enumeration by looking in the documentation that was installed with XNA Game Studio Express. We use ResourceUsage.WriteOnly because we will not be reading from the list (reading would fail with this setting) and it allows the graphics driver to determine the best location in memory to efficiently perform the rendering and write operations. The final parameter of this method tells XNA to handle our memory management automatically. For more information on this enumeration, take look at the documentation. The second statement takes our vertex data we set in our InitializeVertices method and sets our vertex buffer with it.

We can set up our vertexBuffer private member field next:

```
private VertexBuffer vertexBuffer;
```

After these changes, we can compile and run the code on the Xbox 360 and see that our frame rate has done nothing. The conclusion to draw here is that it does not make a difference if we use DrawUserPrimitives or DrawPrimitives methods. It was a good exercise, but for our sample here it did not make a difference. Whichever version is more convenient for us as we develop our game is the one we should use. However, the results could change if we were drawing more vertices. Another performance test could be to add more vertices and indices to see if one scales better than the other. For example, instead of only rendering 4 vertices, you could render 10,000 and see how the two methods compare. Have fun finding the most efficient way to use these methods in your particular situation.

Transformations Revolutions

Just in case it is not clear where these transformation section titles come from, when dealing with matrices it is very hard not to think about *The Matrix* movies. What a great trilogy.

Anyway, the reason we are back yet again to discuss transformations is because we want to gain practical knowledge about transformations and not just the theory we learned about earlier. We need to look at some of the transformation functions that XNA has included in the framework.

In the earlier scenario we had a 3D object that we wanted to scale, rotate (twice), and then translate. We said that we had to do it in a particular order but did not take the discussion any further. Now that we know how to create a 3D object, we can run through the exercise of transforming the object the way we want.

We can make a copy of the demo we just created (XNADemo–DIP) and call it Transformations. We need to rename the assembly title and the GUID again so it will not overwrite the demo with the same GUID on the Xbox 360. We can actually rename each project as well as the solution and change the namespaces if that is preferred.

The scenario from earlier said we wanted to move to a position and scale our object down and then rotate to the left and down some. We said that doing this would need to be done in the correct order because matrix multiplication was not commutative. We are going to modify our code and move our existing rectangle into the distance. Then we will create another rectangle and transform it to get the desired effect.

To start, we need to take a section of code out of our Draw method and create a new method called DrawRectangle. Cut all of the code after we assign the texture to the effect and before we call the Draw method on our base class. Now paste the code into our newly created DrawRectangle method as follows:

```
private void DrawRectangle(ref Matrix world)
{
    effect.World = world;
    effect.Begin();

    //As we are doing a basic effect, there is no need to loop
    //basic effect will only have one pass on the technique
    effect.CurrentTechnique.Passes[0].Begin();  //pass.Begin();

    graphics.GraphicsDevice.DrawIndexedPrimitives(PrimitiveType.TriangleList,
        0, 0, vertices.Length, 0, indices.Length / 3);

    effect.CurrentTechnique.Passes[0].End();

    effect.End();
}
```

The method takes a matrix as a parameter. This is going to be the matrix we transform before sending it to the effect. To demonstrate another way of setting the passes on our `BasicEffect`, we can just grab the first pass on the current technique instead of doing a `foreach` loop because we know there is only one pass we can get by with this optimization.

Now we need to call this method inside of our `Draw` method where we just removed the code. So right above the call to `Draw` on our base class we can add the following code:

```
world = Matrix.Identity;
DrawRectangle(ref world);
```

If we run this, we should get the exact same results as before. We are still rendering one rectangle in the exact same position—the origin of the world. We can remove the member variable world and where we set it at the top of our `Draw` method as we are not using it in this example. Following is our new `Draw` method with the changes mentioned so far:

```
protected override void Draw(GameTime gameTime)
{
    graphics.GraphicsDevice.Clear(Color.CornflowerBlue);

    // TODO: Add your drawing code here
    effect.Projection = projection;
    effect.View = view;

    effect.EnableDefaultLighting();

    effect.TextureEnabled = true;
    effect.Texture = texture;

    world = Matrix.Identity;
    DrawRectangle(ref world);


    base.Draw(gameTime);
}
```

Let's move our existing triangle into the distance. We can move it backward and to the right some. To do this we will need to use the built-in XNA matrix help method `Matrix.CreateTranslation`. We know we are at the origin (0,0,0) and we want to move back and to the right. Remember that XNA uses a right-handed coordinate system so this means that to move the rectangle backward we need to subtract from the z position. To move it right we need to add to the x position. `CreateTranslation` takes in `Vector3` as a parameter so we can set our values into the vector before passing it into the helper function. Change where we set the world matrix to the following:

```
world = Matrix.CreateTranslation(new Vector3(3.0f, 0, -10.0f));
```

We moved the rectangle to the right by 3 units and to the back by 10 units. Now we need to add another rectangle. Let's add one to the same place where this one originally was located. To do this we need to simply pass in `Matrix.Identity` as the code that follows shows:

```
world = Matrix.Identity;
DrawRectangle(ref world);
```

When we run the code we cannot see the rectangle we originally drew because it is further back and this new rectangle is obstructing our view. Let's scale it down a little bit to about 75 percent of what it is currently. To do this we need to call the XNA matrix helper method `Matrix.CreateScale` as follows:

```
world = Matrix.CreateScale(0.75f);
```

By replacing the identity matrix with this `CreateScale` matrix we can see our rectangle is now smaller so we can partially see the one we moved toward the back. A screen shot of this can be seen in Figure 4.5.

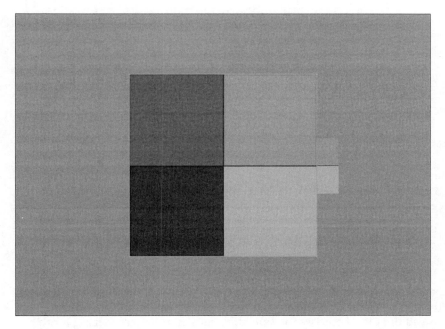

FIGURE 4.5   A smaller rectangle is obstructing the view of a larger rectangle that is further away.

Let's move this rectangle back about 5 units, to the left 3, and down 1 unit. We want to keep the scale that we have in place. We need to multiply our matrices together as discussed earlier, so we change our world matrix again to look like the following code:

```
world = Matrix.CreateScale(0.75f) *
    Matrix.CreateTranslation(new Vector3(-3.0f, -1.0f, -5.0f));
```

We also wanted to rotate our object to one side and downward. We can do that using a couple of other helper methods in the `Matrix` struct. There are three different helper functions and each will rotate one of the three axes. These methods are called `Matrix.CreateRotationX`, `Matrix.CreateRotationY`, and `Matrix.CreateRotationZ`. To add rotation to make the object turn to the side we need to rotate around the y axis. To visualize this take a look at Figure 4.6.

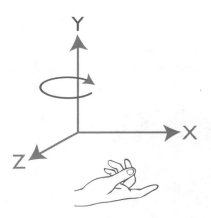

FIGURE 4.6   Rotating around the y axis.

Let's rotate around the y axis by 30 degrees. The rotation helper methods require a value in radians, but the `MathHelper` class allows us to easily convert degrees to radians. So we can rotate 30 degrees around the y axis by using the following code:

```
world = Matrix.CreateScale(0.75f) *
    Matrix.CreateTranslation(new Vector3(-3.0f, -1.0f, -5.0f)) *
    Matrix.CreateRotationY(MathHelper.ToRadians(30.0f));
```

If we run this code we do not see the rectangle. The reason is that we rotated the matrix after we translated it. By doing this, we effectively told it to rotate around the origin (where it was) instead of at its center. By rotating after translating we are making it orbit around where it was. Instead, we want it to rotate around its own center and to do this we need to replace the world matrix with the following code:

```
world = Matrix.CreateScale(0.75f) *
    Matrix.CreateRotationY(MathHelper.ToRadians(30.0f)) *
    Matrix.CreateTranslation(new Vector3(-3.0f, -1.0f, -5.0f));
```

Now when we run this we have rotated around the center of our object to get the desired results. Finally, we wanted to throw in another rotation for good measure. This time we wanted to rotate downward so we need to rotate on the x axis. Assuming we want to rotate it about 15 degrees we can use the following code:

```
world = Matrix.CreateScale(0.75f) *
    Matrix.CreateRotationX(MathHelper.ToRadians(15.0f)) *
    Matrix.CreateRotationY(MathHelper.ToRadians(30.0f)) *
    Matrix.CreateTranslation(new Vector3(-3.0f, -1.0f, -5.0f));
```

The code scales our rectangle, rotates it around the x axis, rotates it around the y axis, and finally it moves the rectangle. By multiplying the matrices in the right order we were able to accomplish the desired effect. The screen shot can be seen in Figure 4.7.

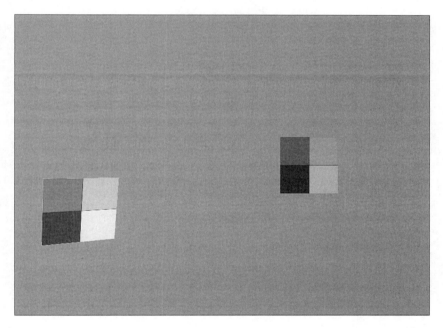

FIGURE 4.7   Applying matrix transformations in the right order will produce the desired effect.

Summary

We covered a lot of ground in this chapter. We discussed the foundation of everything we will do in the 3D worlds we create. We set up a camera to view our 3D world. We discussed basic 3D terminology and how it correlates to XNA. We examined how to use different methods to create 3D objects on the screen with points we manually plotted inside of our code.

We spent quite a bit of time going through the performance checking process to determine what things we could do to improve our code. We put into practice what we learned in the last chapter.

We ended the chapter by actually doing matrix transformations, a concept we learned about at the beginning of the chapter. We applied multiple transformations to one of our objects and saw how important it was to get the multiplication order right when dealing with transformations.

This chapter is very important, as the rest of the book will build on this foundation. Make sure to take time to let it sink in. Reread it, dwell on it, dream about it—OK, maybe that is a little bit too extreme.

CHAPTER 5

Input Devices and Cameras

We created the camera in the last chapter but it did not move. We did not allow any input (other than exiting the demo with the GamePad's Back button, which the template provides for us). We are going to change that now. We are going to learn how to use our input devices (keyboard, mouse, and game pad controller) by working with our camera. To accomplish this we are going to start a game library that we can utilize in our demos and games. Let's get started!

Creating a Game Service

Instead of just throwing input and camera code inside of another demo, we are going to take time to create a library (even if it is just a small one). Before we dig into that, however, we need to discuss game services and how they are used with game components as it will greatly simplify our library architecture.

We have a camera we have been using up to this point. The camera code is actually inside of the game object and although this is perfectly acceptable for smaller demos, we can take the time in this chapter to move the camera into its own game component. We have already moved our FPS code into its own game component and we will end up putting that game component into this library we are creating. In this chapter we are also going to create an input handler. This input handler is going to be a game service.

We learned how to create a game component in the last chapter with our FPS game component. Having a game component makes it easier to manage our code with items broken out into logical pieces. However, we can run into an issue when multiple game components we make need to access the same piece of functionality (or each other). We can see this more easily when thinking about input.

We want to put our code that handles the input into its own game component—it is the XNA way after all. So let's assume we have our input game component done and we have a player game component that needs access to the input device so the player can react to the gamer as they use the input device. To get our player game component (and any other future game component we make) to be able to access the input handler game component, we will turn the input handler game component into a game service.

NOTE

We need to remember what we learned from the last chapter: Too many game components can hurt performance and in those cases we can use a "manager" game component that handles its own objects. The example we used last chapter was creating enemies. Some XNA beginners will actually create an enemy game component for every enemy they have on the screen (or even a bullet game component). They then try to add and remove or set visible and invisible each and every game component. This can bring a system to a crawl as there is overhead associated with a game component and it just is not meant to be used in that way. A better approach is to create an `EnemyManager` or `BulletManager` game component and allow the manager to handle which enemies or bullets are being displayed.

The `Game` object holds collections of services. We have actually been using one already. The `GraphicsDevice` is a game service built into XNA. When we created our FPS game component we needed access to the `GraphicsDevice` so we wrote the following code in the constructor for the FPS code:

```
GraphicsDeviceManager graphics =
    (GraphicsDeviceManager)Game.Services.GetService(
    typeof(IGraphicsDeviceManager));
```

Game components always have a `Game` object passed to them so every game component can obtain access to any game service associated with the game. The preceding code does just that. It creates a reference to the game's `GraphicsDeviceManager` memory. When we create a new solution by selecting a game template, the code generated for us includes a variable that holds the graphics device manager and is called `graphics`. Although we could have made the `graphics` variable public and accessed the data that way, it is much more elegant to use a service. Otherwise, we would probably be creating many publicly accessible properties, which would hurt our game design.

Because XNA used an interface for the graphics device manager object and because they added it to the services collection of the game object, we are able to access it from any piece of code that has access to the game object. We can see this if we look at the preceding code again. It calls out to our game object to which we have a reference and it calls its `Services.GetService` method. This method takes in a type and returns an object. We pass in the type of the interface and get returned the graphics device object. We perform a cast on it so we can work with it intelligently.

We have seen how we used a game service that XNA created for us; let's learn how to actually create a game service. To get started we can copy the Transformations project we created in the last chapter. We can rename the new project InputDemo.

We will create the input game service now inside of this project and then move it along with our FPS game component when we create our library in the next section. We need to add a new game component file to our project, which we can call InputHandler. The first step to making this a game service is to create an interface.

The game services collection can only have one of any particular interface. This is how it knows which object to return when a request is made. This means that if we have more than one object of the same interface and we need to access them both as a game service, we would need to create a different interface for each object. Fortunately, an interface can be empty. This means through inheritance we can quickly make our "duplicate" object inherit from the original object and from the new interface that does not require any additional implementation.

To add our interface we need to add in the following code:

```
public interface IInputHandler { };
```

We could either create a new code file to store this interface or we can put it directly in the input handler file. Currently, our input handler interface is blank, but we will actually be adding properties to it soon. Now we need our game component to inherit from this interface (as well as the GameComponent object it is already inheriting from). We do this by changing our class declaration to the following:

```
public partial class InputHandler
    : Microsoft.Xna.Framework.GameComponent, IInputHandler
```

We also need to make sure our input handler is actually using the XNA Framework's Input namespace:

```
using Microsoft.Xna.Framework.Input;
```

To finish making this game component into a game service we need to actually add it to the game's services collection. We do this in the constructor with the following code:

```
game.Services.AddService(typeof(IInputHandler), this);
```

Adding a service is much like getting a service. We pass in the type of the interface for the object and then we actually pass in our object. We always want to pass in the type of our interface and not the type of our actual class. This way when other objects access the game service, they can simply do it through the interface and not have to explicitly use the object. Of course if needed, we can cast to the actual object if the need arises. We should be able to compile the code at this point. Although it does not do anything differently than it did in the last chapter, we are laying a foundation so we can get started on our library. Let's do that now!

Starting a Library

We have two game components currently (well, one is a skeleton) and are planning on adding more. We should put these into a library that we can easily access from multiple demos and games. We are going to set up a library project to hold our FPS game component as well as the start of the input handler class we just created. To do this we will create a new Windows Game Library project, which we can call XELibrary. While we are at it, we should go ahead and add an Xbox 360 Game Library to our solution as well. Of course, it is possible to do this in either of the ways we discussed in Chapter 2, "XNA and the Xbox 360." However, this book is using the approach of one solution file with two projects.

Now that we have our solution set up with the two projects (or two solutions set up), we can start building our library. To begin we will add the FPS.cs file from our last project. If the game project we were just in (InputDemo) is closed, we should open it in conjunction with our library solution so we can easily get code from it to build our input game component. Let's copy the actual FPS.cs and InputHandler.cs files from our Windows Explorer InputDemo folder into our Visual C# Express XELibrary project. We can then add those items in our other project as well by showing all items, right-clicking them, and adding them to our project. At this point we have started a library that contains our fully made FPS game component and a skeleton of our InputHandler game component. We can remove the Class1.cs file from our projects. We should also make sure our namespace is consistent across the library and can set it to XELibrary. We should be able to build the library project with no compilation errors.

> **NOTE**
>
> As we add items to one project (Windows) we will need to add them to the other project (Xbox 360) as well. From here on, it will be assumed that as we create a project we will create the other platform's counterpart and as we add files to one project it will be assumed that they are added to the other project as well.

Before we start in on our input handler code, we can go ahead and create another game component called Camera. We are going to move the initial camera code we have created to this game component. We will also talk to our input handler game service inside of this game component as well. Let's go ahead and set up a private member field to hold an instance of the input handler because we know we will need it. While we are at it we should also add a variable to hold an instance of our game's graphics device because we will need to set up our camera. We do this by adding the following code to our Camera.cs file:

```
private IInputHandler input;
private GraphicsDeviceManager graphics;
```

Now that we have our fields created we can actually initialize them inside of our constructor as follows:

```
graphics = (GraphicsDeviceManager)Game.Services.GetService(
    typeof(IGraphicsDeviceManager));
input = (IInputHandler)game.Services.GetService(typeof(IInputHandler));
```

Now we can move our `InitializeCamera` method from our `InputDemo` Game1.cs code into our `Camera` class. We need to cut the call to this method from the `Initialize` method inside of our game project. Now we need to paste the call into our camera's `Initialize` method. The updated code in our camera class should look like the following:

```
public override void Initialize()
{
    base.Initialize();
    InitializeCamera();
}

private void InitializeCamera()
{
    float aspectRatio = (float)graphics.GraphicsDevice.Viewport.Width /
        (float)graphics.GraphicsDevice.Viewport.Height;
    Matrix.CreatePerspectiveFieldOfView(MathHelper.PiOver4, aspectRatio,
        1.0f, 10000.0f, out projection);

    Matrix.CreateLookAt(ref cameraPosition, ref cameraTarget,
        ref cameraUpVector, out view);
}
```

We did not modify this code; we simply moved it from our InputDemo game class into our XELibrary camera class. Notice we called `InitializeCamera` after calling `base.Initialize`. This is because we are utilizing the graphics device and it is not available until the main game class finishes with its `Initialize` method.

Our `InitializeCamera` method is using some member fields we have not moved yet. We need to move the following code from our demo to our library:

```
private Matrix projection;
private Matrix view;
private Vector3 cameraPosition = new Vector3(0.0f, 0.0f, 3.0f);
private Vector3 cameraTarget = Vector3.Zero;
private Vector3 cameraUpVector = Vector3.Up;
```

Because we moved our view and projection fields from our demo, the demo will no longer compile until we change our demo's `Draw` method where we set the effect's view and projection so it will display our objects correctly. We could leave them in the game class as public fields and have the `Camera` game component work with them there. A cleaner approach would be to leave the camera self-contained and access those properties from inside of our demo. Let's create and initialize our camera game component inside of our demo. We can use the following code:

```
camera = new Camera(this);
Components.Add(camera);
```

We also need to set up the member field as follows:

```
private Camera camera;
```

We need to clean up our demo project by removing the FPS.cs and InputHandler.cs files as we now have them inside of our game library. Speaking of our game library, we need to actually reference it inside of our project. Because we will be working with both the library and the demo for this chapter the easiest thing for us to do is to close the library solution and then add the projects to the demo solution. We wanted to create the initial library solution first so we can easily access it outside of any particular game or demo we are working on. But when we are making a lot of changes to the library while working on a game or demo we will probably be more efficient if we just associate them inside of the same solution. Of course, this is all a preference. Regardless, we need to add a reference to the library into our demo. We need to make sure to reference the Windows library in the Windows demo and the Xbox 360 library in the Xbox 360 demo.

After having the library projects loaded up inside of our demo solution we now need to add a using statement to the top of our Game1.cs file in our demo project. We need to use the XELibrary as shown here:

```
using XELibrary;
```

If we compile at this point the only errors we should see are inside of our demo's Draw method stating that it has no idea what view and projection are. We are going to fix that now by changing that code to use our camera's view and projection properties. We do not have any properties yet in our Camera object? Well, let's change that. We need to add the following code to our camera game component:

```
public Matrix View
{
    get { return view; }
}

public Matrix Projection
{
    get { return projection; }
}
```

Now we can access them inside of our demo's Draw method. Let's change the properties we set on our effect with the following code:

```
effect.Projection = camera.Projection;
effect.View = camera.View;
```

Now we can successfully compile our code again. Not only that, but we can run it and it will function just like before, but now we have started a library!

Working with Input Devices

We will be populating the stub we created for handling our input. We are going to create a stationary camera and a first person. Both of these cameras will need to respond to user input. We need to learn how to handle input devices and utilize them to move our camera and fully see the worlds we create.

Keyboard

The first input device we will talk about is the keyboard. XNA provides us with helper classes that allow us to easily determine the state of our input devices. We determine the state of our keyboard by declaring a variable to store our keyboard state and then calling the GetState method on the Keyboard helper object. We can then query that variable to determine which key (or keys) is being pressed or released. We can start by adding a private member field to store our keyboard state. We do this via the following code inside of our InputHandler game component:

```
private KeyboardState keyboardState;
```

Then we can find the Update method that was stubbed out for us when the InputHandler game component was created.

```
keyboardState = Keyboard.GetState();
if (keyboardState.IsKeyDown(Keys.Escape))
    Game.Exit();
```

We can put this at the very beginning of the Update method. We are simply storing the state of the keyboard and then checking to see if the Escape key was pressed. If so, we simply exit the program. It doesn't get much simpler than that! So now when we run the program we can exit by pressing the Escape key (instead of having to close the window with our mouse).

Although being able to exit our game easily is important, we still haven't done anything exciting. Let's set up our camera so we swivel back and forth if the left or right keys are pressed. To do this we need to add and initialize a new private member field called cameraReference inside of our Camera game component:

```
private Vector3 cameraReference = new Vector3(0.0f, 0.0f, -1.0f);
```

This camera reference direction will not change throughout the game, but we will be passing it in as a reference so we cannot declare it as a readonly variable. Typically this value will either be (0,0,1) or (0,0,-1). We chose to have a negative z value so we can continue to have our camera face the same way.

Now that we have our camera reference direction set up, we need to apply any movement and rotation to our view of the world. So if the player wants to look left and right we can adjust our view matrix accordingly so that our view of the world is from a certain angle. To look left and right we need to rotate around our y axis. We can add the following code to our Update method right before our call out to the base object's Update method (we are still in our Camera class):

```
Matrix rotationMatrix;
Matrix.CreateRotationY(MathHelper.ToRadians(cameraYaw), out rotationMatrix);
// Create a vector pointing the direction the camera is facing.
Vector3 transformedReference;
Vector3.Transform(ref cameraReference, ref rotationMatrix,
    out transformedReference);
// Calculate the position the camera is looking at.
Vector3.Add(ref cameraPosition, ref transformedReference, out cameraTarget);

Matrix.CreateLookAt(ref cameraPosition, ref cameraTarget, ref cameraUpVector,
    out view);
```

Because we know we will be rotating, we will create a matrix to hold our rotation. With a helper function from XNA we will create a matrix with the appropriate values to rotate our camera on the y axis by a certain number of degrees. We are storing that value in a variable that we will set with our input devices. We will see how we set that value with our keyboard soon. Once we have our matrix with all of the translations, scaling, and rotations that we need (in this case we are only rotating) we can create a transform vector that will allow us to change the target of the camera. We get this transformed vector by using another XNA helper method, `Vector3.Transform`. We then add the transformed camera reference to our camera position, which will give us our new camera target. To do this, we could have used the plus (+) operator like the following code:

```
cameraTarget = cameraPosition + transformedReference;
```

However, it is much more efficient to use the built-in static `Add` method of the `Vector3` struct because it allows us to pass our vectors by reference instead of having to copy the values to memory. Finally, we reset our view with our new camera target. We also need to set the following private member field that we used in the code:

```
private float cameraYaw = 0.0f;
```

Now we are to the point where we can compile the code, but our newly added code does not do anything for us. This is because we are never changing our rotation angle. It stays at 0 on every frame. Let's change that now with our keyboard. Inside of our `InputHandler` class, we need to update our `IInputHandler` interface to expose the keyboard state we retrieved earlier. Let's add the following code inside of our interface:

```
KeyboardState KeyboardState { get; }
```

Now, we need to implement that property inside of the class. An easy way to do this is to right-click IInputHandler where we derived from it and select Implement Interface. We will be doing this a couple of times and each time it will create a region so we will have to clean up the code and remove the extra regions the IDE provides for us. Now we need to change the get value to retrieve our internal `keyboardState` value as follows:

```
public KeyboardState KeyboardState
{
    get { return(keyboardState); }
}
```

Now that we have exposed our keyboard state we can utilize it inside of our `Camera` object. We need to add the following code to our `Update` method right above the previous code inside of our camera object:

```
if (input.KeyboardState.IsKeyDown(Keys.Left))
    cameraYaw += spinRate;
if (input.KeyboardState.IsKeyDown(Keys.Right))
    cameraYaw -= spinRate;

if (cameraYaw > 360)
    cameraYaw -= 360;
else if (cameraYaw < 0)
    cameraYaw += 360;
```

We also need to make sure camera is using the XNA Framework's `Input` namespace because we are accessing the `Keys` enumeration:

```
using Microsoft.Xna.Framework.Input;
```

Finally, we add this constant to the top of our camera class:

```
private const float spinRate = 2.0f;
```

In our update code we utilized the current keyboard state we already captured and checked to see if either the left arrow or right arrow on the keyboard was pressed. If the player wants to rotate to the left then we add our spin rate constant to our current camera yaw angle. (Yaw, pitch, and roll are terms borrowed from flight dynamics. Because we are using a right-handed coordinate system, this means that yaw is rotation around the y axis, pitch is rotation around the x axis, and roll is rotation around the z axis.) If the player wants to rotate to the right then we subtract our spin rate constant from our current camera yaw angle. Finally we just check to make sure that we do not have an invalid rotation angle.

There is one last thing we need to do before we can run our code again. We need to actually add our input handler game component to our game's collection of components. We can declare our member field as follows:

```
private InputHandler input;
```

Now we can actually initialize that variable and add it to the collection inside of our constructor with this code:

```
input = new InputHandler(this);
Components.Add(input);
```

We can compile and run the code and move knowing that our left and right arrows rotate the camera. When running we can see that our objects are just flying by. It almost seems they are blinking we are turning so fast. This is because we are calling our `Update` statement as fast as possible. We can modify the game code where we are initializing our fps variable to use a fixed time step:

```
fps = new FPS(this, false, true);
```

For the preceding code to work we need to add another constructor to our FPS code. We are doing this is so we don't need to actually pass in our target elapsed time value if we want it to be the default.

```
public FPS(Game game, bool synchWithVerticalRetrace, bool isFixedTimeStep)
    : this(game, synchWithVerticalRetrace, isFixedTimeStep,
            game.TargetElapsedTime) { }
```

Now when we run the code we can see the objects move by at a consistent and slower rate. This is because the `Update` method is now only getting called 60 times a second instead of whatever rate our machine was running at.

We will notice, however, that as it renders the rectangles that our screen is "choppy." The reason is that we are not letting XNA only draw during our monitor's vertical refresh. We could do this by setting our second parameter to true and we would see the screen rotate at a nice even pace with the screen drawing nicely. However, a better way to handle this is by utilizing the elapsed time between calls to our methods. We need to retrieve the elapsed time since the last time our `Update` method was called and then multiply our `spinRate` by this delta of the time between calls. We will change the camera code snippet to match the following:

```
float timeDelta = (float)gameTime.ElapsedGameTime.TotalSeconds;

if (input.KeyboardState.IsKeyDown(Keys.Left))
    cameraYaw += (spinRate * timeDelta);
if (input.KeyboardState.IsKeyDown(Keys.Right))
    cameraYaw -= (spinRate * timeDelta);
```

We can modify our game code to call the default constructor again:

```
fps = new FPS(this);
```

Now we are just creeping along. This is because our spin rate is so low. We had it low because we were relying on the update method to be called 60 times per frame, so we were basically rotating our camera 120 degrees per second. To get the same effect we simply set our `spinRate` to 120. The reason is we are now multiplying it by the time difference between calls. At this point we can safely set our units and know they will be used on a per-second basis. Now that we have our `spinRate` utilizing the delta of the time between calls we are safe to run at any frame rate and have our objects drawn correctly based on the amount of time that has elapsed.

We can have it always run at 60 fps in release mode and run as fast as possible in debug mode by modifying our game code as follows:

```
#if DEBUG
    fps = new FPS(this);
#else
    fps = new FPS(this, true, false);
#endif
```

This allows us to run as fast as we can in debug mode while consistently moving our objects no matter the frame rate. It allows us to force XNA to only update the screen during the monitor's vertical retrace, which would drop us to 60 fps or whatever rate the monitor is refreshing at.

Making a game update itself consistently regardless of the frame rate can make the game more complex. We need to calculate the elapsed time (time delta) since the last frame and use that value in all of our calculations. With the fixed step mode that XNA provides we could cut down on development time and rely on the fact that the update code will be called 60 times a second. This is not sufficient if we are writing a library that can be plugged into games, as those games might not run at a consistent frame rate.

Game Pad

The Microsoft Xbox 360 wired controller works on the PC. XNA provides us with helper classes that make it very easy to determine the state of our game pad. The template already provided one call to the game pad helper class. This call is also in the Update method. Let's take a look at what is provided for us already.

```
if (GamePad.GetState(PlayerIndex.One).Buttons.Back == ButtonState.Pressed)
    this.Exit();
```

The template is calling the built-in XNA class GamePad and calling its GetState method passing in which player's controller they want to check. The template then checks the Back button on that controller to see if it has been pressed. If the controller's Back button has been pressed, the game exits. Now, that was pretty straightforward. To be consistent we can use our input class to check for the condition.

Before we can do that, we need to update our interface and add the appropriate property as well as actually getting the game pad state just like we did for our keyboard. Let's jump to our input handler code and do some of these things. We can start by adding a property to get to our list of game pads in our interface:

```
GamePadState[] GamePads { get; }
```

Now we can create the member field and property to get that field like the following code:

```
private GamePadState[] gamePads = new GamePadState[4];
public GamePadState[] GamePads
{
    get { return(gamePads); }
}
```

We need to initialize each game pad state and can do that in the Update method of the input handler object:

```
gamePads[0] = GamePad.GetState(PlayerIndex.One);
gamePads[1] = GamePad.GetState(PlayerIndex.Two);
gamePads[2] = GamePad.GetState(PlayerIndex.Three);
gamePads[3] = GamePad.GetState(PlayerIndex.Four);
```

Now, let's remove the code that checks to see if the Back button is pressed on player one's game pad from our demo. We can add this code in the Update method of our InputHandler game component to get the same effect:

```
if (gamePads[0].Buttons.Back == ButtonState.Pressed)
    Game.Exit();
```

Let's update our yaw rotation code inside of the camera game component so that we can get the same result with our controller. We can modify our existing code that checks for left and right to also handle input from our controller. So we modify our two conditional statements that set the cameraYaw to also check the right thumb stick state of the game pad we are examining:

```
if (input.KeyboardState.IsKeyDown(Keys.Left) ||
    (input.GamePads[0].ThumbSticks.Right.X < 0))
{
    cameraYaw += (spinRate * timeDelta);
}
if (input.KeyboardState.IsKeyDown(Keys.Right) ||
    (input.GamePads[0].ThumbSticks.Right.X > 0))
{
    cameraYaw -= (spinRate * timeDelta);
}
```

The thumb stick x and y axis provide a float value between -1 and 1. A value of 0 means there is no movement. A value of -0.5 means the stick is pushed to the left halfway. A value of 0.9 would be the stick is pushed to the right 90 percent of the way.

We did not change the keyboard code, we simply added another "or" condition to handle our controller. We can see it is very simple, as we only needed to check the ThumbSticks.Left property. We check the x axis of that joystick and if it is less than zero the user is pushing the stick to the left. We check to see if it is positive (user pushing to the right) in the second condition. We leave our cameraYaw variable to be set by our spin rate (taking into account our time delta). At this point, regardless if players are using the keyboard or the game pad they will get the same result from the game: The camera will rotate around the y axis. Compile and run the program to try it out. We can also try the game on the Xbox 360 because we have hooked up our game pad code.

At this point we know how to get access to any of the buttons (they are treated the same way as the Back button) and either thumb stick but we have not discussed the D-pad yet.

The D-pad is actually treated like buttons. If we also wanted to allow the player to rotate the camera left or right by using the D-pad, we simply need to add the following as part of our condition:

```
gamePadState.DPad.Left == ButtonState.Pressed
```

Add that condition along with a check for the right D-Pad being pressed to our code. Compile and run the code again and make sure that the demo allows us to look left or right by using the keyboard, thumb stick, and D-pad. The code should now look like the following:

```
if (keyboardState.IsKeyDown(Keys.Left) ||
    (gamePadState.ThumbSticks.Right.X < 0) ||
    (gamePadState.DPad.Left == ButtonState.Pressed))
{
    cameraYaw += spinRate;
}
if (keyboardState.IsKeyDown(Keys.Right) ||
    (gamePadState.ThumbSticks.Right.X > 0) ||
    (gamePadState.DPad.Right == ButtonState.Pressed))
{
    cameraYaw -= spinRate;
}
```

The shoulder buttons are just that—buttons—and we know how to handle those already. We can determine when we press down on the left or right thumb stick because those are also considered buttons. However, the final item we discuss regarding our game pad controller is the triggers. Now, a good use of our triggers for this demo would be to turn on vibration!

Before we actually determine how to use the triggers, we can look at another property of the game pad state we have access to and that is if the controller is actually connected or not. We can check this by getting the value of the IsConnected property.

The trigger values return a float between 0 and 1 to signify how much the trigger is pressed (0 = not pressed; 1 = fully pressed). The Xbox 360 controller has two motors that create its vibration. The motor on the left is a low-frequency motor whereas the motor on the right is a high-frequency motor. We can set the values on both motors in the same method call. We do this by calling the GamePad.SetVibration method. Because this is just something we are doing for our demo and not really a part of the library, we will put this code in our Game1.cs file inside the Update method:

```
if (input.GamePads[0].IsConnected)
{
    GamePad.SetVibration(PlayerIndex.One, input.GamePads[0].Triggers.Left,
        input.GamePads[0].Triggers.Right);
}
```

The first thing we are doing with this new code is checking to see if the game pad is actually connected. If it is connected then we set the vibration of both the left and right motors based on how much the left and right triggers are being pressed. We are calling the GamePad's static `SetVibration` method. There is currently no benefit in wrapping that into a method inside of our input handler.

We can also change the information being displayed in our window title bar to include the left and right motor values. This can help you determine what values you should use as you implement vibration in your games! The following is the code to accomplish that task:

```
this.Window.Title = "left: " +
    input.GamePads[0].Triggers.Left.ToString() + "; right: " +
    input.GamePads[0].Triggers.Right.ToString();
```

Go ahead and add this debug line inside of the `IsConnected` condition and compile and run the code to check the progress. We will no longer be able to see our frame rate with this code so we could just comment out the fps object until we are ready to actually check on our performance.

Mouse (Windows Only)

This input device is only available for Windows, so if we are deploying our game for the Xbox 360 we will need to put the `XBOX360` compilation directive check we learned about in Chapter 2 around any code that references the mouse as an input device. So we will create a private member field with this preprocessor check inside of our `InputHandler` class. We need to set up a private member field to hold our previous mouse state and another one to hold our current mouse state:

```
#if !XBOX360
    private MouseState mouseState;
    private MouseState prevMouseState;
#endif
```

Then in our constructor we tell XNA that we want the mouse icon visible in our window and we store our current mouse state:

```
#if !XBOX360
    Game.IsMouseVisible = true;
    prevMouseState = Mouse.GetState();
#endif
```

In our `Update` method of the input handler game component we need to set the previous state to what our current state is and then reset our current state as follows:

```
#if !XBOX360
    prevMouseState = mouseState;
    mouseState = Mouse.GetState();
#endif
```

Now we need to expose these internal fields so our camera (and any other) object can get their values. First we need to add the properties to our interface as follows:

```
#if !XBOX360
    MouseState MouseState { get; }
    MouseState PreviousMouseState { get; }
#endif
```

Now we can implement those properties in our class:

```
#if !XBOX360
    public MouseState MouseState
    {
        get { return(mouseState); }
    }

    public MouseState PreviousMouseState
    {
        get { return(prevMouseState); }
    }
#endif
```

In our camera's Update method we want to get the latest state of our mouse and compare the current X value to the previous X value to determine if we moved the mouse left or right. We also want to check if the left mouse button is pushed before updating our cameraYaw variable. Of course, all of this is wrapped in our compilation preprocessor condition as follows:

```
#if !XBOX360
    if ((input.PreviousMouseState.X > input.MouseState.X) &&
        (input.MouseState.LeftButton == ButtonState.Pressed))
    {
        cameraYaw += (spinRate * timeDelta);
    }
    else if ((input.PreviousMouseState.X < input.MouseState.X) &&
        (input.MouseState.LeftButton == ButtonState.Pressed))
    {
        cameraYaw -= (spinRate * timeDelta);
    }
#endif
```

We can compile and run the code and test the latest functionality on Windows. If the preprocessor checks are in place correctly, we should be able to deploy this demo to the Xbox 360 as well, although it will not do anything different than it did before we added the mouse support.

Creating a Stationary Camera

Now that we know how to utilize our input, we can get working on implementing our stationary camera. We actually have most of this done, but we need to add pitching as well as the yaw we already have. One use for a stationary camera is to look at an object and follow it by rotating as needed. This is commonly used in racing game replay mode.

Before we dig into the camera changes, though, let's add a few more rectangles to our world. We can do this by adding the following code to the end of our demo's `Update` method:

```
world = Matrix.CreateTranslation(new Vector3(8.0f, 0, -10.0f));
DrawRectangle(ref world);

world = Matrix.CreateTranslation(new Vector3(8.0f, 0, -6.0f));
DrawRectangle(ref world);

world = Matrix.CreateRotationY(Matrix.CreateTranslation(new Vector3(3.0f, 0, 10.0f));
DrawRectangle(ref world);
```

We should also change our cull mode to `None` so that as we rotate around that we will always see our rectangles. We can do that by calling the following code at the top of our game's `Draw` method:

```
graphics.GraphicsDevice.RenderState.CullMode = CullMode.None;
```

To get our camera updated we need to modify our camera class a little bit. First we need to declare a private member field as follows:

```
private float cameraPitch = 0.0f;
```

Now we can modify the `Update` method to set our camera pitch. Remember, pitching refers to rotating around the x axis. To calculate this we simply take the code we did for calculating the yaw and replace our reference to the y axis with the x axis. The following is the code to check our keyboard and game pad:

```
if (input.KeyboardState.IsKeyDown(Keys.Down) ||
    (input.GamePads[0].ThumbSticks.Right.Y < 0))
{
    cameraPitch -= (spinRate * timeDelta);
}
if (input.KeyboardState.IsKeyDown(Keys.Up) ||
    (input.GamePads[0].ThumbSticks.Right.Y > 0))
{
    cameraPitch += (spinRate * timeDelta);
}
```

No surprises there, and we need to do the same thing with our mouse code. Inside of the `#if !XBOX360` compilation directive we already have we can add the following code:

```
if ((input.PreviousMouseState.Y > input.MouseState.Y) &&
    (input.MouseState.LeftButton == ButtonState.Pressed))
{
    cameraPitch += (spinRate * timeDelta);
}
else if ((input.PreviousMouseState.Y < input.MouseState.Y) &&
    (input.MouseState.LeftButton == ButtonState.Pressed))
{
    cameraPitch -= (spinRate * timeDelta);
}
```

We want to clamp our values so we do not rotate over 90 degrees in either direction:

```
if (cameraPitch > 89)
    cameraPitch = 89;
if (cameraPitch < -89)
    cameraPitch = -89;
```

Finally, we need to update our rotation matrix to include our pitch value. Here is the updated calculation:

```
Matrix rotationMatrix;
Matrix.CreateRotationY(MathHelper.ToRadians(cameraYaw), out rotationMatrix);
//add in pitch to the rotation
rotationMatrix = Matrix.CreateRotationX(MathHelper.ToRadians(cameraPitch)) *
    rotationMatrix;
```

The last statement is the only thing we added. We just added our pitch to the rotation matrix that was already being used to transform our camera. The full `Update` listing can be found in Listing 5.1.

LISTING 5.1   Our stationary camera's `Update` method

```
public override void Update(GameTime gameTime)
{
    float timeDelta = (float)gameTime.ElapsedGameTime.TotalSeconds;

    if (input.KeyboardState.IsKeyDown(Keys.Left) ||
        (input.GamePads[0].ThumbSticks.Right.X < 0))
    {
        cameraYaw += (spinRate * timeDelta);
    }
    if (input.KeyboardState.IsKeyDown(Keys.Right) ||
        (input.GamePads[0].ThumbSticks.Right.X > 0))
```

LISTING 5.1   Continued

```
    {
        cameraYaw -= (spinRate * timeDelta);
    }

    if (input.KeyboardState.IsKeyDown(Keys.Down) ||
        (input.GamePads[0].ThumbSticks.Right.Y < 0))
    {
        cameraPitch -= (spinRate * timeDelta);
    }
    if (input.KeyboardState.IsKeyDown(Keys.Up) ||
        (input.GamePads[0].ThumbSticks.Right.Y > 0))
    {
        cameraPitch += (spinRate * timeDelta);
    }


#if !XBOX360
    if ((input.PreviousMouseState.X > input.MouseState.X) &&
        (input.MouseState.LeftButton == ButtonState.Pressed))
    {
        cameraYaw += (spinRate * timeDelta);
    }
    else if ((input.PreviousMouseState.X < input.MouseState.X) &&
        (input.MouseState.LeftButton == ButtonState.Pressed))
    {
        cameraYaw -= (spinRate * timeDelta);
    }

    if ((input.PreviousMouseState.Y > input.MouseState.Y) &&
        (input.MouseState.LeftButton == ButtonState.Pressed))
    {
        cameraPitch += (spinRate * timeDelta);
    }
    else if ((input.PreviousMouseState.Y < input.MouseState.Y) &&
        (input.MouseState.LeftButton == ButtonState.Pressed))
    {
        cameraPitch -= (spinRate * timeDelta);
    }
#endif

    //reset camera angle if needed
    if (cameraYaw > 360)
        cameraYaw -= 360;
    else if (cameraYaw < 0)
```

LISTING 5.1   Continued

```
        cameraYaw += 360;

    //keep camera from rotating a full 90 degrees in either direction
    if (cameraPitch > 89)
        cameraPitch = 89;
    if (cameraPitch < -89)
        cameraPitch = -89;

    Matrix rotationMatrix;
    Matrix.CreateRotationY(MathHelper.ToRadians(cameraYaw),
        out rotationMatrix);
    //add in pitch to the rotation
    rotationMatrix = Matrix.CreateRotationX(MathHelper.ToRadians(cameraPitch))
        * rotationMatrix;
    // Create a vector pointing the direction the camera is facing.
    Vector3 transformedReference;
    Vector3.Transform(ref cameraReference, ref rotationMatrix,
        out transformedReference);
    // Calculate the position the camera is looking at.
    Vector3.Add(ref cameraPosition, ref transformedReference, out cameraTarget);

    Matrix.CreateLookAt(ref cameraPosition, ref cameraTarget, ref cameraUpVector,
        out view);

    base.Update(gameTime);
}
```

Creating a First Person Camera

We can build on our stationary camera by adding a first person camera. The main thing
we want to do is to add in a way to move back and forth and to each side. Before we
start, we should create a new camera class and inherit from the one we have. We can call
this new class FirstPersonCamera. The following is the Update method for this new class:

```
public override void Update(GameTime gameTime)
{
    // TODO: Add your update code here
    //reset movement vector
    movement = Vector3.Zero;

    if (input.KeyboardState.IsKeyDown(Keys.A) ||
        (input.GamePads[0].ThumbSticks.Left.X < 0))
    {
        movement.X—;
```

```
        }
        if (input.KeyboardState.IsKeyDown(Keys.D) ||
            (input.GamePads[0].ThumbSticks.Left.X > 0))
        {
            movement.X++;
        }

        if (input.KeyboardState.IsKeyDown(Keys.S) ||
            (input.GamePads[0].ThumbSticks.Left.Y < 0))
        {
            movement.Z++;
        }
        if (input.KeyboardState.IsKeyDown(Keys.W) ||
            (input.GamePads[0].ThumbSticks.Left.Y > 0))
        {
            movement.Z—;
        }

        //make sure we don't increase speed if pushing up and over (diagonal)
        if (movement.LengthSquared() != 0)
            movement.Normalize();

        base.Update(gameTime);
}
```

The conditional logic should look familiar. It is identical to our stationary camera, except we changed where we were reading the input and what values it updated. We are reading the A, S, W, D keys and the left thumb stick. We are not looking at the mouse for movement. The value we are setting is a movement vector. We are only setting the X (left and right) and Z (back and forth) values. At the end of the conditions we are normalizing our vector as long as the length squared of the vector is not zero. This makes sure that we are not allowing faster movement just because the user is moving diagonally. There is no more code in the `FirstPersonCamera` object. The rest of the changes were made back on our original camera object.

We declared the movement as a protected member field of type `Vector3` called movement inside of our original `Camera` object. We also declared a constant value for our movement speed. Both of these are listed here:

```
protected Vector3 movement = Vector3.Zero;
private const float moveRate = 120.0f;
```

We also set the access modifier of our input field to protected so our `FirstPersonCamera` could access it:

```
protected IInputHandler input;
```

Finally we updated the last part of our `Update` method to take the movement into account when transforming our camera:

```
//update movement (none for this base class)
movement *= (moveRate * timeDelta);

Matrix rotationMatrix;
Vector3 transformedReference;
Matrix.CreateRotationY(MathHelper.ToRadians(cameraYaw), out rotationMatrix);

if (movement != Vector3.Zero)
{
    Vector3.Transform(ref movement, ref rotationMatrix, out movement);
    cameraPosition += movement;
}

//add in pitch to the rotation
rotationMatrix = Matrix.CreateRotationX(MathHelper.ToRadians(cameraPitch)) *
    rotationMatrix;

// Create a vector pointing the direction the camera is facing.
Vector3.Transform(ref cameraReference, ref rotationMatrix,
    out transformedReference);
// Calculate the position the camera is looking at.
Vector3.Add(ref cameraPosition, ref transformedReference, out cameraTarget);

Matrix.CreateLookAt(ref cameraPosition, ref cameraTarget, ref cameraUpVector,
    out view);
```

Besides just moving our local variables closer together, the only things that changed are the items in bold type. We take our movement vector and apply our move rate to it (taking into account our time delta, of course). The second portion is the key. We transformed our movement vector by our rotation matrix. This keeps us from just looking in a direction but continuing to move straight ahead. By transforming our movement vector by our rotation matrix we actually move in the direction we are looking! Well, the movement actually happens in the next statement when we add this movement vector to our current camera position. We wrapped all of this in a condition to see if any movement happened because we do not want to take a performance hit to do the math if we did not move.

Another thing to note is that because we were creating a first person camera we only transformed our movement vector by the yaw portion of our rotation matrix. We did not include the pitch, as that would have allowed us to "fly." If we did want to create a flying camera instead, we could simply move this following statement before the code that is bold:

```
//add in pitch to the rotation
rotationMatrix = Matrix.CreateRotationX(MathHelper.ToRadians(cameraPitch)) *
    rotationMatrix;
```

Creating a Split Screen

Now that we know how to set up our camera and accept input, we can look into how our code will need to change to handle multiple players in a split-screen game. To start, we need to make a copy of the InputDemo project we just finished. We can rename the project SplitScreen. After we have our solution and projects renamed (complete with our assembly GUID and title) we can look at the code we will need to change to accomplish a split-screen mode of play.

To create a split screen, we need to two different viewports. We have only been using one up until now and we actually retrieved it in our camera's Initialization method. We simply grabbed the GraphicsDevice.Viewport property to get our camera's viewport. Because we want to display two screens in one we need to define our two new viewports and then let the cameras (we will need two cameras) know about them so we can get the desired effect. To start we will need to add the following private member fields to our Game1.cs code:

```
private Viewport defaultViewport;
private Viewport topViewport;
private Viewport bottomViewport;
private separatorViewport;
private bool twoPlayers = true;
private FirstPersonCamera camera2;
```

Then at the end of our LoadGraphicsContent method we will need to define those viewports and create our cameras and pass the new values. We do this in the following code:

```
if (twoPlayers)
{
    defaultViewport = graphics.GraphicsDevice.Viewport;
    topViewport = defaultViewport;
    bottomViewport = defaultViewport;

    topViewport.Height = topViewport.Height / 2;

    separatorViewport.Y = topViewport.Height - 1;
    separatorViewport.Height = 3;

    bottomViewport.Y = topViewport.Height + 1;
    bottomViewport.Height = (bottomViewport.Height / 2) - 1;

    camera.Viewport = topViewport;
```

```
camera2 = new FirstPersonCamera(this);
camera2.Viewport = bottomViewport;
camera2.Position = new Vector3(0.0f, 0.0f, -3.0f);
camera2.Orientation = new Vector3(0.0f, 0.0f, 1.0f);
camera2.PlayerIndex = PlayerIndex.Two;
Components.Add(camera2);
}
```

We discussed briefly that we would need more than one camera to pull this off. This is because we have our view and projection matrices associated with our camera class (which we should). It makes sense that we will have two cameras because the camera is showing what the player is seeing. Each player needs his or her own view into the game.

Our initial camera is still set up in our game's constructor but our second camera will get added here. Our first camera gets the default viewport associated with it. The first thing the preceding code is doing is checking to see if we are in a two-player game. For a real game, this should be determined by an options menu or something similar, but for now we have just initialized the value to true when we initialized the twoPlayer variable.

Inside of the two-player condition the first thing we do is set our default viewport to what we are currently using (the graphic device's viewport). Then we set our top viewport to the same value. We also initialize our bottomViewport to our defaultViewport value. The final thing we do with our viewports is resize them to account for two players. We divide the height in two (we are making two horizontal viewports) on both. We then set our bottom viewport's Y property to be one more than the height of our bottom. This effectively puts the bottom viewport right underneath our top viewport.

While still in the two-player condition we change our first camera's viewport to use the top viewport. Then we set up our second camera by setting more properties. Not only do we set the viewport for this camera to the bottom viewport we have, but we also set a new camera position as well as the orientation of the camera. Finally, we set the player index.

None of these properties is exposed from our camera object, so we need to open our Camera.cs file and make some changes to account for this. First, we need to add a new private member field to hold our player index. We just assumed it was player 1 before. We can set up our protected (so our FirstPersonCamera class can access it) index as an integer as follows:

```
protected int playerIndex = 0;
```

Now, we can actually modify our input code that controls our camera to use this index instead of the hard-coded value 0 for our game pads. In the camera's Update method we can change any instance of input.GamePads[0] to input.GamePads[playerIndex]. We also need to do the same for the FirstPersonCamera object. We did not update the keyboard code and will not for the sake of time. However, to implement multiple users where both can use the keyboard we should create a mapping for each player and check accordingly. In general, it is a good practice to have a keyboard mapping so that if gamers do not like the controls we have defined in our games then they have a way to change them so it works more logically for them. The same can be said about creating a mapping for the game pads but many games simply give a choice of a couple of layouts. Because the code does not implement a keyboard mapping, the only way for us to control the separate screens differently is by having two game pads hooked up to our PC or Xbox 360.

After we have changed our camera to take the player index into consideration before reading values from our game pad, we can add the following properties to our code:

```
public PlayerIndex PlayerIndex
{
    get { return ((PlayerIndex)playerIndex); }
    set { playerIndex = (int)value; }
}

public Vector3 Position
{
    get { return (cameraPosition); }
    set { cameraPosition = value; }
}

public Vector3 Orientation
{
    get { return (cameraReference); }
    set { cameraReference = value; }
}

public Vector3 Target
{
    get { return (cameraTarget); }
    set { cameraTarget = value; }
}
public Viewport Viewport
{
    get
    {
        if (viewport == null)
            viewport = graphics.GraphicsDevice.Viewport;

        return ((Viewport)viewport);
    }
    set
    {
        viewport = value;
        InitializeCamera();
    }
}
```

We are simply exposing the camera's position, orientation (reference), and target variables. For the player index property we are casting it to a `PlayerIndex` enumeration type. The final property is the `Viewport` property. We first check to see if our viewport variable is null and if so we set it to the graphics device's viewport. When we set our `Viewport` property, we also call our `InitializeCamera` method again so it can recalculate its view and projection matrices. We need to set up a private member field for our viewport. We will allow it to have a default null value so we can declare it as follows:

```
private Viewport? viewport;
```

Because we are utilizing the `Viewport` type we will need to add the following using statement to our code:

```
using Microsoft.Xna.Framework.Graphics;
```

The only thing left for us to do now is to actually update our game's drawing code to draw our scene twice. Because we are going to have to draw our scene twice (once for each camera) we will need to refactor our `Draw` code into a `DrawScene` method and pass in a camera reference. Our new code for the new `Draw` method is as follows:

```
protected override void Draw(GameTime gameTime)
{
    graphics.GraphicsDevice.Viewport = camera.Viewport;
    DrawScene(gameTime, camera);

    if (twoPlayers)
    {
        graphics.GraphicsDevice.Viewport = camera2.Viewport;
        DrawScene(gameTime, camera2);
        //now clear the thick horizontal line between the two screens
        graphics.GraphicsDevice.Viewport = separatorViewport;
        graphics.GraphicsDevice.Clear(Color.Black);
    }

    base.Draw(gameTime);
}
```

We took all of the code that was inside of this method and put it into a new method `DrawScene(GameTime gameTime, Camera camera)`. The code we put into the `DrawScene` method did not change from how it looked when it resided inside of the `Draw` method.

The first thing we do with the preceding code is set our graphics device's viewport to be what our camera's viewport is. We then draw the scene passing in our camera. Then we check to see if we have two players; if so we set the viewport appropriately and finally draw the scene for that camera. We can run our application and see that it is using a split screen! The screen shot of this split screen demo can be seen in Figure 5.1.

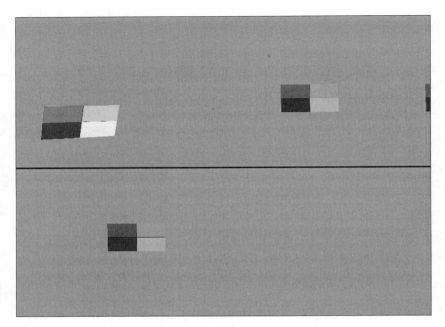

FIGURE 5.1   SplitScreen demo shows how we can create two cameras that can be controlled by two different gamepads.

Summary

Another chapter is behind us. We have learned about XNA game services and how they, along with game components, can really add benefit to our overall game architecture. We started a small library that currently handles our camera (which we can currently switch between stationary and first person), our input devices, and our frame rate counter component.

We discussed how to utilize the keyboard, game pad, and mouse to get input from our gamer to move our camera around. We learned specifically how to write a stationary camera that only rotates and created a functioning first person camera.

We updated our camera functionality to handle two players. We added a split-screen functionality by creating two different cameras and viewports the cameras could use.

In the next chapter we are actually going to load 3D objects to our screen, which will allow us to move in a much better looking world. Play some games, rest the mind, and come back strong as we jump right into working with the content pipeline.

PART III

Content Pipeline

IN THIS PART

Loading and Texturing 3D Objects

We are going to be learning about the Content Pipeline in this part of the book. XNA provides out-of-the-box support for loading 3D objects, textures, effects, Extensible Markup Language (XML), and XACT projects. We discuss 3D objects and textures in this chapter. We will learn how to load 3D objects into our world and learn about different texturing techniques.

Understanding the Content Pipeline

The Content Pipeline can be used to solve a very real problem: The content we create for games is typically not game ready. For example, 3D content is usually stored in a proprietary format and there is a need to convert the data before loading it into the game. This is where Content Pipeline helps out. In general, it can take different files as input, massage them to get them into a type that we can work with, and then compile them into a format that can easily be loaded when our game starts.

The XNA Framework Content Pipeline is made up of several components. First is the Content Importer, which is responsible for reading the data that is loaded into the solution. If there is data in the file the Content Importer does not know how to map to the content DOM, then the data is not stored. It only keeps the data it cares about. Once the importer is done reading in the data, it passes it along to the Content DOM, which stores the strongly typed data. It is then passed from the Content DOM to a Content Processor, which then passes it to a Content Compiler. If the compilation fails we get a nice message inside of the IDE that tells us what happened: We do not have to wait and see if it is going to load at runtime, and this is a huge improvement over how things used to work. The compiler actually builds files that are read in at runtime. These files typically have an .xnb file extension. Audio files actually create .xgs, .xwb, and .xsb files for the actual sound project, wave bank, and sound bank content. We discuss the sound and how it relates to the Content Pipeline in the next chapter. The Content Pipeline is smart enough to not recompile any content that has not changed since the last build. Finally, after all of the content is compiled into files, they are read in via the Content Manager at runtime so our games can consume the content. We have been using the Content Manager since our very first application in Chapter 2, "XNA and the Xbox 360." We created an instance to the Content Manager in our game's constructor like the following:

```
content = new ContentManager(Services);
```

Fortunately, when we use the Content Manager we do not need to actually dispose of our objects, as it handles disposing of our content itself. It does this in the following code, which is always included in our new game projects:

```
protected override void UnloadGraphicsContent(bool unloadAllContent)
{
    if (unloadAllContent == true)
    {
        content.Unload();
    }
}
```

The code simply calls the Unload method on the instance of the content manager. This then goes through each of the objects that have been loaded and disposes of them. We discuss the counter part of this method in the next section. The LoadGraphicsContent method does the actual loading of the data.

As we add content to our project that is recognizable as XNA Framework content, it goes through the process just described. The Properties window inside of the Visual C# Express IDE will show an asset name that we can modify. If we add content types that are not recognized, we can change the XNA Framework Content boolean value to true. We would then need to fill in the Content Importer and Content Processor properties, specifying how to turn the unknown content type into a format that XNA can recognize. This would require a custom importer and processor that we discuss building in Chapter 8, "Extending the Content Pipeline," where we will learn about extending the pipeline.

Loading 3D Models

The XNA Framework's Content Pipeline handles loading .X and .FBX files automatically when they are pasted into the Solution Explorer (or included in the project). This is when the Content Pipeline goes through the process described in the previous section of importing, processing, and compiling the data. We then can use our game class and the Content Manager to read the model information.

We will start by creating a new project, which we can call Load3DObject. We can create both the Windows and Xbox 360 game projects. After getting our solution set up, we can then add an existing project to our solution—the XELibrary from last chapter. Once we import both the Windows and the Xbox 360 XELibrary projects, we need to reference them inside of the game projects we created. We reference the XELibrary in our Windows project and the XELibrary_Xbox360 in our Xbox 360 game project.

After we have our initial setup of our solution file completed, we can jump right in and add a using statement at the top of our Game1.cs class to access our library:

```
using XELibrary;
```

We can set up our private member fields to access the game components in our library:

```
private FPS fps;
private FirstPersonCamera camera;
private InputHandler input;
```

The following is our constructor, where we initialize the variables we just set:

```
public Game1()
{
    graphics = new GraphicsDeviceManager(this);
    content = new ContentManager(Services);

    input = new InputHandler(this);
    Components.Add(input);
    camera = new FirstPersonCamera(this);
    Components.Add(camera);

#if DEBUG
    //draw 60 fps and update as often as possible
    fps = new FPS(this, true, false);
#else
    fps = new FPS(this, true, false);
#endif
    Components.Add(fps);
}
```

With just that little bit of coding (and setup) we now have access to all of the code in our library. We automatically have a first person camera now and we can handle input as well as display our frame rate. Game components aren't too shabby.

As we add content to our pipeline we could pretty easily clutter up our Solution Explorer pane with all of the files. To help alleviate that problem, we are going to create a Contents folder with subfolders under it. To start, we will add two subfolders—Models and Textures—under the Content folder. This is not required, but it really helps keep the clutter minimal. After doing this we will need to make sure we include that folder inside of our Xbox 360 solution, otherwise the content files won't compile and won't be deployed and will cause the demo to not load.

Now with the preliminary work out of the way, we can actually get down to business and load a 3D object. Find the Spacewar project that we extracted back in Chapter 1, "Introducing the XNA Framework and XNA Game Studio Express," and under the Contents\Models\ folder we need to copy the asteroid1.x file and copy it into our Solution Explorer's Contents\Models\ folder. When we do this, XNA Game Studio Express flags it as XNA Framework Content. Now we can compile the code, which will also kick off the Content Pipeline. The Content Pipeline kicked off the Content Importer, shoved the data into the DOM, and then called the Content Processor, which passed it to the Content Compiler. So when we compile our game, it not only compiles our code, but also the content.

The Content Compiler threw an error, "Missing asset … \Content\Textures\asteroid1.tga," because the .X file we loaded has a reference to a texture inside of it. It references a sibling folder by the name of Textures. The following is a portion of the asteroid1.x file where it references the texture in the texture's sibling folder:

```
Material phong1SG {
    1.0;1.0;1.0;1.000000;;
    18.000000;
    0.000000;0.000000;0.000000;;
    0.000000;0.000000;0.000000;;
    TextureFilename {
        "..\\textures\\asteroid1.tga";
    }
}
```

We have that folder, but we did not grab the .tga texture from the Spacewar project. Let's do that now and paste it into our Textures folder. Once we do this we can compile again and it should compile without issues. After it compiles successfully, we can browse to our /bin/x86/content/models/ and /textures/ folders to see there are a couple of files that were created at the time we compiled. The Content Compiler took the files and compiled them into the .xnb files we see here. The compiler gave us an error when it could not find the texture that was associated with the .X file. We have corrected that and our code (and content) now compiles successfully.

We could run the code but nothing would be on our screen because we have not actually told XNA to load and draw the object. We can get that ball rolling by creating a private member field in our Game1.cs class as follows:

```
private Model model;
```

Now we can initialize this variable by actually loading our model in our code. We do this inside of the LoadGraphicsContent method. The following code has the entire method:

```
protected override void LoadGraphicsContent(bool loadAllContent)
{
    if (loadAllContent)
    {
        // TODO: Load any ResourceManagementMode.Automatic content
        model = content.Load<Model>(@"Content\Models\asteroid1");
    }

    // TODO: Load any ResourceManagementMode.Manual content
}
```

The only line we added was the statement inside of the condition, but it is important to discuss this entire method, as we have just breezed over it in the past chapters. This method is where we will load all of our graphics content. We have two options when we load our content: We can let XNA handle the memory management of the resources automatically by loading our content inside of the condition or we can maintain the memory management ourselves. This method as well as its counterpart, UnloadGraphicsContent, gets called at appropriate times. What are these appropriate times? This is a good time to discuss the logic flow of XNA.

The XNA Framework's logic flow works something like this:

1. The Main application calls the Game Constructor.

2. The Game Constructor will create any game components and call their constructors.

3. The XNA Framework calls the game's Initialize method.

4. The XNA Framework calls each of the game component's Initialize methods.

5. The XNA Framework calls each of the Drawable game component's LoadGraphicsContent methods.

6. The XNA Framework calls the game's LoadGraphicsContent method.

7. The XNA Framework calls the game's Update method.

8. The XNA Framework calls each of the game component's Update methods.

9. The XNA Framework calls the game's Draw method.

10. The XNA Framework calls each of the Drawable game component's Draw methods.

11. Steps 7 through 10 are repeated many times each second.

12. If the device is lost (user moved the window to another monitor, screen resolution is changed, window is minimized, etc.) then a call to UnloadGraphicsContent is made.

13. If the device is reset then we start back at step 6 again.

14. The gamer exits the game.

15. The XNA Framework calls the game's Dispose method.

16. The game's `Dispose` method calls the base object's `Dispose` method, which causes ...

17. The XNA Framework calls each of the game component's `Dispose` methods.

18. The XNA Framework calls the game's `UnloadGraphicsContent` method.

19. The game's `Dispose` method gets focus back and the game exits.

Something to note about how the XNA Framework calls the game component's `Initialize` method (and `LoadGraphicsContent` for drawable game components) is this only happens once when the game's `Initialize` method is kicked off by the framework. If game components are added later, their `Initialize` (and `LoadGraphicsContent`) methods will not be called. This is important to understand when managing game components.

At this point we have loaded our 3D content. We have created a private member field to store the model we added. We actually loaded our model in our code and initialized our variable. Now we just need to draw the model on the screen. We need to add the following method to draw a model:

```
private void DrawModel(ref Model m, ref Matrix world)
{
    Matrix[] transforms = new Matrix[m.Bones.Count];
    m.CopyAbsoluteBoneTransformsTo(transforms);

    foreach (ModelMesh mesh in m.Meshes)
    {
        foreach (BasicEffect be in mesh.Effects)
        {
            be.EnableDefaultLighting();
            be.Projection = camera.Projection;
            be.View = camera.View;
            be.World = world * mesh.ParentBone.Transform;
        }

        mesh.Draw();
    }
}
```

Our `DrawModel` method takes in a reference to our model as well as a reference to the world matrix we need to apply to our model. The first two statements get the transforms of each bone in the model. A model can have a parent bone with children bones associated with it. This is mainly used in animations, but even if a model does not have animations it might still have bones and so our code should include this unless we know for certain that our model does not have any children. The transforms array will contain a transformation matrix of each mesh of the model that contains its position relative to the parent. By doing this, we can make sure that each `ModelMesh` of the parent `Model` will be drawn at the right location. This actually happens in the last statement inside of our inner foreach loop.

We take the world matrix that the mesh is supposed to be transformed with and we multiply that transformation with the `ModelMesh`'s parent's transformation. This is to make sure that that each `ModelMesh` is drawn correctly with the parent mesh.

We did not need to create our own `BasicEffect` object as XNA will apply one to a mesh we load. We can override this and will see that in Part V of the book when we talk about the High Level Shader Language and make our own effect files. For now, we just ensure that the default lighting is enabled on the effect as well as setting our projection and view matrices to what our Camera game component has updated it to be. When we did this in the last chapter, we only moved where we are setting those values. Instead of having an effect that we are explicitly calling, we are tying into the one that XNA applies to the `Model` when it loads it. This is also happening inside of the inner foreach loop so we could apply different effects to children meshes if we wanted to.

The other thing to notice is the fact that we did not reference our texture anywhere. Because it was inside of the .X file and the Content Compiler stored that information, the Content Manager knew where to look for the texture and load it automatically. We will see how to override the texture through code a little later in this chapter. Let's just get it to draw with the normal texture for now! To do that, we need to actually call our `DrawModel` method inside of our `Draw` method with the following code:

```
world = Matrix.CreateTranslation(new Vector3(0,0,-4000));
DrawModel(ref model, ref world);
```

The model we are loading is rather large and as such we are going to push it way back into the world. In fact, we made a modification to our `Camera` class in our XELibrary. We originally had our near and far planes set up as 0.0001 and 1000.0, respectively. The thing about the plane values is that they are floating points, which means there is a finite amount of precision we can have. We can either have the precision before the decimal point or after the decimal point, but not both. A lot of times programmers will set the far plane to a very high number but when that happens the depth buffer (also known as a z buffer) could have a hard time knowing which objects to draw first. As a result during game play the screen will almost flicker as different vertices are fighting to be drawn first and the z buffer is confused because it cannot take into account the minor differences in the locations of those vertices. Of course, the .0001 near plan we originally had set was not exactly practical either. At this point having a near plane of 1 and a far plane of 10,000 should meet most of our needs without overly stressing our z buffer. We could have our far plane even further without causing an adverse effect on the depth buffer.

Finally, we need to create our private member `world` field that we referenced:

```
private Matrix world;
```

Now we can compile and run our code and we should see our asteroid object sitting right in front of us. This is not extremely exciting, but we have just successfully drawn a .X model complete with a texture.

Texturing 3D Models

Now, let's replace that texture with one we will load on the fly. We could just modify our texture resource if we wanted to, but let's assume that we want to keep that intact and as we load different asteroids we want some to use that brownish texture and some to use our newly created texture, on which we will simply remove the color. So let's fire up our favorite paint program and open up the .tga file and turn it into a grayscale image. If needed, the image asteroid1-grey.tga can be taken from the CD in this chapter's source code. Let's add our newly created image into our Solution Explorer (or we can just include it into our project if we saved the new version in our /Textures/ subfolder from our paint program).

Add the following code in our `LoadGraphicsContent` method:

```
originalAsteroid = content.Load<Texture2D>(@"Content\Textures\asteroid1");
greyAsteroid = content.Load<Texture2D>(@"Content\Textures\asteroid1-grey");
```

Just like adding our model, we can add our texture asset very easily. Of course, now we have to actually declare our private member field:

```
private Texture2D originalAsteroid;
private Texture2D greyAsteroid;
```

Now we can make a couple of changes to our `DrawModel` method. We need to add in another parameter of type `Texture2D` and call it texture. We also need to actually set our effect to use that texture if it was passed in, which can be seen in the following code:

```
if (texture != null)
    be.Texture = texture;
```

This code statement is inside of the inner foreach loop with the rest of the code that sets the properties of our basic effect that is being used by our model. We are simply checking to see if null is passed in; if not, we are setting the texture of the effect. As we saw earlier, the effect is getting applied to the mesh of our model, so we only need to modify our call to our `DrawModel` to pass in the new texture. We will go ahead and just create another asteroid on our screen by replacing our current drawing code with the following:

```
world = Matrix.CreateTranslation(new Vector3(0, 0, -4000));
DrawModel(ref model, ref world, greyAsteroid);

world = Matrix.CreateTranslation(new Vector3(0, 0, 4000));
DrawModel(ref model, ref world, originalAsteroid);
```

The first line did not change, but it is added here for readability purposes. The second statement we are actually passing in is our new texture. The last two statements are placing another asteroid behind us and resetting the texture to the original one. We can run this program and spin our camera to see both asteroids being drawn.

Now, let's apply some transformations to our asteroids. We can add some rotation to get them to do a little more than they are right now. To do this, we just need to replace our Draw code with the following:

```
world = Matrix.CreateRotationY(MathHelper.ToRadians(
        270.0f * (float)gameTime.TotalGameTime.TotalSeconds)) *
    Matrix.CreateTranslation(new Vector3(0, 0, -4000));
DrawModel(ref model, ref world, greyAsteroid);

world = Matrix.CreateRotationY(MathHelper.ToRadians(
        45.0f * (float)gameTime.TotalGameTime.TotalSeconds)) *
    Matrix.CreateRotationZ(MathHelper.ToRadians(
        45.0f * (float)gameTime.TotalGameTime.TotalSeconds)) *
    Matrix.CreateTranslation(new Vector3(0, 0, 4000));
DrawModel(ref model, ref world, originalAsteroid);
```

Even with the code broken to fit on the page, we can still see that we only have four statements, just like before. The only two that changed are our code that modified the world matrix. This makes sense because we want to rotate our asteroids. We start by looking at our first world transformation and can see that we are simply rotating it around the y axis by 270 degrees * the number of seconds our game has been running. This effectively makes it continuously render every frame. After rotating we still translate it like we did before, moving it 4,000 units into our world. The second world transformation is similar except we are only rotating by 45 degrees instead of 270 degrees. We are also rotating around the x axis by the same amount. This should give us a decent wobble effect. Finally we are translating 4,000 units behind us just like before. We can compile and run our program and see our asteroids are moving (well, rotating in place).

Summary

We were introduced to the Content Pipeline in this chapter. We saw just how easy it was to take content from the pipeline and load into our demo. We discussed how to organize our game content, especially in larger projects.

We loaded a 3D .X file into our demo after modifying the .X file directly to change the location where it was looking for the texture. We discussed texturing techniques and how to override textures that are already set up in our 3D objects. We saw how to load the same 3D object more than once and apply different textures to each instance. Finally, we added some translation to our objects to get a better effect.

CHAPTER 7

Sounds and Music

Stop and think for a moment what your favorite game would be like if it did not have sound. Music sets the atmosphere for our games and sound effects adds to the realism of our games. In this chapter we discuss how to get music and sounds into our demos and games.

To do this we will need to use the Microsoft Cross-Platform Audio Creation Tool (XACT), which Microsoft provides for us. The tool can be found in our Programs/Microsoft XNA Game Studio Express/Tools menu. Once we have the tool opened we will create wave banks and sound banks and discuss global settings. We will then actually create a sound manager that we can add to our library.

Microsoft Cross-Platform Audio Creation Tool (XACT)

Unlike textures and 3D models, we do not simply put our raw wave files into the Content Pipeline directly. Instead we use XACT to bundle them together and add effects to the different sounds. The XACT tool allows us to associate categories with our sounds. When we set a sound to have a category of Music, it allows the Xbox 360 to ignore the music if the gamer has a playlist playing on his or her Xbox 360.

Before we open the actual tool we need to open up the XACT Auditioning Utility, which is found in the same location as XACT itself. We only need to do this if we actually want to audition (listen to) the sounds we are making inside of XACT. This can, of course, be beneficial, especially when we want to add effects to the file. With that said, XACT is not a sound editing software package. It takes completed wave files and puts them in a format that XNA can read and use. We can do simple effects like change the pitch and volume but the tool is not designed to be a wave file editor.

We first need to hook our XACT tool up to the Auditioning Utility we launched before. The Auditioning Utility must be run before the XACT tool is run. To play our sounds we need to tell XACT to connect to the Auditioning Utility by clicking the Audition menu item and then clicking the Connect To (machine) item. After we have successfully connected, the Auditioning Utility will say "XACT tool is now connected...."

When we open the tool we will see an empty project to which we can add .wav files. After adding the files we can then set them up as sounds and create cue names for them that we can kick off inside of our code. We can modify properties to get different effects from the sounds.

Wave Banks

To get started we can create a new wave bank from inside XACT. To create a wave bank, we can follow these steps:

1. Right-click Wave Banks and select New Wave Bank. This can be seen in Figure 7.1.

2. Inside of the Wave Bank empty pane, right-click and select Insert Wave File(s).

3. Find a wave file from the Spacewar project. We can use the Theme.wav file from MySpacewarWin1\Content\Audio\Waves\Music.

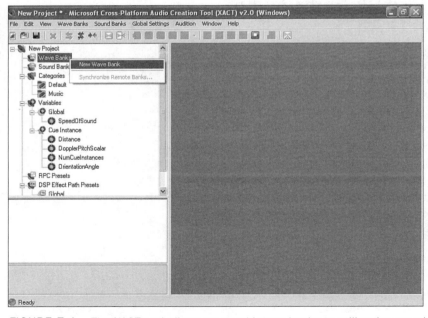

FIGURE 7.1   The XACT tool allows us to add wave banks to utilize the sounds in our games.

4. Because we have our Auditioning Tool set up and XACT connected to it, we can simply select the wave file and press the spacebar to hear it play. We could also right-click and select Play, or click Play in the toolbar. As with most graphical user interfaces (GUIs) there are many ways to accomplish the same task. This book only lists one way in most cases.

We can go ahead and add in a few other wave files as well. Let's follow the preceding steps to enter all of the collision wave files from Spacewar. We can open them all up at one time in the Open dialog box.

Sound Banks

Even though we have the wave file loaded inside our XACT project, we still could not use it in our game. We have to create a sound bank first. To create a sound bank we can follow these steps:

1. Right-click Sound Banks and select New Sound Bank. Just like the wave bank, we could also accomplish this through the toolbar or the main menu items.

2. Our work pane just filled up with our Sound Bank window. We will need to work with the Wave Bank window as well as the Sound Bank window so we will want to position them so we can see them both. One way to do this is to click Tile Horizontally inside of the Window menu item.

3. Now that we can see both windows we need to drag our wave file from the wave bank into the sound bank, inside the top left pane (sounds frame).

4. A cue for the sound needs to be created in order for our code to utilize it. We can create a cue by dragging the sound from the top left pane (sounds frame) into the bottom left pane (cues frame).

This is the bare minimum we need to do to play sounds in our games. To hear the sound we can select it and press the spacebar. We can press Escape to stop the sound. To get sound effects and music into our games, these steps will work. In the next sections we discuss more advanced ways to manipulate our sounds to get them ready for our game.

Understanding Variations

To accomplish something more than just playing sounds we need to understand variations. With variations we can assign many waves to a track and we can create different events for those tracks to create a sound. We can assign many sounds to a cue. We can then set up how those sounds or waves are to be played. We will be utilizing XACT to create different variations and then we are going to write a library component that a demo can use to play these cues.

We can close out our existing XACT instance and open up a new one. We need to create a wave bank and a sound bank to put our waves in. On this book's CD, under this chapter's folder there is a subfolder entitled Sounds. We need to add all of these waves into our wave bank. After adding in the waves we need to create some sounds. We are going to add the different sounds and create different variations so we can learn how to use some of the XACT features by example.

1. We can drag the Attention and Explosion sounds directly into our cues frame (bottom left pane) because we are going to play these sounds as is.

2. We can drag the Axe_throw sound directly into our cues frame and rename the cue to Bullet. We can do this by right-clicking the name in the cues frame and selecting Rename. At this point, the screen should resemble Figure 7.2.

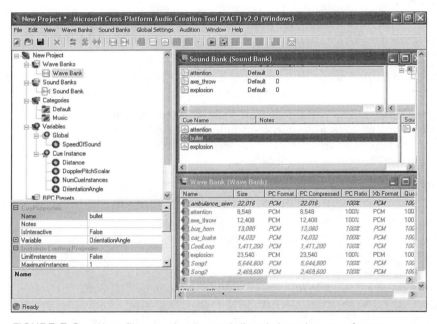

FIGURE 7.2   Wave files can be dragged directly into the cues frame.

3. To start our more complicated tasks let's drag our CoolLoop wave into our cues frame.

4. In the top right pane (tracks frame) we can see that XACT created a track with a play event that include our wave name. We want to make sure this sound loops so we click the Play Wave tree node of the Track 1 root to select it.

5. In the properties window we can see LoopEvent under the PlayWave Properties. The default value is No but we could either loop it a certain number of times by selecting Finite and then entering the number of times to loop in the LoopCount property or we can have it loop forever by selecting Infinite. We are going to let this sound loop forever so we select Infinite. We can see this in Figure 7.3.

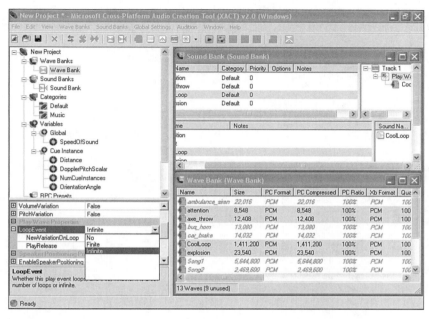

FIGURE 7.3   We can set our play event on a track to loop indefinitely.

6. Because this loop is going to be music we can click the CoolLoop's sound icon and drag it on top of the Music category on the left side of the window. When this is successful we will see the Category change from Default to Music.

7. Next up we are going to add multiple sounds into one cue. We will use Synth_beep_1 to start us off. Let's drag that wave into our cues frame.

8. Now we want to make sure that the sound name is selected (in our sounds frame) so the track frame is showing the play event for track 1.

9. We need to drag Synth_beep_2 and Synth_beep_3 waves and drop them on our play event inside of track 1. We need to be careful to not drag over the cues frame as it will make the tracks frame empty (it deselects the sound from the sound pane). We drag the files by clicking on the icon (XACT does not allow us to drag by the name of the wave). We can see where we need to release the cursor in Figure 7.4. The final result after releasing the cursor and completing our drop operation can be seen in Figure 7.5.

10. Rename this cue from Synth_beep_1 to Hit.

11. With Hit as our active cue, we can press the spacebar to hear it play (assuming we are connected to the Auditioning Utility). Let's hit the spacebar several times in a row very fast. We can hear one sound being played every time we hit the spacebar regardless if the previous sound was played. We see they are not played at the same time by "pressing play" once. By putting our different waves directly into a play event we are giving XACT a list of waves to play from when we call play. It does not play them all at once (but we will see how to do that in a moment).

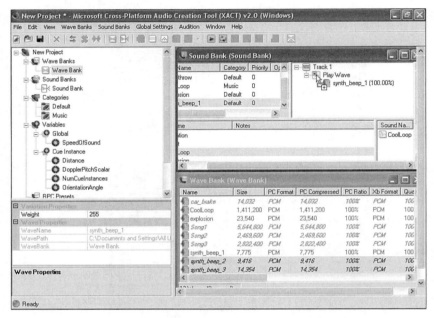

FIGURE 7.4   We can drag our waves directly into a play event on a sound's track.

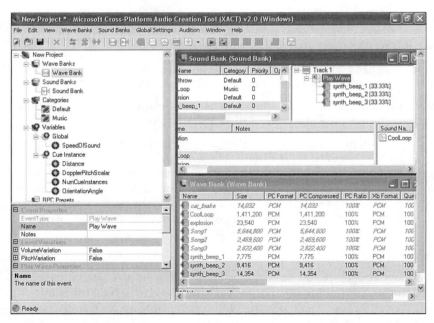

FIGURE 7.5   The waves show up underneath one play event inside of a track when we add them.

12. Because we do not want this particular cue to play more than one sound at a time we can change the `LimitInstances` property in the Instance Limiting Properties section of our properties window to True. We will need to have our cue name selected to do this. Now when we press the spacebar multiple times it will not start playing until the last sound has finished.

13. We can hear the sounds are random but we want them to play in the order we specified in the play event of our track. To do this we need to select Ordered in the `PlayListType` property in the Variation Playlist Properties section of the property frame. We need to do this when we have the cue selected. Changing this value to Ordered causes XACT to play the sounds in the order we specified. If we wanted it to start with a random entry and then do them in order, we could have selected Ordered From Random.

14. Now when we play the sounds, they play in order and only play one at a time. However, we want the sounds to be queued up so that if we press the spacebar five times, it will play all of the waves in the sound with each one starting as soon as the previous one finishes. To do this we need to change the `BehaviorAtMax` property to Queue instead of FailToPlay. This can be useful for queuing up things like voiceover audio that we would never want to play simultaneously. This is shown in Figure 7.6.

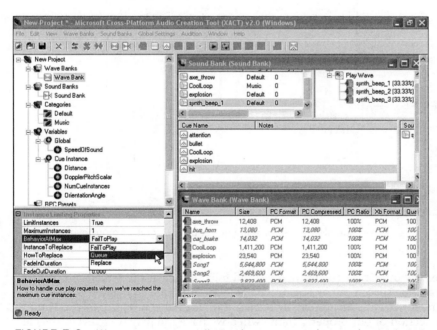

FIGURE 7.6   We can queue up calls to play our cues when we have `LimitInstances` turned on.

15. Now we are going to make a crash cue. To start, let's drag Ambulance_siren from our waves into our cues and rename the cue to Crash.

16. Inside of our tracks frame, with our Ambulance_siren sound selected from the sound frame, right-click and add a new track.

17. Now we can add a play event to the track we just added by right-clicking the track and selecting Add Event > Play Wave.

18. We need to drag the Car_brake wave into the play event of the track we just created. Remember not to drag across the cue frame, as the contents of the track frame will disappear.

19. We need to repeat steps 16 through 18 with the wave files Bus_horn and Explosion. When this step is completed we should have a total of four tracks, each with its own play event that has a wave file associated with it. We have expanded the Sound Banks window in Figure 7.7 so we can see the end result.

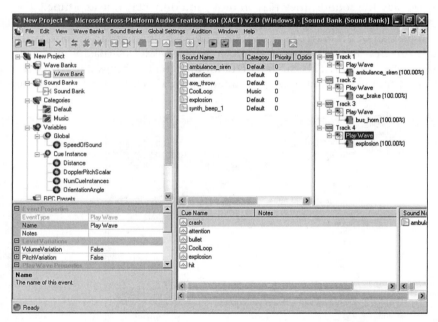

FIGURE 7.7   We can create multiple tracks for a sound, each with one or more events in our tracks frame.

20. Now if we play our Crash cue we will hear all four sounds at the same time. We want them to be spaced out as to simulate an accident. We can delay the time at which different tracks start to play by setting the TimeStamp property in the Timing Properties section of our property frame when we have the play wave event selected. Our Car_brake wave can be left alone as it is a little longer of a sound file. We should modify the rest of the values as follows:

    Bus_horn: 0.300
    Explosion: 1.000
    Ambulance_siren: 1.600

Now when we play the cue we can hear something that resembles a car colliding with a bus, creating a large explosion and the fastest EMT response time ever!

21. Now we want to make a variant of our explosion sound. We are going to make a gunshot sound without requiring an additional wave file to be used. To do this we are going to drag our Explosion sound (top right pane) into the empty white space inside of the same sound pane so it will create a copy of itself. It should have called itself Explosion 2. Let's drag that Explosion 2 from the sounds frame into our cues frame and rename the cue to Gunshot.

22. When we play Gunshot, it does not sound any different than Explosion. Let's change that by adding a Pitch event to our only track for the Explosion 2 sound in our tracks frame. We add this event just like we added the play event earlier, by right-clicking the track and selecting Add Event > Pitch.

23. Now we need to actually modify the pitch to get the desired sound effect. To do this we need to make sure our Pitch event is selected and then change the Constant value. We can find this value in our properties frame under Pitch Properties/Setting Type (Equation)/EquationType (Constant). Let's change the pitch to 50.00 as shown in Figure 7.8. Now if we play the cue we will hear something that resembles a gunshot instead of an explosion. We did not have to add another large wave file to accomplish this effect.

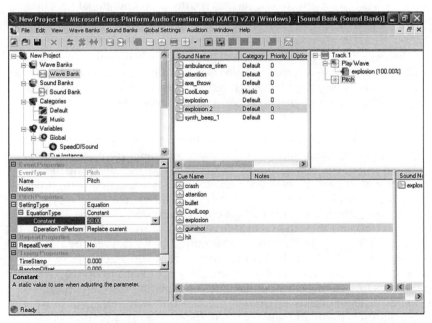

FIGURE 7.8   We can add a pitch event to our track and set the pitch value in our properties frame.

24. Next, we are going to create a cue with multiple sounds. We need to right-click inside of our cues frame and select New Cue. We can name this cue Complex.

25. Drag the Explosion sound down on top of the Complex cue. Let's do the same thing with the Synth_beep_1 sound. Remember, this Synth_beep_1 sound has its own sound variations already as it plays three different waves in order.

26. We need to change the PlayList type for this Complex cue to Random. This way it will just play a sound randomly even if the one it picks was just played.

27. The final thing we will do is add a music playlist. Unfortunately, XACT does not have a way to give us typical playlist functionality so we will have to put that into our code. For now, though, we can at least add our songs to this playlist. We will start by dragging our Song1, Song2, and Song3 waves into our sounds frame.

28. We will also drag those sounds to our music category.

29. Now we need to drag our Song1, Song2, and Song3 sounds from our sounds frame into the cues frame.

30. We can now save our project, calling it Chapter7.

That was a lot of examples, but it was worth going through because at this point we have good idea of how to do a lot of sound manipulation to prepare cues for our games. Our games will always reference the cue value.

There are other actions XACT allows us to do, such as setting local and global variables, setting up transitions through interactive audio settings, and setting up runtime parameter controls (RPCs).

We can create RPCs when a simple pitch or volume change across the board will not do. Perhaps we would like to add some reverb, or maybe we would like to modify the volume as a cue plays up and down. Doing any of these things requires setting up an RPC, which can be done by right-clicking the RPC tree node and selecting New RPC Preset as shown in Figure 7.9.

Then we can drag that preset over to one of our sounds in the sounds frame. To test with, we can make a copy of our CoolLoop sound and then add our preset to this new sound by dragging the RPC on top of the new sound we just created. We can open the RPC preset by double-clicking it. Because there is only one sound it is associated with, it will play that one. At the top of the RPC dialog box we can select other sounds (if we have added the RPC to multiple sounds). A default volume curve has been added for us. We can move the points around and then the vertical horizontal bar that is the same color as our curve can be moved left and right. The bar can be moved or we can modify the variable above beside the curve declaration. This is the variable that we can change in our code to cause the sound to react exactly how we want. We might want to do this, for example, to dim the background music when dialogue is happening between characters. We can pass a value to the global variable that will produce the sound identical to what we are hearing as we audition the sound with our RPC added. We can add more curves (pitch and reverb) by right-clicking the Volume item at the top of the dialog box and selecting Add New Curve. We can add nodes to our curve by right-clicking inside of the main white area and selecting Add. A screen shot of this dialog box is shown in Figure 7.10. Have fun coming up with a totally different CoolLoop 2 sound!

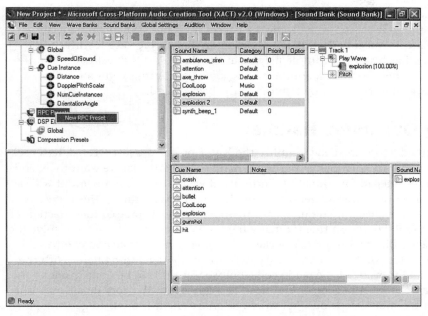

FIGURE 7.9   We can add runtime parameter controls and apply them to sounds to produce different effects.

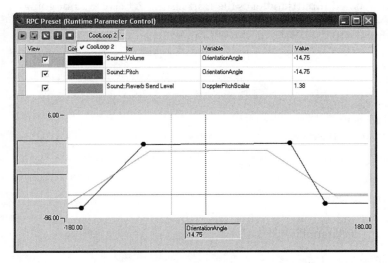

FIGURE 7.10   The RPC dialog box allows us to add new curves and nodes to manipulate the values.

We can pause and resume all sounds in a category. This means that we could organize our sounds in such a way that sounds that are used in our playing state can all be assigned to a category we can define. Then through the code we can pause that category and it will pause all sounds that are playing. This way we do not need to worry ourselves with making sure all the sounds stop when someone pauses the game. When we associate a sound with the Music category the Xbox 360 can mute that and replace it with the playlist the gamer has his or her console playing at the time. This is a really nice feature because no matter how good our soundtrack is, at some point gamers will most likely want to play our games with their own music in the background.

Updating Our Input Handler

Before we actually dig into the code to utilize the XACT project we just created, let's back up a minute and take another look at our input handler. In particular we want to extend our keyboard and gamepad functionality. Currently, if we try to trigger any event with a key press or a button push we will get the event kicked off several times. This is because for every frame we are checking in our Update method, if a key is pressed for a fraction of a second the method will return true for many frames. We already know how to solve the problem because we did it with our Mouse class. We stored the old state and compared it to the new state to see what has changed. We need to do the same thing here. With the mouse code, we did it inside of the demo code, but we want this to be done inside of the library so our game and demo code do not need to worry about the gory details. We will not be updating the mouse code but that would be an excellent exercise to go through once we are done with the chapter.

To get started, we need to open up the InputHandler.cs code file inside of our XELibrary project. The code for our updated InputHandler.cs file is in Listing 7.1. We are not going to do a deep dive on the code in this chapter (this is devoted to sound after all), but we are going to quickly examine what has been modified from a distant view.

LISTING 7.1   InputHandler.cs

```
using System;
using System.Collections.Generic;
using Microsoft.Xna.Framework;
using Microsoft.Xna.Framework.Input;

namespace XELibrary
{
    public interface IInputHandler
    {
        KeyboardHandler KeyboardState { get; }

        GamePadState[] GamePads { get; }
        ButtonHandler ButtonHandler { get; }

#if !XBOX360
        MouseState MouseState { get; }
        MouseState PreviousMouseState { get; }
```

LISTING 7.1   Continued

```
#endif
    };

    public partial class InputHandler
        : Microsoft.Xna.Framework.GameComponent, IInputHandler
    {
        public enum ButtonType { A, B, Back, LeftShoulder, LeftStick,
                                 RightShoulder, RightStick, Start, X, Y }

        private KeyboardHandler keyboard;
        private ButtonHandler gamePadHandler = new ButtonHandler();
        private GamePadState[] gamePads = new GamePadState[4];

#if !XBOX360
        private MouseState mouseState;
        private MouseState prevMouseState;
#endif

        public InputHandler(Game game)
            : base(game)
        {
            // TODO: Construct any child components here
            game.Services.AddService(typeof(IInputHandler), this);

            //initialize our member fields
            keyboard = new KeyboardHandler();
            gamePads[0] = GamePad.GetState(PlayerIndex.One);
            gamePads[1] = GamePad.GetState(PlayerIndex.Two);
            gamePads[2] = GamePad.GetState(PlayerIndex.Three);
            gamePads[3] = GamePad.GetState(PlayerIndex.Four);

#if !XBOX360
            Game.IsMouseVisible = true;
            prevMouseState = Mouse.GetState();
#endif
        }

        public override void Initialize()
        {
            base.Initialize();
        }

        public override void Update(GameTime gameTime)
        {
```

LISTING 7.1   Continued

```
        keyboard.Update();

        gamePadHandler.Update();

        if (keyboard.IsKeyDown(Keys.Escape))
            Game.Exit();

        if (gamePadHandler.WasButtonPressed(0, ButtonType.Back))
            Game.Exit();

#if !XBOX360
        //Set our previous state
        prevMouseState = mouseState;
        //Get our new state
        mouseState = Mouse.GetState();
#endif

        base.Update(gameTime);
    }

    #region IInputHandler Members
    public KeyboardHandler KeyboardState
    {
        get { return (keyboard); }
    }

    public ButtonHandler ButtonHandler
    {
        get { return (gamePadHandler); }
    }

    public GamePadState[] GamePads
    {
        get { return(gamePads); }
    }

#if !XBOX360
    public MouseState MouseState
    {
        get { return(mouseState); }
    }

    public MouseState PreviousMouseState
    {
```

LISTING 7.1   Continued

```
            get { return(prevMouseState); }
        }
#endif
        #endregion
    }

    public class ButtonHandler
    {
        private GamePadState[] prevGamePadsState = new GamePadState[4];
        private GamePadState[] gamePadsState = new GamePadState[4];

        public ButtonHandler()
        {
            prevGamePadsState[0] = GamePad.GetState(PlayerIndex.One);
            prevGamePadsState[1] = GamePad.GetState(PlayerIndex.Two);
            prevGamePadsState[2] = GamePad.GetState(PlayerIndex.Three);
            prevGamePadsState[3] = GamePad.GetState(PlayerIndex.Four);
        }

        public void Update()
        {
            //set our previous state to our new state
            prevGamePadsState[0] = gamePadsState[0];
            prevGamePadsState[1] = gamePadsState[1];
            prevGamePadsState[2] = gamePadsState[2];
            prevGamePadsState[3] = gamePadsState[3];

            //get our new state
            //gamePadsState = GamePad.State .GetState();
            gamePadsState[0] = GamePad.GetState(PlayerIndex.One);
            gamePadsState[1] = GamePad.GetState(PlayerIndex.Two);
            gamePadsState[2] = GamePad.GetState(PlayerIndex.Three);
            gamePadsState[3] = GamePad.GetState(PlayerIndex.Four);
        }

        public bool WasButtonPressed(int playerIndex,
                                     InputHandler.ButtonType button)
        {
            int pi = playerIndex;
            switch(button)
            { //start switch
            case InputHandler.ButtonType.A:
            {
                return(gamePadsState[pi].Buttons.A == ButtonState.Pressed &&
```

LISTING 7.1   Continued

```
                    prevGamePadsState[pi].Buttons.A == ButtonState.Released);
        }
        case InputHandler.ButtonType.B:
        {
            return(gamePadsState[pi].Buttons.B == ButtonState.Pressed &&
                prevGamePadsState[pi].Buttons.B == ButtonState.Released);
        }
        case InputHandler.ButtonType.Back:
        {
            return(gamePadsState[pi].Buttons.Back == ButtonState.Pressed &&
                prevGamePadsState[pi].Buttons.Back == ButtonState.Released);
        }
        case InputHandler.ButtonType.LeftShoulder:
        {
            return(gamePadsState[pi].Buttons.LeftShoulder ==
                                            ButtonState.Pressed &&
                prevGamePadsState[pi].Buttons.LeftShoulder ==
                                            ButtonState.Released);
        }
        case InputHandler.ButtonType.LeftStick:
        {
            return(gamePadsState[pi].Buttons.LeftStick ==
                                            ButtonState.Pressed &&
                prevGamePadsState[pi].Buttons.LeftStick ==
                                            ButtonState.Released);
        }
        case InputHandler.ButtonType.RightShoulder:
        {
            return(gamePadsState[pi].Buttons.RightShoulder ==
                                            ButtonState.Pressed &&
                prevGamePadsState[pi].Buttons.RightShoulder ==
                                            ButtonState.Released);
        }
        case InputHandler.ButtonType.RightStick:
        {
            return(gamePadsState[pi].Buttons.RightStick ==
                                            ButtonState.Pressed &&
                prevGamePadsState[pi].Buttons.RightStick ==
                                            ButtonState.Released);
        }
        case InputHandler.ButtonType.Start:
        {
            return(gamePadsState[pi].Buttons.Start ==
                                            ButtonState.Pressed &&
```

LISTING 7.1   Continued

```
                        prevGamePadsState[pi].Buttons.Start ==
                                              ButtonState.Released);
        }
        case InputHandler.ButtonType.X:
        {
            return(gamePadsState[pi].Buttons.X == ButtonState.Pressed &&
                prevGamePadsState[pi].Buttons.X == ButtonState.Released);
        }
        case InputHandler.ButtonType.Y:
        {
            return(gamePadsState[pi].Buttons.Y == ButtonState.Pressed &&
                prevGamePadsState[pi].Buttons.Y == ButtonState.Released);
        }
        default:
            throw (new ArgumentException());
        } //end switch
    }
}


public class KeyboardHandler
{
    private KeyboardState prevKeyboardState;
    private KeyboardState keyboardState;

    public KeyboardHandler()
    {
        prevKeyboardState = Keyboard.GetState();
    }

    public bool IsKeyDown(Keys key)
    {
        return (keyboardState.IsKeyDown(key));
    }

    public bool IsHoldingKey(Keys key)
    {
        return(keyboardState.IsKeyDown(key) &&
            prevKeyboardState.IsKeyDown(key));
    }

    public bool WasKeyPressed(Keys key)
    {
        return(keyboardState.IsKeyDown(key) &&
            prevKeyboardState.IsKeyUp(key));
```

LISTING 7.1   Continued

```
    }

    public bool HasReleasedKey(Keys key)
    {
        return(keyboardState.IsKeyUp(key) &&
            prevKeyboardState.IsKeyDown(key));
    }

    public void Update()
    {
        //set our previous state to our new state
        prevKeyboardState = keyboardState;


        //get our new state
        keyboardState = Keyboard.GetState();
    }
  }
}
```

The first thing to notice is that we added two more classes at the end of our file:
KeyboardHandler and ButtonHandler. These objects each have an Update method that
gets called by our main Update method inside of InputHandler. The Update method stores
the previous state and resets the new state. This is the key to it all. We simply check our
new state against our old state to see if keys or buttons have been pressed or released. We
have helper functions that our game code can call to check if the key was pressed or a
button was pressed. These helper functions just query the previous and new states of the
appropriate input device and return a boolean value. With this implemented we do not
run into the issue of getting multiple events kicked off because the gamer is holding the
button down. It also gives us a base from which to start working. We left our most current
state available, as we still need that for our triggers and Dpad. Dpad could also be put into
this handler because it is treated as a button, but that along with wrapping up the mouse
information is not in the code. This should be a good starting point if either of those is
needed, though.

Plugging in Our Sound Manager

Finally we can get to our sound manager code. We discussed XACT and how we can use it
to create sound projects that our games can consume. We also extended our input
handler code and now we are ready to dive into the code that will allow us to play the
sounds we set up in our XACT project.

To begin, we need to create a new game component code file inside of our XELibrary
called SoundManager.cs. The code for this class can be found in Listing 7.2.

LISTING 7.2   SoundManager.cs

```csharp
using System;
using System.Collections.Generic;
using Microsoft.Xna.Framework;
using Microsoft.Xna.Framework.Audio;

namespace XELibrary
{
    public partial class SoundManager : Microsoft.Xna.Framework.GameComponent
    {
        public bool RepeatPlayList = true;
        private AudioEngine engine;
        private WaveBank waveBank;
        private SoundBank soundBank;

        private Dictionary<string, Cue> cues = new Dictionary<string, Cue>();
        private Dictionary<string, AudioCategory> categories =
            new Dictionary<string, AudioCategory>();

        private string[] playList;
        private int currentSong;
        private Cue currentlyPlaying;

        public SoundManager(Game game, string xactProjectName)
            : this(game, xactProjectName, xactProjectName)
        { }

        public SoundManager(Game game, string xactProjectName,
                            string xactFileName)
            : this(game, xactProjectName, xactFileName, @"Content\Sounds\")
        { }

        public SoundManager(Game game, string xactProjectName,
                            string xactFileName, string contentPath)
            : base(game)
        {
            xactFileName = xactFileName.Replace(".xap", "");

            engine = new AudioEngine(contentPath + xactFileName + ".xgs");
            waveBank = new WaveBank(engine, contentPath + "Wave Bank.xwb");
            soundBank = new SoundBank(engine, contentPath + "Sound Bank.xsb");
        }

        public override void Initialize()
        {
```

LISTING 7.2   Continued

```
        base.Initialize();
    }

    public override void Update(GameTime gameTime)
    {
        engine.Update();

        if (currentlyPlaying != null) //are we playing a list?
        {
            //check current cue to see if it is playing
            //if not, go to next cue in list
            if (!currentlyPlaying.IsPlaying)
            {
                currentSong++;

                if (currentSong == playList.Length)
                {
                    if (RepeatPlayList)
                        currentSong = 0;
                    else
                        StopPlayList();
                }

                //may have been set to null, if we finished our list
                if (currentlyPlaying != null)
                {
                    currentlyPlaying = soundBank.GetCue(
                        playList[currentSong]);
                    currentlyPlaying.Play();
                }
            }
        }

        base.Update(gameTime);
    }

    protected override void Dispose(bool disposing)
    {
        soundBank.Dispose();
        waveBank.Dispose();
        engine.Dispose();

        playList = null;
        currentlyPlaying = null;
```

LISTING 7.2   Continued

```
            cues = null;
            soundBank = null;
            waveBank = null;
            engine = null;
            base.Dispose(disposing);
        }

        public void SetGlobalVariable(string name, float amount)
        {
            engine.SetGlobalVariable(name, amount);
        }

        private void CheckCategory(string categoryName)
        {
            if (!categories.ContainsKey(categoryName))
                categories.Add(categoryName, engine.GetCategory(categoryName));
        }

        public void SetVolume(string categoryName, float volumeAmount)
        {
            CheckCategory(categoryName);

            categories[categoryName].SetVolume(volumeAmount);
        }

        public void PauseCategory(string categoryName)
        {
            CheckCategory(categoryName);

            categories[categoryName].Pause();
        }

        public void ResumeCategory(string categoryName)
        {
            CheckCategory(categoryName);

            categories[categoryName].Resume();
        }

        public bool IsPlaying(string cueName)
        {
            if (cues.ContainsKey(cueName))
                return (cues[cueName].IsPlaying);
```

7

LISTING 7.2   Continued

```
        return (false);
    }

    public void Play(string cueName)
    {
        Cue prevCue = null;

        if (!cues.ContainsKey(cueName))
            cues.Add(cueName, soundBank.GetCue(cueName));
        else
        {
            //store our cue if we were playing
            if (cues[cueName].IsPlaying)
                prevCue = cues[cueName];

            cues[cueName] = soundBank.GetCue(cueName);
        }

        //if we weren't playing, set previous to our current cue name
        if (prevCue == null)
            prevCue = cues[cueName];

        try
        {
            cues[cueName].Play();
        }
        catch (InstancePlayLimitException)
        {
            //hit limit exception, set our cue to the previous
            //and let's stop it and then start it up again ...
            cues[cueName] = prevCue;

            if (cues[cueName].IsPlaying)
                cues[cueName].Stop(AudioStopOptions.AsAuthored);

            Toggle(cueName);
        }
    }

    public void Pause(string cueName)
    {
        if (cues.ContainsKey(cueName))
            cues[cueName].Pause();
    }
```

LISTING 7.2   Continued

```
public void Resume(string cueName)
{
    if (cues.ContainsKey(cueName))
        cues[cueName].Resume();
}

public void Toggle(string cueName)
{
    if (cues.ContainsKey(cueName))
    {
        Cue cue = cues[cueName];

        if (cue.IsPaused)
        {
            cue.Resume();
        }
        else if (cue.IsPlaying)
        {
            cue.Pause();
        }
        else //played but stopped
        {
            //need to reget cue if stopped
            Play(cueName);
        }
    }
    else //never played, need to reget cue
        Play(cueName);
}

public void StopAll()
{
    foreach (Cue cue in cues.Values)
        cue.Stop(AudioStopOptions.Immediate);
}

public void Stop(string cueName)
{
    if (cues.ContainsKey(cueName))
        cues[cueName].Stop(AudioStopOptions.Immediate);
    cues.Remove(cueName);
}
```

LISTING 7.2   Continued

```
public void StartPlayList(string[] playList)
{
    StartPlayList(playList, 0);
}

public void StartPlayList(string[] playList, int startIndex)
{
    if (playList.Length == 0)
        return;

    this.playList = playList;

    if (startIndex > playList.Length)
        startIndex = 0;

    StartPlayList(startIndex);
}

public void StartPlayList(int startIndex)
{
    if (playList.Length == 0)
        return;

    currentSong = startIndex;
    currentlyPlaying = soundBank.GetCue(playList[currentSong]);
    currentlyPlaying.Play();
}

public void StopPlayList()
{
    if (currentlyPlaying != null)
    {
        currentlyPlaying.Stop(AudioStopOptions.Immediate);
        currentlyPlaying = null;
    }
}

    }
}
```

The sound manager can play playlists. The game can simply call a list of cues to be played and the sound manager will continue to loop through the list until the game tells it not to. The sound manager allows us to set global variables so we can modify item cues that had an RPC associated with them. We can play, pause, and stop any cue in our sound manager as well.

This library component assumes that the name of the XACT project is the same name as the file. It also assumes that there is only one sound bank and one wave bank and that they keep their default names. This is handled in the constructor if there is a need to change the functionality. It assumes the location of the XACT project file is Content\Sounds, but that can be changed by calling the appropriate constructor.

During our `Update` method we call the sound engine's `Update` method as it needs to do things every so often like buffer the sounds. During our `Update` call we also handle all of our logic to determine if we are playing a playlist and, if so, if it is actually playing or if we need to advance to the next song. Of course, a playlist does not need to be only music.

We expose functionality that allows us to process actions on categories. This way we can set up our sound effects in one category (like Default) and our music in another category (like Music) and apply different sound volumes to each one differently through a user interface we could display to gamers. Perhaps they do not like their music so loud and their sound effects really loud. With the sounds associated with different categories we can use the code in this class to pause, resume, stop, and even change the volume on an entire category at one time. This means all of the sounds in that category can be altered with one call instead of many calls, one for each sound we had individually.

We store our list of categories and cues in a dictionary for easy access. This way we are not constantly instantiating new objects. Most of the time sounds will last the entire life of our game (or at least level) so it makes sense to store the data this way.

Creating a Sound Demo

Now we need to add in another Windows game project to our XELibrary solution. We can call this new project SoundDemo. We can also set up our solution for our Xbox 360 project if we want to test it on the console. Now we need to make sure our game is referencing the XELibrary project.

Once we have our XELibrary referenced correctly, we can start writing code to test out our new sound class (and updated input class). We need to use the library's namespace at the top of our game class as follows:

```
using XELibrary;
```

We should also add a folder called Content with a Sounds subfolder to our solution. We can then paste our XACT project file into our Sounds folder. The wave files should be put in the folder, but do not need to be included in the project. When we compile our code later, the Content Pipeline will find all of the waves from the wave bank and wrap them into a wave bank .xwb file. It also creates a sound bank .xsb file while the audio engine is stored in Chapter7.xgs (as that is what we had as our XACT project name).

We will now add in our `InputHandler` game component so we can kick off sound events based on our input. We need to declare our private member field to hold the component as well as adding it to our game's components collection:

```
private InputHandler input;
private SoundManager sound;

public Game1()
{
    graphics = new GraphicsDeviceManager(this);
    content = new ContentManager(Services);

    input = new InputHandler(this);
    Components.Add(input);

    sound = new SoundManager(this, "Chapter7");
    Components.Add(sound);
}
```

We passed in "Chapter7" to our constructor because that is what we called our XACT project. The next thing we need to do is set up our playlist. We can do this inside of our Initialize method because we added the sound component in our constructor:

```
string[] playList = { "Song1", "Song2", "Song3" };
sound.StartPlayList(playList);
```

The code tells our sound manager we will be playing three different songs. The library will keep checking to see if they are playing. If not, it will automatically play the next one, looping back to the beginning song when it reaches the end of the list.

Now we can actually populate our Update method to check for our input to play all of the sounds and songs we set up in XACT. We need to add the following code to our Update method:

```
if (input.KeyboardState.WasKeyPressed(Keys.D1) ||
        input.ButtonHandler.WasButtonPressed(0, InputHandler.ButtonType.A))
    sound.Play("gunshot");
if (input.KeyboardState.WasKeyPressed(Keys.D2) ||
        input.ButtonHandler.WasButtonPressed(0, InputHandler.ButtonType.B))
    sound.Play("hit");
if (input.KeyboardState.WasKeyPressed(Keys.D3) ||
        input.ButtonHandler.WasButtonPressed(0,
            InputHandler.ButtonType.LeftShoulder))
    sound.Play("attention");
if (input.KeyboardState.WasKeyPressed(Keys.D4) ||
        input.ButtonHandler.WasButtonPressed(0,
            InputHandler.ButtonType.LeftStick))
    sound.Play("explosion");
if (input.KeyboardState.WasKeyPressed(Keys.D5) ||
        input.ButtonHandler.WasButtonPressed(0,
            InputHandler.ButtonType.RightShoulder))
```

```
    sound.Play("bullet");
if (input.KeyboardState.WasKeyPressed(Keys.D6) ||
        input.ButtonHandler.WasButtonPressed(0,
            InputHandler.ButtonType.RightStick))
    sound.Play("crash");
if (input.KeyboardState.WasKeyPressed(Keys.D7) ||
        input.ButtonHandler.WasButtonPressed(0, InputHandler.ButtonType.X))
    sound.Play("complex");
if (input.KeyboardState.WasKeyPressed(Keys.D8) ||
        input.ButtonHandler.WasButtonPressed(0, InputHandler.ButtonType.Y))
    sound.Toggle("CoolLoop");
if (input.KeyboardState.WasKeyPressed(Keys.D9) ||
        input.ButtonHandler.WasButtonPressed(0,
            InputHandler.ButtonType.LeftShoulder))
    sound.Toggle("CoolLoop 2");

if (input.KeyboardState.WasKeyPressed(Keys.P) ||
    input.ButtonHandler.WasButtonPressed(0, InputHandler.ButtonType.Start))
{
    sound.Toggle("CoolLoop");
}

if (input.KeyboardState.WasKeyPressed(Keys.S) ||
        (input.GamePads[0].Triggers.Right > 0))
    sound.StopPlayList();
```

We are simply checking to see if different keys were pressed or different buttons were pushed. Based on those results we play different cues that we set up in the XACT project. A good exercise for us would be to run the demo and reread the section of this chapter where we set up all of these sounds and see if they do what we expect when we press the appropriate keys or buttons. In particular we can press the B button or number 2 key repeatedly and see that the "hit" cue is queuing up as we told it to limit itself to only playing once and to queue failed requests. We can also click down on our right thumb stick or press the number 6 key to hear our crash. If the playlist is hindering our hearing of the sounds we can stop it by pressing the S key or pushing on our right trigger.

The final piece of code for our sound demo is where we can set a global variable for the RPC we set up as well as the volume of our default category cues. To start, we need to add two more private member fields:

```
private float currentVolume = 0.5f;
private float value = 0;
```

Now we can finish up our Update method with the following code:

```
if (input.KeyboardState.IsHoldingKey(Keys.Up) ||
        input.GamePads[0].DPad.Up == ButtonState.Pressed)
```

```
    currentVolume += 0.05f;
if (input.KeyboardState.IsHoldingKey(Keys.Down) ¦¦
        input.GamePads[0].DPad.Down == ButtonState.Pressed)
    currentVolume -= 0.05f;

currentVolume = MathHelper.Clamp(currentVolume, 0.0f, 1.0f);
sound.SetVolume("Default", currentVolume);

if (input.KeyboardState.WasKeyPressed(Keys.NumPad1))
    value = 5000;
if (input.KeyboardState.WasKeyPressed(Keys.NumPad2))
    value = 25000;
if (input.KeyboardState.WasKeyPressed(Keys.NumPad3))
    value = 30000;
if (input.KeyboardState.WasKeyPressed(Keys.NumPad4))
    value = 40000;
if (input.KeyboardState.WasKeyPressed(Keys.NumPad5))
    value = 50000;
if (input.KeyboardState.WasKeyPressed(Keys.NumPad6))
    value = 60000;
if (input.KeyboardState.WasKeyPressed(Keys.NumPad7))
    value = 70000;
if (input.KeyboardState.WasKeyPressed(Keys.NumPad8))
    value = 80000;
if (input.KeyboardState.WasKeyPressed(Keys.NumPad9))
    value = 90000;
if (input.KeyboardState.WasKeyPressed(Keys.NumPad0))
    value = 100000;

if (input.GamePads[0].Triggers.Left > 0)
    value = input.GamePads[0].Triggers.Left * 100000;

sound.SetGlobalVariable("SpeedOfSound", value);
```

This completes our sound demo code and now if we run it and press the Up and Down arrow keys or on the Dpad we can hear the volume of the sounds associated with our "Default" category go up and down. We clamp our value between 0 and 1 because that is what the engine takes to set the volume. This is an example of how checking for the input state without considering the previous state can get us into trouble. The code will turn the volume up and down very quickly because it is getting back a true on every call every frame. Feel free to add Dpad to the updated InputHandler code.

Not only does this code let us test the volume settings, it also lets us set a global variable. In the XACT project, if we used SpeedOfSound as one of the parameters when setting up our curve then we can actually modify the way the cue sounds here at runtime. That is pretty powerful.

Summary

We covered a lot in this chapter. We discussed how to use the XACT tool. We saw that we could set up categories for our sounds. We learned to set up our sounds by first adding waves to our project. We discussed variations at the sound level and the cue level. We went through several examples to set up those variants. We then used those variants in a demo we made and saw how we could manage some of the sounds via our code.

We also fixed up our input handler code as we needed it to effectively write a demo to test our sounds. We discussed the new SoundManager class we added to our library. We saw how it handles the references to the cues so we can just pass in a string and not have to clutter up our game code.

We saw how the Content Pipeline can read in an XACT file to generate files that can be consumed on the Xbox 360 and Windows. The Content Pipeline is a great way to do things. In the next chapter we will look at extending the pipeline so we can bring in our own file types or process existing file types in a different way.

7

CHAPTER 8

Extending the Content Pipeline

We have learned how to use the Content Pipeline out of the box. We have seen how easy it is to load our objects and consume them inside of our game code. Sometimes, though, we need more. Sometimes we need to load in content that is custom to our game engine or content that we care about that others do not. We might just need to get a little more data about an object than the default processors obtain. In any and all of these cases we need to extend the Content Pipeline to be able to access our content at runtime with ease. Running everything through the Content Pipeline makes our resources accessible on the Xbox 360 platform. We cannot simply copy files to read from onto the console as everything needs to be compiled up front. We spend this chapter discussing how to extend the pipeline.

Creating a Skybox

We want to add a skybox to our code. We are going to create a project that will contain the content, content processor, and content compiler. After creating this project we will create another file inside of our XELibrary to read the skybox data. Finally, we will create a demo that will utilize the XELibrary's Skybox Content Reader, which the Content Manager uses to consume the skybox.

Before we actually create the project we should first examine a skybox and its purpose in games. A skybox keeps us from having to create complex geometry for objects that are very far away. For example, we do not need to create a sun or a moon or some distant city when we use a skybox. We can create six textures that we can put into our cube. Although there are skybox models we could use, for this chapter we are going to build our own skybox. It is simply a cube and we already have the code in place to create a cube. We know how to create rectangles and we know how to position them where we want them. We can create six rectangles that we can use as our skybox. When each texture is applied to each side of the skybox we get an effect that our world is much bigger than it is. Plus, it looks much better than the cornflower blue backdrop we currently have!

Creating the Skybox Content Object

To start, let's create a new Windows library project called SkyboxPipeline. There is no need to create an Xbox 360 version of the project because this will only be run on the PC. This SkyboxPipeline project will have three files. The first file is the SkyboxContent.cs code file, shown in Listing 8.1.

LISTING 8.1   SkyboxContent.cs holds the design time class of our skybox

```
using System;
using Microsoft.Xna.Framework.Content.Pipeline.Processors;
using Microsoft.Xna.Framework.Content.Pipeline.Graphics;

namespace SkyboxPipeline
{
    public class SkyboxContent
    {
        public ModelContent Model;
        public Texture2DContent Texture;
    }
}
```

The SkyboxContent object holds our skybox data at design time. We need to add a reference to Microsoft.Xna.Framework.Content.Pipeline to our project to utilize the namespaces needed.

Creating the Skybox Processor

The SkyboxContent object is utilized by the processor, shown in Listing 8.2.

LISTING 8.2   SkyboxProcessor.cs actually processes the data it gets as input from the Content Pipeline

```
using System;
using System.Collections.Generic;
using Microsoft.Xna.Framework;
using Microsoft.Xna.Framework.Content.Pipeline;
using Microsoft.Xna.Framework.Content.Pipeline.Graphics;
using Microsoft.Xna.Framework.Content.Pipeline.Processors;
```

LISTING 8.2   Continued

```
namespace SkyboxPipeline
{
    [ContentProcessor]
    class SkyboxProcessor : ContentProcessor<Texture2DContent, SkyboxContent>
    {
        private int width = 1024;
        private int height = 512;
        private int cellSize = 256;

        public override SkyboxContent Process(Texture2DContent input,
                                       ContentProcessorContext context)
        {
            MeshBuilder builder = MeshBuilder.StartMesh("XESkybox");

            CreatePositions(ref builder);

            AddVerticesInformation(ref builder);

            // Create the output object.
            SkyboxContent skybox = new SkyboxContent();

            // Finish making the mesh
            MeshContent skyboxMesh = builder.FinishMesh();

            //Compile the mesh we just built through the default ModelProcessor
            skybox.Model = context.Convert<MeshContent, ModelContent>(
                skyboxMesh, "ModelProcessor");

            skybox.Texture = input;

            return skybox;
        }

        private void CreatePositions(ref MeshBuilder builder)
        {
            Vector3 position;

            //— — — —-front plane
            //top left
            position = new Vector3(-1, 1, 1);
            builder.CreatePosition(position); //0

            //bottom right
```

LISTING 8.2   Continued

```
        position = new Vector3(1, -1, 1);
        builder.CreatePosition(position); //1

        //bottom left
        position = new Vector3(-1, -1, 1);
        builder.CreatePosition(position); //2

        //top right
        position = new Vector3(1, 1, 1);
        builder.CreatePosition(position); //3

        //————back plane
        //top left
        position = new Vector3(-1, 1, -1); //4
        builder.CreatePosition(position);

        //bottom right
        position = new Vector3(1, -1, -1); //5
        builder.CreatePosition(position);

        //bottom left
        position = new Vector3(-1, -1, -1); //6
        builder.CreatePosition(position);

        //top right
        position = new Vector3(1, 1, -1); //7
        builder.CreatePosition(position);
    }

    private Vector2 UV(int u, int v, Vector2 cellIndex)
    {
        return(new Vector2((cellSize * (cellIndex.X + u) / width),
            (cellSize * (cellIndex.Y + v) / height)));
    }

    private void AddVerticesInformation(ref MeshBuilder builder)
    {
        //texture locations:
        //F,R,B,L
        //U,D

        //Front
        Vector2 fi = new Vector2(0, 0); //cell 0, row 0
```

LISTING 8.2   Continued

```
//Right
Vector2 ri = new Vector2(1, 0); //cell 1, row 0

//Back
Vector2 bi = new Vector2(2, 0); //cell 2, row 0

//Left
Vector2 li = new Vector2(3, 0); //cell 3, row 0

//Upward (Top)
Vector2 ui = new Vector2(0, 1); //cell 0, row 1

//Downward (Bottom)
Vector2 di = new Vector2(1, 1); //cell 1, row 1

int texCoordChannel = builder.CreateVertexChannel<Vector2>
    (VertexChannelNames.TextureCoordinate(0));

//————front plane first column, first row

//bottom triangle of front plane
builder.SetVertexChannelData(texCoordChannel, UV(0, 0, fi));
builder.AddTriangleVertex(4); //-1,1,1
builder.SetVertexChannelData(texCoordChannel, UV(1, 1, fi));
builder.AddTriangleVertex(5); //1,-1,1
builder.SetVertexChannelData(texCoordChannel, UV(0, 1, fi));
builder.AddTriangleVertex(6); //-1,-1,1

//top triangle of front plane
builder.SetVertexChannelData(texCoordChannel, UV(0, 0, fi));
builder.AddTriangleVertex(4); //-1,1,1
builder.SetVertexChannelData(texCoordChannel, UV(1, 0, fi));
builder.AddTriangleVertex(7); //1,1,1
builder.SetVertexChannelData(texCoordChannel, UV(1, 1, fi));
builder.AddTriangleVertex(5); //1,-1,1

//————·right plane
builder.SetVertexChannelData(texCoordChannel, UV(1, 0, ri));
builder.AddTriangleVertex(3);
builder.SetVertexChannelData(texCoordChannel, UV(1, 1, ri));
builder.AddTriangleVertex(1);
builder.SetVertexChannelData(texCoordChannel, UV(0, 1, ri));
builder.AddTriangleVertex(5);
```

8

LISTING 8.2   Continued

```
builder.SetVertexChannelData(texCoordChannel, UV(1, 0, ri));
builder.AddTriangleVertex(3);
builder.SetVertexChannelData(texCoordChannel, UV(0, 1, ri));
builder.AddTriangleVertex(5);
builder.SetVertexChannelData(texCoordChannel, UV(0, 0, ri));
builder.AddTriangleVertex(7);

//————-back pane //3rd column, first row
//bottom triangle of back plane
builder.SetVertexChannelData(texCoordChannel, UV(1, 1, bi)); //1,1
builder.AddTriangleVertex(2); //-1,-1,1
builder.SetVertexChannelData(texCoordChannel, UV(0, 1, bi)); //0,1
builder.AddTriangleVertex(1); //1,-1,1
builder.SetVertexChannelData(texCoordChannel, UV(1, 0, bi)); //1,0
builder.AddTriangleVertex(0); //-1,1,1

//top triangle of back plane
builder.SetVertexChannelData(texCoordChannel, UV(0, 1, bi)); //0,1
builder.AddTriangleVertex(1); //1,-1,1
builder.SetVertexChannelData(texCoordChannel, UV(0, 0, bi)); //0,0
builder.AddTriangleVertex(3); //1,1,1
builder.SetVertexChannelData(texCoordChannel, UV(1, 0, bi)); //1,0
builder.AddTriangleVertex(0); //-1,1,1

//————-left plane
builder.SetVertexChannelData(texCoordChannel, UV(1, 1, li));
builder.AddTriangleVertex(6);
builder.SetVertexChannelData(texCoordChannel, UV(0, 1, li));
builder.AddTriangleVertex(2);
builder.SetVertexChannelData(texCoordChannel, UV(0, 0, li));
builder.AddTriangleVertex(0);

builder.SetVertexChannelData(texCoordChannel, UV(1, 0, li));
builder.AddTriangleVertex(4);
builder.SetVertexChannelData(texCoordChannel, UV(1, 1, li));
builder.AddTriangleVertex(6);
builder.SetVertexChannelData(texCoordChannel, UV(0, 0, li));
builder.AddTriangleVertex(0);

//————upward (top) plane
builder.SetVertexChannelData(texCoordChannel, UV(1, 0, ui));
builder.AddTriangleVertex(3);
builder.SetVertexChannelData(texCoordChannel, UV(0, 1, ui));
builder.AddTriangleVertex(4);
```

LISTING 8.2   Continued

```
            builder.SetVertexChannelData(texCoordChannel, UV(0, 0, ui));
            builder.AddTriangleVertex(0);

            builder.SetVertexChannelData(texCoordChannel, UV(1, 0, ui));
            builder.AddTriangleVertex(3);
            builder.SetVertexChannelData(texCoordChannel, UV(1, 1, ui));
            builder.AddTriangleVertex(7);
            builder.SetVertexChannelData(texCoordChannel, UV(0, 1, ui));
            builder.AddTriangleVertex(4);

            //————downward (bottom) plane
            builder.SetVertexChannelData(texCoordChannel, UV(1, 0, di));
            builder.AddTriangleVertex(2);
            builder.SetVertexChannelData(texCoordChannel, UV(1, 1, di));
            builder.AddTriangleVertex(6);
            builder.SetVertexChannelData(texCoordChannel, UV(0, 0, di));
            builder.AddTriangleVertex(1);

            builder.SetVertexChannelData(texCoordChannel, UV(1, 1, di));
            builder.AddTriangleVertex(6);
            builder.SetVertexChannelData(texCoordChannel, UV(0, 1, di));
            builder.AddTriangleVertex(5);
            builder.SetVertexChannelData(texCoordChannel, UV(0, 0, di));
            builder.AddTriangleVertex(1);
        }
    }
}
```

The SkyboxProcessor contains a lot of code, but the vast majority of it is actually building and texturing our skybox. We can go ahead and create this file in our pipeline project now.

To begin we used the [ContentProcessor] attribute for our class so the Content Pipeline could determine which class to call when it needed to process a resource with our type. We inherit from the ContentProcessor class stating that we are going to be taking a Texture2D as input and outputting our skybox content type. In the Process method we take in two parameters: input and context. To create our skybox we are going to pass in a single texture in our game projects. The processor creates a new MeshBuilder object, which is a helper class that allows us to quickly create a mesh with vertices in any order we wish and then apply different vertex information for those vertices that can contain things like texture coordinates, normals, colors, and so on. For our purposes we will be storing the texture. We create our actual eight vertices of our skybox cube in the CreatePositions method. We are simply passing a vertex position into the CreatePosition method of the MeshBuilder method.

Next up is our call to AddVerticesInformation. This method contains the bulk of the code but it is not doing anything fancy. It is simply creating triangles in the mesh by passing the vertices index values to the AddTriangleVertex method of the MeshBuilder object. These vertices need to be called in the right order. We can think of this as building the indices of the mesh. The idea is that we created our unique vertices (in CreatePositions) and although we could have stored the value CreatePosition returned to us, we know that it will return us the next number starting with 0. Instead of using up memory for the index being passed back, we just made a note in the comment next to that vertex so we could build our triangles.

Before we actually add a vertex to a triangle of our mesh, we pass in our vertex channel information. We created a vertex channel before we started creating triangles with the following code:

```
int texCoordChannel = builder.CreateVertexChannel<Vector2>
    (VertexChannelNames.TextureCoordinate(0));
```

We can have multiple vertex channels. Although we are only going to store texture coordinates, we could also store normals, binormals, tangents, weights, and colors. Because we could store all of these different pieces of information we need to tell the vertex channel which type of data we are storing. We then store an index to that particular channel. Once we have that channel index we can call the SetVertexChannelData method for each triangle vertex we add. In fact, set the channel data for the builder before adding the vertex. If we had more than one vertex channel to apply to a vertex, we would call all of them in succession before finally calling the AddTriangleVertex method. The following code shows the order in which this needs to take place:

```
builder.SetVertexChannelData(texCoordChannel, UV(0, 0, fi));
builder.AddTriangleVertex(4);
```

SetVertexChannelData takes in the vertex channel ID followed by the appropriate data for that channel. When we set up the vertex channel to handle texture coordinates we did so by passing the generic Vector2 because texture coordinates have an x and a y component. This means that the SetVertexChannelData for our texture coordinate channel is expecting a type of Vector2.

For this texture mapping code to make sense, we need to discuss how the texture asset we are going to pass into our demo or game needs to be laid out. Instead of requiring six different textures to create a skybox, we are requiring only one with each plane of the cube to have a specific location inside of the texture. The texture size is 1024 x 512 to keep with the power-of-two restriction most graphic cards make us live by. We put four textures on the top row and two textures on the bottom row. The top row will have the cube faces Front, Right, Back, and Left in that order. The bottom row will have Up (Top) and Down (Bottom). If we have skyboxes in other formats we can use a paint program to get them in this format. We can also use tools to generate skybox images and output them into this format or one we can easily work with. The great thing about this being an extension of the Content Pipeline is that we have free reign over how we want to read in data and create content that our games can easily use. If we stick with the current single texture it leaves part of the texture unused. We could utilize these two spots for something else. For example, we could create one or two cloud layers to our skybox, so instead of just rendering a cube, it would render a cube with two additional layers that could prove to be a nice effect. We could use it for terrain generation by reading in the values from a gray-scaled image in one of those spots to create a nice ground layout. We do not discuss terrain generation in this book, but there are many excellent articles on the Web about generating terrains.

Now that we know how the texture is laid out we can discuss some of the details of the code that is applying the texture to the different panels of the cube. In the following code we declared a variable to hold our index of the right panel in the texture:

```
//Right
Vector2 ri = new Vector2(1, 0); //cell 1, row 0
```

We are storing 1,0 in a vector signifying that the right panel's portion of the large texture is in the first cell in row zero (this is zero based). In Chapter 4, "Creating 3D Objects," we discussed how to texture our rectangle (quad) by applying different u and v coordinates to the different vertices of our rectangle. We are using the exact same concept here. The only difference is that we have to take into account the fact that we are extracting multiple textures from our one texture. For example, to texture the right-side panel of our skybox using just one texture we could simply tell the top left vertex to use texture coordinates 0,0 and the bottom right vertex to use texture coordinate 1,1. However, our right-side panel's texture is not the entire texture we have in memory; instead it is from pixels 256,0 to 512,256. We can see this in Figure 8.1 where the right panel texture is not grayed out.

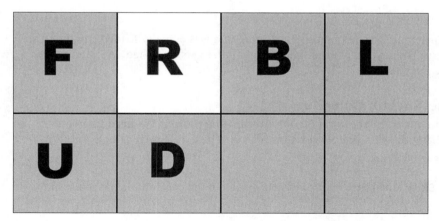

FIGURE 8.1   Our skybox texture is made up of six cells (Front, Right, Back, Left, Up, Down).

To handle the offset issue we created a UV method that takes in the typical 0 and 1 along with index cell from which we need to get our updated u and v coordinates. The UV method that calculates our u and v values is as follows:

```
private Vector2 UV(int u, int v, Vector2 cellIndex)
{
    return(new Vector2((cellSize * (cellIndex.X + u) / width),
        (cellSize * (cellIndex.Y + v) / height)));
}
```

This method simply takes in the u and v coordinates we would normally map on a full texture along with the cell index we want to access in the texture and it returns the calculated u and v coordinates. The cellSize, width, and height are private member fields. We take the size of the cell, 256, and multiply that by the sum of our x value of our cell index and the u value passed in. We take that value and divide it by width to come up with the correct u position of the large texture. We do the same thing to get our v value. We pass those actual values to SetVertexChannelData so it will associate the right texture coordinates with that vertex.

After actually creating the Skybox vertices and setting up all of the triangles needed and applying our texture coordinates, we can finally save the mesh. We do this by calling the FinishMesh method on our MeshBuilder object, which returns a MeshContent type back to us. This is convenient as that is the type of object we need to pass to the default ModelProcessor to process our mesh (just as if we loaded a .X file through the Content Pipeline). This is done with the following code:

```
MeshContent skyboxMesh = builder.FinishMesh();
skybox.Model = context.Convert<MeshContent, ModelContent>(
    skyboxMesh, "ModelProcessor");
```

After setting our texture to the texture (our input) that was actually loaded to start this process, we return the skybox content and the compiler gets launched. We discuss the compiler in the next section.

Creating the Skybox Compiler

This brings us to our third and final file for our pipeline project. We need to create another code file with the name SkyboxCompiler.cs. The code for this file is found in Listing 8.3.

LISTING 8.3   SkyboxCompiler.cs compiles and writes out the content it is passed from the processor

```
using System;
using System.Collections.Generic;
using Microsoft.Xna.Framework;
using Microsoft.Xna.Framework.Content.Pipeline.Graphics;
using Microsoft.Xna.Framework.Content.Pipeline.Processors;
```

LISTING 8.3   Continued

```
using Microsoft.Xna.Framework.Content.Pipeline.Serialization.Compiler;

namespace SkyboxPipeline
{
    [ContentTypeWriter]
    public class SkyboxWriter : ContentTypeWriter<SkyboxContent>
    {
        protected override void Write(ContentWriter output, SkyboxContent value)
        {
            output.WriteObject(value.Model);
            output.WriteObject(value.Texture);
        }

        public override string GetRuntimeType(TargetPlatform targetPlatform)
        {
            return "XELibrary.Skybox, " +
                "XELibrary, Version=1.0.0.0, Culture=neutral";
        }

        public override string GetRuntimeReader(TargetPlatform targetPlatform)
        {
            return "XELibrary.SkyboxReader, " +
                "XELibrary, Version=1.0.0.0, Culture=neutral";
        }
    }
}
```

We start off this class much like the last in that we associate an attribute with it. This time we need to use the [ContentTypeWriter] attribute as it tells the Content Pipeline this is the compiler or writer class. We inherit from the ContentTypeWriter with the generic type of SkyboxContent (which we created in the first file of this project). This way when the Content Pipeline gets the skybox content back from the processor it knows where to send the data to be compiled.

We override the Write method and save our skybox as an .xnb file. The base class does all of the heavy lifting and all we need to do is write our object out. The next method, GetRuntimeType, tells the Content Pipeline the actual type of the skybox data that will be loaded at runtime. The last method, GetRuntimeReader, tells the Content Pipeline which object will actually be reading in and processing the .xnb data. The contents of these two methods are returning different classes inside of the same assembly. They do not need to reside in the same assembly, but it definitely made sense in this case. We store the runtime type and runtime reader in a separate project. We do not add them to the pipeline project because the pipeline project is Windows dependent and our actual skybox type and reader object needs to be platform independent. We are going to set up these two classes inside of our XELibrary so our games and demos will already have access to our library, and it makes sense to have our Skybox content reader in the same place.

Creating the Skybox Reader

Let's copy and open our Load3DObject project from Chapter 6, "Loading and Texturing 3D Objects." Our XELibrary should already be inside of this project and we can add a SkyboxReader.cs file to our XELibrary projects. This file will contain both our `Skybox` type and our `SkyboxReader` type. We could have created separate files if we desired. If we had them in different assemblies, however, we would need to update our `GetRunttimeType` and `GetRuntimeReader` methods in our content writer. The code contained in SkyboxReader.cs can be found in Listing 8.4.

LISTING 8.4   SkyboxReader.cs inside of our XELibrary allows for our games to read the compiled .xnb files generated by the Content Pipeline

```
using System;
using System.Collections.Generic;
using Microsoft.Xna.Framework;
using Microsoft.Xna.Framework.Graphics;
using Microsoft.Xna.Framework.Content;

namespace XELibrary
{
    public class SkyboxReader : ContentTypeReader<Skybox>
    {
        protected override Skybox Read(ContentReader input, Skybox existingInstance)
        {
            return new Skybox(input);
        }
    }

    public class Skybox
    {
        private Model skyboxModel;
        private Texture2D skyboxTexture;

        internal Skybox(ContentReader input)
        {
            skyboxModel = input.ReadObject<Model>();
            skyboxTexture = input.ReadObject<Texture2D>();
        }

        public void Draw(Matrix view, Matrix projection, Matrix world)
        {
```

LISTING 8.4   Continued

```
        foreach (ModelMesh mesh in skyboxModel.Meshes)
        {
            foreach (BasicEffect be in mesh.Effects)
            {
                be.Projection = projection;
                be.View = view;
                be.World = world;
                be.Texture = skyboxTexture;
                be.TextureEnabled = true;
            }
            mesh.Draw(SaveStateMode.SaveState);
        }
    }
}
}
```

Our `SkyboxReader` class is pretty small. It derives from the `ContentTypeReader` and uses a Skybox type that we will see in a moment. We override the `Read` method of this class, which gets passed in the skybox data as input as well as an existing instance of the object that we could write into if needed. We take the input and actually create an instance to our `Skybox` object by calling the internal constructor.

Inside of the `Skybox` class we take the input that was just passed to us and store the model embedded inside. We expose a `Draw` method that takes in view, projection, and world matrices as parameters. We then treat the model as if we loaded it from the pipeline (because we did) and set the basic effect on each mesh inside of the model to use the projection, view, and world matrices passed to the object. Finally, we actually draw the object onto the screen.

Using the Skybox

We have gone through a lot of work, but we are almost done. All we need to do now is actually use this `Skybox` object inside of our game. Let's open the Game1.cs file and add this private member field:

```
private Skybox skybox;
```

Now we need to add a skybox texture to our content folder. Let's create another subfolder under Content and call it Skyboxes. This is not required but it might be helpful to remind us to change the processor type, which we will see how to do shortly. For now, we need to actually add an image to this Skyboxes subfolder. We can find one on this book's CD under the Load3DObject\Content\Skyboxes\skybox.tga inside of the Chapter 8 source code folder. Copy this texture and paste it into the Skyboxes folder through Solution Explorer. Inside of the properties window we need to tell XNA Game Studio Express which importer and processor we want it to use when loading this content. We will leave the importer alone as it is defaulted to Texture – XNA Framework. See the sidebar "Creating a Custom Content Pipeline Importer."

We will change the `Content Processor` property, but before we do we need to tell our project that there is a custom processor of which it needs to be aware. We do this by double-clicking the Properties tree node under our game projects. Inside of our project properties we can open the last tab on the bottom: Content Pipeline. We can click Add and browse to our pipeline project, then add the assembly in the bin folder.

We will add this exact same assembly (under the x86 subfolder) to our Xbox 360 game project as well. This is because the assembly is only run on our PC when we are actually building our project. However, we do need to make sure that our XELibrary_Xbox360 assembly has the same name as our Windows assembly. This is important because we have told the `SkyboxWriter` where to find the `Skybox` type and the `SkyboxReader` object. We told it XELibrary, not XELibrary_Xbox360.

Alternatively, we could have left the assembly names different and added a condition to our `GetRuntimeReader` method in our `SkyboxCompiler` class. We could have returned a different string depending on the target platform that is passed into that method.

Now that we have added our Content Pipeline extension to our game projects we can select `SkyboxProcessor` from the list of content processors that are available in the property window when we have our skybox texture selected.

CREATING A CUSTOM CONTENT PIPELINE IMPORTER

An example of setting up a custom importer is the following code:

```
[ContentImporterAttribute(".ext", DefaultProcessor = "SomeCustomProcessor")]
public class CustomImporter : ContentImporter<CustomType>
{
    public override CustomType Import(string filename,
        ContentImporterContext context)
    {
        byte[] data = File.ReadAllBytes(filename);

        return (new CustomType(data));
    }
}
```

This code is a theoretical importer that would be inside of the pipeline project if we needed to import a type of file that the Content Pipeline could not handle. We could open up the file that was being loaded by the Content Pipeline and extract the data to our `CustomType` that could handle the data. This `CustomType` would also be used as the input inside of our processor object (where we used `Texture2DContent`). The reason we did not make our own importer is because the XNA Framework's Content Pipeline can handle texture files automatically.

We are finally ready to run our game. We should see a star-filled background instead of our typical CornflowerBlue background. We have successfully built a Content Pipeline extension that takes a texture file and creates a skybox for us automatically. There is no limit to the things we can accomplish because of the Content Pipeline's opened architecture. We could create a level editor and save it in any format and load it in at compile time to our game. We could write an importer for our favorite 3D model file type and work directly with the files. There are many opportunities to use the Content Pipeline. Whenever we can take a hit up front at build time instead of runtime is always a good thing.

Debugging the Content Pipeline Extension

Extending the pipeline is excellent, but what happens when something goes awry? We cannot exactly step through the code because this is a component being loaded and run by the IDE … or can we? Fortunately, we can. We discuss how to do that in this section.

If we have the SkyboxPipeline solution opened, we can close it and then add the project to our Load3DDemo solution. This is not required to debug, but it can make it easier to make sure the IDE is using the latest changes to the pipeline processor. Alternatively, we could compile and change the stand-alone SkyboxPipeline solution and then compile the Load3DDemo. Again, it really is just personal preference.

The goal is to make sure our SkyboxPipeline code gets compiled before our game code. To do this we can either add the dependency directly to our game code or we can add it to our XELibrary knowing that our game code already has a dependency on the XELibrary. We can right-click our XELibrary projects (one at a time) and select Project Dependencies. We can then add the check box to our SkyboxPipeline project. From now on, when we compile, the solution will compile the SkyboxPipeline first, followed by the XELibrary and finally compile our Load3DObject project.

Now that the SkyboxPipeline project is open, we can add the following line of code at the top of the Process method inside of our SkyboxProcessor class:

```
System.Diagnostics.Debugger.Launch();
```

This will actually launch the debugger so we can step through the code to see what is happening. If we run our program with this line of coded added, the CLR debugger will get executed. We can then walk through the code like any other. We cannot edit and continue just like we cannot do that on the Xbox 360. Regardless, being able to step through the code at runtime is very beneficial. We can set break points wherever we need to. This is an excellent way to visualize exactly which pieces of code are calling other pieces and see the general flow of the Content Pipeline.

TIP

The CLR Debugger 2.0 is not installed with Visual C# Express. It can be downloaded from http://www.microsoft.com/downloads/details.aspx?familyid=38449A42-6B7A-4E28-80CE-C55645AB1310&displaylang=en.

Summary

In this chapter we learned how to extend the Content Pipeline to load data at design time or compile time instead of at runtime. We learned about skyboxes and actually created a pipeline component that makes a skybox based on a texture. We discussed the different components needed to extend the pipeline including the actual content type of the object we are bringing into the Content Pipeline, the processor to process that object, the writer to compile that object, and finally (in a separate project) a reader to read the object and work with the content manager.

We also learned how to take this new skybox from our pipeline extension and use it in our demo. We discussed how to get the IDE to recognize the newly created Content Pipeline extension and how to set the content properties of our assets to use our importer and processor. Finally, we discussed how to debug our Content Pipeline through the CLR debugger. There are many things we can do with a content processor that will make our job of writing games easier.

We take a break from 3D for the next part of the book, in which we will discuss how to use 2D in XNA. We will be learning the basics, and then create some 2D effects followed by creating a full 2D game.

PART IV
2D in XNA

IN THIS PART

2D Basics

The XNA Framework not only provides easy ways for us to utilize 3D objects, but it also provides excellent 2D support. There are actually a couple of ways we can achieve 2D inside of XNA. There is true 2D, which is sprite manipulation. We will discuss this kind of 2D. The other kind is actually setting up a 3D environment, but locking the camera so that it is always looking at the same angle and cannot be moved—it is a 3D world with a stationary camera.

Whereas 3D uses models to display our scene, 2D uses images to create and animate our scene. The two dimensions are x and y—there is no z in 2D. It is very common to mix 2D and 3D into the same game. Scores, menus, and timers are examples of things that are typically 2D in a 3D world. Even if you are not interested in writing 2D games, the next three chapters will prove beneficial, as there will be things that can be incorporated into your 3D masterpieces.

Sprite Batches

First we need to understand the term *sprite*. A sprite is an image. XNA represents sprites with a `Texture2D` object. We load them just like we load textures for our 3D applications, as they are both images and get processed the same way. The difference is that in 3D we texture an object with the image, whereas in 2D we draw the image (or part of the image) on the screen. We saw an example of drawing part of an image in the last chapter. We applied different parts of an image to our skybox. The concept is the same, but the process is a little different. Really, we just pass in whole numbers instead of floats. Sprites are represented by x and y and as such have int values. It is impossible to draw something at pixel location 0.3, 0.3. If these types of values are passed in, XNA will do some anti-aliasing to make it appear that it is partially in the pixel area but the actual image location is rounded to a whole number.

We discussed the 3D coordinate system earlier and now we discuss the 2D coordinate system. The top left of the screen is the origin of the screen (0,0). The x axis runs horizontally at the top of the screen and the y axis runs vertically down the left side of the screen. It is identical to how a texture's coordinate system is used. The difference is that instead of running from 0.0 to 1.0 like in a texture, the values run from 0 to the width and height of the screen. So if the resolution is 1024 x 768, the x values would run from 0,0 to 1024,0. The y values would run from 0,0 to 0,768. x runs from left to right and y runs from top to bottom. The bottom right pixel of the screen would be 1024,768. This can be seen in Figure 9.1.

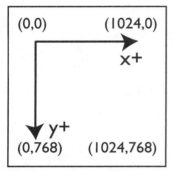

FIGURE 9.1   The 2D coordinate system origin is the top left of the screen.

Although the origin of the screen is 0,0 the origin of a sprite may or may not be. The default is 0,0 but the origin can be overridden if needed. When we draw sprites to the screen we need to be aware of where the origin of the sprite is because when we pass in a coordinate (via a Vector2 type), XNA will draw the object to that location starting with the origin of the sprite. So if we drew the sprite at location 100,200 and we did not touch the origin of the sprite, then the top left of the sprite would get drawn in 100,200. If we wanted 100,200 to be the center then we would either need to define the origin of our sprite or we would need to offset our position manually. When we rotate our sprites, they will rotate around the origin of the sprite. When we need to rotate our sprites we will typically set the origin of the sprite to be the center of the sprite. This way the sprite will rotate around the center. Otherwise, the sprite would rotate around 0,0. The differences between these two can be seen in Figure 9.2.

We can also scale a sprite. Scaling comes in three different flavors. We can either give a number to scale the entire sprite by or we can just scale one portion of the sprite. The final way we can scale is to specify a source rectangle and then specify a destination rectangle. XNA can scale our source rectangle to fit into our destination rectangle.

Sprite batches are simply batches of sprites. When we draw a lot of sprites on the screen it can put a load on the machine as we have to send a separate instruction to the graphics card each time we draw something to the screen. With a sprite batch we have the ability

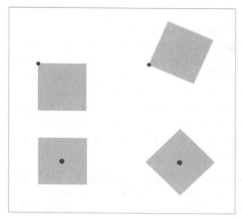

FIGURE 9.2   The origin of the sprite determines how the sprite will be rotated.

to batch up our draw functions to happen within the same settings and send one draw call to the graphics card. When we create a SpriteBatch in our code we can pass in the following values to its Begin method: SpriteBlendMode, SpriteSortMode, and SaveStateMode.

Sprite Blend Modes

The blend mode can be set to AlphaBlend, Additive, and None. The default blend mode is AlphaBlend. AlphaBlend does just that: It blends the sprites drawn (source) with the pixels it is being drawn on (destination) based on the alpha value of both. This includes transparency but can be used to create different effects depending on blend values we provide. We will cover overriding the blending values in the next chapter. Additive is another common blend mode that XNA provides support for with our sprite batches automatically. Finally, None simply does not set any blending modes. It just overwrites the destination area with the source sprite.

Alpha blending is used for normal translucent things like glass, windows, water, and objects that fade in or out. Additive blending, on the other hand, is good to use when creating glowing objects like explosions, sparks, and even magic effects. We will discuss these two blending modes and even more that are not directly supported by sprite batches in the next chapter.

Sprite Sort Modes

The sort mode determines how different sprites that are drawn actually get displayed on the screen. In previous times, game developers had to take great care with how they displayed images to the screen to make sure the background did overwrite their foreground and that textures with alpha values rendered correctly. Although we still need to take care as we approach this task, a lot of work has been done for us so that we need to worry about it less. We still need to be aware of how XNA handles this for us so we can use it effectively and keep our frame rates high.

The sort mode can be set to `BackToFront`, `Deferred`, `FrontToBack`, `Immediate`, and `Texture`. The sort mode defaults to `Deferred` when we call `Begin` with no parameters. `Immediate` is faster than `Deferred`. `Immediate` works a little different than the rest of the sort modes. `Immediate` updates the graphics device settings immediately when the `Begin` method is called. Then as sprites are drawn to the screen they immediately appear with no sorting. This is the fastest method available, but it requires us to sort the images the way we want them to be displayed. We draw the background images first and move up to the foreground. An interesting thing we can do with immediate mode is change our graphics device settings after `Begin` is called and before we actually draw our sprites to the screen. We will discuss this in more detail in the next chapter.

The rest of the sort modes will update the graphics device settings when `End` is called on the `SpriteBatch` instead of `Begin`. This means there is only one call out to the graphics device. The `Deferred` sort mode is like `Immediate` in that it does not do any sorting, it just defers talking to the graphics device until the end of the process.

The next two sort modes are `BackToFront` and `FrontToBack`. When we draw our sprites we can set our layer depth of that sprite. That value is a float between 0.0 and 1.0. The sprites will draw in this order for the two modes. `BackToFront` is typically used for transparent sprites and `FrontToBack` is typically used for nontransparent (opaque) sprites.

Finally, we can pass in `Texture` as a sort mode to our sprite batch's `Begin` method. The `Texture` sort mode will check to see all of the draws that are required and will sort them so that the graphics device does not need to have its texture changed for each draw if possible. For example, if we have five sprites drawing and three of them use the same texture (could be different parts of the same texture) then the graphics device is sent the texture and then the three draws. Then the other two draws occur with their textures. This can really help performance. However, we might need foreground and background images in the same texture. Sorting by texture alone is going to give us good perfor-mance, but we need to also sort by our layer depth. Fortunately, we can set up two sprite batches at the same time (as long as we are not using `Immediate` sort mode).

So we could have our first batch sort by texture and our second batch sort by layer depth (`BackToFront` or `FrontToBack`). We can then draw our items including the layer depth value, and as long as we call `End` on our sprite batches in the appropriate order our screen will display as we expect and the performance will be good as well. Because the `End` method is what actually does the drawing, we need to make sure we call them in order from background to foreground. It is best to draw our opaque sprites first in one batch and then our transparent sprites after that.

Save State Modes

As we complete different tasks inside of our `Draw` method, we might need to change settings on our graphics device. For example, we might want our depth buffer to be on when we are drawing certain items and off when drawing other items. When the sprite batch is executed (when `Begin` is called in `Immediate` sort mode, when `End` is called for all others) the graphics device will have the properties in Table 9.1 modified. We might want to save our properties so we can reset them when the sprite batch is done.

`SaveStateMode.SaveState` does exactly that. The other option is `SaveStateMode.None`, which is the default and does not save any state. It is quicker if we just reset the states ourselves if needed, especially on the Xbox 360.

TABLE 9.1   The `SpriteBatch.Begin` Method Modifies These Graphics Device Properties

Property	Value
RenderState.CullMode	CullCounterClockwiseFace
RenderState.DepthBufferEnable	False
RenderState.AlphaBlendEnable	True
RenderState.AlphaTestEnable	True
RenderState.AlphaBlendOperation	Add
RenderState.SourceBlend	SourceAlpha
RenderState.DestinationBlend	InverseSourceAlpha
RenderState.SeparateAlphaBlendEnabled	False
RenderState.AlphaFunction	Greater
RenderState.ReferenceAlpha	0
SamplerStates[0].AddressU	Clamp
SamplerStates[0].AddressV	Clamp
SamplerStates[0].MagFilter	Linear
SamplerStates[0].MinFilter	Linear
SamplerStates[0].MipFilter	Linear
SamplerStates[0].MipMapLevelOfDetailBias	0
SamplerStates[0].MaxMipLevel	0

When we mix 2D and 3D together we will definitely want to set the following properties before drawing our 3D content:

```
GraphicsDevice.RenderState.DepthBufferEnable = true;
GraphicsDevice.RenderState.AlphaBlendEnable = false;
GraphicsDevice.RenderState.AlphaTestEnable = false;
GraphicsDevice.SamplerStates[0].AddressU = TextureAddressMode.Wrap;
GraphicsDevice.SamplerStates[0].AddressV = TextureAddressMode.Wrap;
```

Practical Sprite Batches

Now that we have learned all about sprite batches, we can write some code to see how to actually make this work. We will make a splash or loading screen we can display when our games load. We will create a demo that allows us retrieve multiple sprites stored in one texture. We will write a small demo that will allow us to quickly change the different blend modes as well as the sort modes so we can see what happens as we modify those settings. Finally, we will create a progress bar that we can use later while we are waiting on our scenes to load.

Splash or Loading Screen Demo

We are going to create a demo called SplashScreenDemo. We need to set up our solution to include our XELibrary project. We are going to make a small modification to our library in this demo, so we need to have the project opened as well. The purpose of this demo is to use our sprite batch knowledge to draw a sprite that covers the entire screen to simulate a splash or loading page.

Once we have our solution created we can jump right into our Game1.cs code. First, we want to define these private member fields:

```
private SpriteBatch spriteBatch;
private Texture2D splashScreen;
private Rectangle titleSafeArea;
private InputHandler input;
```

We need to make sure we have a using statement for our library. Next up is our game's constructor, in which we can use the following code:

```
public Game1()
{
    graphics = new GraphicsDeviceManager(this);
    content = new ContentManager(Services);

    graphics.PreferredBackBufferWidth = 1280;
    graphics.PreferredBackBufferHeight = 720;

    input = new InputHandler(this);
    Components.Add(input);
}
```

We are actually setting the preferred backbuffer width and height. We are doing this because the image we are using for our splash screen is that size. Our Draw method actually allows the image to be put into any rectangle, but for this demo we will just force the aspect ratio to widescreen. We also add our input handler to our game's collection of game components.

Because we were just talking about the actual splash screen image, we should go ahead and add that to our project now. We should create a Content folder with a Textures subfolder. We are only doing that for consistency. It is definitely not a requirement of XNA and we could put all our assets in the main project. We are trying to keep our solution tidy, though, and it is why we create these folders. We can find the image under this chapter's code folder on the CD in the SplashScreenDemo\Content\Textures folder with the name of splashscreen.png.

After we have our image loaded we can continue with our Initialize method. We can add the following code to initialize our title safe area as well as our sprite batch:

```
titleSafeArea = Utility.GetTitleSafeArea(graphics.GraphicsDevice, 0.85f);
spriteBatch = new SpriteBatch(graphics.GraphicsDevice);
```

We have talked about `GetTitleSafeArea` earlier in the book, but we have modified it just a little bit. We only added the parameter `graphicsDevice` to the method so we could use it as a static method in a helper class in our library. Let's jump to our XELibrary project and add a new class called `Utility.cs`. The entire file can be seen in Listing 9.1.

LISTING 9.1   Our new Utility.cs code file inside of our XELibrary project exposes the `GetTitleSafeArea` helper method

```csharp
using System;
using Microsoft.Xna.Framework;
using Microsoft.Xna.Framework.Graphics;

namespace XELibrary
{
    public sealed class Utility
    {
        public static Rectangle GetTitleSafeArea(GraphicsDevice graphicsDevice,
            float percent)
        {
            Rectangle retval = new Rectangle(graphicsDevice.Viewport.X,
                graphicsDevice.Viewport.Y,
                graphicsDevice.Viewport.Width,
                graphicsDevice.Viewport.Height);
#if XBOX360
            // Find Title Safe area of Xbox 360
            float border = (1 - percent) / 2;
            retval.X = (int)(border * retval.Width);
            retval.Y = (int)(border * retval.Height);
            retval.Width = (int)(percent * retval.Width);
            retval.Height = (int)(percent * retval.Height);
            return retval;
#else
            return retval;
#endif
        }
    }
}
```

The method simply takes in a percentage and if running on the Xbox 360 it will determine the safe area in which we can put critical text like we described in Chapter 2, "XNA and the Xbox 360." For Windows, it simply returns the viewport's width and height.

Now we can get back to our game code and update our `LoadGraphicsContent` method with the following statement:

```csharp
splashScreen = content.Load<Texture2D>(@"Contents\Textures\splashscreen");
```

We are loading our resource, which should be very familiar by now. After loading our sprite we can modify our `Draw` method with the following code:

```
spriteBatch.Begin();
spriteBatch.Draw(splashScreen, titleSafeArea, Color.White);
spriteBatch.End();
```

We are simply calling the default `Begin` method on our sprite batch, which sets the blend mode to `AlphaBlend`, the sort mode to `Deferred`, and the save state mode to `None`. We pass in our texture asset, the rectangle on the screen we want to draw the sprite on, and the color we want to tint it with. We do not want to tint it, so we are passing in `White`. Finally we call the `End` method of our sprite batch to actually draw our sprite on the screen.

Drawing Multiple Sprites from One Texture Demo

We need to set up another solution for this demo. We do not need to reference the XELibrary this time. We can call this project MultiSpriteDemo. We are going to display multiple sprites from one texture.

Once we have our solution set up we can open up our game code file and add the following private member fields:

```
private SpriteBatch spriteBatch;
private Texture2D tiledSprite;
```

Once we have our sprite batch and sprite declared we can initialize them inside of our `LoadGraphicsContent` method:

```
spriteBatch = new SpriteBatch(graphics.GraphicsDevice);
tiledSprite = content.Load<Texture2D>(@"Content\Textures\shapes");
```

We can find the shapes.png file under the subfolder MultiSpriteDemo\Content\Textures of this chapter's folder on the CD. If we find ourselves always using the same content in different projects we can add the asset files as links so we do not continue to eat up hard drive space. This also helps if multiple projects are accessing an asset that changes frequently. This is a 512 x 512 image that is broken up into four 256 x 256 cells. This image can be seen in Figure 9.3.

FIGURE 9.3   shapes.png.

Finally we need to add the following code to our Draw method to actually draw our sprites:

```
spriteBatch.Begin();
spriteBatch.Draw(tiledSprite, new Vector2(50, 50),
                        new Rectangle(0, 0, 256, 256), Color.White);
spriteBatch.Draw(tiledSprite, new Vector2(300, 50),
                        new Rectangle(256, 0, 256, 256), Color.White);
spriteBatch.Draw(tiledSprite, new Vector2(50, 300),
                        new Rectangle(0, 256, 256, 256), Color.White);
spriteBatch.Draw(tiledSprite, new Vector2(300, 300),
                        new Rectangle(256, 256, 256, 256), Color.White);
spriteBatch.Draw(tiledSprite, new Vector2(550, 50),
                        new Rectangle(0, 256, 256, 256), Color.White);
spriteBatch.Draw(tiledSprite, new Vector2(550, 300),
                        new Rectangle(0, 256, 256, 256), Color.White);
spriteBatch.End();
```

We call Begin on our sprite batch to get started. After that we call the Draw method on our sprite batch six times. We use the same tiledSprite texture in each call. The second parameter is where we want to draw our sprite on the screen. In the last demo we used a rectangle, but we are using a vector here. The third parameter is the rectangle we are going to use as our source from the texture we have loaded. In the past we have not used this parameter as we have used the entire image for our sprite. Because we are only using a portion of the image we are telling the sprite batch which region we want to draw. Finally, we pass in Color.White again so there is no color modulation effect in place.

The key to the preceding code is the third parameter where we draw only a portion of our rectangle. We know each cell is a 256 x 256 block so we pass in 0,0 for the first cell on the first row. We pass in 256,0 for the second cell on the first row. We pass in 0,256 for the first cell on the second row and finally we pass in 256,256 for the second cell on the second row. We always pass in the same width and height of 256.

We drew each of the cells once and then the cell containing our star an additional two times. They are positioned on the screen based on the second parameter we passed in. Finally, we call the End method on the sprite batch so it will actually pass all of the data to our graphics card. We can run the demo to see the different cells on our screen at the coordinates we specified.

Sprite Batch Blend and Sort Mode Demo

Now, we are going to update the previous project. We can just modify it or make a copy to modify. We will need to reference our XELibrary assembly. We do not need to actually include the project in the solution if we do not want to. We can just add a reference to our project. Of course, we need to add a using statement to the top of our code as well. The name of this project on the CD is SortOrderDemo.

We can start, as usual, by declaring the private member fields we will be using for this demo. In addition to what we already have we need to declare the following:

```
private SpriteBlendMode blendMode = SpriteBlendMode.AlphaBlend;
private SpriteSortMode sortMode = SpriteSortMode.Deferred;
private InputHandler input;
```

We are using our input handler component in this demo so we need to initialize that in our constructor and add it to our game's component collection:

```
input = new InputHandler(this);
Components.Add(input);
```

We created member fields earlier to hold our blend mode and our sort mode. We are going to set those modes based on input we get from our gamepad and keyboard. To do this, we will want to replace our Update method with the following code:

```
protected override void Update(GameTime gameTime)
{
    if (WasPressed(InputHandler.ButtonType.A, Keys.A))
        blendMode = SpriteBlendMode.AlphaBlend;
    if (WasPressed(InputHandler.ButtonType.B, Keys.B))
        blendMode = SpriteBlendMode.Additive;
    if (WasPressed(InputHandler.ButtonType.X, Keys.X))
        blendMode = SpriteBlendMode.None;

    if (WasPressed(InputHandler.ButtonType.LeftShoulder, Keys.D1))
        sortMode = SpriteSortMode.BackToFront;
    if (WasPressed(InputHandler.ButtonType.RightShoulder, Keys.D2))
        sortMode = SpriteSortMode.FrontToBack;
    if (WasPressed(InputHandler.ButtonType.LeftStick, Keys.D3))
        sortMode = SpriteSortMode.Deferred;
    if (WasPressed(InputHandler.ButtonType.RightStick, Keys.D4))
```

```
        sortMode = SpriteSortMode.Immediate;
    if (WasPressed(InputHandler.ButtonType.Y, Keys.D5))
        sortMode = SpriteSortMode.Texture;

    base.Update(gameTime);
}

private bool WasPressed(InputHandler.ButtonType buttonType, Keys keys)
{
    return(WasPressed(0, buttonType, keys));
}

private bool WasPressed(int playerIndex, InputHandler.ButtonType buttonType,
    Keys keys)
{
    if (input.ButtonHandler.WasButtonPressed(playerIndex, buttonType) ||
        input.KeyboardState.WasKeyPressed(keys))
        return (true);
    else
        return (false);
}
```

We added an overloaded method called WasPressed that takes in the player's index (or optionally defaults to 0 [player 1]), and the button we want to check along with the keys we want to check. The method simply calls our input handler to check if the buttons or keys were pressed. The Update method uses the WasPressed method to check for different buttons and keys and sets our blend mode along with our sort mode as needed.

Finally, we can update the contents of our Draw method with the following code:

```
graphics.GraphicsDevice.Clear(Color.CornflowerBlue);
spriteBatch.Begin(blendMode, sortMode, SaveStateMode.None);

//only affects the code if we are using the Immediate sort mode
graphics.GraphicsDevice.RenderState.DestinationBlend =
    Blend.InverseDestinationAlpha;

//draw heart
spriteBatch.Draw(tiledSprite, new Rectangle(64, 64, 256, 256),
    new Rectangle(256, 256, 256, 256), Color.White, 0, Vector2.Zero,
    SpriteEffects.None, .10f);

//draw circle
spriteBatch.Draw(tiledSprite, new Rectangle(0, 0, 256, 256),
    new Rectangle(256, 0, 256, 256), Color.White, 0, Vector2.Zero,
    SpriteEffects.None, .15f);

//draw shape
```

```
spriteBatch.Draw(tiledSprite, new Rectangle(128, 128, 256, 256),
    new Rectangle(0, 0, 256, 256), Color.White, 0, Vector2.Zero,
    SpriteEffects.None, .05f);

//draw star
spriteBatch.Draw(tiledSprite, new Rectangle(192, 192, 256, 256),
    new Rectangle(0, 256, 256, 256), Color.White, 0, Vector2.Zero,
    SpriteEffects.None, .01f);

Window.Title = "Sort Order Demo - " + blendMode.ToString() + " : " +
    sortMode.ToString();


spriteBatch.End();
base.Draw(gameTime);
```

The first thing we do in our `Draw` code after clearing our graphics device is call `Begin` on our sprite batch. We are passing in the member fields we used in our `Update` method. This way we can control how our scene is rendered by pressing different buttons. We can see how the blending modes work and how the sorting mode works in real time.

After executing our `Begin` method we call the sprite batch's `Draw` method to display our sprites. These draw methods are similar to our last demo. We used a different overload, which requires us to pass in a rectangle for our destination location instead of just a vector. We had to use this one because we wanted to set our layer depth value, which is the last value of the method. We could also choose a rotation angle and a point of origin, but we will discuss that in the next chapter.

Right after we call `Begin` on our sprite batch we set the `DestinationBlend` value. We will talk more about this in the next chapter, but for now we can see that we can override the default blend mode when we are in immediate sort mode. The reason is that the `Begin` method (for `Immediate` mode) calls the graphics device immediately, whereas the other sort modes do not call the graphics device until the `End` method is executed, which will override anything we have inside of the sprite batch.

We can run the demo and push the appropriate buttons or keys to see the results. The demo will launch in deferred mode and the sprites will be displayed in the order they are in the code: heart, circle, shape, and star, as shown in Figure 9.4. If we go into an immediate sort mode we will see the different blend state we set. If switch to the `BackToFront` sort mode we can see it uses the layer depth values we created because the shapes are in the order of circle, heart, shape, and star. It drew the highest value on the screen first and ended with the lowest value (causing the lowest value to be "closer" than the largest value), as shown in Figure 9.5. Sorting `FrontToBack` does the opposite and outputs the star first and finishes up with the circle, as shown in Figure 9.6.

We can also press the appropriate buttons and keys to change our blending state. If we select `None`, then we get to see the full textures complete with black where it was transparent. If we select `Additive`, we see the pixels added together to create rather "bright" sprites. This demo should help us see exactly how the sort mode works inside of our sprite batch.

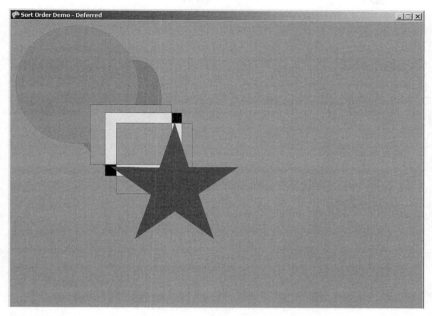

FIGURE 9.4   SpriteSortMode.Deferred does not sort the images drawn and displays them in the order they were drawn in the code.

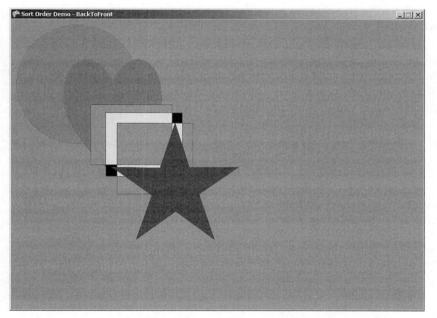

FIGURE 9.5   SpriteSortMode.BackToFront sorts the images based on the layer depth values, with the highest number being farthest from the screen.

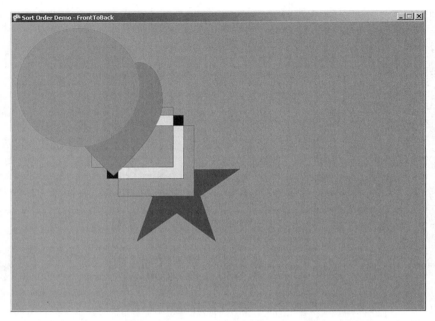

FIGURE 9.6   SpriteSortMode.FrontToBack sorts the images based on the layer depth values, with the lowest number being farthest from the screen.

Progress Bar Demo

Now that we understand how to use the blend modes and sort modes and we have a firm grasp on drawing a portion of a texture on the screen, we can create a new project called ProgressBarDemo. We can open up our XELibrary project because we will be modifying our library. We are going to add a new game component to our library called ProgressBar.cs. We need to set up the following private member fields of our progress bar game component:

```
private readonly Vector2 initializationVector = new Vector2(-99, -99);
private Vector2 currentPosition;
private Vector2 originalPosition;
private Vector2 position;
//background area of our texture (256 - 63 = 193)
private Rectangle progressBarBackground = new Rectangle(63, 0, 193, 32);
//foreground of our texture
private Rectangle progressBarForeground = new Rectangle(0, 0, 63, 20);
// where we want our foreground to show up on our background
private Vector2 progressBarOffset = new Vector2(7, 6);
public float MoveRate = 90.0f;
```

The first variable we set up was our initialization vector. We do this so we can tell if our Draw method has ever been called before. We are going to create our own Draw method and will not be inheriting from DrawableGameComponent because we want to pass in an instance of our sprite batch and we cannot change the signature of the Draw method inside of DrawableGameComponent. We will get to our Draw method in a moment, but for now we need to initialize our variables inside of our constructor with the following two statements:

```
content = new ContentManager(game.Services);
Enabled = false;
```

We are going to have content inside of our game component, so we need to obtain a reference to our game's content manager. We also set the Enabled flag of our game component to false. We explicitly need the caller to enable us when they want us to draw the progress bar. This brings us to the next section of code where we override the event that tells us that the Enabled property has changed:

```
protected override void OnEnabledChanged(object sender, EventArgs args)
{
    if (Enabled)
        currentPosition = originalPosition = initializationVector;

    base.OnEnabledChanged(sender, args);
}
```

When the game enables our game component, we initialize our original and current position of the actual progress bar foreground. Next up is the Load method, which will actually load the progress bar texture from the content manager:

```
public void Load(Vector2 position)
{
    progressBar = content.Load<Texture2D>(@"Content\Textures\progressbar");
    this.position = position;
}
```

Fortunately, XNA allows us to load content inside of our game components. We do not have to rely on our game to hold the resources as we can add the content directly inside of our component project. We need to create a Content folder with a Textures subfolder. We can then add the progressbar.png file to the Textures folder. This file can be found under the XELibrary project's Content\Textures folder on this book's CD for this chapter.

Our Load method loaded our progress bar texture, and it also stored the position that the component should be drawn. The game will pass in the position to this method and we will use the value to draw the progress bar at the correct place on the screen.

When we set up our member fields we created rectangles to specify where in our texture the progress bar background and foreground are. We also set up an offset of where we want to draw the foreground on our background. We will be using these values in our Draw method, which is as follows:

```
public void Draw(GameTime gameTime, SpriteBatch spriteBatch, Color color)
{
    if (!Enabled)
```

```
    return;

if (progressBar == null)
    throw (new ApplicationException("You must call Load before calling Draw"));

spriteBatch.Draw(progressBar, originalPosition, progressBarBackground,
    Color.White);
spriteBatch.Draw(progressBar, currentPosition + progressBarOffset,
    progressBarForeground, color);
}
```

We pass in the game time, the sprite batch we are supposed to draw to, the top left position of the screen where we want to draw our progress bar, and finally the color that we want to tint our progress bar's foreground. The first thing we check in this function is that our component is enabled. If it is not, we simply return. The next thing we check for is to make sure our progressBar texture has been created. If it is has not, we throw an error letting the developer know he or she needs to call the component's Load method before calling the Draw method.

Now we actually draw our progress bar onto the screen. We have two different calls to the sprite batch passed in. One draws the background at the original position passed in and the other draws the foreground at the current position. We store the original position just in case the game decides to change positions in the middle of our drawing. As we draw our foreground we are using the color passed in to tint our white progress bar. This way our progress bar can be any color we want. We determine the position to draw our foreground by adding our offset vector to our current position vector. This way we can center the foreground vertically and push it over a little so it is not flushed to the left when it starts out.

Our Update method will actually update the current position that the Draw method is using. Our Update method is as follows:

```
public override void Update(GameTime gameTime)
{
    if (currentPosition == initializationVector) //first time in
        currentPosition = originalPosition = position;
    else
        currentPosition += new Vector2(MoveRate *
            (float)gameTime.ElapsedGameTime.TotalSeconds, 0);

    //have we reached the end (or the beginning) of our area?
    //If so reverse direction
    if (currentPosition.X > originalPosition.X +
            (progressBarBackground.Width - progressBarForeground.Width - 15)
        || currentPosition.X < position.X)
    {
        MoveRate = -MoveRate;
```

```
    }

    base.Update(gameTime);
}
```

We check to see if this is the first time our `Update` method has been called. We do this by checking our current position's value. If it is still set to the initialization value, then we know this is the first time we have been called since we have been enabled. At this point we reset our current and original positions to match the position passed into the `Load` method.

If this is not the first time our `Update` method has been called then we update our `currentPosition` by the public member field `MoveRate` we declared. We set this up as public to allow our game to override how fast or slow the progress bar should move. To translate our foreground position we are simply adding a vector that contains the product of our move rate and the elapsed total seconds of our game time. Remember, we do this so that when our frame rate changes we still get nice, even flow.

The last check we do in our `Update` method tests to see if our foreground is about to be moved outside of our progress bar's background rectangle. If so, we simply reverse our direction by changing our `MoveRate` value. This way our progress bar foreground will simply bounce back and forth inside of our background.

Now that we are done adding the component to our library, we can open our game code and add the following private member fields:

```
private Vector2 position = new Vector2(150, 150);
private SpriteBatch spriteBatch;
private ProgressBar progressBar;
private InputHandler input;
```

We start by setting up the position at which we want to draw our component on the screen. Next, we set up our sprite batch, our progress bar game component, and our input handler game component. Next we need to set up our game components inside of our constructor:

```
input = new InputHandler(this);
Components.Add(input);

progressBar = new ProgressBar(this);
Components.Add(progressBar);
```

This code should be very familiar by now as we are just adding our game components to our game's component collection. Now we can actually initialize our sprite batch by calling the following code inside of our `LoadGraphicsContent` method:

```
spriteBatch = new SpriteBatch(graphics.GraphicsDevice);
progressBar.Load(position);
progressBar.Enabled = true;
```

After creating our sprite batch, we also load our progress bar so it can grab its asset and be ready to draw when we are. We next add the following to our Update code to actually enable (or disable) our progress bar when the Start button or spacebar is pressed:

```
if (input.ButtonHandler.WasButtonPressed(0, InputHandler.ButtonType.Start) ||
    input.KeyboardState.WasKeyPressed(Keys.Space))
{
    progressBar.Enabled = !progressBar.Enabled;
}
```

We finish up our game class by adding the following to our Draw code:

```
spriteBatch.Begin();
progressBar.Draw(gameTime, spriteBatch, Color.Blue);
spriteBatch.End();
```

We are drawing our progress bar on the screen at position 50,50 and we are tinting the color of the foreground to blue. With just a little bit of code we have a reusable progress bar we can use in our games on our splash and load screens now!

Using Sprite Fonts

The XNA Framework 1.0 Refresh includes built-in font support. We can use any TrueType font in our games. It also allows use of bitmaps, which can either be drawn by hand or be generated with the Bitmap Font Make Utility (ttf2bmp). This utility can be found on XNA Creators Club Online at http://creators.xna.com/Headlines/utilities/archive/2007/04/26/Bitmap-Font-Maker-Utility.aspx.

BE CAREFUL NOT TO DISTRIBUTE COPYRIGHTED FONTS

Most font files are licensed pieces of software. They are not typically sold. Most do not allow distribution of fonts in any applications, even games. This even includes distributing bitmap reproductions of the fonts and many of the fonts that are distributed with Microsoft Windows. Be careful not to distribute any copyrighted fonts with your game.

Importing TrueType Fonts

We want our library to handle fonts, so we will add a TrueType font to our XELibrary project. We need to create a Fonts subfolder under our Content folder in our XELibrary project. We can import TrueType fonts by following these steps:

1. Right-click the Fonts subfolder and click Add.

2. Click New Item and choose Sprite Font. We can name our file Arial.spritefont. This will open the newly created .spritefont XML file.

3. In the .spritefont XML file we can change the `FontName` element to the friendly name of the font we want to load, Arial.

4. (Optional) We can change the `Size` element to be the point size we want the font to be. We can also scale the font, which we will see later.

5. (Optional) We can change the `Spacing` element, which specifies the number of pixels there should be between each character in our font.

6. (Optional) We can change the `Style` element, which specifies how the font should be styled. This value is case sensitive and can be the following values: Regular, Bold, Italic, or Bold Italic.

7. The `CharacterRegions` element contains the start and end characters that should be generated and available for drawing.

Now that we have added this spritefont file, when we compile our code the compiler will generate the resource needed so we can utilize the font in our game. The XML file is simply a description to the compiler as to which TrueType font to grab and which characters to create in the .xnb file.

Creating Bitmap Fonts

Not only can we use TrueType font resources, we can make our own bitmap fonts to be used. To do this we need to actually create the bitmap. We can either do it by hand or by using the Bitmap Font Maker Utility mentioned at the beginning of this section. After getting the base bitmap generated, we can modify it in our favorite paint program.

The background of the image must be a fully opaque, pure magenta color (R: 255, G: 0, B: 255, A: 255). It needs to include an alpha channel that specifies which parts of the characters are visible. Once the image is created or modified we can import the image into our Fonts subfolder. XNA Game Studio Express will think it is just a normal texture so we need to modify the Content Processor value in our properties panel to be Font Texture.

Drawing 2D Text

Now that we have our font imported we can actually use it. We are not going to create a demo for this. Instead, we are going to modify our ProgressBarDemo project and have it display the text Loading ... right above the progress bar. We need to add the following private member fields:

```
private Vector2 loadingPosition = new Vector2(150, 120);
private SpriteFont font;
```

We already added the font to our XELibrary project. We could have added it to our game, but it is most likely we will want to print text out on the screen in the future so now we have it loaded and don't need to worry about it any more. However, we need to actually load the font to our game. We do this just like any other content inside of our `LoadGraphicsContent` method:

```
font = content.Load<SpriteFont>(@"Content\Fonts\Arial");
```

Finally, inside of our `Draw` method, above our call to end our sprite batch, we need to add the following statement:

```
spriteBatch.DrawString(font, "Loading ...", loadingPosition, Color.White);
```

We can run our ProgressBarDemo and see the word Loading ... displayed above our progress bar. Things are shaping up nicely!

Summary

We were introduced to 2D concepts in this chapter, spending the majority of the time covering sprites and sprite batches. We learned the importance of the blend modes and sort modes for our sprites when dealing with our sprite batch. We saw the different graphics device state changes that happen when we call a sprite batch. We learned how to have the sprite batch save the state and reset it automatically, and we discussed some common values we could reset manually if we were mixing 3D with 2D.

We spent a good a portion of this chapter creating demos to help firm up our understanding of these concepts. We created a splash screen that we could also use the same concept for if creating a loading screen, especially if we add the progress bar component. In addition to those two demos, we saw how to actually draw part of a texture as a sprite to save the amount of textures we have. We created a demo that allowed us to quickly see the changes the different blend and sort modes had on our scene. We finished the chapter by adding in the ability to draw fonts on our screen. With these 2D basics down, we can move on to writing 2D effects in the next chapter.

CHAPTER 10

2D Effects

After learning the basics we can now get into some more exciting 2D content creation—effects. In this chapter we are going to discuss cel animation, rotating and scaling our sprites as well as different blend modes available to use when dealing with sprite batches. We will learn how to fade to a particular color as well. We will finish out the chapter discussing fire and creating explosions.

Cel Animation

In the last chapter we saw how to render portions of a texture into multiple sprites. In this section we are going to use the same principle to create cel animation. This is taking a texture with multiple rows and columns and looping them to create an animation. This is typically done for characters in the game and really any objects that require animation in 2D. For example, we could have a texture that included five cels of a stick figure jumping. Cel one could contain him right before he jumped, cel three would have him in the middle of the air, and the last cel would show him landing. We would want to display those cels in order in a rapid fashion to make it appear that our stick man just jumped.

To get started we are going to create a demo called CelAnimation. We will be including our XELibrary in this project because we will be creating a cel animation helper class. Once our solution is set up we create a new game component that we call CelAnimationManager. The code for this new class is given in Listing 10.1.

LISTING 10.1 CelAnimationManager.cs

```csharp
#region Using Statements
using System;
using System.Collections.Generic;
using Microsoft.Xna.Framework;
using Microsoft.Xna.Framework.Graphics;
using Microsoft.Xna.Framework.Content;
#endregion

namespace XELibrary
{
    public sealed partial class CelAnimationManager
        : Microsoft.Xna.Framework.GameComponent
    {
        private Dictionary<string, CelAnimation> animations =
            new Dictionary<string, CelAnimation>();
        private Dictionary<string, Texture2D> textures =
            new Dictionary<string, Texture2D>();
        private ContentManager content;

        private string contentPath;

        public CelAnimationManager(Game game, string contentPath)
            : base(game)
        {
            this.contentPath = contentPath;

            if (this.contentPath.LastIndexOf('\\') <
                this.contentPath.Length - 1)
            {
                this.contentPath += "\\";
            }

            content = new ContentManager(game.Services);
        }

        public override void Initialize()
        {
            base.Initialize();
        }

        public void AddAnimation(string animationKey, string textureName,
                                 CelCount celCount, int framesPerSecond)
        {
            if (!textures.ContainsKey(textureName))
```

LISTING 10.1   Continued

```
        {
            textures.Add(textureName, content.Load<Texture2D>(
                contentPath + textureName));
        }

        int celWidth = (int)(textures[textureName].Width /
            celCount.NumberOfColumns);
        int celHeight = (int)(textures[textureName].Height /
            celCount.NumberOfRows);

        int numberOfCels = celCount.NumberOfColumns *
            celCount.NumberOfRows;

        //we create a cel range by passing in start location of 1,1
        //and end with number of column and rows
        //2,1  =   1,1,2,1  ;    4,2  =  1,1,4,2
        AddAnimation(animationKey, textureName,
            new CelRange(1, 1, celCount.NumberOfColumns,
            celCount.NumberOfRows), celWidth, celHeight,
            numberOfCels, framesPerSecond);
    }

    public void AddAnimation(string animationKey, string textureName,
        CelRange celRange, int celWidth, int celHeight,
        int numberOfCels, int framesPerSecond)
    {
        CelAnimation ca = new CelAnimation(textureName, celRange,
            framesPerSecond);

        if (!textures.ContainsKey(textureName))
        {
            textures.Add(textureName, content.Load<Texture2D>(
                contentPath + textureName));
        }

        ca.CelWidth = celWidth;
        ca.CelHeight = celHeight;

        ca.NumberOfCels = numberOfCels;

        ca.CelsPerRow = textures[textureName].Width / celWidth;

        if (animations.ContainsKey(animationKey))
            animations[animationKey] = ca;
```

LISTING 10.1   Continued

```
        else
            animations.Add(animationKey, ca);
    }

    public void ToggleAnimation(string animationKey)
    {
        if (animations.ContainsKey(animationKey))
        {
            animations[animationKey].Paused =
                !animations[animationKey].Paused;
        }
    }

    public override void Update(GameTime gameTime)
    {
        foreach(KeyValuePair<string,CelAnimation> animation in animations)
        {
            CelAnimation ca = animation.Value;

            if (ca.Paused)
                continue; //no need to update this animation,check next one

            ca.TotalElapsedTime +=
                (float)gameTime.ElapsedGameTime.TotalSeconds;
            if (ca.TotalElapsedTime > ca.TimePerFrame)
            {
                ca.Frame++;

                //min: 0, max: total cels
                ca.Frame = ca.Frame % (ca.NumberOfCels);

                //reset our timer
                ca.TotalElapsedTime -= ca.TimePerFrame;
            }
        }
        base.Update(gameTime);
    }

    public void Draw(GameTime gameTime, string animationKey,
        SpriteBatch batch, Vector2 position)
    {
        Draw(gameTime, animationKey, batch,
            animations[animationKey].Frame, position);
    }
```

LISTING 10.1   Continued

```
public void Draw(GameTime gameTime, string animationKey,
    SpriteBatch batch, int frame, Vector2 position)
{
    Draw(gameTime, animationKey, batch,
        animations[animationKey].Frame, position, Color.White);
}

public void Draw(GameTime gameTime, string animationKey,
    SpriteBatch batch, int frame, Vector2 position, Color color)
{
    if (!animations.ContainsKey(animationKey))
        return;

    CelAnimation ca = animations[animationKey];

    //first get our x increase amount
    //(add our offset-1 to our current frame)
    int xincrease = (ca.Frame + ca.CelRange.FirstCelX - 1);
    //now we need to wrap the value so it will loop to the next row
    int xwrapped = xincrease % ca.CelsPerRow;
    //finally we need to take the product of our wrapped value
    //and a cel's width
    int x = xwrapped * ca.CelWidth;

    //to determine how much we should increase y, we need to look
    //at how much we increased x and do an integer divide
    int yincrease = xincrease / ca.CelsPerRow;
    //now we can take this increase and add it to
    //our Y offset-1 and multiply the sum by our cel height
    int y = (yincrease + ca.CelRange.FirstCelY - 1) * ca.CelHeight;

    Rectangle cel = new Rectangle(x, y, ca.CelWidth, ca.CelHeight);
    batch.Draw(textures[ca.TextureName], position, cel, color);
    }
}

public class CelAnimation
{
    private string textureName;
    private CelRange celRange;
    private int framesPerSecond;
    private float timePerFrame;

    public float TotalElapsedTime = 0.0f;
```

LISTING 10.1   Continued

```
        public int CelWidth;
        public int CelHeight;
        public int NumberOfCels;
        public int CelsPerRow;
        public int Frame;
        public bool Paused = false;

        public static CelAnimation Create(string textureName,
            CelRange celRange, int framesPerSecond)
        {
            CelAnimation ca = new CelAnimation();
            ca.textureName = textureName;
            ca.celRange = celRange;
            ca.framesPerSecond = framesPerSecond;
            ca.timePerFrame = 1.0f / (float)framesPerSecond;
            ca.Frame = 0;

            return (ca);
        }

        public string TextureName
        {
            get { return (textureName); }
        }

        public CelRange CelRange
        {
            get { return (celRange); }
        }

        public int FramesPerSecond
        {
            get { return (framesPerSecond); }
        }

        public float TimePerFrame
        {
            get { return (timePerFrame); }
        }
    }

    public struct CelCount
    {
        public int NumberOfColumns;
```

LISTING 10.1   Continued

```
        public int NumberOfRows;

        public CelCount(int numberOfColumns, int numberOfRows)
        {
            NumberOfColumns = numberOfColumns;
            NumberOfRows = numberOfRows;
        }
    }

    public struct CelRange
    {
        public int FirstCelX;
        public int FirstCelY;
        public int LastCelX;
        public int LastCelY;

        public CelRange(int firstCelX, int firstCelY, int lastCelX,
            int lastCelY)
        {
            FirstCelX = firstCelX;
            FirstCelY = firstCelY;
            LastCelX = lastCelX;
            LastCelY = lastCelY;
        }
    }
}
```

The CelAnimationManager.cs file has two classes and two structs inside of it. Typically, we have one class per file, but we wanted them all listed here together so we could discuss them easily. Our game will talk to at least one of the two structs and the manager class. Our manager class exposes two different AddAnimations methods that our games can use to create animation textures. The first is the most simplistic to set up but it requires that the texture contain only one animation. The signature for this method is shown here:

```
public void AddAnimation(string animationKey, string textureName,
    CelCount celCount, int framesPerSecond)
```

It allows us to pass in an animation key, along with a texture name, the number of rows and columns our texture contains, and finally the rate per second at which we would like our animation to be drawn. We store the animation key inside of an animations dictionary. We do the same thing with the textures by storing them in their own dictionary so we do not need to have multiple textures when we have multiple animations that share the same texture. This will be obvious as we get into the other overload of this method. By passing in the number of columns and rows in our texture, the cel animation manager can determine how many cels are in the texture.

10

The second overload of our `AddAnimation` method is a little more complex. We can see the parameters we pass into this method here:

```
public void AddAnimation(string animationKey, string textureName,
    CelRange celRange, int celWidth, int celHeight, int numberOfCels,
    int framesPerSecond)
```

Just like the other overload, we pass in the animation key and the texture name and the frames per second we want our animation to play at. We do not pass in the `CelCount` struct that tells us how many rows and columns are in the texture; instead we pass in the `CelRange` struct that tells us which cel our animation starts with and which cels it ends with. We also need to tell the method how large our cel width and height is because it cannot determine that based on the texture size (as we are not using the entire texture). Finally, we need to tell the method exactly how many cels it is that we are rendering. This could be computed, but it is not something difficult for the game to be passed in. The `CelCount` is basically identical to `Vector2`. The properties have changed to make it more intuitive for our situation. Also, the `CelRange` struct is basically identical to a `Rectangle` struct.

Our cel animation manager's constructor takes in the path to where the textures that contain the animation are located. The path should have a trailing backslash when it is passed in, but the code will append one if needed. It is assumed the texture content will be loaded inside of the game.

The manager actually holds a collection of `CelAnimation` objects in a dictionary. This class stores all of the relevant information about itself so the manager does not need to. It keeps track of which frame it is currently on as well as how many cels it has, its texture name, how many frames a second it is supposed to be drawn, along with some other information. We can look at one of the `AddAnimation` methods to see how the manager adds a cel animation to its dictionary and prepares it to be drawn:

```
public void AddAnimation(string animationKey, string textureName,
    CelRange celRange, int celWidth, int celHeight, int numberOfCels,
    int framesPerSecond)
{
    CelAnimation ca = new CelAnimation(textureName, celRange,
        framesPerSecond);

    if (!textures.ContainsKey(textureName))
    {
        textures.Add(textureName, content.Load<Texture2D>(
            contentPath + textureName));
    }

    ca.CelWidth = celWidth;
    ca.CelHeight = celHeight;
```

```
    ca.NumberOfCels = numberOfCels;

    ca.CelsPerRow = textures[textureName].Width / celWidth;

    if (animations.ContainsKey(animationKey))
        animations[animationKey] = ca;
    else
        animations.Add(animationKey, ca);
}
```

The first thing we do is create an instance of our CelAnimation object, passing it in required information about the animation. Next, we check to see if the texture name this animation is using is already in our list before adding it. Next, we set some more properties on our cel animation object, and finally we either add it to our dictionary or reset our dictionary with the new object.

Inside of our Update method, we loop through our animation dictionary and as long as the animation is not paused we add to our timer (much like we did for our FPS code) and if enough time has elapsed we add to our frame number. We make sure we do not exceed the number of cels we have in our animation. Finally, we reset our time.

The last piece of this cel animation manager object is the Draw method. It actually does not contain much code, but it does all of the work of rendering the correct cel. First, it makes sure that an animation by that key actually exists in the collection. If it does not, it just returns but it could just as easily throw an error. If the animation does exist, the manager obtains a reference to it. Next is where it handles the math to calculate which cel to display. The code to do this is as follows:

```
//first get our x increase amount (add our offset-1 to our current frame)
int xincrease = (ca.Frame + ca.CelRange.FirstCelX - 1);
//now we need to wrap the value so it will loop to the next row
int xwrapped = xincrease % ca.CelsPerRow;
//finally we need to take the product of our wrapped value and a cel's width
int x = xwrapped * ca.CelWidth;

//to determine how much we should increase y, we need to look at how much we
//increased x and do an integer divide
int yincrease = xincrease / ca.CelsPerRow;
//now we can take this increase and add it to our Y offset-1 and multiply
//the sum by our cel height
int y = (yincrease + ca.CelRange.FirstCelY - 1) * ca.CelHeight;

Rectangle cel = new Rectangle(x, y, ca.CelWidth, ca.CelHeight);
batch.Draw(textures[ca.TextureName], position, cel, color);
```

10

The first thing we do is determine how much our x index should increase by looking at our current frame and adding our first cel's x offset. It is zero based, so we subtract one. Then we perform a mod function to make sure it will wrap around if needed. Then we can set the x location of our texture to what we just wrapped multiplied by the width of our cels.

Next, we perform similar calculations to get our y value. Instead of performing a mod function on the increased value of x, we do an integer divide giving us just the whole number available. This will return a 0 for the first row, 1 for the next row, and so on. We take that value and add our first cel's y offset. Again, it is zero based so we subtract one. Finally we multiply the value with the height of our cels.

We take the x and y values we just calculated and create a rectangle that we will pass to our sprite batches' Draw method as our source rectangle. We also pass in the position at which the game told us to draw this animation. The code also allows our game to tint the animations if needed because it allows us to pass in the color.

Now that we have discussed the cel animation manager, let's use it in our demo. Let's open the Game1.cs code and make sure we have all of our references (and using clauses, etc) set up. Once we do, we can add the following member fields to the top of our code:

```
private SpriteBatch spriteBatch;
private CelAnimationManager cam;
```

Then in our constructor we need to add it to our collection of components and pass in the location of the animation textures we will be using:

```
cam = new CelAnimationManager(this, @"Content\Textures\");
Components.Add(cam);
```

Let's go ahead and add the MrEye.png and the complex.png textures to our Content\Textures folder. The files can be found on the CD that accompanies the book under this project's folder. The next code we need to add goes into our LoadGraphicsContent method. We will create our sprite batch and then actually call the AddAnimation methods of our CelAnimationManager:

```
spriteBatch = new SpriteBatch(graphics.GraphicsDevice);

cam.AddAnimation("enemy1", "MrEye", new CelCount(4, 2), 8);
cam.AddAnimation("enemy2", "MrEye", new CelCount(4, 2), 12);
cam.AddAnimation("enemy3", "MrEye", new CelCount(4, 2), 6);

cam.AddAnimation("complex1","complex",new CelRange(1, 1, 2, 1), 64, 64, 2, 2);
cam.AddAnimation("complex2","complex",new CelRange(3, 1, 1, 3), 64, 64, 7, 8);
cam.AddAnimation("complex3","complex",new CelRange(2, 3, 1, 4), 64, 64, 4, 2);
cam.AddAnimation("complex4","complex",new CelRange(2, 4, 4, 4), 64, 64, 3, 5);
```

The enemy methods use the shorter signature of our overloaded AddAnimation method. The MrEye texture uses an entire texture. It is a 1024 x 512 texture with a total of eight cels (four on two rows). So we can just pass in the number of columns (four) and the number of rows (two) through our `CelCount` struct into the `AddAnimation` method. We then simply pass in how fast we want our animation to run. The value is measured in fps.

TIP

Certain graphics cards require that textures be a power of two in size. For example, 512 is a power of two because we can keep dividing it by two and never end up with a fraction. On the other hand, 768 is not a power of two.

The complex methods use the larger signature and need more information. It allows us to have multiple animations in the same texture to save on space. The image we are loading can be seen in Figure 10.1.

FIGURE 10.1   The `CelAnimationManager` allows us to utilize one texture to contain multiple animations.

We pass the `AddAnimation` method cel 1,1 to start and cel 2,1 to end for our first animation. We then pass in the cel width and height of our animation (in this case both are 64). We then pass in the total number of cels that are inside of our animation. Finally, we pass in how fast we want the animation to play just like the other method. We can run this code and see the animations.

Rotating and Scaling

We are going to create a small rotation and scaling demo as an example of what we talked about in the last chapter. We can create a new solution and call it RotateAndScaleDemo. This is going to be a very simple program. We need to create a sprite batch and a texture. We can load our texture called circular from the CD included with this book. We need to set up our class variables as follows:

```
private SpriteBatch spriteBatch;
private Texture2D circular;
private Rectangle destination;
private Rectangle source;
```

10

```
private float rotation;
private Vector2 origin;
private float scale;
```

Next, we can replace our LoadGraphicsContent code with the following:

```
if (loadAllContent)
{
    // TODO: Load any ResourceManagementMode.Automatic content
    spriteBatch = new SpriteBatch(graphics.GraphicsDevice);
    circular = content.Load<Texture2D>(@"Content\Textures\circular");
}

destination = new Rectangle(graphics.PreferredBackBufferWidth / 2,
    graphics.PreferredBackBufferHeight / 2, circular.Width, circular.Height);
origin = new Vector2(circular.Width / 2, circular.Height / 2);
source = new Rectangle(0, 0, circular.Width, circular.Height);

rotation = 1.0f;
scale = 0.5f;
```

We simply create our sprite batch and load up a texture. Then we set up a destination where we will be placing our sprite on the screen. We are going to center it, so we take the dimensions of our preferred back buffer and divide them by two. We set the width and height to match that of our texture so it does not stretch. Next, we declare an origin that we will use for our sprite. If we do not set an origin, it defaults to 0,0 (the top left of the texture). We set it to be the center of our texture by dividing the texture's width and height by two. We then need to set our source rectangle, which is used to grab a portion (or all) of the texture we are drawing. We are grabbing the entire texture. Finally we set our rotation to 1.0 and our scale to 0.5.

Inside of our Update method we can add this statement so that our rotation value will continually be updated:

```
rotation += .05f;
```

Finally, we can add the following code to our Draw method and run the demo:

```
spriteBatch.Begin();
spriteBatch.Draw(circular, destination, source, Color.White, rotation, origin,
    SpriteEffects.None, 0.0f);
spriteBatch.Draw(circular, new Vector2(100,600), null, Color.White, -rotation,
    new Vector2(256,256), scale, SpriteEffects.None, 0.0f);
spriteBatch.Draw(circular, new Vector2(600, 100), null, Color.White, -rotation,
    new Vector2(256, 256), scale, SpriteEffects.None, 0.0f);
spriteBatch.Draw(circular, new Vector2(300, 300), null, Color.White, rotation,
    new Vector2(0, 0), scale, SpriteEffects.None, 0.0f);
spriteBatch.End();
```

The code draws four sprites. The first one it draws is at its normal size (512,512) and passes in the rotation that is being updated. The origin is the one we set up earlier (center of the texture). The next two sprites are similar, except we explicitly set the origin. We can tweak these values to examine how XNA rotates our sprites. We also switched the rotation by negating the rotation value. The last sprite we drew with the origin set to the default 0,0 location. We can see this looks like it is orbiting because it is rotating around the top left of the texture. We applied our scale of 0.5 for all of the sprites except the first one. We can modify the scale variable to see the effect it has on our demo.

Blending Mode Example

We will use the preceding code and tweak it a little bit to show some interesting blending effects. Let's replace the contents of our previous Draw method with the following code:

```
spriteBatch.Begin(SpriteBlendMode.AlphaBlend, SpriteSortMode.Immediate,
    SaveStateMode.None);
graphics.GraphicsDevice.RenderState.SourceBlend = Blend.DestinationColor;
graphics.GraphicsDevice.RenderState.DestinationBlend = Blend.SourceColor;
spriteBatch.Draw(circular, destination, source, Color.White, rotation, origin,
    SpriteEffects.None, 0.0f);
spriteBatch.End();

spriteBatch.Begin(SpriteBlendMode.AlphaBlend, SpriteSortMode.Immediate,
    SaveStateMode.None);
graphics.GraphicsDevice.RenderState.SourceBlend = Blend.One;
graphics.GraphicsDevice.RenderState.DestinationBlend = Blend.One;
spriteBatch.Draw(circular, new Vector2(600, 100), null, Color.White, -rotation,
    new Vector2(256, 256), scale, SpriteEffects.None, 0.0f);
spriteBatch.End();

spriteBatch.Begin(SpriteBlendMode.AlphaBlend, SpriteSortMode.Immediate,
    SaveStateMode.None);
graphics.GraphicsDevice.RenderState.SourceBlend = Blend.DestinationColor;
graphics.GraphicsDevice.RenderState.DestinationBlend = Blend.SourceAlpha;
spriteBatch.Draw(circular, new Vector2(100,600), null, Color.White, -rotation,
    new Vector2(256,256), scale, SpriteEffects.None, 0.0f);
spriteBatch.End();

spriteBatch.Begin(SpriteBlendMode.AlphaBlend, SpriteSortMode.Immediate,
    SaveStateMode.None);
graphics.GraphicsDevice.RenderState.SourceBlend = Blend.InverseSourceColor;
graphics.GraphicsDevice.RenderState.DestinationBlend =
    Blend.InverseDestinationColor;
spriteBatch.Draw(circular, new Vector2(300, 300), null, Color.White, -rotation,
    new Vector2(0, 0), scale, SpriteEffects.None, 0.0f);
spriteBatch.End();
```

We wrapped each of the sprites we drew into its own immediate mode sprite batch calls. We did this so we could easily see some interesting effects by explicitly setting the source and destination blend modes of our render state. This way we are not just limited to alpha blending or additive blending when dealing with sprite batches. We can play with the values to see the effects it has on our sprites.

Fade to Color

We are going to create another simple demo. In fact, we can continue to modify the code we have open. This demo will wait one second after the program launches and then start to do a fade to black, although we could fade to any color we want. First, we want to add the following member fields to our code:

```
private float fadeAmount;
private Texture2D fadeTexture;
```

Next, in our `LoadGraphicsContent` method we want to create a texture that we can store in our `fadeTexture` variable. We can do this with the following code:

```
fadeTexture = CreateFadeTexture(graphics.GraphicsDevice.Viewport.Width,
    graphics.GraphicsDevice.Viewport.Height);
```

We are calling a method that requires us to pass in the width and height of the texture it will create. We are passing in the width and height of our viewport so it will fill the entire screen. Now we can actually look at this method to see how it creates a texture through code:

```
private Texture2D CreateFadeTexture(int width, int height)
{
    Texture2D texture = new Texture2D(
        graphics.GraphicsDevice, width, height, 1,
        ResourceUsage.None,
        SurfaceFormat.Color,
        ResourceManagementMode.Automatic);

    int pixelCount = width * height;
    Color[] pixelData = new Color[pixelCount];
    Random rnd = new Random();

    for (int i = 0; i < pixelCount; i++)
    {
        //could fade to a different color
        pixelData[i] = Color.Black;
    }

    texture.SetData(pixelData);

    return (texture);
}
```

The key to this code is the very first statement. XNA provides a constructor to the `Texture2D` object that allows us to create a texture on the fly! We simply pass in the graphics device, the width and the height of the texture, and the number of mipmaps we will have (we have set it to 1). We also have to pass how we will be using this resource and the surface format we will be using, as well as if we will be managing the memory or letting the framework handle it automatically.

We are not specifying any particular usage for this code. Most have to do with the Vertex Buffer, which we discussed earlier. The Xbox 360 has Linear and Tiled, which determines how it is stored in memory. There is also `ResolveTarget`, which allows us to use a texture that will get the contents of our back buffer, which we will talk about in Chapter 13, "Advanced HLSL." We pass in `Color` as our surface format as we know that is available on all hardware.

After creating our texture we can actually define it inside of our code. For this case, we are simply going to set all the pixels to a single color, black. To this, we add an array of unsigned integers. Unsigned types allow us to have very large numbers without having to allocate memory for a long time, as an unsigned type does not store negative numbers, effectively doubling the maximum positive number the type can hold. We initialize our array to be the width times height of our texture so we have enough room to store each pixel. Then inside the for loop, we simply set each pixel. In this case, we are setting them all to black. This could be any color and, in fact, we could create random colors for each pixel.An easy way to get to a particular pixel in a texture is to use the following formula in our array:

```
Color pixelvalue = pixeldata[(y * width) + x];
```

Although we did not need that formula in this example, it is a very clean way of easily passing in an x and y value to get or set a particular pixel in a texture. The array starts at position 0,0 of our texture and each pixel is stored consecutively from left to right. When it gets to the end of the texture, it grabs the value from the first pixel in the next row and just continues down until it has stored all of the values. This is the way we used to access the data on old graphics cards. In fact, we will be using this in the next section as we create fire old school style.

As we look back at the code we see that the only thing left to do is to take this pixel data we generated and actually apply it to our texture through the `SetData` method. There is a counterpart to this method called `GetData`. Both are generic methods that allow us to set and get the data in multiple formats. Not only can we use unsigned integers, but we can also use the XNA `Color` type.

The next code we will update will be in our `Update` method. We will add the following code to the bottom of that method:

```
//start fading out after 2 seconds
if (gameTime.TotalGameTime.Seconds > 2)
    fadeAmount += (.0005f * gameTime.ElapsedGameTime.Milliseconds);
```

10

```
//reset fade amount after a short time to see the effect again
if (fadeAmount > 2.0f) //two seconds passed?
    fadeAmount = 0.0f;
```

We are simply updating a value holding our fade amount. Because we don't actually have anything to kick this off, we are just doing it after the game has been around for two seconds. Then we start to gradually add to this fade amount each frame. The next condition simply removes the fading amount after a couple of seconds so we can see the effect again. An interesting flicker effect we can make is to change the .0005f to 0.1f. This will make it fade very quickly (in about 10 frames) and get to the 2.0 value very quickly (in about 20 frames) so we get an interesting flashing screen effect.

Finally, we need to add the following code to the end of the Draw method:

```
spriteBatch.Begin();
spriteBatch.Draw(fadeTexture, Vector2.Zero,
    new Color(new Vector4(Color.White.ToVector3(), fadeAmount)));
spriteBatch.End();
```

This starts up a new batch (we can leave the origin sprite batch alone to draw like it was doing). This batch always draws our fadeTexture. In a real game, we would only call this code when we were actually going to fade our scene. We can use the texture we created just like any other texture and see it displayed on the screen with our specified tint value. We are still passing in Color.White, but in alpha we are sending in our fade amount. Because we are starting with a small number and making it larger we are fading in our texture, which in effect fades out our scene. If we wanted to fade in our scene we could reverse our fade amount to start out a 1.0 and gradually work itself to 0. We could also use this fading code as is to fade in a particular sprite or something else. We do not need to create a sprite to cover the entire scene in that case. We can just fade in (or out) the sprite we are concerned with. With just a little code we can get a nice transition effect.

Making Fire Old School Style

Making fire in real life can be dangerous business, but in games it is excellent! The code we will be writing in this section is actually not optimal for use in a real game. It is more of a history lesson than anything else. We will be able to learn more about texture manipulation, which we touched on in the last section, but this actual implementation crawls on many machines and really does poorly on the Xbox 360. Fortunately, to get this type of effect with today's hardware is similar but we just have to use effects, which we cover in Chapter 12, "HLSL Basics," and Chapter 13 of this book. With that disclaimer out of the way, let's get started by creating a new project called FireDemo. We can add a reference to our XELibrary. We will not be changing our library for this demo so we can just create a reference if we do not want to include the actual project. We can create an Xbox 360 project, but it does not perform well at all.

We can get started with our code by declaring the following private member fields:

```
private SpriteBatch sb;
private Texture2D fire;
private InputHandler input;
private FPS fps;
private uint[] pixelData;
private uint[] firePalette;
private Random rand = new Random();
```

We then need to update our constructor to use our game components and to force the back buffer to a certain width and height:

```
graphics.PreferredBackBufferHeight = 256;
graphics.PreferredBackBufferWidth = 512;

fps = new FPS(this);
Components.Add(fps);

input = new InputHandler(this);
Components.Add(input);
```

Next is our LoadGraphicsContent method, which will contain the following code inside of the loadAllContent condition:

```
sb = new SpriteBatch(graphics.GraphicsDevice);

//256x1 image
Texture2D fireTexture = content.Load<Texture2D>(@"Content\Textures\FireGrade");

//initialize our array to store the palette info
firePalette = new uint[fireTexture.Width * fireTexture.Height];

//storing image data in our fireTexture
fireTexture.GetData<uint>(firePalette);

//now we can create our fire texture
fire = CreateFireTexture(128, 128);
```

We are initializing our sprite batch like we have done so many times now. We are loading a 256 x 1 texture from our content. This texture can be found on the CD. It is simply a single-line image that has a gradient color strip ranging from black to red to orange to yellow to white, so we can easily get a "fire palette" instead of generating one in our code. We store these palette data in our firePalette variable, which we initialize to hold all of the pixels of our texture. Then we actually call GetData from the fire palette texture and each pixel is placed inside of our array in the order we discussed last section. Finally, we create our own texture that we will be rendering to the screen. We are calling a method much like we did in the last section to create the texture for us. We can look at that method now:

```
private Texture2D CreateFireTexture(int width, int height)
{
    Texture2D texture = new Texture2D(
        graphics.GraphicsDevice, width, height, 1,
        ResourceUsage.None,
        SurfaceFormat.Color,
        ResourceManagementMode.Manual);

    int pixelCount = width * height;
    pixelData = new uint[pixelCount];

    for (uint i = 0; i < pixelCount; i++)
        pixelData[i] = Color.Black.PackedValue;

    //set bottom 16 rows to fiery colors
    for (int y = height - 1; y > height - 16; y—)
    {
        for (int x = 0; x < width; x++)
        {
            pixelData[(y * width) + x] = GetRandomFireColor();
        }
    }

    texture.SetData(pixelData);

    return (texture);
}
```

The first statement is familiar to us because we just used it in the last section. We then set up our structure to hold the pixel data for the fire texture we are making. It needs to contain enough room for our texture's pixels. We loop through all of the pixels, setting each one to black. We did this in the last section as well, but we did not discuss the PackedValue property on the Color struct. This property represents a color in an unsigned integer, which is really useful when we are working with textures this way, as they do not require a tremendous amount of memory and this is great when we think about how big our textures could be!

TIP

2048 x 2048 sized textures are the largest that work reliably across all shader-based Windows cards. Many can go up to 4096 and Xbox 360 supports textures up to 8192.

After initializing all of our pixels we then set the bottom 16 rows of our texture to fiery colors. We could optimize the top loop to not set these 16 rows but because this is not something we really plan to use, we skip that optimization here.

We can look closely at these 16 rows to which we are assigning values. We are in a nested for loop with the outer loop handling rows and the inner loop handling columns. We can see the formula we mentioned in the last section is being used here. We are setting a particular piece of texture to a color by taking the sum of our x value with the product of our y value and the width of the texture. This way we can easily access our 2D image in a 1D array. After completing our loops, we actually set the texture's pixel data. We finish up by returning the texture to the calling method.

The way we are setting the color on those last 16 rows of pixels is through a method called GetRandomFireColor, shown here:

```
private uint GetRandomFireColor()
{
    return (firePalette[rand.Next(0, 256)]);
}
```

This one line simply gets a random number from 0 to 255 and uses that as an index to our fire palette. The firePalette actually contains the uint color associated with the index of the palette.

Next, we want to add a call to the following method in our Update method:

```
UpdateFire();
```

This method does all of the work and brings the system to a crawl. Again, we could spend time optimizing it but because there is a much better way to handle a fire effect like this, we will pass. The UpdateFire method is as follows:

```
private void UpdateFire()
{
    int height = fire.Height;
    int width = fire.Width;

    uint left, right, bottom, top;
    uint colorIndex;
    int xRight, xLeft, yBelow, yAbove;

    for (int y = 0; y < height; y++)
    {
        for (int x = 0; x < width; x++)
        {
            xRight = x + 1;
            yBelow = y + 1;
            xLeft = x - 1;
            yAbove = y - 1;

            //make sure our values are within range
            if (xRight >= width)
```

10

```
            xRight = 0;
        if (yBelow >= height)
            yBelow = height - 1;

        if (xLeft < 0)
            xLeft = width - 1;
        if (yAbove < 0)
            yAbove = 0;

        //we need to get uint value of each surrounding color
        right = pixelData[(y * width) + xRight];
        left = pixelData[(y * width) + xLeft];
        bottom = pixelData[(yBelow * height) + x];
        top = pixelData[(yAbove * height) + x];

        //we now have the uint value of the colors stored
        //we need to find our palette value for this color
        //and do an average and reset the color
        colorIndex = (FindColorIndex(right) + FindColorIndex(left) +
                    FindColorIndex(top) + FindColorIndex(bottom)) / 4;

        colorIndex -= 3; //could make a random number

        if (colorIndex > 255) //went "negative" (unsigned)
            colorIndex = 0;

        //finally, we can set this pixel to our new color
        pixelData[(yAbove * width) + x] = firePalette[colorIndex];
    }
}

//now, it is time to animate our fire
AnimateFire(width, height);
}
```

The code is long but not really that complex. The overall concept is that we loop through each pixel and find the neighbors of each pixel (to the right, left, top, and bottom) and then average those colors together to come up with the new color for the pixel above the one we are on. We then keep the flame from rising too high by deducting the index of the pixel color a little bit. We finally set the color of the pixel above us to our new color.

To explain this method further we can see that we are calculating our pixel positions that are neighboring the current pixel in our for loops. We hold our left and right values beside our current pixel x location and the above and below values around our current y pixel location. If we are on an edge, we wrap to the other side to get the value.

To actually obtain our new color value we take each pixel location and obtain the color for each. Because we do not have an easy way to handle our palette, we have a method that loops through our palette and finds the index based on the color passed into the method FindColorIndex. We take the average of these four indices and store that in the colorIndex variable. We then subtract three from our index (this could be a random number if we wanted to allow the flame to rise or fall in different ways) to find our final index. We make sure our index is in a valid range and finally set the color associated with that palette index to the pixel directly above the pixel we are processing.

After we have finished looping through all of the pixels we make a call to the AnimateFire method. Before examining that method we quickly look at the FindColorIndex method we referenced earlier. The following method simply loops through our palette to find the appropriate index of the color being passed in:

```
uint FindColorIndex(uint color)
{
    for (uint i = 0; i < firePalette.Length; i++)
    {
        if (color == firePalette[i])
            return (i);
    }

    throw(new ApplicationException(color.ToString() + " not in palette"));
}
```

At this point our code will animate the pixels on the texture, however it will get to a point where nothing will update because everything will be averaged out. This is why we have the AnimateFire method at the bottom. This method takes all of the pixels on the bottom row of the texture and changes them. This way the main UpdateFire method actually has something to update. The AnimateFire method is as follows:

```
private void AnimateFire(int width, int height)
{
    int newColorIndex;

    //we could work with just one pixel at a time,
    //but we will work with five for a broader flame
    for (int x = 0; x < width - 5; x += 5)
    {
        // we are only going to modify the bottom row
        int y = height - 1;

        //we get our palette index for the color we just set on the
        //bottom row we then either add or subtract a substantial 64 to or from
        //that index
        newColorIndex = (int)FindColorIndex(
            pixelData[(y * width) + x]) + (rand.Next(-64, 64));
```

```
        //now we make sure our palette index is within range
        if (newColorIndex > 255)
            newColorIndex = 255;
        if (newColorIndex < 0)
            newColorIndex = 0;

        //Because we are stepping through our loop by a factor of 5
        //we can set all adjacent rows from here and over 4 additional
        //space and set those pixels to the same color.
        //an interesting effect is to change line 4 (x + 2) with
        //Color.Navy.PackedValue; It makes it look like it has a
        //really hot blue center
        uint ci = (uint)newColorIndex;
        pixelData[(y * width) + x] = firePalette[ci];
        pixelData[(y * width) + x + 1] = firePalette[ci];
        pixelData[(y * width) + x + 2] = firePalette[ci];
        pixelData[(y * width) + x + 3] = firePalette[ci];
        pixelData[(y * width) + x + 4] = firePalette[ci];
    }
}
```

Fortunately, this code is very straightforward and we can see that we loop the entire width of our texture for the last row (y = height − 1) of our texture. We find the index in our palette of this color and then add or subtract 64 from that index making sure we keep within the 0 to 255 range. This gives a new pseudo-random index that this pixel should now become.

When we loop through this bottom row, we are actually looking at every fifth pixel, so we are setting all five pixels: the one we are on as well as the four to the right of us. In this case, we are setting them all to the same color value. This produces nice wide flames. We could change this effect if we desired.

So far we have created code that creates a texture and then updates that texture on every frame. The creation consists of blacking out the entire texture and then setting the last 16 rows to some random colors in our fire palette. The update consists of reading in the pixel values of our texture and averaging the indices of the colors to come up with a new color for the pixel above the one we are reading in. We also reset the bottom row of our texture with new colors so the process can continue endlessly.

This brings us to the final piece of code in our fire demo. We have to actually draw our texture on the screen. Of course this is the simplest piece because that is what we have been doing for the last two chapters! The Draw method code is as follows:

```
protected override void Draw(GameTime gameTime)
{
    graphics.GraphicsDevice.Clear(Color.Black);

    fire.SetData<uint>(pixelData);
```

```
    int h = graphics.GraphicsDevice.Viewport.Height - fire.Height;
    // TODO: Add your drawing code here
    sb.Begin(SpriteBlendMode.Additive);

    //bottom left
    sb.Draw(fire, new Vector2(0, 0), null, Color.White, 0, Vector2.Zero,
        2.0f, SpriteEffects.None, 0);

    //bottom right
    sb.Draw(fire, new Vector2(256, 0), null, Color.White, 0, Vector2.Zero,
        2.0f, SpriteEffects.FlipHorizontally, 0);

    //top left
    sb.Draw(fire, new Vector2(0, 0), null, Color.White, 0, Vector2.Zero,
        2.0f, SpriteEffects.FlipVertically, 0);

    //top right
    sb.Draw(fire, new Vector2(256, 0), null, Color.White, 0, Vector2.Zero,
        2.0f, SpriteEffects.FlipVertically | SpriteEffects.FlipHorizontally,0);

    //left
    sb.Draw(fire, new Vector2(128,128), null, Color.White, MathHelper.PiOver2,
        new Vector2(64, 64), 2.0f, SpriteEffects.FlipHorizontally, 0);


    //right
    sb.Draw(fire, new Vector2(512-128, 128), null, Color.White,
        MathHelper.PiOver2, new Vector2(64, 64), 2.0f,
        SpriteEffects.FlipVertically, 0);

    sb.End();

    base.Draw(gameTime);
}
```

After clearing our device (to black because fire looks so much better on black than corn-flower blue), take the array of pixel colors and call SetData on the fire texture. We do the call here instead of in our Update method so we only set it right before we draw it and not on every update. We are going to be repeating our small 128 x 128 texture on the screen for a total of six textures. We are basically going to make a frame of fire. Because our textures are going to be overlapping and we have cleared our background to black, we can easily set our blend mode to Additive. As we discussed earlier, this will allow our images to draw on top of each other without interfering with each other. With additive blending, it treats black as transparent.

Now we will actually draw our texture six times. We will draw it twice (side by side) on the bottom, twice (side by side) on the top, and then one on left and right. We will also scale the textures by two so they appear 256 x 256. If we actually tried to make the update method work with 256 x 256 pixels it would be hard for the CPU to handle it. We also rotate our left and right textures as needed.

For some of the textures we add a `SpriteEffect`. This enumeration simply allows us to flip a texture vertically, horizontally, both, or not at all. The enumeration does not have "both" but we can bit OR `FlipVertically` and `FlipHorizontally` together to get the desired result.

Now we have successfully created a fire effect old school style! Fortunately, there are much faster ways of doing this now. We can use pixel shaders to get much better results. We discuss pixel shaders in detail in Part V of this book.

Explosions

What would a chapter on effects be without some explosions? We are going to create some explosion effects by animating more sprites. This means we need to actually have a texture that contains explosions. Fortunately, there is an application that Cliff Harris of Positech Games has provided free of charge that will allow us to generate explosion textures. The application can be found at http://www.geocities.com/starlinesinc/. With this great tool and our cel animation library file, we are equipped to create great-looking explosions in our games.

We need to create a new solution named ExplosionDemo. We will need to reference our XELibrary project so we can use the cel animation class we built at the beginning of this chapter. We need to add our `using` clause and set up our Xbox 360 project as usual.

After we get our demo solution created we can dive into our Game1.cs file and add the following private member fields to get started:

```
private SpriteBatch spriteBatch;
private InputHandler input;
private CelAnimationManager cam;
```

We can then add our input and cel animation management game components to our constructor. This should be engraved in our memories by now, so there is no need to write the code. After we initialize our fame components and add them to our game component collection we can add the following code to our `LoadGraphicsContent` method:

```
spriteBatch = new SpriteBatch(graphics.GraphicsDevice);
cam.AddAnimation("explosion", "explode_1b", new CelCount(4,4), 16);
cam.AddAnimation("explosion2", "explode_1b", new CelCount(4, 4), 16);
cam.AddAnimation("explosion3", "explode_3b", new CelCount(4, 4), 12);
cam.AddAnimation("explosion4", "explode_4b", new CelCount(4, 4), 20);
cam.AddAnimation("explosion5", "explode_3b", new CelCount(4, 4), 12);
cam.AddAnimation("explosion6", "explode_4b", new CelCount(4, 4), 20);
```

```
cam.AddAnimation("bigexplosion", "bigexplosion", new CelCount(4, 4), 18);
```

We are simply initializing our sprite batch and then adding seven different animations to be drawn later. To refresh on the animation code, the first parameter is the name of the animation and needs to be unique so we can easily access it later. The second parameter is the name of the texture and we can see that we use the same texture in some of these animations. The third parameter is taking the size (in cels columns by rows) of our texture. The final parameter is the number of cels we want to render per second. These textures can be found on the CD. The Bigexplosion texture was made using Paint.NET by adding in the other three images and doubling their size and then using the additive blend method available in that program for each layer. Then it was saved as a .png file to be loaded here. The explosion generator tool is excellent!

Finally, to get some great explosion effects we only need to draw them on the screen. All the heavy lifting has been accomplished by the cel animation class we created earlier.

```
protected override void Draw(GameTime gameTime)
{
    graphics.GraphicsDevice.Clear(Color.Black);

    spriteBatch.Begin(SpriteBlendMode.Additive, SpriteSortMode.Immediate,
        SaveStateMode.None);

    cam.Draw(gameTime, "explosion", spriteBatch, new Vector2(32, 32));
    cam.Draw(gameTime, "explosion2", spriteBatch, new Vector2(40, 40));
    cam.Draw(gameTime, "explosion3", spriteBatch, new Vector2(64, 32));
    cam.Draw(gameTime, "explosion4", spriteBatch, new Vector2(64, 64));
    cam.Draw(gameTime, "explosion5", spriteBatch, new Vector2(28, 40));
    cam.Draw(gameTime, "explosion6", spriteBatch, new Vector2(40, 64));

    cam.Draw(gameTime, "bigexplosion", spriteBatch, new Vector2(150, 150));
    spriteBatch.End();

    base.Draw(gameTime);
}
```

We clear the device to black and set our blend mode to Additive just like we did for our fire demo. We are doing this because we are going to draw multiple explosions in relatively the same spot to create the illusion of a massive explosion followed by a chain reaction of explosions. We are also going to display our larger explosion that was created by

10

massaging the output of the generator in a paint program at a different location. Now we can have nice-looking explosions in our games by using this simple technique to create an explosion effect.

Summary

We started this chapter by adding a very helpful class to our growing library. We created a class to handle animating a texture that is made up of cels. We allowed different ways to pass in data to create our animation ranging from as simple as one animation in one texture to as complex as multiple animations in one texture. We allow sending in a value that tells the animator how many cels a second it should draw on the screen.

After creating that class and testing it with a demo, we created another demo that showed us how easy it is to rotate and scale sprites in XNA. We saw how to set the origin of our sprite and how that affects if the sprite rotates around the center or not. We then discussed the different blending modes of XNA and modified our demo to display the objects in different blending modes. We saw how easy it was to change the blending modes on our render state after calling creating our sprite batch in immediate mode.

Fading to a particular color can be a nice transition effect and we saw a very easy way to accomplish that effect. We also discussed a technique to fade something into the scene. We could easily use the same code concept to fade that object in as a certain color.

We spent some time discussing an old technique to manipulate pixel data to create a fire effect. We saw the algorithm needed to pull off the effect and saw some modifications we could make. It was nice going down memory lane, but we know there are better ways to create fire that we learn about a little later in the book. We finished up this chapter by discussing how to make realistic-looking explosion effects in our games.

We touched on quite a few different subjects through the different examples of this chapter. To make anything we learn stick with us, it is beneficial to use it in examples and prototypes. This is what we are going to do in the next chapter. We will learn some new techniques like parallax scrolling, but will see how to implement the items we already learned to create a nice, simple 2D game.

CHAPTER 11

Creating a 2D Game

We have enough basics under our belt that we can actually create a small 2D game. In this chapter we use the knowledge we have gained so far and add a little bit more and create a parallax side scrolling game complete with collision detection.

Setting Up the Game Skeleton

To get started, we need to create our solution and project files and add the XELibrary project as well. We can call this game SimpleGame as it will be a rather basic but complete game.

After we have our environment set up, we can jump right into our Game1.cs code. To begin with, as usual, we create some member fields we know we will need:

```
public enum GameState { StartMenu, Scene }
public GameState State = GameState.StartMenu;
private InputHandler input;
private SpriteBatch sb;
private Texture2D startMenu;
private Vector2 centerVector;
private int viewportWidth;
private int viewportHeight;
```

Because this is going to be slightly more complicated than a demo in that we have to maintain our game state, we have set up an enum variable to define the different states in which our game can find itself. For now, we can only be in two states: StartMenu and Scene (or playing). We then declared a variable to actually hold our current game state and initialized it to the start menu state. We are going to use input in this game and will be using the sprite batch as we have been, so we set up those variables. We also declared a variable in which to hold our start menu texture. Finally, we have some reference variables we are creating so we do not have to continue to query our graphics device for the information.

We discuss states at length in Chapter 15, "Finite State Machines and Game State Management." For now, it is enough to know that our game can be in different states and we need to do different things (draw certain things on our screen, update different objects, etc.) depending on which state our game is in.

After declaring our variables we need to initialize and set up our input handler in our constructor. This should be standard procedure by now, so we will not bother listing the code here. After that, we need to get our viewport's width and height values in our `Initialize` method as follows:

```
viewportHeight = graphics.GraphicsDevice.Viewport.Height;
viewportWidth = graphics.GraphicsDevice.Viewport.Width;
```

Now we can load up our graphics content by adding the following code in our `LoadGraphicsContent` method inside of the `loadAllContent` condition:

```
sb = new SpriteBatch(graphics.GraphicsDevice);
startMenu = content.Load<Texture2D>(@"Content\Textures\startmenu");
centerVector = new Vector2((viewportWidth - startMenu.Width) / 2,
    (viewportHeight - startMenu.Height) / 2);
```

The first two lines should be very familiar as we are initializing our sprite batch and loading a texture called Startmenu. The third line is simply storing a vector so we will not have to calculate it every frame. It finds the position we need to draw our start menu texture at to center it inside of the viewport. Next, we update our `Update` method with the following code:

```
float elapsedTime = (float)gameTime.ElapsedGameTime.TotalSeconds;

switch (State)
{
    case GameState.Scene:
        {
            UpdateScene(gameTime);
            break;
        }
    case GameState.StartMenu:
        {
            UpdateStartMenu(elapsedTime);
            break;
        }
}
```

We are simply checking in which state our game is to determine what we need to update. The starting point for these methods is as follows:

```
private bool WasPressed(int playerIndex, InputHandler.ButtonType button, Keys keys)
{
    if (input.ButtonHandler.WasButtonPressed(playerIndex, button) ||
            input.KeyboardState.WasKeyPressed(keys))
        return (true);
    else
        return (false);
}

private void UpdateScene(GameTime gameTime)
{
    if (WasPressed(0, InputHandler.ButtonType.Start, Keys.Enter))
    {
        State = GameState.StartMenu;
    }
}

private void UpdateStartMenu(float elapsedTime)
{
    if (WasPressed(0, InputHandler.ButtonType.Start, Keys.Enter))
    {
        State = GameState.Scene;
    }
}
```

The first method is simply a helper method that allows us to easily determine if a button or key was pressed in the same call so we do not clutter up our code. The other two methods are doing the exact same thing at this point and that is checking to see if Start has been pressed; if so it changes the game state. Now we can look at our Draw method, which will start out looking like this:

```
protected override void Draw(GameTime gameTime)
{
    graphics.GraphicsDevice.Clear(Color.Black);

    sb.Begin(SpriteBlendMode.Additive, SpriteSortMode.Immediate,
        SaveStateMode.None);

    float elapsedTime = (float)gameTime.ElapsedGameTime.TotalSeconds;

    if (State == GameState.StartMenu)
        DrawStartMenu(elapsedTime);

    base.Draw(gameTime);

    sb.End();
}
```

We clear our back buffer to black and we start our sprite batch so we can draw to the screen. We then check to see if we should draw our start menu. We do not have a switch statement here, as we will be drawing everything through our game components. We could turn the start menu into its own game component, but there is not very much code and we can live with it being directly inside of our game class. The thing to notice about this method is the fact that we are calling our `base.Draw` method inside of our sprite batch's `begin` and `end` methods so we can pass our sprite batch to our game components and they can draw using the same sprite batch object we have set up. We are going to be setting this game up using `Immediate` mode with `Additive` blending and we are not going to be saving our render state.

Our `DrawStartMenu` method only has one line of code that draws the start menu texture in the center of the screen:

```
sb.Draw(startMenu, centerVector, Color.White);
```

We need to add in a start menu asset to our Content\Textures folder. This should be old hat by now, but we can find the startmenu.png file on this book's CD under this chapter's folder. Once we have successfully added our asset we should be able to compile and run our game skeleton. All the code does at this point is display the start menu and toggle between our two game states when we press Start (or Enter). Our scene state (the state we go into when we are playing the game) does not have anything in it currently and so we just toggle between our start screen and a black screen.

Creating Parallax Scrolling

Let's actually make our `DrawScene` method do something; perhaps it could draw the scene. The game we are going to make is going to be a side scroller that looks 3D. The idea with parallax scrolling is that we have a distant view of something (like mountains or clouds) way off in the distance. This faraway plane scrolls at a pretty slow rate. Then we have one or more background planes that each scroll faster than the one before it. We then render our player and enemies and an immediate background that all moves at the same rate. Optionally, we could create a foreground plane that scrolls even faster than our main playing plane. The purpose of scrolling the planes at different rates is that it causes the illusion of those planes being off in the distance.

To start with we are going make our `DrawScene` method actually draw our scrolling backgrounds. We are going to create a `ScrollingBackgroundManager` to go inside of our XELibrary project. The code for this new class can be found in Listing 11.1.

LISTING 11.1   ScrollingBackgroundManager.cs goes inside of our XELibrary as it can handle generic parallax scrolling backgrounds

```
using System;
using System.Collections.Generic;
using Microsoft.Xna.Framework;
using Microsoft.Xna.Framework.Graphics;
using Microsoft.Xna.Framework.Content;
```

LISTING 11.1   Continued

```
namespace XELibrary
{
    public interface IScrollingBackgroundManager { }

    public class ScrollingBackgroundManager
        : Microsoft.Xna.Framework.GameComponent
    {
        private Dictionary<string, ScrollingBackground> backgrounds =
            new Dictionary<string, ScrollingBackground>();
        private Dictionary<string, Texture2D> textures =
            new Dictionary<string, Texture2D>();
        private ContentManager content;

        private string contentPath;

        private int screenWidth;
        private int screenHeight;

        private float scrollRate;

        public ScrollingBackgroundManager(Game game, string contentPath)
            : base(game)
        {
            this.contentPath = contentPath;

            if (this.contentPath.LastIndexOf('\\') < this.contentPath.Length-1)
                this.contentPath += "\\";

            content = new ContentManager(game.Services);
            game.Services.AddService(
                typeof(IScrollingBackgroundManager), this);
        }

        public override void Initialize()
        {
            base.Initialize();

            GraphicsDeviceManager graphics =
                (GraphicsDeviceManager)Game.Services.GetService(
                typeof(IGraphicsDeviceManager));

            screenWidth = graphics.GraphicsDevice.Viewport.Width;
            screenHeight = graphics.GraphicsDevice.Viewport.Height;
        }
```

LISTING 11.1   Continued

```
public void AddBackground(string backgroundKey, string textureName,
    Vector2 position, float scrollRateRatio)
{
    AddBackground(backgroundKey, textureName, position, null,
        scrollRateRatio, Color.White);
}

public void AddBackground(string backgroundKey, string textureName,
    Vector2 position, Rectangle? sourceRect, float scrollRateRatio,
    Color color)
{
    ScrollingBackground background = new ScrollingBackground(
        textureName, position, sourceRect, scrollRateRatio, color);

    if (!textures.ContainsKey(textureName))
    {
        textures.Add(textureName, content.Load<Texture2D>(
            contentPath + textureName));
    }

    if (backgrounds.ContainsKey(backgroundKey))
        backgrounds[backgroundKey] = background;
    else
        backgrounds.Add(backgroundKey, background);
}

public override void  Update(GameTime gameTime)
{
    foreach (KeyValuePair<string, ScrollingBackground> background
                                                in backgrounds)
    {
        ScrollingBackground sb = background.Value;

        sb.Position.X += (sb.ScrollRate *
            (float)gameTime.ElapsedGameTime.TotalSeconds);
        sb.Position.X = sb.Position.X % textures[sb.TextureName].Width;
    }

    base.Update(gameTime);
}

public void Draw(float elapsedTime, string backgroundKey,
    SpriteBatch batch)
{
```

LISTING 11.1   Continued

```csharp
            ScrollingBackground sb = backgrounds[backgroundKey];
            Texture2D texture = textures[sb.TextureName];

            //Draw the main texture
            batch.Draw(texture, sb.Position, sb.SourceRect,
                sb.Color, 0, Vector2.Zero, 1.0f, SpriteEffects.None, 0f);

            //Determine if we need to scroll left or right
            Vector2 offset;
            if (sb.Positive)
                offset = sb.Position - (new Vector2(texture.Width, 0));
            else
                offset = new Vector2(texture.Width, 0) + sb.Position;
            //now draw the background again at the appropriate offset
            //NOTE: If our Width is larger than two times the size of our
            //texture then the code will need to be modified
            batch.Draw(texture, offset, sb.SourceRect,
                sb.Color, 0, Vector2.Zero, 1.0f, SpriteEffects.None, 0f);
        }

        public void ScrollRate
        {
            get { return(scrollRate); }
        }

        public void SetScrollRate(float scrollRate)
        {
            this.scrollRate = scrollRate;

            foreach (ScrollingBackground sb in backgrounds.Values)
                sb.ScrollRate = scrollRate * sb.ScrollRateRatio;
        }
    }

    public class ScrollingBackground
    {
        public Rectangle? SourceRect;
        public string TextureName;
        public Vector2 Position;
        public float ScrollRateRatio;
        public float ScrollRate;
        public Color Color;

        public bool Positive
```

LISTING 11.1   Continued

```
    {
        get { return (ScrollRate > 0); }
    }

    public ScrollingBackground(string textureName, Vector2 position,
        Rectangle? sourceRect, float scrollRateRatio, Color color)
    {
        TextureName = textureName;
        Position = position;
        SourceRect = sourceRect;
        ScrollRateRatio = scrollRateRatio;
        Color = color;
    }
  }
}
```

The scrolling background manager class works much like the cel animation manager class we created in the last chapter. We add backgrounds to a dictionary and we add textures to a dictionary so we do not waste memory on the same texture. It could prove to be helpful to create a texture manager game service that our components could reference when adding textures. In this case, we will not be sharing textures between our cel animation manager and our scrolling background manager, but seeing patterns like this should make us consider it.

We derive from GameComponent so we have an Update method that gets called automatically. Inside of that method we move our backgrounds based on each of their scroll rate values. Just like we had a cel animation object, we also have a scrolling background object. Each object contains information about itself that the manager has easy access to so it can manipulate each object as needed. We also set this game component up as a game service because we need to access it from other components as we write our game.

Some of the properties the scrolling background object include are the texture name, the position of the texture, how fast it should scroll, any color tinting values, and a source rectangle value that allows us to have multiple backgrounds inside of one texture.

We did not inherit from DrawableGameComponent because we need to pass in specific information to our Draw method. Our scrolling background manager will draw a scrolling background based on the background key it is given (again, much like our cel animation manager). The key piece of the code is the last part of our Draw method. After drawing our main texture, we then determine where to draw an additional texture to create our scrolling effect. We check to see if we are scrolling left or right and based on that we either put the next copy of the background we are drawing to one side or the other. Remember, the position of the background is getting set in our Update method.

Now that we have another class added to our library, we can plug it into our game code so when we press Start we actually see something. However, before jumping to our game code, we actually want to create an additional game component to have our games handle our backgrounds. Now, we are adding this game component to our actual game project and not our library because this is specific to our game. We are putting it inside of a component so we can keep our game code separated in a logical place and maintain it easier.

We are going to create a game component called `Background`. We need to derive from `DrawableGameComponent`. Let's make sure we add a `using` statement for our XELibrary so we can access our `ScrollingBackgroundManager` class. Inside of this file, we can create a member field to hold our scrolling background manager and a sprite batch:

```
private ScrollingBackgroundManager sbm;
private SpriteBatch sb;
```

We can also initialize our scrolling background manager object and add it to our components in our constructor. We can also cast our game object to our specific `SimpleGame` object type. This allows us to access the game state.

```
public Background(Game game, string contentPath)
    : base(game)
{
    // TODO: Construct any child components here
    sbm = new ScrollingBackgroundManager(game, contentPath);
    game.Components.Add(sbm);

    simpleGame = (SimpleGame)game;
}
```

Our constructor takes in the game instance like all game components do, but it also receives the content path so we can get to our textures as needed. We can load game components inside of game components like we are doing here. We also set the game component to be disabled because our game launches with the start menu active first and we do not want any kind of update code to be running when it does not need to.

We need to add a `using` statement to use the `Graphics` namespace of the XNA Framework. We will also need to create a custom `Load` method that our game needs to call:

```
public void Load(SpriteBatch spriteBatch)
{
    sb = spriteBatch;
}
```

This method takes in a sprite batch as a parameter. This way our components can all share the same sprite batch to draw on. This is better than creating many different sprite batches for each of our components. It also gives us more control as we can draw everything in immediate mode. We would have problems if we started up an immediate mode batch in our game and then created a different sprite batch and called End on that batch before we finished with our Immediate mode batch.

Next, we are going to look at the code we need to add inside of our LoadGraphicsContent method. We need to keep this inside of our loadAllContent condition. The code that goes into the bottom of the condition is as follows:

```
int viewportWidth = GraphicsDevice.Viewport.Width;
int viewportHeight = GraphicsDevice.Viewport.Height;
int textureWidth = 1024;
int cloudHeight = 512;
int cityHeight = 256;
int foregroundHeight = 128;
int streetHeight = 128;
int cloudY = 0;
int streetY = cloudHeight;
int foregroundY = streetY + streetHeight;
int cityY = foregroundY + foregroundHeight;

sbm.SetScrollRate(-75.0f); //75 pixels a second

sbm.AddBackground("clouds1", "background",
    Vector2.Zero,
    new Rectangle(0, cloudY, textureWidth, cloudHeight),
    0.4f, Color.White);

sbm.AddBackground("clouds2", "background",
    new Vector2(128, 0),
    new Rectangle(0, cloudY, textureWidth, cloudHeight),
    0.6f, new Color(255, 255, 255, 127));

sbm.AddBackground("street", "background",
    new Vector2(0, viewportHeight - streetHeight),
    new Rectangle(0, streetY, textureWidth, streetHeight),
    1.0f, Color.White);

sbm.AddBackground("foreground", "background",
    new Vector2(0, viewportHeight - foregroundHeight),
    new Rectangle(0, foregroundY, textureWidth, foregroundHeight),
    1.5f, Color.White);

sbm.AddBackground("city", "background",
    new Vector2(0, viewportHeight - cityHeight - streetHeight + 64),
    new Rectangle(0, cityY, textureWidth, cityHeight),
    0.8f, Color.White);
```

To start dissecting this code we see that the first thing we do is create several variables storing height and y values. These values are the position of the background in our texture. We only have one 1024 x 1024 background texture and are creating a total of five backgrounds from that one texture. For these values to make sense, we can look at the background image in Figure 11.1. Let's go ahead and add the texture background.png into our project (under our typical Content\Textures folder).

FIGURE 11.1   We are able to pack multiple backgrounds into one texture.

After initializing our variables that make it easier for us to work with our background coordinates, we actually add our backgrounds to our scrolling background manager. We add two different cloud backgrounds but they are really accessing the same location from our texture. We are passing in the initial position of 0,0 to draw one background and then we are offsetting the other cloud background by 128 pixels to the right. For the second cloud background, we are actually setting the alpha channel of our color modulation parameter to about halfway transparent. This way we can get an interesting depth effect for our clouds. It would be even better if the two cloud textures were not the same. We could modify our manager to allow a SpriteEffect and flip it horizontally or vertically to get a nice effect. However, the example, as is, gets the point across. We also set different speeds for the cloud backgrounds. The one farthest away moves slower than the one that is closer. Everything is relative to the speed we set a couple of statements earlier.

The next three statements simply set more backgrounds at different speeds from different sources in our texture and places them in different locations in our scene.

Finally, to get our scrolling backgrounds to draw on our scene, we need to add the following code to our background game component's `Draw` method:

```
float elapsedTime = (float)gameTime.ElapsedGameTime.TotalSeconds;

sbm.Draw(elapsedTime, "clouds1", sb);
sbm.Draw(elapsedTime, "clouds2", sb);

GraphicsDevice.RenderState.SourceBlend = Blend.SourceAlpha;
GraphicsDevice.RenderState.DestinationBlend = Blend.InverseSourceAlpha;
sbm.Draw(elapsedTime, "city", sb);
sbm.Draw(elapsedTime, "street", sb);
```

Remember, when we set up our sprite batch in our game's `Draw` method, we set the blend mode to additive and we will set our sort mode to immediate, which means our objects draw in the order in which we send them. By using immediate mode we can also switch blend modes in the middle of drawing our sprites. We do that here. We draw our two cloud backgrounds in additive blending mode (as they are being drawn on top of each other) but then we switch to normal alpha blending mode to draw the remaining pieces of our scene.

NOTE

Typically we would not use additive blending for our clouds, as different cloud textures could produce unwanted results. It would easily oversaturate the colors. It would be better to use alpha blending and make sure our cloud textures included an alpha channel. However, for demonstration purposes we set our clouds up to be drawn with additive blending.

We saw that when the default `SpriteBatch.Begin` method is called, different render states get modified. These states were listed in Table 9.1 in Chapter 9, "2D Basics." In that table, we saw that the source blend state was set to `SourceAlpha` and the destination blend state was set to `InverseSourceAlpha`. We set those values manually here because we are in immediate mode using an additive blending and we want to get back into an alpha blending mode.

Finally, let's add the needed code to our game class. After we declare our variable to hold our background we need to set up our background in our game's constructor method as follows:

```
background = new Background(this, @"Content\Textures\");
background.Enabled = background.Visible = false;
Components.Add(background);
```

When we start out, we disable the game component because we will be in our start menu mode to begin with. We need to call the background's `Load` method to pass it our sprite batch. We do this at the bottom of our `loadAllContent` condition in our `LoadGraphicsContent` method:

```
background.Load(sb);
```

Let's add our foreground "background." We need to do this after everything else has drawn on the screen, so we cannot do it in our background's game component. We will do it inside of our `Draw` method in our game code after we call our `base.Draw` method:

```
//Display our foreground (after game components)
if (State == GameState.Scene)
    sbm.Draw(elapsedTime, "foreground", sb);
```

By calling the `Draw` method on our scrolling background manager after we call our `base.Draw` method, we ensure that this will be last thing drawn on the screen (unless a particular `DrawOrder` on a component is set). We need to add a variable to hold our `ScrollingBackgroundManager` game component. We have called it `sbm`. Next, we need to initialize it inside of our constructor, but because our `Background` game component already created it, we just need to reference it. We can do that because it is a game service. We need to add this code to our game's `Initialize` method:

```
sbm = (ScrollingBackgroundManager)Services.GetService(
                          typeof(IScrollingBackgroundManager));
```

We added that statement after calling `base.Initialize` so that the background component has a chance to load it.

Switching States

Now, we need to correctly switch out between our two states (`StartMenu` and `Scene`). We already have a stub created for our `UpdateStartMenu` method. We need to replace the contents of our `WasPressed` condition with the following code:

```
ActivateGame();
```

Next we can actually create the method as follows:

```
private void ActivateGame()
{
    background.Visible = background.Enabled = true; //start updating scene
    State = GameState.Scene;
}
```

That is all there is to creating scrolling backgrounds. We took it a step further and created multiple scrolling backgrounds to create a parallax scroller. If we wanted to create a typical scrolling background we would only need to modify our scroll rate based on our player's movement.

At this point, if we run it and press the Start button or Enter key, we will see our background scrolling. We want to be able to get back to our start menu so we need to hook up the code to make that happen. To start we need to replace the contents of the `WasPressed` condition inside of the `UpdateScene` method:

```
ActivateStartMenu();
```

Now we can create this method:

```
public void ActivateStartMenu()
{
    //stop updating scene backgrounds
    background.Visible = background.Enabled = false;
    State = GameState.StartMenu;
}
```

We will be updating these two methods (`ActivateStartMenu` and `ActivateGame`) as we create more components our game will use. This is where we will hide and show, disable and enable our different game components. Our background game component is just the first. We need to go ahead and call the `ActivateStartMenu` method at the end of our `loadAllContent` condition inside of our `LoadGraphicsContent` method.

If we run our code now we can see that we can toggle between our start menu and our scene as expected. The problem, though, is that even though we have changed our background component to be disabled and not visible when we move from our scene into our start menu, the background is still scrolling. We can look at the truck and watch as we go in and out of our scene and see that it is still updating in the background. The reason is because even though we disabled our background component, the back end scrolling background manager component was not disabled. We need to hook into the `Enable` property of our background component so we can correctly set our scrolling background manager's `Enable` property using the following code:

```
protected override void OnEnabledChanged(object sender, EventArgs args)
{
    base.OnEnabledChanged(sender, args);
    sbm.Enabled = this.Enabled;
}
```

Game components allow us to tie into the `Enabled` and `Visible` properties. When they change, the changed event is kicked off. We can override the preceding method to set our scrolling backorder manager game component's `Enabled` property.

Drawing Our Hero

We have a game with simple state management that allows us to switch back and forth from a start screen to our game scene. The next step we need to take is to actually draw our main character on the screen. We can see the code for the player game component we will be adding to our game in Listing 11.2.

LISTING 11.2   Player.cs

```
using System;
using System.Collections.Generic;
using Microsoft.Xna.Framework;
using Microsoft.Xna.Framework.Input;
using Microsoft.Xna.Framework.Graphics;

using XELibrary; // for input handler

namespace SimpleGame
{
    public class Player : Microsoft.Xna.Framework.DrawableGameComponent
    {
        public string CurrentAnimation = "hero";
        public Vector2 Position;

        private float kickTime = 0.0f;
        private bool kicking = false;

        private InputHandler input;
        private CelAnimationManager cam;
        private SpriteBatch sb;

        public bool Attacking
        {
            // could OR ( ¦¦ ) a bunch of other actions if we had them
            get { return (kicking); }
        }

        public Player(Game game) : base(game)
        {
            input = (InputHandler)game.Services.GetService(
                typeof(IInputHandler));
            cam = (CelAnimationManager)game.Services.GetService(
                typeof(ICelAnimationManager));
            Visible = Enabled = false;
        }

        public void Load(SpriteBatch spriteBatch)
        {
            sb = spriteBatch;
        }

        public void SetPause(bool paused)
        {
```

LISTING 11.2   Continued

```
        cam.ToggleAnimation(CurrentAnimation, paused);
    }

    public override void Update(Microsoft.Xna.Framework.GameTime gameTime)
    {
        if (WasPressed(0, InputHandler.ButtonType.A, Keys.Space))
        {
            kickTime = 0;
            kicking = true;
        }

        if (kicking)
        {
            CurrentAnimation = "hero-kick";
            kickTime += (float)gameTime.ElapsedGameTime.TotalSeconds;
            if (kickTime > 0.5f)
                kicking = false;
        }
        else
            CurrentAnimation = "hero";

        base.Update(gameTime);
    }

    protected override void LoadGraphicsContent(bool loadAllContent)
    {
        cam.AddAnimation("hero", "hero", new CelCount(4, 4), 16);
        cam.AddAnimation("hero-kick", "hero-kick", new CelCount(4, 1), 8);

        base.LoadGraphicsContent(loadAllContent);
    }

    public override void Draw(GameTime gameTime)
    {
        float elapsedTime = (float)gameTime.ElapsedGameTime.TotalSeconds;

        cam.Draw(elapsedTime, CurrentAnimation, sb, Position);

        base.Draw(gameTime);
    }

    private bool WasPressed(int playerIndex,
        InputHandler.ButtonType button, Keys keys)
    {
```

LISTING 11.2   Continued

```
            if (input.ButtonHandler.WasButtonPressed(playerIndex, button) ||
                    input.KeyboardState.WasKeyPressed(keys))
                return (true);
            else
                return (false);
        }

        public void SetPause(bool paused)
        {
            cam.ToggleAnimation(CurrentAnimation, paused);
        }
    }
}
```

Our player game component has two public fields: `CurrentAnimation` and `Position`. Although in this game we will not be changing the player's position, it would be an easy modification and we will leave it here in case we want to make that modification later. The `CurrentAnimation` string holds the cel animation key of the animation our player is displaying. We set up our cel animation in our `LoadGraphicsContent` method.

We currently only have two different animations for our hero, which are him running and him kicking. A real game would have more, but this allows us to see how we can switch between the different animations. We have an `Attacking` property that tells us if our player is attacking or not. This currently is only returning our kicking variable, but if we had other actions such as punching, swinging a machete, and so on, we could just "OR" them all together with this one property. This will allow us to handle our collision detection appropriately. We discuss collision detection later in this chapter.

We modified our `CelAnimationManager` to be a game service so we could access it in multiple components. We access the `InputHandler` and the `CelAnimationManager` both in our constructor. This game component and most we will be creating for this game have their own `Load` method that must be called manually. This `Load` method will be used to pass around our sprite batch.

To change our cel animation manager to a game service we need to create an interface (it can be blank) and then inherit from the interface. Then inside of the constructor we need to add it to our game's `Services` collection. We did this for our scrolling background manager if we need a reference on how to set it up.

We have a helper method for checking input in our class called `WasPressed`. This method allows us to pass in a player index, the button we want to check, and the key we want to check. This helps make our code a little cleaner. We could actually add it directly to our `InputHandler` class because we also needed to use it in our main game class.

Because this is a drawable game component, not only do we have the `Update` method, but we also have the `Draw` method. In our `Update` method we are checking to see if we are pressing the kick button or key. If we are, then we change our animation to our kick texture and set up a timer so we know how long to play our animation. It would be more robust to update our cel animation manager to allow us to call it and tell it to render the animation one time only (or a certain number of times). Time and space do not allow us to do it here, so we just improvise with a timer in our game code. We do that here and also when we draw our explosions a little later. When we are finished kicking, we revert back to our main hero animation (which is the hero running full speed ahead). The Draw method simply calls our cel animation manager and tells it to draw our current animation at the position we specify. All of our player code is nicely contained in one source file.

We need to create our player variable with our Player type and we need to actually initialize it and add it to our components in the game's constructor as follows:

```
player = new Player(this);
player.Position = playerPosition;
Components.Add(player);
```

It is important that the preceding code is placed before initializing our background game component. This is because the Components collection will get called in the order the items were added. We could override this with the DrawOrder property.

We need to declare our playerPosition member field as Vector2 with the values 64,350. Instead of having numbers sprinkled all through our code we can create constants or variables (whichever is more appropriate) at the top of our code files for easy access. Now, as our backgrounds are relatively small, we are hard-coding our width and height for this game to be 640 x 480. These are also set at the top of SimpleGame:

```
private Vector2 playerPosition = new Vector2(64, 350);
private int width = 640;
private int height = 480;
```

We use the width and height properties in our constructor to force our aspect ratio so we do not have to do any extra calculation for our character placement.

```
graphics.PreferredBackBufferWidth = width;
graphics.PreferredBackBufferHeight = height;
```

Before we can check how our player looks, we need to add the actual textures to our project. The textures hero.png and hero-kick.png can be found in the usual manner. We need to call the Load method in our player component so we can initialize the sprite batch. We do that inside of our LoadGraphicsContent method:

```
player.Load(sb);
```

Now we need to update our ActivateStartMenu method to enable our hero and make him visible:

```
player.Visible = player.Enabled = false;
player.SetPause(true);
```

We want to do the exact opposite in our `ActivateGame` method:

```
player.Visible = player.Enabled = true;
player.SetPause(false);
```

The `SetPause` method calls the `ToggleAnimation` method in our cel animation manager. However, we do not have that particular overloaded method and we need to add that to our CelAnimationManager.cs file:

```
public void ToggleAnimation(string animationKey, bool paused)
{
    if (animations.ContainsKey(animationKey))
        animations[animationKey].Paused = paused;
}
```

Finally, we need to add a `CelAnimationManager` object to our `SimpleGame` class. We then need to initialize it inside of our constructor. This should be done before initializing our player game component because our player game component relies on the cel animation manager. We now have our hero running on the screen. If we run the game at this point we will see our player is running and he is getting paused correctly. We can also press the spacebar or the A button to get him to kick.

Drawing Our Enemies

Our hero looks a little lonely, so we need to give him some competition. We can add in some enemies in this section. We are going to use an enemy manager that will control our enemies. Our `EnemyManager` will be a game component that will have a collection of Enemy objects. The code for these two classes can be found in Listing 11.3.

LISTING 11.3   EnemyManager.cs

```
using System;
using System.Collections.Generic;
using Microsoft.Xna.Framework;
using Microsoft.Xna.Framework.Graphics;

using XELibrary; //for cel animation manager

namespace SimpleGame
{
    public partial class EnemyManager
        : Microsoft.Xna.Framework.DrawableGameComponent
    {
        private readonly int maxXPosition = 800;
        private readonly int minXPosition = 650;
        private readonly float collisionDistance = 64.0f;
        private int yPosition = 350;
```

LISTING 11.3   Continued

```
private int xPosition = 650;

private Enemy[] enemies;
private int totalEnemies;
private int enemiesThisLevel;
private int maxEnemies;

private SpriteBatch sb;
private Random rand;
private CelAnimationManager cam;

public bool EnemiesExist
{
    get { return (totalEnemies < enemiesThisLevel); }
}

public EnemyManager(Game game)
    : base(game)
{
    // TODO: Construct any child components here
    rand = new Random();

    cam = (CelAnimationManager)game.Services.GetService(
        typeof(ICelAnimationManager));
}

public void Load(SpriteBatch spriteBatch, int maxEnemies,
    int enemiesThisLevel, float speed)
{
    sb = spriteBatch;

    this.enemiesThisLevel = enemiesThisLevel;
    this.totalEnemies = 0;
    this.maxEnemies = maxEnemies;

    Vector2 position = new Vector2();
    enemies = new Enemy[maxEnemies];
    for (int i = 0; i < maxEnemies; i++)
    {
        position.X = GetNextPosition(); //off screen
        position.Y = yPosition;

        enemies[i] = new Enemy();
        enemies[i].Active = true;
```

LISTING 11.3   Continued

```
            enemies[i].Position = position;
            enemies[i].Velocity = new Vector2(-speed, 0.0f);
        }
    }

    public void SetPause(bool paused)
    {
        cam.ToggleAnimation("robot", paused);
    }

    public void ToggleAnimation()
    {
        cam.ToggleAnimation("robot");
    }

    private float GetNextPosition()
    {
        xPosition += rand.Next(50, 100);
        if (xPosition > maxXPosition)
            xPosition = minXPosition;
        return (xPosition);
    }

    protected override void LoadGraphicsContent(bool loadAllContent)
    {
        cam.AddAnimation("robot", "robot", new CelCount(4, 4), 16);

        base.LoadGraphicsContent(loadAllContent);
    }

    public int CollidedWithPlayer(Vector2 playerPosition)
    {
        for (int i = 0; i < enemies.Length; i++)
        {
            Enemy enemy = enemies[i];
            if (enemy.Active)
            {
                float distance =(playerPosition - enemy.Position).Length();
                //within collision distance?
                if (distance < collisionDistance)
                    return (i);
            }
        }
        return (-1);
```

LISTING 11.3   Continued

```csharp
    }

    public Vector2 Die(int enemyIndex)
    {
        Enemy enemy = enemies[enemyIndex];
        enemy.Active = false;
        Vector2 oldPosition = enemy.Position;

        if (totalEnemies + maxEnemies < enemiesThisLevel)
        {
            Vector2 position = new Vector2();
            position.X = GetNextPosition(); //off screen
            position.Y = yPosition;
            enemy.Position = position;
            enemy.Active = true;
        }
        totalEnemies++;

        return (oldPosition);
    }

    public override void Update(GameTime gameTime)
    {
        float elapsed = (float)gameTime.ElapsedGameTime.TotalSeconds;
        for (int i = 0; i < enemies.Length; i++)
        {
            Enemy enemy = enemies[i];
            if (enemy.Active)
            {
                enemy.Position += (enemy.Velocity * elapsed);
            }
        }
        base.Update(gameTime);
    }

    public override void Draw(GameTime gameTime)
    {
        GraphicsDevice.RenderState.SourceBlend = Blend.SourceAlpha;
        GraphicsDevice.RenderState.DestinationBlend =
                                        Blend.InverseSourceAlpha;

        float elapsedTime = (float)gameTime.ElapsedGameTime.TotalSeconds;
        for (int i = 0; i < enemies.Length; i++)
        {
```

LISTING 11.3   Continued

```
                Enemy enemy = enemies[i];
                if (enemy.Active)
                    cam.Draw(elapsedTime, "robot", sb, enemy.Position);
            }

        base.Draw(gameTime);
        }
    }

    public class Enemy
    {
        public Vector2 Position;
        public Vector2 Velocity;
        public bool Active;
    }
}
```

We will first talk about our Enemy class. This is a very simple class that has three public fields: Position, Velocity, and Active. The position will hold this particular enemy's position. The velocity holds the direction and speed of our enemy. Finally, the active flag determines if any logic should be done on this enemy. Instead of creating and destroying a bunch of Enemy objects, we create a list and then just set them to not active when they die and reset them when they are created.

We have a Load method that not only allows us access to the game's sprite batch, but it also tells us how many enemies we need to create, the total enemies to generate, and the speed at which they move. This makes it ideal to set up these properties when we load levels. Although we will not be creating levels in this simple game, it would not be much of a challenge to create a level manager with the needed information that could then populate our enemy manager's Load method.

We allow pausing our enemy sprite animation much like we did with our player. We create our enemies either at the time our Load method is called or when a previous enemy dies and we have not reached our total number of enemies specified in the Load method. When we update our enemies we just iterate through our array and set their positions. We set the enemy position by randomly finding their x position through our GetNextPosition method. We do not do anything sophisticated so the current code allows our enemies to stack up on each other. We could add better logic to make sure we do not set an enemy's position to one that is already used.

During our Draw method we set our render state to make sure we are in alpha blended mode and we loop through our enemies and draw each one (assuming it is active). We have two other methods in our EnemyManager class: Die and CollidedWithPlayer. We discuss the CollidedWithPlayer method in the next section. The Die method will be called if the game determines that a collision has happened and the player was attacking.

If that happens, the game will call the enemy manager's `Die` method passing in the particular enemy that needs to die.

We always have the maximum number of enemies generated so as soon as one dies, another one is created off screen. Before we generate a new one, we make sure we should by checking to see if there are more enemies to create based on the values passed into the `Load` method. The `Die` method first sets the enemy's active flag to false. It then stores its position. If more enemies are needed another enemy is generated. Finally, the total number of enemies that have died is increased. We use this value to determine if there are any more enemies around. Our property `EnemiesExist` returns the condition if our total numbers of enemies is less than the enemies created for this level.

Before we dig into the collision code and collision detection concepts in general, let's utilize our enemy manager game component inside of our game. Of course we need to create a member variable (enemies) and then intialize it and add it to our game component collections inside of our constructor right after we add our player game component.

Inside the `ActivateStartMenu` method, we need to disable our enemies and keep them from drawing on our screen. We also pause their animation for good measure:

```
enemies.Visible = enemies.Enabled = false; //stop updating enemies
enemies.SetPause(true);
```

Inside the `ActivateGame` method, we need to activate the enemy manager again. In fact, if we are getting into our game state, we need to load our enemies but it would be nice to allow our gamer to pause the game. This means we need a way to know if the game is starting from a paused state or a new game state. Let's add the following code to handle this in our `ActiveGame` method:

```
if (!paused)
    enemies.Load(sb, 5, 20, 120.0f); //should be read by level (level 1)
enemies.Visible = enemies.Enabled = true; // resume updating enemies
enemies.SetPause(false);
```

We are going to use a boolean variable to determine if our game was paused or not. If it was not paused, then we are going to call the `Load` method of our `EnemyManager`. In a real game we would actually create a level manager and pass in data based on our level information. For example, level 1 would have a total of 5 enemies on the screen at once, with a total of 20 enemies for the level, and the enemies move at a rate of 120 pixels per second. We could have our levels store different values for those and each time we finish a level, the next level's data are sent to the enemy manager.

We need to declare and initialize the `paused` field to `false`. In our `UpdateScene` method inside of the `WasPressed` condition, right before we call our `ActivateStartMenu` method we need to set the `paused` variable to `true`. We need to set it to false inside of the `UpdateStartMenu` method, at the end of our `WasPressed` condition after the call to `ActivateGame`. Making these changes will pause our game when we press the Start button while playing and then resume the game when we are looking at our start menu.

11

We need to actually load our enemy textures to our project. The texture is called robot.png and can be found on the CD. We can copy that to the same location as our other textures. We can run our game and see our enemies are drawing on the screen (five of them) and coming toward us. We have not spaced them out at all and let them generate their x position randomly so they could be all over each other. For this example, though, it is good enough for us to test out our concepts. The problem is that they run right past us because we have not set up any kind of collision detection.

Handling Collision Detection

In general, collision detection is the process of checking certain objects to see if they have collided with other objects. Algorithms to do this can be very simplistic (like ours is for this game) or very complex. A collision detection algorithm can really drop a game's frame rate. The algorithm consists of searching for objects and comparing objects.

One possible algorithm is to loop through all objects checking if they collide with each other. Another is checking only certain portions of the screen (in 2D) or our world (in 3D) where we know the player is. There are many ways to store our scene objects. We can simply store them in a list, like this game, or put them into a tree structure that we can quickly scan using an algorithm to check only certain objects. The idea is that we could easily exclude certain objects to check based on their position in the tree.

One possibility is to split up the screen or world into quadrants and only check the quadrant we care about. This can break down if we have bullets flying everywhere and most of the world has objects that can react (glass shatters, metal dents, water cooler gushes water, etc.) to being hit by a bullet. In these cases, it is all about checking the immediate objects close to the bullet we are testing. We would iterate through all our bullets, checking for objects close by and handling the collision. There is no reason to test if the bullet collided with an object across the room.

Different methods are appropriate for different needs. There are many ways to store our game objects so we can quickly search them. We will not even begin to scratch the surface of possibilities, but it will really pay off to do some research in this area.

The key to remember is that perfect is the enemy of good enough. This means that if your game can get by with a more simplistic collision detection algorithm, by all means use it. If it needs more robust collision detection capabilities, benchmarking different algorithms is key.

Not only are there different ways to search for objects to test for the collision, there is the actual testing that can cause a slowdown in frame rates. For our game we are simply getting a vector between our player and the enemy we are checking. We have both positions as vectors and we can simply subtract those two vectors to determine how far away they are from each other. We can think of this as a bounding sphere with a certain radius around our objects and if we get within a certain range, we flag that we have a collision. Sometimes this is good enough. Other times, we need per-pixel collision detection in 2D or vertex collision detection in 3D.

Any detection we perform can adversely affect performance and we need to be aware of the cost and determine how well it scales. If we only will ever have 100 objects in our scene, then our algorithm only needs to be good enough to handle those 100. If that increases, our algorithm might need to change so we do not drop frames.

We only have five enemies on the screen at a time and we are only checking for collision against one player, so we pass our player's position to our enemy manager, which loops through all of the enemies and does a simple vector distance check to determine if we are colliding. The code takes the difference between the player's position and the enemy's position and checks the length of that vector. In our case, if the length is less than 64 units (pixels in this case), we return that we have collided and in this implementation we return the index of the enemy we collided with.

A COLLISION DETECTION OPTIMIZATION

An easy optimization we can perform immediately is to not calculate the length of the vector as that involves a medium-expensive square root computation. Instead, we can use the `Vector2.DistanceSquared` method, which bypasses the square root computation, and compare this value with the square of our collision radius. We could replace our EnemyManager's CollidedWithPlayer method with the following:

```
public int CollidedWithPlayer(Vector2 playerPosition)
{
    for (int i = 0; i < enemies.Length; i++)
    {
        Enemy enemy = enemies[i];
        if (enemy.Active)
        {
            float distance = Vector2.DistanceSquared(playerPosition,
                enemy.Position);
            if (distance < collisionDistance * collisionDistance)
                return (i);
        }
    }

    return (-1);
}
```

Inside of our game object, we check to see if the player is attacking or not. If the player is not, we lose because the enemy touched us. If the player is attacking, the enemy dies. We need to set up our collision test inside of our game. We need to create the following method:

```
private void CheckForCollisions(GameTime gameTime)
{
    int enemyIndex = enemies.CollidedWithPlayer(player.Position);
    if (enemyIndex != -1)
```

```
    {
        if (player.Attacking)
        {
            //die robot
            Vector2 enemyPosition = enemies.Die(enemyIndex);
        }
        else
        {
            background.Enabled = false;
            enemies.SetPause(true);
            enemies.Enabled = false;
            player.SetPause(true);
            player.Enabled = false;
        }
    }
}
```

We see that we call the CollidedWithPlayer method we set up in our enemy manager that checks the distance between the two sprites' positions. If we collided, we check to see if the player was attacking. If so, we destroy the robot. If the player was not attacking when the collision took place, we disable our background, player, and enemies game components.

We need to actually call our CheckForCollisions method inside of our UpdateScene method. Now on every update of our game while we are in the Scene state, we will see if we have collided with an enemy.

At this point we are correctly detecting if the player is colliding with any of the enemy robots. We have our enemies actually dying and disappearing when they are kicked. If there are more enemies to be created, they are created off screen correctly. If the player collides with a robot and the player is not attacking, the game is stopped and must be restarted to continue.

Winning and Losing

Now that we have successfully detected our collisions we need to do something when we successfully kill all of the enemies or when we get destroyed. Let's set two more game states for these events. We will add Lost and Won to our GameState enum.

We need to add the following code to the false condition inside of our CheckForCollisions method:

```
State = GameState.Lost;
```

Now we need to add the following code to the UpdateScene method under our call to CheckForCollisions:

```
if (!enemies.EnemiesExist)
{
    //Level over  (would advance level here and on last level state won game)
    enemies.SetPause(true);
    enemies.Enabled = false;
    player.SetPause(true);
    player.Enabled = false;
    background.Enabled = false;
    State = GameState.Won;
}
```

We check our property to see if any more enemies exist after checking for collisions. If no more exist then we are done with the level (and because this game only has one level, we are done with the game). We set our state to Won to signify that we won.

Adding Transitions

We are going to create a transition effect of fading our screen out if we win or lose. If we win we will fade to black; if we lose we will fade to red. Then our fading game component will manage its fading cycle and when it is completed it will call our game's ActivateStartMenu to get us back into a playable state.

Let's add some more conditions to our game's update switch. We currently only check for Scene and StartMenu, but now we can add Won and Lost to the list:

```
case GameState.Won:
    {
        //Game Over - You Won!
        if (!fade.Enabled)
        {
            fade.Color = Color.Black;
            fade.Enabled = true;
        }
        break;
    }
case GameState.Lost:
    {
        if (!fade.Enabled)
        {
            fade.Color = Color.Red;
            fade.Enabled = true;
        }
        break;
    }
```

The code is pretty simple as we have a fade game component that we are enabling if it is not already enabled and we set a property of what color we want to fade to. We can see the code for our FadeOut game component in Listing 11.4.

LISTING 11.4   FadeOut.cs

```csharp
using System;
using System.Collections.Generic;
using Microsoft.Xna.Framework;
using Microsoft.Xna.Framework.Graphics;

namespace SimpleGame
{
    public partial class FadeOut : Microsoft.Xna.Framework.DrawableGameComponent
    {
        private Texture2D fadeTexture;
        private float fadeAmount;
        private double fadeStartTime;
        private SimpleGame simpleGame;

        public Color Color;
        private SpriteBatch sb;

        public FadeOut(Game game)
            : base(game)
        {
            simpleGame = (SimpleGame)game;
            this.Enabled = false;
            this.Visible = false;

            DrawOrder = 999;
        }

        public void Load(SpriteBatch spriteBatch)
        {
            sb = spriteBatch;
        }

        public override void Update(GameTime gameTime)
        {
            // TODO: Add your update code here
            if (fadeStartTime == 0)
            {
                fadeStartTime = gameTime.TotalGameTime.TotalMilliseconds;
                Visible = true;
            }
```

LISTING 11.4   Continued

```
        fadeAmount += (.25f *(float)gameTime.ElapsedGameTime.TotalSeconds);

        if(gameTime.TotalGameTime.TotalMilliseconds > fadeStartTime + 4000)
        {
            fadeAmount = 0;
            fadeStartTime = 0;
            Visible = Enabled = false;

            simpleGame.ActivateStartMenu();
        }

        base.Update(gameTime);
    }

    protected override void LoadGraphicsContent(bool loadAllContent)
    {
        fadeTexture = CreateFadeTexture(
            GraphicsDevice.Viewport.Width, GraphicsDevice.Viewport.Height);

        base.LoadGraphicsContent(loadAllContent);
    }

    public override void Draw(GameTime gameTime)
    {
        GraphicsDevice.RenderState.SourceBlend = Blend.SourceAlpha;
        GraphicsDevice.RenderState.DestinationBlend =
                                            Blend.InverseSourceAlpha;


        Vector4 color = Color.ToVector4();
        color.W = fadeAmount; //set transparancy
        sb.Draw(fadeTexture, Vector2.Zero, new Color(color));

        base.Draw(gameTime);
    }

    private Texture2D CreateFadeTexture(int width, int height)
    {
        Texture2D texture = new Texture2D(GraphicsDevice, width, height, 1,
        ResourceUsage.None, SurfaceFormat.Color ,
            ResourceManagementMode.Automatic);

        int pixelCount = width * height;
        Color[] pixelData = new Color[pixelCount];
        Random rnd = new Random();
```

LISTING 11.4   Continued

```
            for (int i = 0; i < pixelCount; i++)
            {
                pixelData[i] = Color.White;
            }

            texture.SetData(pixelData);

            return (texture);
        }
    }
}
```

Most of this code should look very familiar as we did this in the last chapter. The key points to see here are the fact that we set the DrawOrder of our component to a high number, 999. This will make this component draw last on our screen so we can get the effect we are looking for. In our Update method we fade our texture in 25 percent at a time each second. Once we have passed four seconds we reset our fade variables and then activate our game's start menu, which gets us out of our current state and back to our start menu state.

We need to actually use the FadeOut component in our SimpleGame class. Let's create the fade member field and initialize it as normal in our constructor. We also need to call the Load method passing in the sprite batch. We can now run our game and see that we handle our lose state as well as our won state appropriately.

Adding Explosions

We have all of our game logic in place and are correctly switching between our game states and handling our collision detection. Now, we need to add a little flare to the game. When we kick an enemy and it just disappears, it would be nice to make a little explosion effect. We are going to do that now.

We can see the code for our new ExplosionManager game component in Listing 11.5.

LISTING 11.5   ExplosionManager.cs

```
using System;
using System.Collections.Generic;
using Microsoft.Xna.Framework;
using Microsoft.Xna.Framework.Graphics;
using XELibrary;

namespace SimpleGame
{
    public class ExplosionManager
        : Microsoft.Xna.Framework.DrawableGameComponent
    {
```

LISTING 11.5   Continued

```
private Dictionary<int, Explosion> explosions =
    new Dictionary<int, Explosion>(5);
private CelAnimationManager cam;
private SpriteBatch sb;
private SimpleGame simpleGame;

public ExplosionManager(Game game) : this(game, 0) { }
public ExplosionManager(Game game, int maxExplosions) : base(game)
{
    simpleGame = (SimpleGame)game;

    cam = (CelAnimationManager)game.Services.GetService(
                            typeof(ICelAnimationManager));
    if (maxExplosions > 0)
        SetMaxNumberOfExplosions(maxExplosions);
}

public void Load(SpriteBatch spriteBatch)
{
    sb = spriteBatch;
}

public override void Update(GameTime gameTime)
{
    if (simpleGame.State == SimpleGame.GameState.Scene)
    {
        //Check For Explosions
        int markForDeletion = -1;
        foreach (KeyValuePair<int, Explosion> explosion in explosions)
        {
            //have we been playing our explosion for over a second?
            if (gameTime.TotalGameTime.TotalMilliseconds >
                explosion.Value.TimeCreated + 100)
            {
                markForDeletion = explosion.Key;
                break;
            }
        }

        if (explosions.ContainsKey(markForDeletion))
            explosions.Remove(markForDeletion);
    }

    base.Update(gameTime);
}
```

LISTING 11.5   Continued

```
protected override void LoadGraphicsContent(bool loadAllContent)
{
    //add our explosions
    cam.AddAnimation("explosion", "explode_1", new CelCount(4, 4), 16);
    cam.AddAnimation("explosion2", "explode_1", new CelCount(4, 4), 16);
    cam.AddAnimation("explosion3", "explode_3", new CelCount(4, 4), 12);
    cam.AddAnimation("explosion4", "explode_4", new CelCount(4, 4), 20);
    cam.AddAnimation("explosion5", "explode_3", new CelCount(4, 4), 12);
    cam.AddAnimation("explosion6", "explode_4", new CelCount(4, 4), 20);

    cam.AddAnimation("bigexplosion", "bigexplosion", new CelCount(4, 4), 18);

    base.LoadGraphicsContent(loadAllContent);
}

public override void Draw(GameTime gameTime)
{
    float elapsedTime = (float)gameTime.ElapsedGameTime.TotalSeconds;

    switch (simpleGame.State)
    {
        case SimpleGame.GameState.Scene:
            {
                foreach (Explosion explosion in explosions.Values)
                {
                    cam.Draw(elapsedTime, "explosion4", sb,
                        explosion.Position);
                }
                break;
            }
        case SimpleGame.GameState.StartMenu:
            {
                //we can add our explosions to make our title page pop
                cam.Draw(elapsedTime, "explosion", sb,
                    new Vector2(32, 32));
                cam.Draw(elapsedTime, "explosion2", sb,
                    new Vector2(40, 40));
                cam.Draw(elapsedTime, "explosion3", sb,
                    new Vector2(64, 32));
                cam.Draw(elapsedTime, "explosion4", sb,
                    new Vector2(64, 64));
                cam.Draw(elapsedTime, "explosion5", sb,
                    new Vector2(28, 40));
                cam.Draw(elapsedTime, "explosion6", sb,
                    new Vector2(40, 64));
```

LISTING 11.5   Continued

```
                        cam.Draw(elapsedTime, "explosion", sb,
                            new Vector2(432, 32));
                        cam.Draw(elapsedTime, "explosion2", sb,
                            new Vector2(440, 40));
                        cam.Draw(elapsedTime, "explosion3", sb,
                            new Vector2(464, 32));
                        cam.Draw(elapsedTime, "explosion4", sb,
                            new Vector2(464, 64));
                        cam.Draw(elapsedTime, "explosion5", sb,
                            new Vector2(428, 40));
                        cam.Draw(elapsedTime, "explosion6", sb,
                            new Vector2(440, 64));

                        cam.Draw(elapsedTime, "bigexplosion", sb,
                            new Vector2(250, 330));
                        break;
                }
            }
            base.Draw(gameTime);
        }

        public void StartExplosion(int explosionKey, Vector2 position,
            double time)
        {
            explosions.Add(explosionKey, new Explosion(position, time));
        }

        public void SetMaxNumberOfExplosions(int maxExplosions)
        {
            explosions = new Dictionary<int, Explosion>(maxExplosions);
        }
    }

    public class Explosion
    {
        public double TimeCreated;
        public Vector2 Position;

        public Explosion(Vector2 position, double timeCreated)
        {
            Position = position;
            TimeCreated = timeCreated;
        }
    }
}
```

Most of the code in our `ExplosionManager` should look familiar. We set up a dictionary to hold our collection of explosions. We load up our cel animation manager with our different explosion textures. We require the game to set our sprite batch through the `Load` method.

We have an `Explosion` class that has two public fields that are set through its constructor. We store the time the explosion was created as well as the position of the explosion. This way the explosion manager can handle the life span of our explosion and draw it on the screen in the appropriate position.

Our explosion manager checks our game state to determine if it should draw the active explosions for our game scene or if it should draw our start menu explosions. We want the start screen to have a little more pop than it currently does, so we are going to add a few explosions around the texture.

In our update code, we check the time our explosions were created and compare that to our current time to determine if we should continue to draw them. If enough time has passed, we remove them from our collection. We could have set this code up exactly like we have our enemy manager code, but we can see different ways to handle the same task.

We need to update our game code to use the explosion manager. First, we need to declare a variable to hold our explosion manager and then we need to add the game component to our component collection. We can call our variable `explosionManager`. We can use the default constructor when we initialize our game component. We also need to call `Load` on our explosion manager inside of the `LoadGraphicsContent` method and pass in our sprite batch.

Next, we need to add this statement to our "not paused" condition inside of our `ActivateGame` method:

```
explosionManager.SetMaxNumberOfExplosions(5); //should be read by level
```

We are hard-coding a value of 5 in here just like we are for the line before it when we set up our enemy manager. The idea is that we would have a level and we would pass in the number of enemies to be created at one time into this method. The reason is that every time we kill off an enemy we create an explosion. We need to have as many explosions as we do enemies at any given point.

We can see the code for that inside of the `player.Attacking` condition in the `CheckForCollisions` method:

```
explosionManager.StartExplosion(enemyIndex, enemyPosition,
    gameTime.TotalGameTime.TotalMilliseconds);
```

We call our explosion manager's start explosion method, which takes in the key of the explosion we are creating (in this case it is the enemy's index), the position we want the explosion to draw (in this case it is the same position as our enemy), and finally the current game time in milliseconds. Now, when we collide with our enemy and are kicking, we will see an explosion on the screen when the enemy disappears.

Before we run our game again to see the progress, we need to add the explosion textures we referenced inside of our project. We can find the following files on the CD: bigexplosion.png, explosion_1.png, explosion_2.png, and explosion_4.png.

Let's run the game to see the explosions we have set up. We see our start menu screen has the explosions we added. As we play the game and collide with our enemies we can see the explosions being created. An improvement would be to center the explosions to the center of the enemy position. They are currently being drawn at the top left (0,0) of the enemy.

Adding Sounds

We can add in some sounds to help the game out some. We already have our sound manager class from Chapter 7, "Sounds and Music," so we do not need to write any new code for that. Instead of going through the hassle of creating another XACT project, we will simply copy the XACT project and sound files from our Chapter 7 Sound Demo project folder. We should create a Sounds subfolder in our Content folder in our project to store the files. We only need to have the XACT project included in the project with the wave files just in the same directory, but not in the solution itself.

We need to declare our sound manager variable and we need to initialize it in our constructor like all of our other game components:

```
sound = new SoundManager(this, "Chapter7");
Components.Add(sound);
```

Now, we can create our playlist just like we did in the SoundDemo project by adding the following code to our Initialize method:

```
string[] playList = { "Song1", "Song2", "Song3" };
sound.StartPlayList(playList);
```

Finally, we should play the explosion sound we set up back in Chapter 7. We should do this right after we start our explosion when our enemy dies, so we need to add the following statement at the end of the player.Attacking condition inside of the CheckForCollisions method:

```
sound.Play("explosion");
```

Now, we have our songs playing and when we kick a robot we not only see an explosion but we hear one, too.

Summary

In this chapter, we created a simple, but complete game. We learned how to scroll our background and to even create parallax scrolling. We discussed different blending options again and saw examples of how we can use them together in a game. We looked at changing states at a high level. We had some simple collision detection to check to see if we collided with our enemies. We utilized the fading transition we learned about in the last chapter but modified it so we could fade to any color. We also incorporated our explosions into our game. We finished out the chapter by hooking up our sound manager and using the sounds we created in Chapter 7.

PART V

High Level Shader Language

IN THIS PART

CHAPTER 12

HLSL Basics

Before 2001 the only way to talk to the graphics hardware was through the Fixed Function Pipeline (FFP) provided in DirectX. Graphics card manufacturers started allowing access through assembly code directly to their hardware. This was needed because the graphics cards were so much more complex than they were when the DirectX application programming interface (API) originally came out. It used to be enough to have an API that allowed us to set different properties and settings to get the graphics cards to work the way we wanted. However, as the cards became more complex, the DirectX API, specifically the FFP, also had to become more complex.

Instead of continuing to add functions to the FFP, Microsoft provided a way through their API to execute assembly code on the graphics cards directly. This assembly code is called a shader. The graphics cards have vertex shader instructions as well as pixel shader instructions. Vertex shaders are executed on every vertex in the visible scene. Pixel shaders are executed on all of the visible geometry in the scene.

VERTEX SHADERS VERSUS PIXEL SHADERS

Vertex shaders are executed on every vertex of our object. When we are drawing a face (triangle) of a 3D object the vertex shader will be executed for all three vertices that make up that triangle. When we are drawing a 2D sprite the vertex shader will run four times for each vertex that make up that sprite—one vertex in each corner to make the rectangle.

Pixel shaders, on the other hand, execute on every visible pixel of the geometry in the scene. If the triangle of the 3D object we drew is close to the camera so that it takes up most of the screen, the pixel shader will be run for every pixel that the triangle is visible on. On the other hand, if the 3D object is far away so that it does not even make up an entire pixel, the pixel shader will not be run at all—not even one time. For the 2D sprite, it will be run for every pixel that is visible on the screen. If it is a full-screen sprite, then every single pixel on the screen will be run through the pixel shader. We will see several examples of this in the next chapter as we look at postprocessing effects that are done through pixel shaders.

Assembly language is great. It allows us to get down to the hardware level and move data on particular registers and we can have complete control over how it is processed. However, writing assembly code can be time consuming. NVIDIA, one of the graphics cards leaders, came out with a language called Cg, which stood for C for Graphics. As the name implies, Cg was a higher level C-like language that developers could use for their games instead of using assembly language.

Microsoft created a standard high-level language that is called the High Level Shader Language (HLSL). The two languages are similar because they actually started out as the same language. It was a joint project between NVIDIA and Microsoft. For some reason the project ended up forking into two separate final products. The advantage of HLSL for XNA programmers is that the XNA Framework can load in the .fx files automatically as the Content Pipeline compiles it for us automatically.

HLSL is language that allows us to talk at a high level to the graphics card so we do not need to use assembly code to access the hardware. However, on the Xbox 360 we can still use assembler directly inside of the HLSL syntax if we want to.

HLSL is an integral part of XNA. The FFP no longer exists in XNA. We can only get data on the screen using HLSL. Of course, until now we have been able to get our demos and game on the screen but we have used the `BasicEffect` XNA helper class. To help developers get up to speed quicker, Microsoft added this helper class to XNA. It allows us to write to the graphics card without understanding HLSL. However, all the `BasicEffect` helper class is doing is passing the data through to an internal shader.

Effects give us the ability to render the same geometry in different ways. For example, we can have the exact same content and display it differently depending on how far away the camera is or based on the gamer's hardware capabilities.

Understanding the Shader Process

Before we get into the details of how to pass our application data from our XNA application to the graphics card we need to discuss the process flow in general, which is shown in Figure 12.1. We will take a little time to explain the flow so we can understand what shaders provide for us.

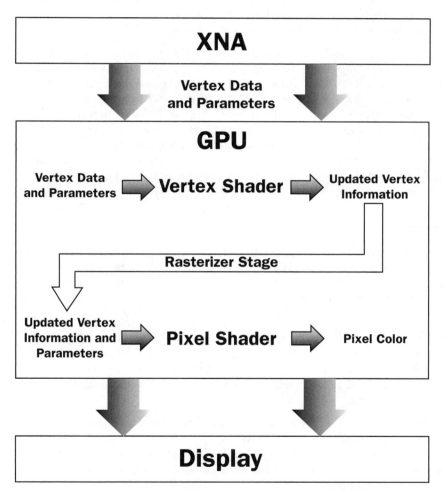

FIGURE 12.1   This shows the flow of data from our XNA game to the graphics card and finally onto the rendering surface.

It helps to keep in mind that our end goal is to get our scene to display on the screen. We are trying to get pixels on our screen to look a certain way with different colors to form an image of our scene. We create our vertex information (either through creating it manually or by loading in a 3D file) and we texture the vertex. We then pass that vertex data (position, normals, textures, etc.) to the graphics card. Our graphics cards have a graphics processing unit (GPU), sometimes referred to as a video processing unit (VPU). The GPU is just like our CPU except it runs at a lower clock speed, but is able to process many vertices and pixels in parallel, which makes it much faster for doing graphics and rendering work.

After we pass our vertex data from our application to the GPU, the GPU can perform tasks on the data to get it to appear a certain way on the screen. It can be as simple as determining the colors from the texture being used to as complex as translating vertices and doing multiple passes of the pixel shader to create very interesting effects.

The way the GPU processes our vertex information and displays our scene is through the vertex and pixel shaders. (In DirectX 10, there are geometry shaders, but those are not supported under the current XNA Framework or on Xbox 360.) Once the GPU gets the vertex information and any parameters our XNA application passes to it, the vertex shader is executed. The vertex shader will "shade" the vertex and transform it to a format we specify using a transformation we specify. The rasterization process then occurs, which converts the primitives (triangles mainly) into the pixels that will need to be rendered on the screen. The pixel shader processes each pixel that is to be rendered on the screen and produces a color for that pixel. Finally, the pixels are sent to the frame buffer, which is sent to the display.

HLSL Syntax

Although we do not go into a lot of detail about the HLSL language syntax, we will touch on the high points and explain the mapping between the C# type and the HLSL type when appropriate. We not only discuss the types of data in HLSL, but also semantics, intrinsic functions, loops, and conditions.

Variable Types

Just like C#, HLSL allows us to declare variables of different types. Most use the same keyword as their C# counterpart. Examples of these are int, float, bool, struct, in, out, return, void, string, true, and false. There are more, of course, but those are the common ones we will be using.

Vectors can be defined several ways. Typically we see them listed as float3 for a vector with three components and float4 for a vector with four components. We could also declare a vector with the vector keyword. We can access the different components of the vector in different ways. We can access them like an array or through their component directly; for example, if we had a vector to hold a color value like:

```
float4 color;
```

We could access the red portion of the color by writing either of the next two lines:

```
float red = color[0];
float samered = color.r;
```

Vectors have two component namespaces: r,g,b,a and x,y,x,w. We could also get the red value from our color by writing the following valid line of code:

```
float anotherred = color.x;
```

If we wanted the red and green components of our color to store them in a vector with two components we could write the following code:

```
float2 something = color.xy;
float2 somethingelse = { color[0], color[1] };
```

When we access multiple components at the same time, like the first statement just shown, it is called swizzling. Although we can swizzle our components in the same name-space, the following is invalid code because we cannot combine component namespaces:

```
//bad code - we can't combine component namespaces
float2 wontcompile = color.xg;
```

We can set up matrices with the matrix keyword or by using floatRxC where R(ows) and C(olumns) can be any values. To define a 4 x 4 matrix we could use either of the following declarations:

```
float4x4 whatIsTheMatrix;
matrix <float, 4, 4> theMatrixHasYou;
```

The following code shows how we would access a particular row and column of a matrix:

```
matrix a = worldViewProjection;
float b = a._m11;
float c = a[0][0];
```

In HLSL we have storage class modifiers that we can associate with our variables. These determine how the variables are used. The storage class modifiers are as follows:

```
extern

shared

static

uniform

volatile
```

The extern modifier allows our application to have access to our global variables. We can set and get those variables inside of our XNA code. The default for global variables is extern. The static modifier, on the other hand, does not allow us access to the global variable. Local variables can also have the static storage class modifier, which means that the value it has persists while each vertex or pixel is being shaded. There is also a shared modifier that allows multiple effect files to share the value. The last two modifiers are uniform and volatile. The volatile storage class modifier lets the HLSL compiler know that the global variable data will change frequently. The `uniform` modifier does the opposite and lets the compiler know that the data will not change. This is the default of our global variables. This is important because if we did not mark our variables as uniform (again, this is the default) then the shader would have many more instructions per vertex. Instead, the compiler does a preshader compilation and will execute those items to be executed once on the CPU and then do the per-vertex/pixel calculations on the GPU. This is very much the desired effect.

TIP

In practice you will probably never need to use these modifiers as the defaults generally do the right thing.

Setting up variables is a lot like C#. There is an additional step we need to take when setting up variables, though. HLSL has something known as semantics, which we discuss in the next section.

Semantics

Semantics are used to link our input with the output of the graphics pipeline function that was just executed. For example, there are semantics used to link our output from our application to the vertex shader input. These are called vertex input semantics. After the vertex shader is done processing the vertices, it has passed to the rasterization stage, which we saw in Figure 12.1. These are called vertex output semantics.

The pixel shader receives data from both the vertex shader and the rasterization stage. These are called pixel input semantics. After the pixel shader is done, it sends the data to the correct render target and the pixel shader output color is linked to the alpha blend stage. These are called pixel output semantics. We discuss the syntax of semantics in the next section as we talk about structs.

Structs

We have to specify structs to hold our input and output data. For example, the vertex input struct that is populated from our XNA application could look something like this:

```
struct VertexInput //Application Data
{
    float4 Position : POSITION0;
    float3 Normal : NORMAL;
    float4 TextureCoords : TEXCOORD0;
};
```

We set up our structs much in the same way as we do in C#. The only difference is the semantics. We discussed semantics in the last section but we did not actually get to see their syntax. Our effect is expecting our game to pass in the position of the vertex, the normal of the vertex, and the texture coordinates of the vertex. It then maps all of those types to a specific register so when it gets to the next stage in the pipeline it will be able to read in the appropriate values. A list of all the vertex input semantics can be found in Table 12.1.

TABLE 12.1   Vertex Input Semantic List

Vertex Shader Input Semantic	Description
BINORMAL[n]	Binormal
BLENDINDICES[n]	Blend indices
BLENDWEIGHT[n]	Blend weights
COLOR[n]	Diffuse and specular color
NORMAL[n]	Normal vector
POSITION[n]	Vertex position in object space
PSIZE[n]	Point size
TANGENT[n]	Tangent
TESSFACTOR[n]	Tessellation factor
TEXCOORD[n]	Texture coordinates

A struct that holds our vertex output data would look something like this:

```
struct VertexOutput
{
    float4  Position : POSITION0;
    float4  TexCoord : TEXCOORD0;
};
```

We can see it is set up the same as our input struct. The main thing to note about the vertex output is that it must return at least one vertex. All of the vertex output semantics can be found in Table 12.2.

TABLE 12.2   Vertex Output Semantic List

Vertex Shader Output Semantic	Description
COLOR[n]	Diffuse or specular color. Any vertex shader prior to vs_3_0 should clamp a parameter that uses this semantic between 0 and 1, inclusive. A vs_3_0 vertex shader has no restriction on the data range.
	vs_1_1 through vs_1_3 only support two-color interpolators. vs_1_4 supports six and eight colors with subsequent versions.
FOG	Vertex fog. Not supported on Xbox 360 or with vs_3_0.
POSITION	Position of a vertex in homogenous space. Compute position in screen space by dividing (x,y,z) by w. Every vertex shader must write out a parameter with this semantic.
PSIZE	Point size.
TEXCOORD[n]	Texture coordinates. This is actually an all-purpose semantic meaning that we can pass any data (not just texture coordinates) with this semantic.

The vertex output data is passed to the rasterization stage and then passed to the pixel shader. Our pixel shader also takes a struct as its input. An example of one follows:

```
struct PixelInput // Rasterization Data
{
    float4 Color : COLOR0;
};
```

A list of pixel shader input semantics can be found in Table 12.3.

TABLE 12.3   Pixel Input Semantic List

Pixel Shader Input Semantic	Description
COLOR[n]	Diffuse or specular color. For shaders prior to vs_3_0 and ps_3_0, this data ranges between 0 and 1, inclusive. Starting with ps_3_0, there is no restriction on the data range.
TEXCOORD[n]	Texture coordinates.
VFACE	Floating-point scalar that indicates a back-facing primitive. A negative value faces backward, whereas a positive value faces the camera. This is only valid with ps_3_0.
VPOS	Contains the current pixel (x,y) location. This is only valid with ps_3_0.

Finally, we can see an example of a pixel shader output struct:

```
struct PixelOutput // Pixel Output Data
{
    float4 Color : COLOR0;
    float Depth : DEPTH;
};
```

The pixel shader must return the color of the pixel at the very least. Both of the pixel shader output semantics can be found in Table 12.4.

TABLE 12.4   Pixel Output Semantic List

Pixel Shader Output Semantic	Description
COLOR[n]	Output color. Any pixel shader prior to ps_3_0 should clamp a parameter that uses this semantic between 0 and 1, inclusive. For ps_3_0 shaders, the data range is dependent on the render target format.
DEPTH[n]	Output depth.

We now have seen examples of the different structs we need to pass data around our shaders. We also saw the available semantics listed for each of those structs.

Intrinsic Functions

We can define our own functions in HLSL much like we do in C#, but there are also a lot of built-in functions, which are called intrinsic functions. Table 12.5 lists all of the intrinsic functions available in HLSL. These functions are listed here for easy reference in case the DirectX 9 SDK documentation is not handy. However, there is even more information about each function inside of the documentation.

TABLE 12.5   Intrinsic Functions Available in HLSL

Syntax	Description
value abs(value a)	Absolute value (per component).
acos(x)	Returns the arccosine of each component of x. Each component should be in the range [-1, 1].
all(x)	Tests if all components of x are nonzero.
any(x)	Tests if any component of x is nonzero.
asin(x)	Returns the arcsine of each component of x. Each component should be in the range [-pi/2, pi/2].
atan(x)	Returns the arctangent of x. The return values are in the range [-pi/2, pi/2].
atan2(y, x)	Returns the arctangent of y/x. The signs of y and x are used to determine the quadrant of the return values in the range [-pi, pi]. atan2 is well-defined for every point other than the origin, even if x equals 0 and y does not equal 0.
ceil(x)	Returns the smallest integer that is greater than or equal to x.
clamp(x, min, max)	Clamps x to the range [min, max].
clip(x)	Discards the current pixel, if any component of x is less than zero. This can be used to simulate clip planes, if each component of x represents the distance from a plane.
cos(x)	Returns the cosine of x.
cosh(x)	Returns the hyperbolic cosine of x.
cross(a, b)	Returns the cross-product of two 3D vectors a and b.
D3DCOLORtoUBYTE4(x)	Swizzles and scales components of the 4D vector x to compensate for the lack of UBYTE4 support in some hardware.
ddx(x)	Returns the partial derivative of x with respect to the screen-space x coordinate.
ddy(x)	Returns the partial derivative of x with respect to the screen-space y coordinate.
degrees(x)	Converts x from radians to degrees.
determinant(m)	Returns the determinant of the square matrix m.
distance(a, b)	Returns the distance between two points, a and b.

(continues)

TABLE 12.5   Continued

Syntax	Description
dot(a, b)	Returns the · product of two vectors, a and b.
exp(x)	Returns the base-e exponent.
exp2(value a)	Base 2 Exp (per component).
faceforward(n, i, ng)	Returns -n * sign(·(i, ng)).
floor(x)	Returns the greatest integer that is less than or equal to x.
fmod(a, b)	Returns the floating point remainder f of a / b such that a = i * b + f, where i is an integer, f has the same sign as x, and the absolute value of f is less than the absolute value of b.
frac(x)	Returns the fractional part f of x, such that f is a value greater than or equal to 0, and less than 1.
frexp(x, out exp)	Returns the mantissa and exponent of x. frexp returns the mantissa, and the exponent is stored in the output parameter exp. If x is 0, the function returns 0 for both the mantissa and the exponent.
fwidth(x)	Returns abs(ddx(x)) + abs(ddy(x)).
isfinite(x)	Returns true if x is finite, false otherwise.
isinf(x)	Returns true if x is +INF or -INF, false otherwise.
isnan(x)	Returns true if x is NAN or QNAN, false otherwise.
ldexp(x, exp)	Returns x * 2exp.
length(v)	Returns the length of the vector v.
lerp(a, b, s)	Returns a + s(b - a). This linearly interpolates between a and b, such that the return value is a when s is 0, and b when s is 1.
lit(n · l, n · h, m)	Returns a lighting vector (ambient, diffuse, specular, 1): ambient = 1;diffuse = (n · l < 0) ? 0 : n · l; specular = (n · l < 0) || (n · h < 0) ? 0 : (n · h * m);
log(x)	Returns the base-e logarithm of x. If x is negative, the function returns indefinite. If x is 0, the function returns +INF.
log10(x)	Returns the base-10 logarithm of x. If x is negative, the function returns indefinite. If x is 0, the function returns +INF.
log2(x)	Returns the base-2 logarithm of x. If x is negative, the function returns indefinite. If x is 0, the function returns +INF.
max(a, b)	Selects the greater of a and b.
min(a, b)	Selects the lesser of a and b.
modf(x, out ip)	Splits the value x into fractional and integer parts, each of which has the same sign and x. The signed fractional portion of x is returned. The integer portion is stored in the output parameter ip.

Syntax	Description
mul(a, b)	Performs matrix multiplication between a and b. If a is a vector, it is treated as a row vector. If b is a vector, it is treated as a column vector. The inner dimension acolumns and brows must be equal. The result has the dimension arows x bcolumns.
noise(x)	Not yet implemented.
normalize(v)	Returns the normalized vector v / length(v). If the length of v is 0, the result is indefinite.
pow(x, y)	Returns xy.
radians(x)	Converts x from degrees to radians.
reflect(i, n)	Returns the reflection vector v, given the entering ray direction i, and the surface normal n, such that $v = i - 2n * (i \cdot n)$.
refract(i, n, R)	Returns the refraction vector v, given the entering ray direction i, the surface normal n, and the relative index of refraction R. If the angle between i and n is too great for a given R, refract returns (0,0,0).
round(x)	Rounds x to the nearest integer.
rsqrt(x)	Returns 1 / sqrt(x).
saturate(x)	Clamps x to the range [0, 1].
sign(x)	Computes the sign of x. Returns -1 if x is less than 0, 0 if x equals 0, and 1 if x is greater than zero.
sin(x)	Returns the sine of x.
sincos(x, out s, out c)	Returns the sine and cosine of x. sin(x) is stored in the output parameter s. cos(x) is stored in the output parameter c.
sinh(x)	Returns the hyperbolic sine of x.
smoothstep(min, max, x)	Returns 0 if x < min. Returns 1 if x > max. Returns a smooth Hermite interpolation between 0 and 1, if x is in the range [min, max].
value sqrt(value a)	Square root (per component).
step(a, x)	Returns (x >= a) ? 1 : 0.
tan(x)	Returns the tangent of x.
tanh(x)	Returns the hyperbolic tangent of x.
tex1D(s, t)	1D texture lookup. s is a sampler or a sampler1D object. t is a scalar.
tex1D(s, t, ddx, ddy)	1D texture lookup, with derivatives. s is a sampler or sampler1D object. t, ddx, and ddy are scalars.
tex1Dbias(s, t)	1D biased texture lookup. s is a sampler or sampler1D object. t is a 4D vector. The mip level is biased by t.w before the lookup takes place.
tex1Dgrad(s, t, ddx, ddy)	1D gradient texture lookup. s is a sampler or sampler1D object. t is a 4D vector. The gradient values (ddx, ddy) select the appropriate mipmap level of the texture for sampling.

(continues)

TABLE 12.5   Continued

Syntax	Description
tex1Dlod(s, t)	1D texture lookup with level of detail (LOD). s is a sampler or sampler1D object. t is a 4D vector. The mipmap LOD is specified in t.
tex1Dproj(s, t)	1D projective texture lookup. s is a sampler or sampler1D object. t is a 4D vector. t is divided by its last component before the lookup takes place.
tex2D(s, t)	2D texture lookup. s is a sampler or a sampler2D object. t is a 2D texture coordinate.
tex2D(s, t, ddx, ddy)	2D texture lookup, with derivatives. s is a sampler or sampler2D object. t, ddx, and ddy are 2D vectors.
tex2Dbias(s, t)	2D biased texture lookup. s is a sampler or sampler2D object. t is a 4D vector. The mip level is biased by t.w before the lookup takes place.
tex2Dgrad(s, t, ddx, ddy)	2D gradient texture lookup. s is a sampler or sampler2D object. t is a 4D vector. The gradient values (ddx, ddy) select the appropriate mipmap level of the texture for sampling.
tex2Dlod(s, t)	2D texture lookup with LOD. s is a sampler or sampler2D object. t is a 4D vector. The mipmap LOD is specified in t.
tex2Dproj(s, t)	2D projective texture lookup. s is a sampler or sampler2D object. t is a 4D vector. t is divided by its last component before the lookup takes place.
tex3D(s, t)	3D volume texture lookup. s is a sampler or a sampler3D object. t is a 3D texture coordinate.
tex3D(s, t, ddx, ddy)	3D volume texture lookup, with derivatives. s is a sampler or sampler3D object. t, ddx, and ddy are 3D vectors.
tex3Dbias(s, t)	3D biased texture lookup. s is a sampler or sampler3D object. t is a 4D vector. The mip level is biased by t.w before the lookup takes place.
tex3Dgrad(s, t, ddx, ddy)	3D gradient texture lookup. s is a sampler or sampler3D object. t is a 4D vector. The gradient values (ddx, ddy) select the appropriate mipmap level of the texture for sampling.
tex3Dlod(s, t)	3D texture lookup with LOD. s is a sampler or sampler3D object. t is a 4D vector. The mipmap LOD is specified in t.
tex3Dproj(s, t)	3D projective volume texture lookup. s is a sampler or sampler3D object. t is a 4D vector. t is divided by its last component before the lookup takes place.
texCUBE(s, t)	3D cube texture lookup. s is a sampler or a samplerCUBE object. t is a 3D texture coordinate.
texCUBE(s, t, ddx, ddy)	3D cube texture lookup, with derivatives. s is a sampler or samplerCUBE object. t, ddx, and ddy are 3D vectors.
texCUBEbias(s, t)	3D biased cube texture lookup. s is a sampler or samplerCUBE object. t is a 4D vector. The mip level is biased by t.w before the lookup takes place.

Syntax	Description
texCUBEgrad(s, t, ddx, ddy)	3D gradient cube texture lookup. s is a sampler or samplerCUBE object. t is a 4D vector. The gradient values (ddx, ddy) select the appropriate mipmap level of the texture for sampling.
tex3Dlod(s, t)	3D cube texture lookup with LOD. s is a sampler or samplerCUBE object. t is a 4D vector. The mipmap LOD is specified in t.
texCUBEproj(s, t)	3D projective cube texture lookup. s is a sampler or samplerCUBE object. t is a 4D vector. t is divided by its last component before the lookup takes place.
transpose(m)	Returns the transpose of the matrix m. If the source is dimension mrows x mcolumns, the result is dimension mcolumns x mrows.

In general, these methods are used identical to how C# methods are used. They have a return value and take in parameters. There are a lot of functions, and that is a good thing. Some of the more frequently used functions are clamp, which clamps a value within the range specified; saturate, which is identical to clamp with an implied value range of 0 and 1; dot, which computes the dot product of two vectors; cross, which computes the cross-product of two vectors; normalize, which returns the normalized vector; and tex2D, which allows us to get a color from a vertex by passing in a sampler and the position of the texture we want the color of. Samplers are required whenever we need to use textures. A sampler has a direct relation to the part of the hardware where the texture is stored.

Loops and Conditions

We are almost done hitting the highlights of the syntax but we need to discuss loops and conditions, the shader's flow control. HLSL has many of the same flow controls that C# includes: if, while, do, and for. They really are identical to their C# counterparts. When the if statement only has one line, the curly braces are optional just like C#. Fortunately, there is nothing new in regard to our loop and conditions inside of HLSL compared to how they are structured in C#.

Vertex Shaders

Now that we have discussed how vertex and pixel shaders are used and saw some of the syntax of the language we can actually look at some real shader code. We start by looking at a simple vertex shader. Then we look at a pixel shader and finally we look at the techniques and passes needed to execute these shaders.

We can start by discussing an actual vertex shader. This shader is going to be very simple because we are going to process our vertex position and texture coordinates.

```
VertexOutput vertexShader(VertexInput input)
{
    VertexOutput output;
```

```
        WorldViewProjection = mul(mul(World, View), Projection);
        output.Position = mul(input.Position, WorldViewProjection);
        output.TexCoord = input.TexCoord;
        return( output );
}
```

We take a parameter called input of type `VertexInput`. We return a `VertexOutput` value.
Those structs look like this:

```
struct VertexInput
{
    float4 Position : POSITION;
    float2 TexCoord : TEXCOORD0;
};

struct VertexOutput
{
    float4 Position : POSITION;
    float2 TexCoord : TEXCOORD0;
};
```

Our `vertexShader` function calculates the world view projection matrix based on the
world, view, and projection matrices being passed into the shader from our application.
After multiplying the matrices together, it then sets the output position by transforming
the position passed to us with our `worldviewprojection` matrix. Afterward, it simply does
a pass through of the texture coordinate information. The vertex information is then
passed to the rasterization stage and then on to our pixel shader.

TIP

The position is being passed in as a float4 even though the C# code provides Vector3
values. There is no need to "fix" the shader to input a float3. This is done on purpose
and the GPU automatically fills in the fourth component with the 1 value to make the
projection work properly.

Pixel Shaders

Pixel shaders allow us to manipulate each and every pixel being rendered. This is very
powerful. We can see an actual pixel shader here:

```
float4 pixelShader(PixelInput input) : COLOR
{
    return( tex2D(TextureSampler, input.TexCoord) * AmbientColor);
}
```

We are passed in our pixel input struct and return a color (a 4D vector). The single statement in this pixel shader is getting the red, green, blue, and alpha values from the texture using the texture coordinates passed in. Here is the `PixelInput` struct, in which we can see we need the texture coordinates passed in:

```
struct PixelInput
{
    float2 TexCoord : TEXCOORD0;
};
```

After getting our color for that texture location, we are multiplying each component of our color with our ambient color passed in from our application. This produces a new color that we return. This color will ultimately be passed through to the buffer that gets put onto our screen.

Techniques

Now that we have our shaders created we need to actually call them inside of our effect file. When our game uses an effect, it passes in a technique. The technique can have one or more passes (we discuss passes in the next section). Effects can have multiple techniques. A technique is really just a name and a container of our pass(es).

```
technique Default
{
    ...
}
```

Techniques can have any name. This book will typically have one technique per effect file and call it default.

Passes

Each pass in a technique will define which vertex and pixel shader should be used. The game typically will either loop through all of the passes in a technique or it will just call one directly. If more than one pass is contained in the technique we can have our scenes go through a couple of different changes before actually rendering to the screen by looping through the passes. We set up our passes in the following way:

```
pass P0
{
    VertexShader = compile vs_1_1 vertexShader();
    PixelShader = compile ps_1_1 pixelShader();
}
```

The preceding block is inside of the technique code block. This is what kicks off our shaders. Our application specifies a technique and then specifies a pass. When the effect is processed, it searches for a vertex and pixel shader and processes them.

Inside of our pass we can also set render states. For example, we can set the following values:

```
CullMode = none;
AlphaBlendEnable = false;
FillMode = Wireframe;
```

Those are just a few, but most render states we can set directly inside of XNA we can also set in our HLSL code.

Passing Application Data to the GPU

Our shaders need to have data passed to them to do any work. The main piece of information needed is our vertex data. Not only do we need to send in our vertex data, but we also need to send in some of the matrices. It could be our world, view, projection, or our world view projection matrix. We also can send in our textures and any other data we determine our shaders need from our game.

Before we can pass any information to our effect, we need to initialize a variable for it. We do this with the XNA `Effect` class as follows:

```
Effect effect;
```

Then we need to load our effect file. Fortunately, this is just as easy as loading our textures or any other resource because the Content Pipeline knows how to read them in. Therefore, the code to load our effect is:

```
effect = content.Load<Effect>(@"Content\Effects\AmbientTexture");
```

It is very easy to load our effect, so let's see what hurdles we need to jump over to pass data to our actual effect file to use. We can jump straight into a code snippet to see the complexity:

```
effect.Parameters["Texture"].SetValue(texture);
effect.Parameters["Projection"].SetValue(camera.Projection);
effect.Parameters["View"].SetValue(camera.View);
effect.Parameters["World"].SetValue(world * mesh.ParentBone.Transform);
```

That is really not complex at all. We access our global variables from our effect file by accessing the `Parameters` collection of our effect. We pass in the name of our variable as the key to the collection and then call the `SetValue` method to actually set the value of the variable. We do not need to cast our value to any type—thanks to method overloading it just works.

HLSL Demo

Now we can actually create a demo using all of this knowledge. To start with, we can load up our Load3DObject demo from Chapter 6, "Loading and Texturing 3D Objects." In the

Draw method of our code we are currently using the `BasicEffect` class that XNA provides for us. We are going to update the code to use an effect file we will create.

To start, we can actually create our HLSL effect file. Inside of our project we need to create another folder under Contents called Effects. After we create that folder, we can add a new file. We can select a text file and call it AmbientTexture.fx. The code we need to enter into the file is as follows:

```
float4x4 World  : WORLD;
float4x4 View;
float4x4 Projection;

float4 AmbientColor : COLOR0;

float4x4 WorldViewProjection : WORLDVIEWPROJECTION;
texture Texture;
sampler TextureSampler = sampler_state
{
    texture = <Texture>;
    magfilter = LINEAR;
    minfilter = LINEAR;
    mipfilter = LINEAR;
    AddressU = mirror;
    AddressV = mirror;
};

struct VertexInput
{
    float4 Position : POSITION;
    float2 TexCoord : TEXCOORD0;
};

struct VertexOutput
{
    float4 Position : POSITION;
    float2 TexCoord : TEXCOORD0;
};

VertexOutput vertexShader(VertexInput input)
{
    VertexOutput output;
    WorldViewProjection = mul(mul(World, View), Projection);
    output.Position = mul(input.Position, WorldViewProjection);
    output.TexCoord = input.TexCoord;
    return( output );
}
```

```
struct PixelInput
{
    float2 TexCoord : TEXCOORD0;
};

float4 pixelShader(PixelInput input) : COLOR
{
    return( tex2D(TextureSampler, input.TexCoord) * AmbientColor);
}

technique Default
{
    pass P0
    {
        VertexShader = compile vs_1_1 vertexShader();
        PixelShader = compile ps_1_1 pixelShader();
    }
}
```

We have already discussed most things in this shader. We will go over the items we did not discuss already. To start, we declare some variables to hold the matrices that our game will pass in. Then we declare our ambient color as a `float4`. When we process a texture from our scene, we need to set up a variable to hold our texture. We also need to set up a sampler so our HLSL code can actually sample that texture. We already discussed our vertex input and output structs as well as our pixel input structs. Instead of using a pixel output struct, we are just returning the color data because that is all that is required.

Now in our game code, we need to declare our effect:

```
private Effect effect;
```

Next, we need to actually load the effect into our content manager. We can do that inside of our `LoadGraphicsContent` method as follows:

```
effect = content.Load<Effect>(@"Content\Effects\AmbientTexture");
```

Now, we need to set our first parameter for this effect. We have an `AmbientColor` variable that we need to set, so we can do that now. We will not change our ambient light color every frame. In fact, we are just going to set it once, so we can set it up right after creating our effect. We need to add this line of code to set our variable:

```
effect.Parameters["AmbientColor"].SetValue(0.8f);
```

Finally, we need to replace the inner foreach loop in the `Draw` method. Before we had this:

```
foreach (BasicEffect be in mesh.Effects)
{
    be.EnableDefaultLighting();
```

```
    if (texture != null)
        be.Texture = texture;

    be.Projection = camera.Projection;
    be.View = camera.View;
    be.World = world * mesh.ParentBone.Transform;
}
```

Remember, XNA sets up a `BasicEffect` for each mesh we load so we can simply set properties on the basic effect and be on our way. In this case, though, we want to replace that functionality with our own HLSL effect. We see that we are setting the texture, the camera's projection, and view. We are also setting the world matrix on the mesh. We need to do all of these things in our new effect as well, so let's replace the preceding code with the following code:

```
foreach (ModelMeshPart mp in mesh.MeshParts)
{
    if (texture != null)
        effect.Parameters["Texture"].SetValue(texture);

    effect.Parameters["Projection"].SetValue(camera.Projection);
    effect.Parameters["View"].SetValue(camera.View);
    effect.Parameters["World"].SetValue(world * mesh.ParentBone.Transform);
    mp.Effect = effect;
}
```

We can see this is very similar. The first thing to notice is that we are now looping through our mesh parts instead of our mesh effects. Our mesh part has an effect property that we need to set. We are using lights (although it is a simple ambient light) and there is no need to set that value because our effect file is always using the ambient value. We see we are setting our texture just like before, as well as our camera projection and view. After setting our world just like before we set this mesh part's effect to our effect. We can now run the application and basically get the same results that we got from the basic effect.

Actually, the basic effect has a little better lighting structure, as it is using three directional lights and we are using a simple ambient light. There is plenty of material available on the Internet that shows how to set up directional lights, so we do not go into the details here. Instead, we will wrap up this chapter so we can cover some information in the next chapter that is not quite so abundant on the Web.

Summary

In this chapter, we discussed the purpose of shaders and went over the syntax needed to create a shader. We broke out each part of a shader and explained what it was used for. We then actually created a full effect file complete with a technique and pass. We modified an existing application to use our new effect we created in this chapter instead of the BasicEffect built into XNA. At this point we understand the basics of the HLSL syntax and how to structure a shader to use in our games. In the next chapter, we take it a step further and discuss vertex displacement as well as postprocessing effects.

CHAPTER 13

Advanced HLSL

In the last chapter we learned the basics of HLSL. In this chapter, we take those concepts further by doing vertex displacement in our vertex shaders and by doing postprocessing techniques in our pixel shaders.

Vertex displacement is simply changing the position of our vertices through our vertex shader. Postprocessing is the process of taking a completed (or partial) scene and rendering that scene to a texture. It then takes that texture and processes it with a pixel shader to make some interesting effects.

Vertex Displacement

We are going to create an interesting effect that will allow us to move our vertices around. Shaders are not only used to texture and shade our scene, but can actually transform it as well.

To begin, we are going to use the same Load3DObject code we left off with in the last chapter. We need to load that solution. We are going to modify our effect file to modify the vertex position it is passed in before passing it on to the rasterization stage.

We will be passing another value to our shader to accomplish this. We are going to pass in a timer based on our game time that we will scale down. Using this data our vertex shader will combine this with an offset to determine a new vertex location for the vertex it is shading. Let's set up our variable inside of the effect file by adding the following declaration:

```
float Timer : TIME;
```

We are using the TIME semantic, which signifies we are passing in our game time in seconds to the shader. We also declare an offset of how far out we are going to move our vertex position. We are setting it to 100 because the objects are so large in this demo:

```
float Offset = 100.0f;
```

We are going to use simple sine and cosine functions to create our new vertex position. We need to add the following code at the top of our vertex shader:

```
float4 Pos = float4(input.Position.xyz,1);
float y = Pos.y * Offset + Timer;
float x = sin(y) * Offset;
Pos.x += x;
```

We set our position and then create an offset for our y position. We also add in the amount of time to create a variance of where that position is every frame. We then take that y position and calculate our real x position with the sine of the calculated y.

Now, we can modify our game code to actually pass in our timer parameter. We need to add this statement inside of the inner foreach loop in the DrawModel method:

```
effect.Parameters["Timer"].SetValue(time);
```

We need to set the value of our time variable inside of the Update method, so we can add the following line of code:

```
time += (float)gameTime.ElapsedGameTime.TotalSeconds;
```

We can declare time as a private member field of type float. We are also going to modify the ambient color we are passing in. Of course we do not need to, but this is to show that we can pass in a system-defined color as a Vector4, and an asteroid fluctuating in shape looks cooler when it does not have a typical asteroid color. For this exercise we are going set our asteroid color to red by just changing our ambient light color to red with the following code:

```
effect.Parameters["AmbientColor"].SetValue(Color.Red.ToVector4());
```

The preceding code should replace the existing statement where we set the color to a light gray. The final change we make is to modify our first asteroid so it does not spin. It makes it harder to see our vertex displacement if it is spinning. We need to replace the first world variable initialization with the following statement, which simply removes the y rotation:

```
world =  Matrix.CreateTranslation(new Vector3(0, 0, -4000));
```

We can run the code and see our asteroid is doing a wavy effect. With some imagination and some decent algorithms we could really make our models look different by changing vertex position through the vertex shader. Vertex displacement can also be used to deform objects when they collide. The options are endless with vertex displacement.

We could add in the following line to our shader code to also modify the y position of the vertex:

```
Pos.y += cos(y) * Offset;
```

This will effectively get each vertex to move in a circular motion.

To see the effects better, we can change our render states to turn off culling and set our scene to a wireframe. We could do this inside of our XNA game, but we can also do it inside of our shader. We can add the following code to the beginning of our pass to turn off culling and to render our objects in wireframe mode:

```
CullMode = None;
FillMode = Wireframe;
```

Postprocessing

Postprocessing is a great way to get excellent effects in our games that can really help them look polished. To set up our game to do postprocessing, we have to render our scene to a texture. We then draw that texture over the entire screen after running it through our pixel shader. As a result, our entire scene is generated as before and then it appears as though we are running the entire scene through a filter.

Setting Up Our Game Code

We can easily display a texture on our screen as we learned in the 2D part of this book, but we do not know how to actually render our scene to a texture. We explore the code for doing that soon, but first we should look at the overall flow of the tasks we need to perform to handle postprocessing:

Declare our render target member field.

We initialize our render target inside of the `LoadGraphicsContent` method.

Inside of the `Draw` method, we do the following:

Tell our device to draw to our render target instead of the back buffer.

Clear our device.

Draw our scene as normal (it will draw to our render target).

Resolve render target.

Reset render target back to null (so we will draw on our back buffer).

Clear device.

Start effect.

Start sprite batch in immediate mode.

Start effect pass.

Get generated texture.

Draw generated texture.

End sprite batch.

End effect pass.

End effect.

Although it might seem like a lot of steps, it really is not that bad. We can look at steps we have not touched on previously in more detail. We can do postprocessing on our 2D or 3D scenes; it does not matter because we are ultimately processing a 2D texture anyway.

So that we can easily see our effects, we are going to copy our SimpleGame project from Chapter 11, "Creating a 2D Game." We are going to modify our game so that the game play will be run through a postprocessing filter. We will not be modifying our XELibrary, but we should copy that over so we do not need to modify our solution as it is using it as a project reference.

From the steps earlier, we know we need to declare our render target member field. We also know we will need an effect later on, so we might as well declare that. We can declare those variables at the top of our game code:

```
private RenderTarget2D renderTarget;
private Effect effect;
```

We need to initialize our render target once we have a valid graphics device. We can also load up our effect file. Both of those tasks can be performed inside of the LoadGraphicsContent method as follows:

```
GraphicsDevice device = graphics.GraphicsDevice;
renderTarget = new RenderTarget2D(device, device.Viewport.Width,
    device.Viewport.Height, 1, device.DisplayMode.Format,
    device.PresentationParameters.MultiSampleType,
    device.PresentationParameters.MultiSampleQuality);
effect = content.Load<Effect>(@"Content\Effects\NightTime");
```

The effect we added is called NightTime so we can create an Effects subfolder in our Content folder. We will create a new text file in that folder and call it NightTime.fx later. We set up our render target by passing in our device, the width and height of our target (in this case it is going to be the whole screen so we just used our viewport's width and height) along with the number of mip levels we want to create (one in our case) and the format we will use is the current format of our device. We also pass in our device's multi-sample type and quality.

Next up in our list is modifying the Draw method. We need to tell our device to draw to the render target we just created and initialized instead of rendering to the back buffer like it does normally. To do this, we need to add the following statement at the top of the Draw code:

```
GraphicsDevice device = graphics.GraphicsDevice;
if (State != GameState.StartMenu)
    device.SetRenderTarget(0, renderTarget);
device.Clear(Color.Black);
```

We replaced our first line, `graphics.GraphicsDevice.Clear(Color.Black);`, with the preceding code to do a couple of things in one pass. First, we just created a reference to our device to save us some typing. Then we made sure we are only going to do our effect when we are not in our start menu screen. This is optional, of course. We let the device know that we are going to be rendering to our render target instead of the back buffer by setting the render target on the device. Finally, we clear our device to black, which is actually the next step listed in the preceding steps.

Now that we have our device rendering to our render target, we need to actually draw our scene. The remaining `Draw` code does not change as it is already drawing our scene. At this point, though, it is drawing it to our 2D render target and not our back buffer, which will get put on the screen, so we need to do some things to get scene to show up again. If we ran the code at this point, when we click Start, the screen would freeze. It really is not frozen; it is just the last thing we drew on our screen was the last frame of our start menu before starting the game.

We need to get our scene rendering again, and to do that we need to complete the next step, which is resolving our render target. When we tell our device to resolve itself to our render target, which in this case is a 2D render target, the device will store the scene in memory. We can then get the scene by calling `renderTarget.GetTexture()`, but we are getting ahead of ourselves. After we resolve our render target, we then need to clear the device's render target so that when we draw the texture it will actually show up on the back buffer and our screen. To do both of these things (resolve our render target and clear our device's render target) we add the following code:

```
device.ResolveRenderTarget(0);
device.SetRenderTarget(0, null);
```

After clearing our device, we need to start our effect. We need to start our sprite batch in immediate mode so our effect can be applied as the texture is drawn. Then we need to begin our effect's pass. We can add that code now:

```
device.Clear(Color.Black);
effect.Begin();
sb.Begin(SpriteBlendMode.None, SpriteSortMode.Immediate, SaveStateMode.None);
EffectPass pass = effect.CurrentTechnique.Passes[0];
pass.Begin();
```

Now we can actually draw our render target's texture on the screen. When we called `ResolveRenderTarget` earlier, it applied the surface it was drawing on into our 2D render target. We can get access to that texture by calling the `GetTexture` method. We will do that and finish our effect's pass and close up our sprite batch and our effect in general:

```
sb.Draw(renderTarget.GetTexture(), Vector2.Zero, Color.White);
sb.End();
pass.End();
effect.End();
```

It did not take a lot of code to have our objects drawn onto a texture. We could use the same method to draw a rearview mirror in a racing game, and there are plenty of uses for drawing our scene to a texture. In fact, we could use this technique for any mirror in a game. We could even apply the texture to a 3D object and render that on the screen. It is pretty cool to think of all the ways we could use this and we have not even done our postprocessing effect yet. Let's do that now by creating our NightTime.fx file.

Setting Up Our Effect Code

Our NightTime effect file is actually pretty simple. It does not have a vertex shader because our sprite batch handles passing in a full-screen quad for us. All we need to do is create a pixel shader with our desired effect. As the name of the effect implies, we are going to create a nighttime effect. Really, we are just going to increase the blue color and decrease the red and green colors for each pixel. The entire code for this file is as follows:

```
sampler TextureSampler;

struct PixelInput
{
    float2 TexCoord : TEXCOORD0;
};

float4 pixelShader(PixelInput input) : COLOR
{
    float4 color = tex2D(TextureSampler, input.TexCoord);
    color.b = color.b + color.b * .25;
    color.rg *= .15;
    return( color );
}

technique Default
{
    pass P0
    {
        PixelShader = compile ps_2_0 pixelShader();
    }
}
```

That is very simple. To start, we have to have a sampler so our sprite batch can pass in our texture. We use that texture inside of our pixel shader function by using the intrinsic text2D function. We learned that we pass in the texture coordinate of the pixel we are wanting from our texture and it will return the color of that pixel. We get the coordinates from our sprite batch as well, so it has saved us some work yet again.

The actual effect is only two lines of code:

```
color.b *= 1.25;
color.rg *= .15;
```

We are adding 25 percent to the blue component of our pixel color. We are decreasing our red and green values to 15 percent of what they originally were. This gives us a nice shade of blue that emulates nighttime. If we run our game, we can see we are now running and kicking at night.

More Postprocessing Examples

Now that we see how easy it is to set up a postprocessing effect, we can take a little time and indulge ourselves by making some attractive effects for our games. Some of these will be practical to use in a game, and others will just be fun to experiment with.

Negative Image

We can get the negative of an image by doing a simple inversion of our colors. This is very simple: We just subtract our color from 1. That is it. We just need to replace the code inside of our pixel shader function with this code:

```
float4 color = 1.0f - tex2D(TextureSampler, input.TexCoord);
return( color );
```

We had to cast our 1 as a float4. This effectively put a 1 in the RGBA components. So we are subtracting 1 from our red, 1 from our green, 1 from our blue, and 1 from our alpha, which does not affect our end result because our sprite batch is being rendered with a blend mode of None. If we were using alpha blending we would want to set our alpha to a fully opaque value

```
color.a = 1.0f;
```

Switching RGB Values

Another simple effect we can make is to switch out our red, green, and blue values. With the following effect, the hero's red shirt will become green:

```
float4 color = tex2D( TextureSampler, input.TexCoord);
return( color.brga );
```

Without using our swizzle we would have had to create a temporary value to store one of the colors and then swap the rest around. With swizzling we can just modify the order in which we are returning our components. Simply returning color is the same as returning color.rgba, so by returning color.brga we are passing blue as the first component, red as the second, and so on.

We can see that when our hero dies, the screen turns green now instead of red. The sky is red instead of blue, and the grass is red instead of green. This is not necessarily useful in a real game, but it could be—perhaps the goal of a level is to correctly fix the colors by solving some puzzles.

Sharpening the Image

We can sharpen our image, much like the paint programs do, by subtracting color values of surrounding pixels with our pixel and by adding other surrounding pixels' colors in. Before we look at the code, it is important to understand that that we can do arithmetic on the x and y values of our texture coordinates in the same call. This means that input.TexCoord + 1 is the same as input.TexCoord.x + 1, input.TexCoord.y + 1. Also, we are not required to sample in pixel increments. In other words, we can use floats if appropriate to sample a part of a pixel. We can see how we do this in the following code to sharpen our image:

```
float sharpAmount = 15.0f;
float4 color = tex2D( TextureSampler, input.TexCoord);
color += tex2D( TextureSampler, input.TexCoord - 0.0001) * sharpAmount;
color -= tex2D( TextureSampler, input.TexCoord + 0.0001) * sharpAmount;
return( color );
```

We sample a small offset and increase the intensity of the color by multiplying it by 15. That is our sharpening amount. We can adjust this value to get different effects.

Blurring an Image

Next on the list of effects is blurring. We actually did this already in our sharpen effect. We just need to leave off our sharp amount and we can use an average of several samples around us. The code for this is as follows:

```
float4 color = tex2D( TextureSampler,
    float2(input.TexCoord.x+0.0025, input.TexCoord.y+0.0025));
color += tex2D( TextureSampler,
    float2(input.TexCoord.x-0.0025, input.TexCoord.y-0.0025));
color += tex2D( TextureSampler,
    float2(input.TexCoord.x+0.0025, input.TexCoord.y-0.0025));
color += tex2D( TextureSampler,
    float2(input.TexCoord.x-0.0025, input.TexCoord.y+0.0025));
color = color / 4;
return( color );
```

Most of the time this is implemented by sampling only four surrounding colors. We can play with our numbers to get the desired effect we are looking for. In this case, as we are adding each color, we just need to make sure we take the average at the end. Otherwise we would have a very bright image because the color values would be so high.

Embossed

We can create an embossed effect by slightly modifying our sharpen image code. Instead of initializing our color by sampling the pixel we are on, we just set the red, green, and blue values to .5 (gray). We also set the alpha channel to 1.0 for fully opaque. Then we basically do the same thing we did for our sharpening effect by sampling an offset and sharpening it by a particular weight amount, then subtracting the same weight amount from another sample. Finally, we take an average of our red, green, and blue components to keep a flat gray look. The end result is the embossed raised effect we were looking for. The code to create this effect is shown here:

```
float sharpAmount = 15.0f;
float4 color;
color.rgb = 0.5f;
color.a = 1.0f;
color -= tex2D( TextureSampler, input.TexCoord - 0.0001) * sharpAmount;
color += tex2D( TextureSampler, input.TexCoord + 0.0001) * sharpAmount;
color = (color.r+color.g+color.b) / 3.0f;
return( color );
```

Grayscale

After doing the embossing effect, it does not seem a stretch to do a grayscale effect. We can do that with the following code:

```
float4 color = tex2D( TextureSampler, input.TexCoord);
color.rgb = dot(color.rgb, float3(0.3, 0.59, 0.11));
return( color );
```

One would think that we could just use the last line from the embossed effect by averaging our red, green, and blue values. Unfortunately, the human eye is more sensitive to green brightness than it is to blue, so there is a standard computation that is used to convert colors to grayscale. It weights the colors differently. After processing the colors with the appropriate weights, our scene is in black and white.

What if we wanted one side to be gray and the other side to be color? We could use the following code:

```
float4 color = tex2D( TextureSampler, input.TexCoord);
if (input.TexCoord.x > 0.5)
    color.rgb = dot(color.rgb, float3(0.3, 0.59, 0.11));
return( color );
```

So if our x texture coordinate was the middle of the screen or further out we would average out the colors, otherwise we would leave the initial color of our texture on the left side of our screen.

What if we wanted to have a gradient effect? Let's say we wanted the left and right of our screen to be gray and the middle of our screen to be fully saturated. To do that, we would just need to use the following code:

```
float4 color = tex2D( TextureSampler, input.TexCoord);
float4 gs = dot(color.rgb, float3(0.3, 0.59, 0.11));
if (input.TexCoord.x > 0.5f)
    color = lerp(gs, color, (1 - input.TexCoord.x) * 2);
else
    color = lerp(gs, color, input.TexCoord.x * 2);

return( color );
```

The first two lines were discussed earlier. We get our color of the pixel based on the texture coordinates. We then calculate the grayscale value for that same pixel. We have the same `if` statement checking to see if we are drawing pixels on the left side of the screen or the right side. If we are drawing on the left side of the screen we lerp (check back to the last chapter for a definition of what this intrinsic function does) between our color value and our grayscale value. We double the x component of our texture coordinate because we want to be fully colored in the middle of our screen. We do the exact same thing on the right side of our screen, except we subtract our texture coordinate from 1 and multiply the result by 2.

Chalk

We are going to modify our sharpen effect again to produce something that looks like a chalk effect. Our sharpening amount will be 100 and our sampling offset will only be 1/1000 instead of 1/10000. The code for this is as follows:

```
float sharpAmount = 100.0f;
float4 color = tex2D( TextureSampler, input.TexCoord);
color += tex2D( TextureSampler, input.TexCoord - 0.001) * sharpAmount;
color -= tex2D( TextureSampler, input.TexCoord + 0.001) * sharpAmount;
return( color );
```

Wavy

We can also modify the position we are going to read from to set our color instead of modifying the color itself. A great way to show this off is to create an effect that makes it appear that our scene is underwater or that we are looking at it through the side of a fish tank. There are subtle x and y movements happening that make the scene wavy. We can see the following code:

```
float y = input.TexCoord.y;
float x = input.TexCoord.x;
y = y + (sin(x*100)*0.001);
float4 color = tex2D(TextureSampler, float2(x,y));
return( color );
```

We get the x and y values passed to us from the application. We then modify our y value by adding in the sine of our x value multiplied by 100. We then divide it by 1,000

(* 0.001). This creates a small wavy effect. For some interesting results, modify the 100 and .001 numbers.

TIP

To make the hero look like he is running up a hill, change 100 to 1 and .001 to 0.1.

Summary

We have seen ways to use vertex shaders to displace our vertices to create interesting effects, as well as pixel shaders to do postprocessing. We were able to modify our example to make our asteroid look like it was morphing with very little code. Shaders are very powerful.

We spent the majority of the chapter covering postprocessing effects and how they can be used on 2D and 3D scenes alike. We went through many examples to show some of the more common effects. This should give us a good starting point to branch out and try more complex things with shaders.

13

PART VI

Physics and Artificial Intelligence

IN THIS PART

Physics Basics

This chapter gives an overview of some important physics principals we might need to model in our games. We do not go through an exhaustive list by any means. Physics in general requires an understanding of calculus, but there will not be any explanation of the math involved to create our games physics. It is very important to understand matrix and vector math to be able to actually write any code that simulates real-world physics in 2D and 3D games.

Kinematics

To start our discussion of physics we will talk about motion dynamics, particularly kinematics. Kinematics is the study of moving objects. It does not take into consideration any forces applied to those objects (that made them move).

To understand the movement of objects, we need to first understand our objects themselves. For starters, objects have a position, velocity, and acceleration. Just like the position of an object, the velocity and acceleration are also represented by vectors. We know that vectors have a magnitude (length) and a direction. The magnitude of the velocity vector contains our speed value.

Many physics formulas are based on time. Fortunately, we have access to our game time in our update method where we will be doing (or calling) all of our physics calculations. We have already used velocity in our demos up until this point. We moved our enemies in Chapter 11, "Creating a 2D Game," a few pixels every second. We made sure that no matter what frame rate our game was running at, we always moved the same distance for every second by taking into account how long it took between our update calls by getting the change in time (delta) between each time our method was executed.

Velocity

We also have handled velocity already. That is how fast we are moving our object. In the preceding paragraph we also discussed how we have used velocity already by having our enemies move at the same pace. Their velocity was constant. If we wanted to vary it, we could add acceleration. Whereas velocity is the rate of change of our distance traveled, acceleration is the rate of change of our velocity. Both are measured by our change in time. In other words, at time stamp A (0 seconds), we are at position 0 meters and at time stamp B (5 seconds) we are at position 25 meters. Our velocity is the rate of change between those two points for the amount of time between our two time stamps; in this case it would be 25 meters per 5 seconds (25 m/5 s) or 5 meters per second (5 m/s). The formula for our velocity can be seen here:

$$v = \Delta s\ /\ \Delta t$$

Δs (delta s) is our change in position between two points, our displacement. Δt is our change in time. Using those values we can compute our velocity. Of course, this also means that we can determine how long it will take us to get somewhere if we know our velocity and our starting and ending points. For example, if we know we are going 5 m/s, our starting position is 0 m, and our ending position is 10 m, we know we will be at our destination in 2 seconds.

Acceleration

Acceleration, on the other hand, is the rate of change of our velocity for our change in time. So, if we were going 0 m/s at time stamp A (0 seconds) and we were going 21 m/s at time stamp B (3 seconds) and 25 m/s at time stamp C (5 seconds), then we can calculate our acceleration for those last two time stamps. Our formula for acceleration is:

$$a = \Delta v\ /\ \Delta t$$

We can plug in our numbers

$$a = 21m/s\ /\ 3s\ =\ 21m\ /\ s\ *\ 1/3s\ =\ 21m/3s*s = 7m/s\ *\ s = 7m/s^2$$
$$a = 4m/s\ /\ 2s = 4m/s\ *\ 1/2s = 4m/2s*s = 2m/s\ *\ s = 2m/s^2$$

So our first measurement shows our average acceleration was 7 m/s^2 and our second measure shows our average acceleration was 2 m/s^2.

We typically want to add acceleration to our objects, which will need to update the object's velocity. This is as simple as adding our two values together to get a new velocity. Now, if we are adding in acceleration we are just changing our velocity each frame.

If our object is traveling at 50 miles per hour (mph) we know it is traveling at 80.45 kilometers per hour (km/h) because there are 1.609 kilometers in 1 mile. If our acceleration is 16.6 m/s^2, then every second we just need to add that value, but we need to make sure we are using the same units of measure, so we need to convert our km/h values to m/s. We know there are 1,000 meters in a kilometer, so we first multiply that value and the product is 80,450 m/h. However, we need to be in seconds, and we know there are 60 seconds in a minute and 60 minutes is an hour, so the 1 hour becomes 3,600 seconds. We are now in the right unit of measure and our velocity is 80,450 m/3,600 s, or 22.35 m/s. If we are at position (50,0,0) and our velocity is only on the x dimension then when the next second rolls around we should be at position 72.35 and the next second our object should be at 94.70. This represents our change in velocity and does not include any acceleration because we are moving at a constant rate.

If we started to accelerate we only need to add that value in. Using C#, the code would look something like this:

```
model.Velocity.X += model.Acceleration.X;
```

The code assumes we have an object called model that has two vectors, velocity and acceleration. We simply continue to increase our velocity by the amount we are accelerating. We also continue to update our position by our velocity as the following statement shows:

```
model.Position.X += model.Velocity.X;
```

So we are not only updating our object's position by our velocity amount, we are also modifying our velocity based on the acceleration value our object contains.

We are going to write a small acceleration demo to help us understand how these concepts look in code. Let's create a new solution and call it AccelerationDemo. We are going to load up a skybox, so we need to make sure our skybox pipeline assembly is close by so we can tell the IDE to use it. On the CD that accompanies this book, it is inside the root of this chapter's folder. After setting that, by double-clicking Properties and selecting Content Pipeline and clicking Add, we can also reference our XELibrary. We will not be adding any code to the library so we can just reference the assembly. We also need to grab the skybox2.tga file from the CD and add it to the Content\Skyboxes folder of our solution. We need to make sure we associate our Content Processor for the skybox image with our custom SkyboxProcessor. We will also need to grab the sphere0.x object and add that to our Content\Models folder.

To start, we need to add the following private member fields to the top of our demo code:

```
private PhysicalObject sphere = new PhysicalObject();
private InputHandler input;
private FirstPersonCamera camera;
private Model model;
private Skybox skybox;
private float maxSpeed = 163.0f;
private float maxReverseSpeed = 25.0f;
private float constantAcceleration = .5f;
private float constantDeceleration = .85f;
```

We also need to make sure we have our using XELibrary; statement included. PhysicalObject is a small class we are going to make. We can keep this in the same file because it is going to be a small class. Let's add the following class to our Game1.cs file:

```
class PhysicalObject
{
    public Vector3 Position;
    public Vector3 Velocity;
    public Vector3 Acceleration;
}
```

We are going to store our object's position, velocity, and acceleration. We need to set up the game components we declared earlier. As usual, we do this in our constructor:

```
input = new InputHandler(this);
Components.Add(input);
camera = new FirstPersonCamera(this);
Components.Add(camera);
```

We need to add this method, and we need to call it from our `Initialize` method:

```
private void InitializeValues()
{
    sphere.Position = new Vector3(-15.0f, 0, -500);
    sphere.Velocity = Vector3.Zero;
    sphere.Acceleration = Vector3.Zero;
}
```

Now, we need to load our model and skybox content in our `LoadGraphicsContent` method:

```
model = content.Load<Model>(@"Content\Models\sphere0");
skybox = content.Load<Skybox>(@"Content\Skyboxes\skybox2");
```

Now, we need to draw our skybox and our sphere in the `Draw` method:

```
skybox.Draw(camera.View, camera.Projection, Matrix.CreateScale(2000.0f));
Matrix world = Matrix.CreateScale(10.0f) *
                Matrix.CreateTranslation(sphere.Position);
DrawModel(ref model, ref world);
```

We scaled our skybox by 2,000 units and our sphere by 10 units. Our skybox is a light-colored cement texture and our sphere has no color or texture. We need to create a `DrawModel` method. This method is not new. However, so we can more easily see our ball we are just going to change our ambient color on the basic effect to red so it will shade our ball a red color.

```
private void DrawModel(ref Model m, ref Matrix world)
{
    Matrix[] transforms = new Matrix[m.Bones.Count];
    m.CopyAbsoluteBoneTransformsTo(transforms);
```

```
    foreach (ModelMesh mesh in m.Meshes)
    {
        foreach (BasicEffect be in mesh.Effects)
        {
            be.EnableDefaultLighting();
            be.AmbientLightColor = Color.Red.ToVector3();

            be.Projection = camera.Projection;
            be.View = camera.View;
            be.World = world * mesh.ParentBone.Transform;
        }
        mesh.Draw();
    }
}
```

Next is the update code that will actually allow us to speed up and slow down our sphere. We need to add the following code to our Update method:

```
if (input.KeyboardState.WasKeyPressed(Keys.Enter))
    InitializeValues();

float elapsed = (float)gameTime.ElapsedGameTime.TotalSeconds;

//increase acceleration
if (input.KeyboardState.IsHoldingKey(Keys.Space))
{
    sphere.Acceleration.X += (constantAcceleration * elapsed);
}
//decrease acceleration (brake)
else if (input.KeyboardState.IsHoldingKey(Keys.B))
{
    sphere.Acceleration.X -= (constantDeceleration * elapsed);
}
else //coast
{
    sphere.Acceleration.X = 0;
}

sphere.Velocity.X += sphere.Acceleration.X;

if (sphere.Velocity.X > maxSpeed)
    sphere.Velocity.X = maxSpeed;
if (sphere.Velocity.X < -maxReverseSpeed)
    sphere.Velocity.X = -maxReverseSpeed;
```

```
sphere.Position = sphere.Position + (elapsed * sphere.Velocity);

Window.Title = "Acceleration: " + sphere.Acceleration.X.ToString() + " Position: "
+ sphere.Position.X.ToString() + " Velocity: " + sphere.Velocity.X.ToString();
```

If we press the Enter key, we reinitialize our variables just in case our sphere goes far away and we lose it. Next, we check to see if the spacebar is being held down. If it is, we increase our acceleration. If the B key is being pressed, we apply the brake and slow down the sphere and actually let it go into reverse. If we are neither accelerating nor braking, then we are coasting and we set our acceleration value to zero.

We then add our acceleration value to our velocity value and make sure that we have not increased our speed over the maximum speed we have set up. We also check to make sure we are not reversing the sphere any faster than we allowed either.

Finally, we set our new position by adding our new velocity to our current position. We display the current values of our position, velocity, and acceleration in our window title so we can see the values easily.

We can run this demo and see that our sphere is sitting still. To make it move, we only need to press the spacebar or the B key. If we lose sight of our sphere, we can press the Enter key to reset the values. This demo shows how we can set the acceleration based on input and modify our velocity based on the acceleration we set.

Force

Force changes the acceleration of an object. For example, when we hit a baseball the acceleration of the ball is changed because we applied force (in the form of swinging a bat) to the ball. If the ball was pitched to us, then it had a positive acceleration coming toward us; when we hit it we changed the acceleration to the negative direction.

Force is a very important concept in physics. This is understandable because it is constantly in effect. For example, even when we are sitting down there is a force of gravity keeping us in the chair. The first example with the baseball is considered contact force, as an object (the bat) made contact with the ball to make it change its acceleration. Gravity is considered a field force (or a force-at-a-distance) because it does not have to have contact with the object while applying force. Gravity causes items to be drawn to the Earth's core. This is why we can sit (and stand) and not float about. This is why we have weight. It is all because of gravity. If there were an object on the floor it would be sitting on the floor because of gravity. If we tried to pick it up, we would have to apply enough force to counteract the force that gravity is applying to it. In outer space, objects float around and are very light because regardless of their mass (assuming it is not as large as a planet) they do not weigh much at all because there is no force pushing them down.

Mass is the amount of physical matter an object comprises. With the force of gravity our mass has weight. The more mass an object has, the more it weighs on Earth. The larger the mass, the more force is applied against that object to bring it toward the Earth's core. When we try to move an object, we have to apply enough force to accelerate the object.

If we do not apply as much force to lift the object upward as gravity is applying to the object downward, the object will not move.

Newton's Second Law of Motion describes the relationship between an object's mass and acceleration with the force applied to the object. The formula is:

```
F = ma
```

We know that acceleration is a vector, and force is a vector as well. This makes sense as we think about the fact that when we hit that baseball it can go in multiple directions (pop fly, foul ball, etc.). This is because we are creating acceleration when we apply force to the object at different angles. Our mass is a scalar value (one dimension) and not a vector (multiple dimensions). We could also write the preceding formula as:

```
a = F/m
```

In our previous code example we had an invisible force acting on our sphere that was generating the acceleration of the sphere. Newton's First Law of Motion basically states that objects that are in motion stay in motion and objects that are sitting still stay still. Our previous demo shows this as well, as if we do not press any keys to accelerate our sphere it stays at rest. Once we do apply some force to the object, it accelerates and stays in motion.

Collisions

This section is going to be pretty detailed. It is something that is best read with a physics textbook handy to get the full effect. It is not required though, and the actual code is easier to understand than the math involved. Regardless, it is very beneficial to understand the reason why this works so we can do further research to determine the best way to model other important physics needed in our games.

Momentum

When the objects stay in motion, it is because of momentum. Objects in motion have momentum. Momentum is used to measure our object's mass and velocity. The formula to calculate momentum is:

```
p = mv
```

p is our object's momentum and we know that m is our object's mass and v is the velocity. The reason we know about mass is because of our force formula. We can substitute our formula for acceleration in our formula for force:

```
F = ma = m Δv / Δt
```

Now we can multiply our change in time on both sides, which produces:

```
FΔt = ma = m Δv
```

Impulse

FΔt is called an impulse. We can do some vector math and multiply our mass by our change in velocity (the right side of our equation) and see that it can be represented by:

FΔt = Δ(mv)

Therefore, we know that our impulse is equal to the change in momentum, which can be written as follows:

FΔt = Δp

Conservation of Momentum

When objects collide their momentum changes. To be more precise, the magnitude of the momentum remains the same just in the opposite direction. This is how we can model our collision response. We can reflect our objects off of each other, knowing that whatever their momentum was before they collided will remain, but their direction will be reversed. We just threw two objects into the mix but have only been discussing momentum on a single object. How does this change our momentum formula? Fortunately, it does not. This is called the law of conservation of momentum and it means the total momentum for the objects is constant and does not change. This is true because any momentum changes are equal in magnitude and opposite in direction. This is expressed with the following formula:

$p_1 + p_2 = p_1 + p_2$

Kinetic Energy

Now we can discuss Newton's Third Law of Motion, which basically says that for every action there is an equal and opposite reaction. Whatever momentum one object decreases, the other object increases. As momentum is transferred from one object to another there is another physical property that takes place—kinetic energy. Kinetic energy is energy associated with moving objects. It is the amount of energy needed to make an object that is sitting still move. It is also the amount of energy needed to make an object moving stop and sit still. The formula for kinetic energy is:

$E_k = 1/2 \; m \; v^2$

When a collision occurs and the amount of kinetic energy is unchanged it is considered to be an elastic collision. When kinetic energy is lost it is considered to be an inelastic collision. Objects that collide in the real world will deform and cause a loss of kinetic energy. If the objects do not deform, no energy is lost.

Coefficient of Restitution

The coefficient of restitution is the measurement of how elastic or inelastic our collision is based on the types of object that are colliding. The formula for coefficient of restitution is:

$$e = (v_{2f} - v_{1f}) / (v_1 - v_2)$$

The coefficient of restitution models the velocity before and after a collision takes place and the loss of kinetic energy happens. The typical value for e is between 0.0 and 1.0 inclusive. A value of 0.0 means the collision is inelastic and 1.0 means the collision is elastic. The values in between will have a proportionate elastic collision effect. The subscripts on the preceding formula are specifying which vectors we are using: 1 and 2 are the two objects and f is the final velocity of that vector after the impact of the collision.

Conservation of Kinetic Energy

We need to discuss the conservation of kinetic energy, which says that the sum of the kinetic energy of two objects before they collide will be equal to the sum of the kinetic energy of the two objects after they collide. The formula for the conservation of kinetic energy is:

$$E_{k1} + E_{k2} = E_{k1} + E_{k2}$$

Broken down into its components, the formula becomes:

$$\tfrac{1}{2} \, m_1 \, v_1^2 + \tfrac{1}{2} \, m_2 \, v_2^2 = \tfrac{1}{2} \, m_1 \, v_{1f}^2 + \tfrac{1}{2} \, m_2 \, v_{2f}^2$$

Solving Our Final Velocities

When we are modeling collisions we need to determine our final velocities (which is what the f in the earlier formula represents). Before we can do that, we need to expand our conservation of momentum formula from earlier. We will break down the momentum p into its components as follows:

$$(m_1 \, v_1) + (m_2 \, v_2) = (m_1 \, v_{1f}) + (m_2 \, v_{2f})$$

Now, we can solve for our final velocity by combining both of our earlier conservation formulas with our coefficient of restitution formula. Our final velocities will equate to:

$$v_{1f} = (\ (e + 1) \ m_2 \, v_2 + v_1(m_1 - e \, m_2) \ ) \ / \ (m_1 + m_2)$$
$$v_{2f} = (\ (e + 1) \ m_1 \, v_1 - v_2(m_1 - e \, m_2) \ ) \ / \ (m_1 + m_2)$$

This uses the conservation of kinetic energy formula with our conservation of momentum formula, along with our coefficient of restitution, which allows us to solve our final velocity for each object. That is all we need to start modeling realistic collisions.

Creating a Collision Response Demo

We have gone through a lot of formulas, but what does any of this look like in code? Let's take a look. We are going to create a new demo called CollisionDemo. We need to reference our XELibrary component as well.

To start, we need to declare the following private member fields:

```
private Model sphere;

private PhysicalObject[] spheres = new PhysicalObject[3];
private float e; //coefficient of restitution

private InputHandler input;
private FirstPersonCamera camera;
private FPS fps;
```

We also need to set up our game components in our constructor as usual:

```
input = new InputHandler(this);
Components.Add(input);
camera = new FirstPersonCamera(this);
Components.Add(camera);
fps = new FPS(this, false, true);
Components.Add(fps);
```

Our `PhysicalObject` class is pretty small, so we can just add this class to our same Game1.cs code:

```
class PhysicalObject
{
    public Vector3 Position;
    public Vector3 Velocity;
    public float Mass;
    public float Radius;
    public Matrix World;
    public Color Color;
}
```

Our physical object has a position, velocity, mass, and a radius. We need these properties to model the object in a real-world manner. The World matrix is the object's world matrix, so we can draw it inside of our 3D world. The color is the color our object will be when it is drawn in the scene.

Now, we need to initialize the array of physical objects that we will be colliding. We currently have set this to three, but we can have as many as we want. We need to add the following loop inside of our `Initialize` method:

```
for (int i = 0; i < spheres.Length; i++)
    spheres[i] = new PhysicalObject();
```

Now we need to add the sphere0.x file from our last demo to this solution as well. We also need to load that model, which we can do in our `LoadGraphicsContent` method:

```
sphere = content.Load<Model>(@"Content\Models\sphere0");
```

We need to initialize the values of our objects. We can call the following method inside of our `Initialize` method:

```
InitializeValues();
```

Our `InitializeValues` method is as follows:

```
private void InitializeValues()
{
    e = 0.85f;

    spheres[0].Position = new Vector3(-90.0f, 0, -300.0f);
    spheres[0].Velocity = new Vector3(60.0f, 0, 0);
    spheres[0].Mass = 1.0f;
    spheres[0].Color = Color.Silver;

    for (int i = 1; i < spheres.Length; i++)
    {
        spheres[i].Position = new Vector3(25.0f + (i * 25), 0, -300);
        spheres[i].Velocity = new Vector3(-5.0f, 0, 0);
        spheres[i].Mass = 4.0f;
        spheres[i].Color = Color.Red;
    }

    spheres[spheres.Length - 1].Velocity = Vector3.Zero;
    spheres[spheres.Length - 1].Mass = 6.0f;
    spheres[spheres.Length - 1].Color = Color.Black;
}
```

The variable holds our coefficient of restitution. A value of .85 means that the collision will be mainly elastic. Remember, 1.0 would be totally elastic and 0.0 would be totally inelastic (objects would not bounce off each other; instead they would stick together).

The next three sections of code are all doing the same thing: setting the physical properties of our objects. We are setting our position, velocity, and mass. We also set our color just so it looks a little better on the screen. Inside of the for loop, we make sure we space our objects far enough apart by spacing them 25 units apart. The last section just resets the last object our for loop set so we can easily change the last object in our chain. We can definitely modify this code to plot our objects all over the world, wherever we want. To be concise, we currently have them in a row along the x axis.

Our `Draw` method will also have a for loop to draw the objects in the right position. We can see this here:

```
for(int i=0; i<spheres.Length; i++)
    DrawModel(ref sphere, ref spheres[i].World, spheres[i].Color);
```

This is similar to our previous Draw methods, except we are storing our world matrix inside of our sphere object so we do not have to do the translations here. We are also passing the color of this object to our DrawModel method. The code for our DrawModel method is as follows:

```
private void DrawModel(ref Model m, ref Matrix world, Color color)
{
    Matrix[] transforms = new Matrix[m.Bones.Count];
    m.CopyAbsoluteBoneTransformsTo(transforms);

    foreach (ModelMesh mesh in m.Meshes)
    {
        foreach (BasicEffect be in mesh.Effects)
        {
            be.EnableDefaultLighting();

            be.AmbientLightColor = color.ToVector3();
            be.Projection = camera.Projection;
            be.View = camera.View;
            be.World = world * mesh.ParentBone.Transform;
        }

        mesh.Draw();
    }
}
```

The only thing that really changed from the way we have used this method in the past is that we actually passed in a color.

Now we can get to the core of our code: the Update method where we actually model the physics we have been talking about in this section. Here is the Update method:

```
protected override void Update(GameTime gameTime)
{
    float elapsedTime = (float)gameTime.ElapsedGameTime.TotalSeconds;

    if (input.KeyboardState.WasKeyPressed(Keys.Enter))
        InitializeValues();

    for (int i = 0; i < spheres.Length; i++)
    {
        spheres[i].World = Matrix.CreateScale(spheres[i].Mass) *
            Matrix.CreateTranslation(spheres[i].Position);

        Vector3 trans, scale;
        Matrix rot;
        MatrixDecompose(spheres[i].World, out trans, out scale, out rot);
```

```
            spheres[i].Radius = scale.Length();
        }

    for (int a = 0; a < spheres.Length; a++)
    {
        for (int b = a + 1; b < spheres.Length; b++)
        {
            if (a == b)
                continue; //don't check against yourself

            float distance = (spheres[a].Position -
                              spheres[b].Position).Length();
            float tmp = 1.0f / (spheres[a].Mass + spheres[b].Mass);

            float collisionDistance = distance - (spheres[a].Radius +
                                      spheres[b].Radius);

            if (collisionDistance <= 0)
            {
                Vector3 velocity1 = (
                    (e + 1.0f) * spheres[b].Mass * spheres[b].Velocity +
                    spheres[a].Velocity * (spheres[a].Mass - (e * spheres[b].Mass))
                    ) * tmp;

                Vector3 velocity2 = (
                    (e + 1.0f) * spheres[a].Mass * spheres[a].Velocity +
                    spheres[b].Velocity * (spheres[b].Mass - (e * spheres[a].Mass))
                    ) * tmp;

                spheres[a].Velocity = velocity1;
                spheres[b].Velocity = velocity2;
            }
        }
        spheres[a].Position = spheres[a].Position +
            (elapsedTime * (spheres[a].Velocity));
    }
    base.Update(gameTime);
}
```

As soon as we start the program, our simulation will run. To reset the scene to all of the initial values, we just have to press the Enter key. The first for loop in our method updates our object's world matrix information. We are scaling our object by the amount of mass we have associated with our object. This is not needed, but it adds a nice visual effect when we run the demo. We also make sure our position is set. We update our position later in this method. While still inside of the first for loop, we also set our object's radius for collision detection. We are really just using the same algorithm we used in our 2D game.

Then we loop through all of our objects, checking each object to every other object each frame. Again, for a small number of objects this method is perfectly acceptable. As we discussed while working on collision detection in our 2D game, there are other ways to manage our objects that can help optimize how we search for our objects to test against collisions. We make sure we are not checking for a collision against our object by just continuing to the next index in our for loop.

For every iteration through our for loop, we calculate the distance between the two objects we are checking by calculating the length of the vector between them. This is identical to the code in our 2D game. Our tmp variable is actually part of our velocity formula.

Next, we calculate collision distance between these two objects. We sum up the radii and take the difference of the distance between our two objects. We can see this in Figure 14.1. If our collision distance reaches zero we have a collision and we do all of the real work of everything we have been discussing this section.

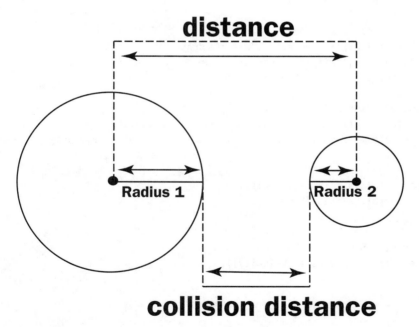

FIGURE 14.1   Calculating the collision distance.

The formula we are using to determine the final velocity of our objects after they collide is listed again here for convenience:

$$v_{1f} = (\ (e + 1)\ m_2\ v_2 + v_1(m_1 - e\ m_2)\ )\ /\ (m_1 + m_2)$$
$$v_{2f} = (\ (e + 1)\ m_1\ v_1 - v_2(m_1 - e\ m_2)\ )\ /\ (m_1 + m_2)$$

Our code that represents these formulas is as follows:

```
float tmp = 1.0f / (spheres[a].Mass + spheres[b].Mass);

Vector3 velocity1 = (
    (e + 1.0f) * spheres[b].Mass * spheres[b].Velocity +
    spheres[a].Velocity * (spheres[a].Mass - (e * spheres[b].Mass))
    ) * tmp;

Vector3 velocity2 = (
    (e + 1.0f) * spheres[a].Mass * spheres[a].Velocity +
    spheres[b].Velocity * (spheres[b].Mass - (e * spheres[a].Mass))
    ) * tmp;
```

We can see it is a direct port. The only difference is that we are calculating the sum of our mass up front and storing the inverse in a tmp variable so we only need to do the division once and then multiply the value for our actual formulas inside of our collision condition in our nested for loop. In the last statement inside of this collision condition, we set the velocity of our objects to the new velocity just calculated. Finally at the end of our outer loop, which iterates through each of our objects, we update the object's position based on its current velocity.

If we run our demo now, we can get a nice collision simulation. There is only one problem: The objects never stop moving! This is because while we labored so hard on the formulas to model the collision itself, we did not take friction into account. Friction, of course, is the force that is ever present on objects that resist their movement. As we slide an object on the ground, friction is generated that basically pushes back against it. As we roll balls, they will roll for a while but will eventually stop because of the frictional force on the ball. Instead of going into the formulas to determine friction we just jump straight to the code because it is very easy to plug into our current demo.

Basically, we just need to subtract our friction amount from our positive velocity vector (or add to our negative vector) to create the new velocity. Of course, we do not want to actually reverse our velocity, so once we reach zero we stop applying the friction force (as there will be none because the object is not moving). This is easy enough to do, so let's get to the code.

First, we need to create another private member field called `friction`:

```
private Vector3 friction;
```

Next, we need to initialize the value at the top of our `InitializeValues` method:

```
friction = new Vector3(-0.025f);
```

We can set our friction value to whatever is appropriate for our environment. We have set up friction as a vector to allow us to have friction in multiple dimensions. Now we need to actually apply the force on our velocity inside of the Update method. We need to put the following code at the bottom of our first for loop in the Update method:

```
ApplyFriction(ref spheres[i].Velocity);
```

The code for that function is as follows:

```
private void ApplyFriction(ref Vector3 velocity)
{
    if (velocity.X < 0)
        velocity.X -= friction.X;
    if (velocity.X > 0)
        velocity.X += friction.X;

    if (velocity.Y < 0)
        velocity.Y -= friction.Y;
    if (velocity.Y > 0)
        velocity.Y += friction.Y;

    if (velocity.Z < 0)
        velocity.Z -= friction.Z;
    if (velocity.Z > 0)
        velocity.Z += friction.Z;
}
```

We are simply updating the velocity vector passed into us by subtracting or adding our friction amount for that component (x, y, or z) of the vector. We do not update our velocity if we are at zero for that axis. When we initialize our friction vector, we set all components to be 0.025, but we could definitely set different values for each component, depending on what we are trying to model. We are also using 3D here because this is a 3D demo, but if we wanted to do it in 2D we could either just ignore the z component or rewrite this to use Vector2—we would also want to change our friction variable to a Vector2 as well.

TIP

Applying friction can also be done by multiplying a constant slightly less than one. Neither approach is fully accurate compared to a real physical model, but both will give realistic results in practice. Applying friction through multiplication involves less code as there is no need to worry about the sign of the velocity and no special handling for zero.

If we run our code, we will see our game is slowing down our objects and they stop after a while due to friction. The scene appears realistic.

A good exercise would be to plot some specific locations for some of these objects. We are only moving in one direction (along the x axis) in this demo, but the code allows for movement in any direction. It only takes us plotting our values correctly and setting our velocities so they will reach the other objects.

To get started, we could just modify our first sphere to have these values for a look at how our objects handle collisions when our velocity has a value in all three components:

```
spheres[0].Position = new Vector3(-25.0f, 5.0f, -430);
spheres[0].Velocity = new Vector3(50.0f, -8.0f, 10);
spheres[0].Mass = 6.0f;
spheres[0].Color = Color.Silver;
```

Well, that ends the rather long section on collision response. This should get us well on our way to creating realistic collisions in our games.

Summary

This was a very technical chapter with lots of formulas and equations. Fortunately, we were able to model some nice real-world physics through it all. We discussed acceleration and velocity in detail, as well as our object's position and how all three of these vectors have a relationship to each other. We discussed force and mass and several of Newton's laws.

We spent a good deal of time on our collision response theory and worked toward a very practical way to apply it in our code. We can now simulate multiple objects colliding in 3D space. We also simulated friction in our code so that our objects look very realistic as they move through our scene. There are many more topics in physics related to game programming that we did not cover, but this chapter provided a good start.

14

CHAPTER 15

Finite State Machines and Game State Management

The next two chapters discuss artificial intelligence (AI). However, this chapter discusses our game engine structure as well. Using finite state machines (FSMs) is critical for believable objects. We discuss FSMs and how we can set up our game itself as an FSM as we structure our game.

Finite State Machine

A finite state machine (FSM) is a machine with a finite set of states. Maybe we should first talk about a state. We discussed this some in Chapter 11, "Creating a 2D Game," where we created the SimpleGame. We had StartMenu, Scene, Won, and Lost as states the game could be in. The finite part simply means that there are a limited number of states. The machine, for our purposes, just means that it is run in software. Therefore, an FSM is piece of software that has a finite number of states that it can be transitioned in and out of.

We had a very simplistic FSM in our 2D game. We just went from our StartMenu to our Scene (playing) state. Then we either went to a Lost or Won state depending on if we kicked all of the enemies or not. Those states just had a timer to fade the screen and then finally, it went back to the StartMenu state to start all over again. We also allowed pausing, which just toggled between our StartMenu state and our Scene state.

A little later in this chapter we will create a more advanced way to handle our game state, but for now we discuss how we can use this same concept to control our objects. We can first think about our enemy objects because they will need to do some thinking. In our 2D game, our enemies only had one thought: Walk to the left. That was it. We just set their velocity and did not do anything else. It was a simple game, after all. In a real game, though, we would want to actually make our enemies think before acting. Perhaps they are not as strong as our hero and need to hide and attack from behind. Perhaps they need to run away when their health gets to a critical level. Perhaps they need to attack as much as possible but then get tired and have to run away. All of these actions are states. Our enemy would have each of these states defined and as the game progressed and an enemy was deployed it would "decide" which state it wanted to be in.

We could even set up a probability table for our different states that would be set on a per-enemy basis. This means that some enemies would attack more and others would retreat. We could assign these probabilities randomly or we could actually create different enemy types (even if they looked the same on the screen), which would inherit from a base enemy object but would override its probability settings. This way as it was deciding which state to be in, an enemy would use its own probability values and determine which state it should go into.

Object-Oriented Design

Once we start thinking about modeling our enemies as objects (which we did to a small degree in our SimpleGame) we can start seeing how we can create some really complex thinking enemies. We can have a base enemy object from which all of our other enemies inherit. Now, we do not want to go overboard with this as we can hurt performance with a lot of virtual methods that need to be overridden. However, we should not sacrifice design to save on performance. The key is balance. Because we are not creating a 3D engine to sell that needs to allow for all sorts of things our consumers might want, we can tighten up our design as we have full control over our code. While we are developing our game, if we decide that we need to inherit from an enemy object, then we can make just the methods we need to override virtual. We have that luxury. If we seal a class, but later realize that we should not have done that, we can easily modify the code to correct the problem. If we were releasing a library however, this would not be appropriate unless breakable changes were clearly communicated. We do not need to worry about that, though, because we have full control over our game code and how our objects will interact with each other.

The main point of this section is to say that we should utilize XNA's game component and game services architecture and when we write our code we should do so in an object-oriented way. It makes the code cleaner and easier to follow and it makes a lot of sense because this is how we see the real world—in objects. Writing code this way really makes it easier to maintain the code.

15

Managing Game States

When we think about our overall game design we should consider the different states our game will be in. When we made the SimpleGame in Chapter 11, we just used an enumerated type that we could pick from to change our game state. This was sufficient for that game, although the method we are going to discuss now would still fit it well without adding a lot of complexity to the game code.

A common question from those starting out making games is this: "How should I structure my game code?" This is a valid question with many different answers, each having its own merit. As with every other aspect of programming, tasks can be in completed many different ways. For this discussion, we use a structure that is not very hard to implement and yields some very nice results in terms of flexibility.

Consider the following as a concrete example of the problem we are trying to solve:

1. Game is loaded and the start or title screen is displayed.

2. Player presses A or Start so the start or title screen is removed and the main menu screen appears.

3. Player selects single player game, the main menu is removed, and a submenu is displayed.

4. The game is a trial game, so a warning message is also displayed prompting the gamer to purchase the game or continue with limited play. The message is displayed on top of our submenu.

5. The player accepts the message and the submenu no longer has the message obstructing the view.

6. The player selects Quick Game from the Single Player menu. The Single Player menu is removed and we start the level by displaying a start level loading screen.

7. When the level finishes loading, the start level screen is removed and we load up our game's scene.

8. The player pauses the game and we bring up a paused screen that overlays our paused game play, which is a little blurred in the background.

Most of those state changes could be done with a simple enumerated type, but there are a couple of situations where a simple enumerated type is not sufficient, such as when we display our message in a modal dialog box that does not allow the gamer to continue until he or she closes the box. However, we do not want to lose sight of the state we were just in. We might use this same message dialog box at other times in our game for a tutorial or hints, and so on. Another example is when the gamer pauses the game. We could just switch our current state with our paused state and then return to our playing state when the pause button is toggled by the gamer, but then we could not display our current game's scene in a blurred (or grayscaled) manner behind our pause screen.

We are going to create a method that will allow us to handle both of those situations and give us the flexibility of having access to the different states from within each state. We are going to create a game state manager class that will control a stack of our different game states. Instead of just switching between states, we are going to implement a stack.

WHAT IS A STACK?

The typical real-world example computer scientists use to explain a stack is a stack of plates. We push and pop items on and off of the stack. In our plates example, we push a plate onto the top of the stack. We can then pop a plate off the top of a stack (but we need to be careful so we don't break it). It is a last in, first out (LIFO) method of processing. We do need to make sure we do not try to pop off a plate if the stack is empty, but that is easy enough to handle.

We are going to use a stack so we can easily handle situations like adding a pause menu on top of our currently playing scene state. This way we can continue to draw our scene even though we are paused. We do not want to update our scene, though, as our enemies would keep coming for us, our timer would continue to count down, and so on. So when we pause, we really do want to pause our game play, but we still want to draw our game scene in its paused state. In fact, we might want to use some of the postprocessing techniques we learned about to blur out, turn gray, or change our scene some other way when we are in a paused state. By using a stack we can accomplish any of those things.

Using a stack for game state management is also beneficial when trying to handle things like dialog boxes, as it effectively pauses the game to give players a hint, tell them the demo's time is up, and so on. Another benefit is multiple menus. We can push a menu state on top of our game play if the user backs out (or pauses) and then offer an options menu and sound options or controller options under that. With a stack we have the flexibility to leave our previous menus displayed, or have our screen replace them. With a simple switch statement on an enumerated type this would not be possible.

Fortunately, with all of this flexibility we do not increase the complexity of our code very much. The principle is an easy one to grasp. We are going to have a game state manager that will manage the different states in our game. It will be implementing a stack to hold our states. Each state will contain logic that determines what happens next. The states themselves will drive the game flow.

Each state will inherit from a base game state abstract class. This abstract class will inherit from the `DrawableGameComponent` class. Each game state that inherits from our abstract state will be a game service. There are two reasons for this. One is that we want our state objects to be singleton objects because we do not want more than one instance of our state created. The second reason we are making it into a game service is because our game state manager will need access to the states.

Our game state manager also inherits from `GameComponent` because it is a game service that our states need a reference to. The game state manager will include an `OnStateChange` event. Normally, other objects would register for an event like this. Instead, we are going to expose the event handler in our game states and have our game manager manage the event registration process for our game states. The exposed event handler in our game states will be called `StateChanged`.

This `StateChanged` method in our game state class can be overridden but by default it will simply check to see if the current state of the game is itself. If it is, it will set its `Enable` and `Visible` properties to true; otherwise it will set them to false. So by default, when a state is loaded, but not at the top of the stack, it will not update itself nor will it draw itself. All active game states will have this event handler executed whenever our game changes state. Each state could also search the stack to see if it contains some other state and if so do some different processing. Because our `StateChanged` event handler will be protected, the actual game states can implement any functionality they want to as the game state changes. We can see that this system is pretty flexible.

Because we want our objects to use the singleton pattern and we want our states to be game services so each state can access other states if needed, we can combine those two requirements because the game service collection can only have one object in its collection with a particular interface. Therefore each one of our states will need its own interface, but we saw earlier that this can be a blank interface. In our situation, we are going to have an `IGameState` interface, but then each one of our states will have its own interface that implements the `IGameState` interface.

We need to be able to make comparisons between our game states. Mainly, we need to make comparisons between our game manager's current state and a particular game state. Enumerated types obviously lend themselves to comparisons easily, but what about actual game state objects? Fortunately, we can just as easily compare our object references and this is why it is important that there is only one instance of the object—so our reference is always the same. We will create a property called `Value`, which is of type `GameState`. This property allows us to perform the comparisons that we need.

Managing Game States Demo

So what exactly does this state game structure look like and how do we actually implement it?

Figure 15.1 shows a partial diagram of our game state structure. We have several interfaces that are just referenced in the diagram. GameStateManager actually has a private stack that holds all of our states. It exposes methods so our states can change state permanently or temporarily by just pushing or popping states on and off the stack. It does not allow direct access to its stack. All of the methods, the property, and the event we see to the side of the GameStateManager are actually in the IGameStateManager interface. We have set up an interface so we can set up our GameStateManager as a game service. This is crucial, as our individual game states will need access to our game state manager.

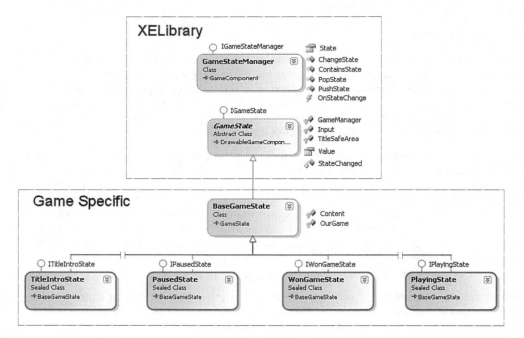

FIGURE 15.1   Our game state design diagram.

GameState is an abstract class that also implements an interface appropriately called IGameState. This interface allows us to use our states as a service, but we need to create individual interfaces for each game state we will have. We can see that in the bottom of Figure 15.1. The property and event handler are in the IGameState interface. The fields are declared inside of the GameState abstract class itself. These fields are ones that all of our states will need access to, and instead of making each one implement them, we let our abstract class do it for us.

Both the GameStateManager class and the GameState class are inside of XELibrary. The rest of the classes are in our game project. This brings us to the BaseGameState, which is optional. The reason it is included here is to make our lives a little easier by exposing two fields that most, if not all, of our game states will need: a reference to the content manager and a reference to our specific game, not the `Microsoft.Xna.Framework.Game` type but our game type like `Game1` or `SimpleGame`. It is not in Figure 15.1, but our actual game class will be the class that declares each game state. Our game class will also expose its own `SpriteBatch`. For situations like this, it is beneficial to have a reference to our actual game, which will become clearer as we get into the code.

Each individual state will inherit from our `BaseGameState` (which inherits from the abstract `GameState` class). Each individual state will also implement its own interface. Each interface will inherit from the `IGameState` interface. All of our individual state interfaces in this demo are empty except our `IFadingState` interface, which exposes a `Color` property that will allow another state to set the color to fade to before pushing it onto the stack.

To start with, we want to create a new project that we can call GameStateDemo. We also know we will be updating our XELibrary, so let's import that project as well. We can copy it from our last chapter. Once we have our solution set up, we can create a new file called interfaces.cs. The code we will be entering into this file is as follows:

```
using System;
using Microsoft.Xna.Framework;
namespace XELibrary
{
    public interface IGameState
    {
        GameState Value { get; }
    }

    public interface IGameStateManager
    {
        event EventHandler OnStateChange;
        GameState State { get; }
        void PopState();
        void PushState(GameState state);
        bool ContainsState(GameState state);
        void ChangeState(GameState newState);
    }
}
```

We can see that it is just as we described before. For several of our `IGameStateManager` methods, we are passing around a reference to our abstract class `GameState`. The code for our `GameState` abstract class is shown here:

```
using System;
using System.Collections.Generic;
using Microsoft.Xna.Framework;
```

```
namespace XELibrary
{
    public abstract partial class GameState : DrawableGameComponent, IGameState
    {
        protected IGameStateManager GameManager;
        protected IInputHandler Input;
        protected Rectangle TitleSafeArea;

        public GameState(Game game)
            : base(game)
        {
            GameManager = (IGameStateManager)game.Services.GetService(
                typeof(IGameStateManager));
            Input = (IInputHandler)game.Services.GetService(
                typeof(IInputHandler));
        }

        protected override void LoadGraphicsContent(bool loadAllContent)
        {
            if (loadAllContent)
            {
                TitleSafeArea = Utility.GetTitleSafeArea(GraphicsDevice, 0.85f);
            }

            base.LoadGraphicsContent(loadAllContent);
        }

        internal protected virtual void StateChanged(object sender, EventArgs e)
        {
            if (GameManager.State == this.Value)
                Visible = Enabled = true;
            else
                Visible = Enabled = false;
        }

        #region IGameState Members
        public GameState Value
        {
            get { return (this); }
        }
        #endregion
    }
}
```

We create a reference to our `GameStateManager` and our `InputHandler` so our states can
have easy access to those objects. We also set our `TitleSafeArea` property for the same

reason. This is, of course, optional. If we determined that only one of our states really needed to be concerned with the title safe area of the screen, then we could take it out and put it directly into the state that needed it. We only set the title safe area property after we know our device has been initialized.

Our `GameState` class also implements the event handler from the `IGameState` interface. This handler is here so we can be notified whenever the game state changes. We will see our `GameStateManager` has an event that will kick off this code (or an overridden version from one of our specific states). By default, our game state will check to see if it is at the top of the stack when it is notified of a changed state event. If our game state is at the top, then it will make sure it is enabled and visible. If it is not, it will disable itself and make itself invisible. We have set both the internal and protected modifiers on this event handler method. The reason for the protected modifier is so our specific derived state classes can override this behavior if needed. The reason for the internal modifier is because we want our `GameStateManager` to handle if the game state should be concerned about a state change or not. Marking the method as internal allows the `GameStateManager` to modify an internal variable of the `GameState` class.

Our `GameState` class inherits from the `DrawableGameComponent` class. We do not need to override the `Update` or `Draw` methods in this class, so we did not include them. Our individual states will most definitely override those methods to perform the tasks they need to.

Finally, our class implements the `Value` property from the interface so our objects can pass around the exact reference of the object. We are not strictly forcing a singleton pattern, but the game services collection does that for us by throwing an error if more than one object implementing the same interface is added to the collection. We know we will only have one instance of our state at any one time, so we can just compare on our value to determine if we are on top on the stack. The `Value` property is the key to comparing our states.

Next, we can look at how our `GameStateManager` is implemented. Although this is not any more complex than our `GameState` class, we break it down into chunks as we talk about it to help us focus on the pieces that are important. To start, we need to set up our using statements:

```
using System;
using System.Collections.Generic;
using Microsoft.Xna.Framework;
using Microsoft.Xna.Framework.Content;
```

Now we can actually get into our class. We start with our private member fields and our constructor:

```
namespace XELibrary
{
    public class GameStateManager : GameComponent, IGameStateManager
    {
```

```
        private Stack<GameState> states = new Stack<GameState>();

        public event EventHandler OnStateChange;

        private int initialDrawOrder = 1000;
        private int drawOrder;

        public GameStateManager(Game game)
            : base(game)
        {
            game.Services.AddService(typeof(IGameStateManager), this);
            drawOrder = initialDrawOrder;
        }
```

We have our private stack that will store all of the active states. We have also declared our event called OnStateChange. The initialDrawOrder and drawOrder fields are needed as we manage our states because each state is a game component and we are tying into the built-in functionality of XNA. However, there is a problem. We have not specified our draw order. We need to set up our draw order and manage it in this class. The initial draw order value could be anything. We have it set as 1,000 and add or subtract 100 from the values. The idea is that we can have up to 10 states at any one time (which is definitely a stretch) and then if we wanted to actually set the draw orders on the other components, that could be done as well. Most of the time this will not be needed, so we should be in good shape. An improvement would be to expose this field as a public property that could be set by our game. The constructor simply registers our object as a service and initializes our drawOrder with the initialDrawOrder value.

Next, we actually look at the methods that push and pop our temporary states onto our stack:

```
public void PopState()
{
    RemoveState();
    drawOrder -= 100;

    //Let everyone know we just changed states
    if (OnStateChange != null)
        OnStateChange(this, null);
}

private void RemoveState()
{
    GameState oldState = (GameState)states.Peek();

    //Unregister the event for this state
    OnStateChange -= oldState.StateChanged;
```

```
//remove the state from our game components
Game.Components.Remove(oldState.Value);

states.Pop();
}
```

The `PopState` method will pop a state from our internal stack. This is actually done by the private `RemoveState` method. The private method finds our current state and unregisters the `OnStateChange` event for that specific state. Finally it removes the state from our game component collection. This might seem like we are breaking the rule of overutilizing game components, but in this situation we will not be changing states that often and even so there will not be that many different states. The main thing we want to shy away from is creating game components for every enemy (or event bullet) in our games. We should have a manager for those.

After our `PopState` method calls the private `RemoveState` method that does all of the things we just talked about, it also subtracts 100 from its draw order so it will be ready to use the correct draw number when another state is pushed back onto the stack. To be more flexible, we could set that value up as a property that could be changed from within our game. We could at the very least set it as a constant. For now, this suffices. Finally, we fire off our `OnStateChange` event so that all of the active game states can know that a state was removed and determine if they should take control of the game or not.

Now we can discuss the counterpart of `PopState` and that is our `PushState` method. This method allows our individual game states (or even our game) to push a new state onto the stack:

```
public void PushState(GameState newState)
{
    drawOrder += 100;
    newState.DrawOrder = drawOrder;

    AddState(newState);

    //Let everyone know we just changed states
    if (OnStateChange != null)
        OnStateChange(this, null);
}
private void AddState(GameState state)
{
    states.Push(state);

    Game.Components.Add(state);

    //Register the event for this state
    OnStateChange += state.StateChanged;
}
```

When a game state is pushed onto the stack we add our magic number of 100 to our draw order. DrawableGameComponents with the highest values get drawn last (which means they will obscure things drawn after it). After updating our draw order value, we set our game state's DrawOrder property so XNA will draw it in the order we want. Next, we call a private method AddState and pass in the state that is to be added to our stack. This method simply pushes the state onto our private stack and then adds the state (which is also a drawable game component) to our game component's collection. This method finishes up by registering the state for the OnStateChange event. The PushState method finishes up by actually firing the event, letting everyone know that the state was just changed.

Having the PopState and PushState methods is what we need, but we also need to replace the entire stack of states with a new state. This is done by the next method. Our ChangeState method allows us to do a permanent state change instead of a temporary one (of just pushing and popping states). We can see the ChangeState method here:

```
public void ChangeState(GameState newState)
{
    //We are changing states, so pop everything ...
    //if we don't want to really change states but just modify,
    //we should call PushState and PopState
    while (states.Count > 0)
        RemoveState();

    //changing state, reset our draw order
    newState.DrawOrder = drawOrder = initialDrawOrder;
    AddState(newState);

    //Let everyone know we just changed states
    if (OnStateChange != null)
        OnStateChange(this, null);
}
```

Because this is an all-out change state request, we pop everything off of the stack. We already have a private method to handle this so we simply call that while there are states in our stack. This is why we have the exposed methods firing our events instead of our private method. When we pop all of these states off, we are not firing a bunch of needless events. Instead we just pop them all off and reset our draw order to our initial value (as well as setting the DrawOrder on the state we are adding) and finally add that state using our predefined method. After we have popped off all of our states and added the one we changed to, we can fire off our OnStateChange to let the new state know that it is up to bat.

Because we do not expose our stack itself, we need to provide a method for our states to see if a certain state exists in the stack. This method can be helpful when a state needs to behave one way when another state is on the stack. It can query to see if the special case needs to be handled by seeing if this other state is in the stack or not. The following

ContainsState method is very simple as it just exposes the Contains method from our stack:

```
public bool ContainsState(GameState state)
{
    return (states.Contains(state));
}
```

The final portion of our GameStateManager code is the property that returns the state that is on the top of the stack:

```
    public GameState State
    {
        get { return (states.Peek()); }
    }
}
}
```

Those three files (Interfaces.cs, GameState.cs, and GameStateManager.cs) are all that we will be adding to our XELibrary. Now, we can move to our actual game project and see what we need to do to start using this game state design. To begin with, we create a folder called GameStates. This is optional, but as our states grow it can be beneficial to have them tucked out of the way. Of course, it might be beneficial to actually have each state in its own folder, complete with its own game components and the logic it uses. This is a personal preference, of course. We can do whatever makes sense for the size of the project we are working on.

The first file we will add to our GameStates folder is the GameStateInterfaces.cs file. This file contents is as follows:

```
using System;
using Microsoft.Xna.Framework.Graphics;
using XELibrary;

namespace GameStateDemo
{
    public interface ITitleIntroState : IGameState { }
    public interface IStartMenuState : IGameState { }
    public interface IOptionsMenuState : IGameState { }
    public interface IPlayingState : IGameState { }
    public interface IPausedState : IGameState { }
    public interface ILostGameState : IGameState { }
    public interface IWonGameState : IGameState { }
    public interface IStartLevelState : IGameState { }
    public interface IYesNoDialogState : IGameState { }
```

```
    public interface IFadingState : IGameState
    {
        Color Color { get; set; }
    }
}
```

We have simply set up a bunch of empty interfaces that all inherit from `IGameState`. This allows our game state objects that we will create in a moment to all be accessed the same way, but it also allows them to be registered as a game service. A game service must have a unique interface. Whenever we determine we need another game state, we need to add a new interface. Our demo will handle each one of these states. The last state, `IFadingState`, does expose a property: `Color`. This allows other states to specify the color to which the screen should fade when this state is loaded.

After setting up our interfaces for each state our game will be using, we can implement our `BaseGameState`. This class is optional, as each individual state could simply inherit from the XELibrary's `GameState` class, but this class is created so our states do not need to have the same code over and over again. The code for our `BaseGameState` is as follows:

```
using System;
using System.Collections.Generic;
using Microsoft.Xna.Framework;
using Microsoft.Xna.Framework.Content;
using XELibrary;

namespace GameStateDemo
{
    public partial class BaseGameState : GameState
    {
        protected Game1 OurGame;
        protected ContentManager Content;

        public BaseGameState(Game game)
            : base(game)
        {
            Content = new ContentManager(game.Services);
            OurGame = (Game1)game;
        }
    }
}
```

This is a very simple class that inherits from `GameState` and exposes two protected fields: `OurGame` and `Content`. We discussed how it is beneficial for our states to have access to our specific game instance and having this hook in place can be good if we find ourselves needing to implement the same code for many of our game states. A good example is our `Content` field. Most of our game states will have to load content so it makes sense to get the content one time and keep using it from the derived classes instead of each one needing to create an instance of the `ContentManager` object.

Now we can take a look at the first state our game will push onto the stack—the TitleIntroState. The purpose of this state would be to display all of the title screens we want to show when our game starts. The demo will not be a game anyway. We are simply setting up a framework that will allow us to easily move between different states of the game. This is very beneficial to set up at the start. To demo this state we are going to load a texture. We can add the Content\Textures folder to our game project and copy the titleIntro.png file from the CD included in this book. The code for this state is as follows:

```
using System;
using System.Collections.Generic;
using Microsoft.Xna.Framework;
using Microsoft.Xna.Framework.Content;
using Microsoft.Xna.Framework.Graphics;
using Microsoft.Xna.Framework.Input;
using XELibrary;

namespace GameStateDemo
{
    public sealed class TitleIntroState : BaseGameState, ITitleIntroState
    {
        private Texture2D texture;

        public TitleIntroState(Game game)
            : base(game)
        {
            game.Services.AddService(typeof(ITitleIntroState), this);
        }

        public override void Update(GameTime gameTime)
        {
            if (Input.WasPressed(0, InputHandler.ButtonType.Back, Keys.Escape))
                OurGame.Exit();

            if (Input.WasPressed(0, InputHandler.ButtonType.Start, Keys.Enter))
            {
                // push our start menu onto the stack
                GameManager.PushState(OurGame.StartMenuState.Value);
            }


            base.Update(gameTime);
        }

        public override void Draw(GameTime gameTime)
        {
            Vector2 pos = new Vector2(TitleSafeArea.Left, TitleSafeArea.Top);
            OurGame.SpriteBatch.Draw(texture, pos, Color.White);
```

15

```
        base.Draw(gameTime);
    }

    protected override void LoadGraphicsContent(bool loadAllContent)
    {
        texture = Content.Load<Texture2D>(@"Content\Textures\titleIntro");
    }

    protected override void UnloadGraphicsContent(bool unloadAllContent)
    {
        if (unloadAllContent)
            texture = null;

        base.UnloadGraphicsContent(unloadAllContent);
    }
    }
}
```

There is nothing special about the code; we are simply loading a texture and drawing it on the screen. We are using the SpriteBatch from our Game1 code (which we have not set up yet). We are also using the GameState's TitleSafeArea property to make sure we render the texture in a TV-friendly manner. Our update method checks to see if the user is trying to exit the game or start the game. If the gamer presses Back (or Escape), the game exits. If the gamer presses Start (or Enter), the game is started by pushing StartMenuState onto the stack. We could have called the ChangedState method, but this allows us to have a small start menu pop up while the main intro and title is still being updated. We are not allowing our main intro and title screen to be updated, though, as we did not override the StateChanged event handler. We will see how to do that in another state we set up. For now, let's move on to our StartMenuState. The code for this state is as follows:

```
using System;
using System.Collections.Generic;
using System.Text;
using Microsoft.Xna.Framework;
using Microsoft.Xna.Framework.Graphics;
using Microsoft.Xna.Framework.Input;
using XELibrary;

namespace GameStateDemo
{
    public sealed class StartMenuState : BaseGameState, IStartMenuState
    {
        private Texture2D texture;

        public StartMenuState(Game game)
```

```
            : base(game)
{
    game.Services.AddService(typeof(IStartMenuState), this);
}

public override void Update(GameTime gameTime)
{
    if (Input.WasPressed(0, InputHandler.ButtonType.Back, Keys.Escape))
    {
        //go back to title / intro screen
        GameManager.ChangeState(OurGame.TitleIntroState.Value);
    }

    if (Input.WasPressed(0, InputHandler.ButtonType.Start, Keys.Enter))
    {
        //got here from our playing state,just pop myself off the stack
        if (GameManager.ContainsState(OurGame.PlayingState.Value))
            GameManager.PopState();
        else //starting game, queue first level
            GameManager.ChangeState(OurGame.StartLevelState.Value);
    }


    //options menu
    if (Input.WasPressed(0, InputHandler.ButtonType.Y, Keys.O))
        GameManager.PushState(OurGame.OptionsMenuState.Value);

    base.Update(gameTime);
}

public override void Draw(GameTime gameTime)
{
    Vector2 pos = new Vector2(TitleSafeArea.Left, TitleSafeArea.Top);
    OurGame.SpriteBatch.Draw(texture, pos, Color.White);

    base.Draw(gameTime);
}

protected override void StateChanged(object sender, EventArgs e)
{
    base.StateChanged(sender, e);

    if (GameManager.State != this.Value)
        Visible = true;
}
```

15

```
    protected override void LoadGraphicsContent(bool loadAllContent)
    {
        texture = Content.Load<Texture2D>(@"Content\Textures\startMenu");
    }

    protected override void UnloadGraphicsContent(bool unloadAllContent)
    {
        if (unloadAllContent)
        {
            texture = null;
        }

        base.UnloadGraphicsContent(unloadAllContent);
    }
  }
}
```

We seal all of our states because we do not have any that need our functionality. Now, we do have a YesNoDialog class we will be creating and it is feasible to think that we could have a DialogState with a YesNoDialog that inherits from the DialogState and some other ChooseWeaponState that might inherit from the DialogState. So we might not want every state to be sealed, but if we are pretty confident we will not be deriving other classes from it, then we should seal the class for a performance gain.

We also register each state as a service in our constructor. This code should be pretty familiar by now. Besides our typical LoadGraphicsContent, UnloadGraphicsContent, Draw, and Update methods we have overridden the StateChange event handler method. We first call our base class so that it will do its normal tasks of enabling and making visible the state if we are on top of the stack and disabling and making invisible otherwise. But then we reset our Visible property even if we aren't on the top of the stack. This way other submenus like our OptionsMenuState can be displayed on top of our main start menu.

Our Update method handles typical start menu actions. If the gamer escapes out of the start menu, we change states to our title menu. At this point, we could just pop but we will also allow getting to this start menu state from our playing state and popping would not be enough.

We can see that we handle a special case if the user presses Enter (to start the game). We first check to see if the playing state is in our stack. If so, then our start menu state was invoked by the playing state and we should just pop ourself off of the stack so the playing state will be on top of the stack again. If the playing state is not on the stack then we are assuming we got here from our title menu so we do a permanent state change to go to our state level state.

The next state we will look at is our Options menu. The code for our OptionsMenuState.cs file is as follows:

```
using System;
```

```
using System.Collections.Generic;
using System.Text;
using Microsoft.Xna.Framework;
using Microsoft.Xna.Framework.Content;
using Microsoft.Xna.Framework.Graphics;
using Microsoft.Xna.Framework.Input;
using XELibrary;

namespace GameStateDemo
{
    public sealed class OptionsMenuState : BaseGameState, IOptionsMenuState
    {
        Texture2D texture;

        public OptionsMenuState(Game game)
            : base(game)
        {
            game.Services.AddService(typeof(IOptionsMenuState), this);
        }

        public override void Update(GameTime gameTime)
        {
            if ((Input.WasPressed(0, InputHandler.ButtonType.Back, Keys.Escape)
            || (Input.WasPressed(0, InputHandler.ButtonType.Start, Keys.Enter))
                GameManager.PopState();

            base.Update(gameTime);
        }

        public override void Draw(GameTime gameTime)
        {
            Vector2 pos = new Vector2(TitleSafeArea.Left + 50,
                TitleSafeArea.Top + 50);
            OurGame.SpriteBatch.Draw(texture, pos, Color.White);

            base.Draw(gameTime);
        }

        protected override void LoadGraphicsContent(bool loadAllContent)
        {
            if (loadAllContent)
            {
                texture = Content.Load<Texture2D>(
                    @"Content\Textures\optionsMenu");
            }
            base.LoadGraphicsContent(loadAllContent);
```

```
        }

        protected override void UnloadGraphicsContent(bool unloadAllContent)
        {
            if (unloadAllContent)
            {
                texture = null;
            }
            base.UnloadGraphicsContent(unloadAllContent);
        }
    }
}
```

The only code of interest is the Update method. We check to see if we should exit the Option menu by checking for either the Escape key or the Enter key (Back button, Start button). We could have multiple menus linked from here. Perhaps an audio options menu or a controller options menu. We would handle them the same way. We would push on the new state and then in that state, let it pop itself off. In the Web world, this is called pogo sticking, as you have to perform so many "clicks" to get to where you want to be. Although this method of having multiple submenus would work and might be the only option in some situations, if it is possible to combine multiple menus so the gamer does not have to go many levels deep that is an advantage.

Next is the StartLevelState code. This code is set up just like the rest we have seen. Instead of listing the entire file the only methods of interest are listed. The Update and StateChanged methods for the StartLevelState can be found here:

```
public override void Update(GameTime gameTime)
{
    if (Input.WasPressed(0, InputHandler.ButtonType.Start, Keys.Enter))
        GameManager.ChangeState(OurGame.PlayingState.Value);
    base.Update(gameTime);
}
protected override void StateChanged(object sender, EventArgs e)
{
    base.StateChanged(sender, e);

    if (GameManager.State == this.Value)
    {
        if (demoMode && !displayedDemoDialog)
        {
            //We could set properties on our YesNoDialog
            //so it could have a custom message and custom
            //Yes / No buttons ...
            //YesNoDialogState.YesCaption = "Of course!";
```

```
            GameManager.PushState(OurGame.YesNoDialogState.Value);
            this.Visible = true;
            displayedDemoDialog = true;
        }
    }
}
```

Our `Update` method is not doing anything special. We simply check for the Enter key (or Start button) and do a permanent change of state to our playing state. Our overridden `StateChanged` method is a little more interesting. The idea here is that our game has not been purchased and we are in a demo mode. As a result, we bring up a dialog box that the gamer must click through to actually start the game. As the game loads a new level, the user will be prompted to purchase the game. We do call the base `StateChanged` method and then we check to see if we are on top of the stack. If we are, we are in demo mode, and we have not displayed the demo dialog box yet, then we push the `YesNoDialogState` (which simulates an annoying pop-up box) onto the stack. We do not do this with the code, but we could set properties to allow us to override the Yes and No caption as well as the message that is being displayed. This way the `YesNoDialogState` can be used for multiple things.

The `YesNoDialogState` does not do anything special. It is simply popping itself off of the stack when the gamer presses Enter or the A button. Its `Update` method is as follows:

```
public override void Update(GameTime gameTime)
{
    if (Input.WasPressed(0, InputHandler.ButtonType.A, Keys.Enter))
        GameManager.PopState(); //we are done ...

    base.Update(gameTime);
}
```

Our `PlayingState` has enough complexity to it (although not very much at all) that we will list the entire code listing:

```
using System;
using System.Collections.Generic;
using System.Text;
using Microsoft.Xna.Framework;
using Microsoft.Xna.Framework.Content;
using Microsoft.Xna.Framework.Graphics;
using Microsoft.Xna.Framework.Input;
using XELibrary;

namespace GameStateDemo
{
    public sealed class PlayingState : BaseGameState, IPlayingState
    {
```

```
SpriteFont font;
Random rand;
Color color;

public PlayingState(Game game)
    : base(game)
{
    game.Services.AddService(typeof(IPlayingState), this);
    rand = new Random();
}

public override void Update(GameTime gameTime)
{
    if (Input.WasPressed(0, InputHandler.ButtonType.Back, Keys.Escape))
        GameManager.PushState(OurGame.StartMenuState.Value);

    // push our paused state onto the stack
    if (Input.WasPressed(0, InputHandler.ButtonType.Start, Keys.Enter))
        GameManager.PushState(OurGame.PausedState.Value);

    if (Input.WasPressed(0, InputHandler.ButtonType.X, Keys.X))
    {
        //simulate game over
        //randomly pick if we win or lose
        if (rand.Next(2) < 1) //lose
            GameManager.PushState(OurGame.LostGameState.Value);
        else //win
            GameManager.PushState(OurGame.WonGameState.Value);
    }

    //simulate activity on the game
    //when updating ...
    if (color == Color.Black)
        color = Color.Purple;
    else
        color = Color.Black;


        base.Update(gameTime);
}

public override void Draw(GameTime gameTime)
{
    OurGame.SpriteBatch.DrawString(font,
        "Playing the game ... playing the game",
        new Vector2(20, 20), color);
```

```
    OurGame.SpriteBatch.DrawString(font,
        "Playing the game ... playing the game",
        new Vector2(20, 120), Color.White);
    OurGame.SpriteBatch.DrawString(font,
        "Playing the game ... playing the game",
        new Vector2(20, 220), Color.Red);

    base.Draw(gameTime);
}

protected override void StateChanged(object sender, EventArgs e)
{
    base.StateChanged(sender, e);

    if (GameManager.State != this.Value)
    {
        Visible = true;
        Enabled = false;
    }
}

protected override void LoadGraphicsContent(bool loadAllContent)
{
    font = Content.Load<SpriteFont>(@"Content\Fonts\Arial");
}
    }
}
```

We start out by setting up a variable to hold a random number along with one to hold our color. We are going to use the random number to simulate winning or losing. We are using the color to "animate" our scene so we can easily tell that our Update method is being called (our state is enabled). We use that color in our Draw method to update the color of one of the lines we are drawing on the screen.

We override our StateChanged method by making sure that we are still drawing on the screen but are not updating. As long as we are in the stack we will draw our scene but we will not update our game (enemies, timers, etc.) unless our state is on top of the stack.

Our Update method will push the StartMenuState back on the stack if the gamer presses the Back button or the Escape key. That state will then either pop itself off so we can continue playing, or change states back to the title screen if they pressed Escape a second time. Our Update method will push the PausedState on the stack if the user paused the game by pressing Start or pressing the Enter key. If the user presses the X button or the X key then we end the game and randomly pick if we win or lose. Based on that random number we either push the LostGameState or the WonGameState.

There are just a few more states to go over before we get to our game code. The next state we will look at is PausedState. We will not even list any code for this one because the only thing of interest is the Update method. All it does is pop itself off the stack if the gamer presses the Enter key (or Start button).

Next are WonGameState and LostGameState. The code for these states is basically identical. The only thing to note for these states is the overridden StateChanged event handler:

```
protected override void StateChanged(object sender, EventArgs e)
{
    if (GameManager.State == this.Value)
    {
        OurGame.FadingState.Color = Color.Red;
        GameManager.PushState(OurGame.FadingState.Value);
    }
}
```

We simply check to see if we are on top of the stack and if so, we set a color (Red for LostGameState, Black for WonGameState) and then push the FadingState onto our stack. We could have kept our fading code as a drawable game component and not have an explicit state for it, but it seemed to make sense in this case. We can look at our last state, the FadingState, now. Our FadingState code is very similar to our previous FadeOut drawable game component. The code is listed here in its entirety:

```
using System;
using System.Collections.Generic;
using System.Text;
using Microsoft.Xna.Framework;
using Microsoft.Xna.Framework.Content;
using Microsoft.Xna.Framework.Graphics;
using Microsoft.Xna.Framework.Input;
using XELibrary;

namespace GameStateDemo
{
    public sealed class FadingState : BaseGameState, IFadingState
    {
        private Texture2D fadeTexture;
        private float fadeAmount;
        private double fadeStartTime;

        private Color color;

        public Color Color
        {
            get { return (color); }
            set { color = value; }
        }
```

```
public FadingState(Game game)
    : base(game)
{
    game.Services.AddService(typeof(IFadingState), this);
}


public override void Update(GameTime gameTime)
{
    if (fadeStartTime == 0)
        fadeStartTime = gameTime.TotalGameTime.TotalMilliseconds;

    fadeAmount += (.25f *(float)gameTime.ElapsedGameTime.TotalSeconds);

    if (gameTime.TotalGameTime.TotalMilliseconds > fadeStartTime+4000)
    {
        //Once we are done fading, change back to title screen.
        GameManager.ChangeState(OurGame.TitleIntroState.Value);
    }
}

public override void Draw(GameTime gameTime)
{
    GraphicsDevice.RenderState.SourceBlend = Blend.SourceAlpha;
    GraphicsDevice.RenderState.DestinationBlend =
                                        Blend.InverseSourceAlpha;
    Vector4 fadeColor = color.ToVector4();
    fadeColor.W = fadeAmount; //set transparancy
    OurGame.SpriteBatch.Draw(fadeTexture, Vector2.Zero,
        new Color(fadeColor));

    base.Draw(gameTime);
}

protected override void StateChanged(object sender, EventArgs e)
{
    //Set up our initial fading values
    if (GameManager.State == this.Value)
    {
        fadeAmount = 0;
        fadeStartTime = 0;
    }
}<$Iprojects;GameStateDemo;FadingState c

protected override void LoadGraphicsContent(bool loadAllContent)
{
```

15

```
        if (loadAllContent)
            fadeTexture = CreateFadeTexture(GraphicsDevice.Viewport.Width,
                GraphicsDevice.Viewport.Height);

        base.LoadGraphicsContent(loadAllContent);
    }

    private Texture2D CreateFadeTexture(int width, int height)
    {
        Texture2D texture = new Texture2D(GraphicsDevice, width, height, 1,
            ResourceUsage.None, SurfaceFormat.Color,
            ResourceManagementMode.Automatic);

        int pixelCount = width * height;
        Color[] pixelData = new Color[pixelCount];
        Random rnd = new Random();

        for (int i = 0; i < pixelCount; i++)
        {
            pixelData[i] = Color.White;
        }
        texture.SetData(pixelData);

        return (texture);
    }
  }
}<$Iprojects;GameStateDemo;FadingState c
```

The logic of this class did not change at all. The only thing we need to focus on is our Update method and our StateChanged event handler. Our Update method is identical to before, except that in our condition once we have waited long enough for our screen to totally become opaque we change our state to our TitleIntroState. When the state changes and we get notified we are making the assumption that we will always be the last state in the list and we initialize fade amount and start time values. Again, this code really did not change much from before. We just plopped it in as a game state. It would have been perfectly acceptable to leave it as a game component, have it work similar to how it did before, and have our WonGameState and LostGameState code do a change state to the TitleIntroState.

One final thing we need to do in our XELibrary is keep our input handler from just exiting our application. We want to add a flag so that when we create our input handler we can let it know if it should handle exiting our application or not. We will change the default behavior to not exit our game. If we are writing a demo, though, it might be beneficial to keep the code in place. We want to replace our current InputHandler's constructor signature with this:

```
private bool allowsExiting;

public InputHandler(Game game) : this(game, false) { }
public InputHandler(Game game, bool allowsExiting)
    : base(game)
        {
            this.allowsExiting = allowsExiting;
```

Then in our Update method we need to wrap our exit conditions with a check of that variable. The code for this is shown here:

```
if (allowsExiting)
{
    if (keyboard.IsKeyDown(Keys.Escape))
        Game.Exit();

    // Allows the default game to exit on Xbox 360 and Windows
    if (gamePadHandler.WasButtonPressed(0, ButtonType.Back))
        Game.Exit();
}
```

We can finally take a look at our game code to see what we need to do to wrap this up. Here are the member fields we need to create:

```
private InputHandler input;
private Camera camera;
private GameStateManager gameManager;

public SpriteBatch SpriteBatch;

public ITitleIntroState TitleIntroState;
public IStartMenuState StartMenuState;
public IOptionsMenuState OptionsMenuState;
public IPlayingState PlayingState;
public IStartLevelState StartLevelState;
public ILostGameState LostGameState;
public IWonGameState WonGameState;
public IFadingState FadingState;
public IPausedState PausedState;
public IYesNoDialogState YesNoDialogState;
```

We have now created a way for our states to easily push other states onto the stack as well as changing states by making each state public. We now initialize all of our states in our constructor:

```
public Game1()
{
```

```
graphics = new GraphicsDeviceManager(this);
content = new ContentManager(Services);

input = new InputHandler(this);
Components.Add(input);

camera = new Camera(this);
Components.Add(camera);

gameManager = new GameStateManager(this);
Components.Add(gameManager);

TitleIntroState = new TitleIntroState(this);
StartMenuState = new StartMenuState(this);
OptionsMenuState = new OptionsMenuState(this);
PlayingState = new PlayingState(this);
StartLevelState = new StartLevelState(this);
FadingState = new FadingState(this);
LostGameState = new LostGameState(this);
WonGameState = new WonGameState(this);
PausedState = new PausedState(this);
YesNoDialogState = new YesNoDialogState(this);

gameManager.ChangeState(TitleIntroState.Value);
}
```

The first part of this code should look very familiar. We are simply initializing our game components and adding them to the collection. This includes our GameStateManager. After that we initialize each one of our states. Remember, each state registers itself as a game service in its constructor. Finally, we "change" our state to our TitleIntroState to kick things off. Things are shaping up nicely.

We initialize our SpriteBatch just like normal so there is no need to show that code. The only thing left is our Draw method, which really is not all that special either. The main thing this shows is that we need to call Begin on our sprite batch and then call our base.Draw method before calling End on our sprite batch:

```
protected override void Draw(GameTime gameTime)
{
    graphics.GraphicsDevice.Clear(Color.CornflowerBlue);
    SpriteBatch.Begin();
    base.Draw(gameTime);
    SpriteBatch.End();
}
```

We now have a nice little demo that allows us to move in and out of the different game states. We should be able to use this as a starting point for our projects. A good exercise would be to plug this framework into the SimpleGame we made in Chapter 11.

Summary

We started the chapter discussing FSMs and their place within our games. We then took the concept and applied it to our actual game structure. We talked in detail about how we could use a stack-based system to manage our different game states to create a nice and clean process flow between our states. This is key to a nice polished game. A lot of times, this is left until the end, but that can have disastrous effects on a game as it might be hard to plug it in after the fact.

We finished out the chapter by looking at all of the code needed to pull off our stack-based game state management system. Although there was good amount of code, it definitely was not difficult and is very easy to use once it is in place. Having a way to manage our game states effectively is huge. We are well on our way to creating excellent games!

AI Algorithms

We discussed finite state machines (FSMs) in the previous chapter, but in this chapter, as we look at common algorithms, we will put the knowledge into motion by having enemies that will move randomly, chase, evade, and move in patterns.

Setting Up Our Demo

We need to create a new solution called AIDemo. We need to reference our XELibrary but do not need to change it. We can either include it as a project or just add it as a reference.

We need to add the sphere0.x file to our Content\Models folder. We can create a private member field called `sphere` to hold our model:

```
private Model sphere;
```

We also need to add a skybox and add our skybox pipeline assembly to our solution's content pipeline properties. We can use the same skybox texture from our acceleration demo in the last chapter and put the texture into the Content\Skyboxes folder. We need to create a private member to hold our skybox:

```
private Skybox skybox;
```

After making sure we have set our skybox2.tga content's content processor property to `SkyboxProcessor`, we need to load our sphere and skybox in our `LoadGraphicsContent` method:

```
sphere = content.Load<Model>(@"Content\Models\sphere0");
skybox = content.Load<Skybox>(@"Content\Skyboxes\skybox2");
```

We can set up our typical input and camera game components next. The camera we should use is our stationary `Camera` object. We need to set up the following private member fields:

```
private InputHandler input;
private Camera camera;
```

We add them to our constructor:

```
input = new InputHandler(this, true);
Components.Add(input);
camera = new Camera(this);
Components.Add(camera);
```

We are allowing our `InputHandler` to exit the demo when the user presses the Back button or the Escape key. This is why we are passing true in as the second parameter of the constructor. We need to set up two new classes, and we can keep these inside of our Game1.cs file as they are small:

```
class Player
{
    public Vector3 Position;
    public Vector3 Velocity;
    public Matrix World;
    public Color Color;
}

class Enemy
{
    public Vector3 Position;
    public Vector3 Velocity;
    public Matrix World;
    public Color Color;
}
```

We will add more properties to our `Enemy` class as we move through the chapter, but this is enough to get us started. We are going to be drawing multiple spheres on the screen. One represents our player and some others represent the enemies. We need to add our faithful `DrawModel` method:

```
private void DrawModel(ref Model m, ref Matrix world, Color color)
{
    Matrix[] transforms = new Matrix[m.Bones.Count];
    m.CopyAbsoluteBoneTransformsTo(transforms);
```

```
    foreach (ModelMesh mesh in m.Meshes)
    {
        foreach (BasicEffect be in mesh.Effects)
        {
            be.EnableDefaultLighting();

            be.AmbientLightColor = color.ToVector3();
            be.Projection = camera.Projection;
            be.View = camera.View;
            be.World = world * mesh.ParentBone.Transform;
        }

        mesh.Draw();
    }
}
```

We can set up our variables to hold our player and enemies:

```
private const int MaxEnemies = 10;
private Player player;
private Enemy[] enemies = new Enemy[MaxEnemies];
```

We can initialize them in our Initialization method:

```
player = new Player();
player.Position = new Vector3(-100, 0, -300);
player.Velocity = Vector3.Zero;
player.World = Matrix.CreateTranslation(player.Position);
player.Color = Color.Black;

for (int i = 0; i < MaxEnemies; i++)
{
    enemies[i] = new Enemy();
    enemies[i].Position = new Vector3((i * 50) + 50, (i * 25) - 50, -300);
    enemies[i].Velocity = Vector3.Zero;
    enemies[i].World = Matrix.CreateTranslation(enemies[i].Position);
}
```

We are spacing our enemies out in a diagonal line. We can go ahead and draw our skybox and spheres by adding this code in our Draw method:

```
skybox.Draw(camera.View, camera.Projection, Matrix.CreateScale(ArenaSize));
//Draw player
DrawModel(ref sphere, ref player.World, player.Color);

//Draw enemies
for (int i = 0; i < MaxEnemies; i++)
```

```
{
    Enemy enemy = enemies[i];
    DrawModel(ref sphere, ref enemy.World, enemy.Color);
}
```

ArenaSize is simply a float constant with the value of 500. If we run our demo at this point we should see our skybox, our player sphere colored black, and our enemy spheres colored white. We set up our camera as the stationary camera so we can rotate but cannot move. We did this because we are going to hook our A, S, W, and D keys to moving our player sphere. We are going to create a new method to do the update:

```
private void UpdatePlayer()
{
    player.Velocity = Vector3.Zero;

    if (input.KeyboardState.IsHoldingKey(Keys.W) ||
        input.GamePads[0].ThumbSticks.Left.Y > 0)
    {
        player.Velocity.Y++;
    }
    else if (input.KeyboardState.IsHoldingKey(Keys.S) ||
        input.GamePads[0].ThumbSticks.Left.Y < 0)
    {
        player.Velocity.Y—;
    }

    if (input.KeyboardState.IsHoldingKey(Keys.D) ||
        input.GamePads[0].ThumbSticks.Left.X > 0)
    {
        player.Velocity.X++;
    }
    else if (input.KeyboardState.IsHoldingKey(Keys.A) ||
        input.GamePads[0].ThumbSticks.Left.X < 0)
    {
        player.Velocity.X—;
    }

    //restrict to 2D?
    if (!restrictToXY)
    {
        if (input.KeyboardState.IsHoldingKey(Keys.RightShift) ||
            input.GamePads[0].Triggers.Right > 0)
        {
            player.Velocity.Z—;
        }
        else if (input.KeyboardState.IsHoldingKey(Keys.RightControl) ||
```

```
            input.GamePads[0].Triggers.Left > 0)
        {
            player.Velocity.Z++;
        }
    }

    //Normalize our vector so we don't go faster
    //when heading in multiple directions
    if (player.Velocity.LengthSquared() != 0)
        player.Velocity.Normalize();

    player.Velocity *= playerMoveUnit;
}
```

We need to add a private member field called `restrictToXY`, which we can set to true. This demo will only move on the x and y axis so we can easily see how our enemies are thinking. We are including the z axis so that when we create a real world we will be closer to the end goal of having thinking enemies that can move in 3D. This `UpdatePlayer` method needs to be called from our `Update` method. There is not a lot going on inside of the method: We are checking if the input is moving our player; if so, we update the velocity. We only do it on the z axis if we are supposed to. Finally, we normalize our vector so we do not move faster when going in multiple directions. The last thing this method does is actually multiply our velocity by our `playerMoveUnit` value, which is a member field that needs to be set to 25. Let's call this method in our `Update` method and finish updating our player's position:

```
float elapsedTime = (float)gameTime.ElapsedGameTime.TotalSeconds;
UpdatePlayer();
player.Velocity *= elapsedTime;
player.Position += player.Velocity;
KeepWithinBounds(ref player.Position, ref player.Velocity);
player.World = Matrix.CreateTranslation(player.Position);
```

After calling the `UpdatePlayer` method, we factor in our calculated elapsed time so we will move at a consistent rate no matter what our frame rate happens to be. We then update our player's position taking into account the current velocity just calculated. We pass our position and velocity into a helper method that will keep us within the boundaries of the arena. Finally, we update our world coordinates so it will be drawn in the correct position. We can add in our helper method:

```
private void KeepWithinBounds(ref Vector3 position, ref Vector3 velocity)
{
    if ((position.X < -ArenaSize) || (position.X > ArenaSize))
        velocity.X = -velocity.X;
    if ((position.Y < -ArenaSize) || (position.Y > ArenaSize))
        velocity.Y = -velocity.Y;
```

```
    if ((position.Z < -ArenaSize) || (position.Z > ArenaSize))
        velocity.Z = -velocity.Z;
    position += velocity;
}
```

This method simply reverses velocity if we hit the wall. We can run our code and move our player around the screen. It is almost 2D because the camera is fixed. This demo is definitely not going to win any awards for camera movement, but we are interested in the AI code.

Chase Algorithm

To start, we are going to have our enemies target us and try to catch us. We can create a method called TrackPlayerStraightLine. This method will make our enemies do exactly that: track our player in the most direct path possible:

```
private void TrackPlayerStraightLine(Enemy enemy)
{
    if (player.Position.X > enemy.Position.X)
        enemy.Velocity.X = moveUnit;
    else if (player.Position.X < enemy.Position.X)
        enemy.Velocity.X = -moveUnit;
    else
        enemy.Velocity.X = 0;

    if (player.Position.Y > enemy.Position.Y)
        enemy.Velocity.Y = moveUnit;
    else if (player.Position.Y < enemy.Position.Y)
        enemy.Velocity.Y = -moveUnit;
    else
        enemy.Velocity.Y = 0;

    //restrict to 2D?
    if (!restrictToXY)
    {
        if (player.Position.Z > enemy.Position.Z)
            enemy.Velocity.Z = moveUnit;
        else if (player.Position.Z < enemy.Position.Z)
            enemy.Velocity.Z = -moveUnit;
        else
            enemy.Velocity.Z = 0;
    }

    enemy.Color = Color.Red;
}
```

The algorithm for tracking is very straightforward. We check to see if the enemy's position is less than the player's position. If it is, we add to our velocity appropriately. The moveUnit is a float that needs to be set to 20 (just a little slower than our player's movement). If it is greater than the player's position, we subtract from our velocity. We do this for all of the axes. We are also setting the color of our enemies to red so we can keep them straight later on when we have other types of enemies on the screen. We can call this method in our Update method:

```
foreach (Enemy enemy in enemies)
{
    TrackPlayerStraightLine(enemy);

    enemy.Velocity *= elapsedTime;
    enemy.Position += enemy.Velocity;
    KeepWithinBounds(ref enemy.Position, ref enemy.Velocity);
    enemy.World = Matrix.CreateTranslation(enemy.Position);
}
```

We track our player relentlessly and make sure we are moving according to our frame rate. We update our position based on our velocity and make sure the enemy stays within the walls of the arena. Finally, we update the enemies' world matrices. We can run the code now and get ready to run.

A Better Chase Algorithm

Although that gets the job done effectively, it is a little unrealistic because the enemies are moving in a very precise manner. We can modify how they turn to track us, which slows them down a little but ultimately makes them look more realistic. We are going to create another method called TrackPlayer:

```
private void TrackPlayer(Enemy enemy)
{
    Vector3 tv = player.Position - enemy.Position;
    tv.Normalize();

    enemy.Velocity = tv * moveUnit;

    enemy.Color = Color.Red;
}
```

With this algorithm we are effectively doing the same thing but this time we are utilizing some vector math to move our enemies in a more realistic manner. Of course, depending on the enemy, the first method we used might work. In this method however, we are computing the vector between our enemy and our player. This is done by taking the difference of our two positions and then normalizing the resulting vector. We then set our velocity to the product of our resulting vector and the movement unit we have defined.

16

We have a much better result with fewer lines of code. It did require a little bit of vector math, but even that is all done by XNA for us. We can replace the `TrackPlayerStraightLine` method with this updated `TrackPlayer` method and run our demo and see some nice results.

Evading Algorithm

Our evading algorithm is identical to our tracking algorithm. The only difference is that we change our resulting vector by switching the order in which we are subtracting our player and enemies' position vectors. The code is as follows:

```
private void EvadePlayer(Enemy enemy)
{
    Vector3 tv = enemy.Position - player.Position;
    tv.Normalize();

    enemy.Velocity = tv * moveUnit;

    enemy.Color = Color.Navy;
}
```

That is really all there is to it. We can replace the call to the `TrackPlayer` method in our `Update` method to this `EvadePlayer` method.

Because we are keeping our spheres within the arena, these evading bots will just move as far away as possible. The one that is on the same y axis will stay where it is, whereas those higher or lower will continue to move higher or lower while fleeing to the right. They do not want to come near the player and so they will basically end up in the corner.

Random Movement

Besides chasing and evading we can also have our enemies move in random motion. To do this we need to add some more properties to the enemy class. We want to change directions every so often (each enemy should have a different timer it uses to determine when to switch directions). The direction should be random for each enemy (each enemy will need a random velocity). The properties we need to add to our `Enemy` class are as follows:

```
public float ChangeDirectionTimer;
public Vector3 RandomVelocity;
public int RandomSeconds;
```

We will create a method called `MoveRandomly` that will have the logic to move our enemies in a random motion:

```
private void MoveRandomly(Enemy enemy, GameTime gameTime)
{
```

```
if (enemy.ChangeDirectionTimer == 0)
    enemy.ChangeDirectionTimer =
        (float)gameTime.TotalGameTime.TotalMilliseconds;

//has the appropriate amount of time passed?
if (gameTime.TotalGameTime.TotalMilliseconds >
    enemy.ChangeDirectionTimer + enemy.RandomSeconds * 1000)
{
    enemy.RandomVelocity = Vector3.Zero;
    enemy.RandomVelocity.X = rand.Next(-1, 2);
    enemy.RandomVelocity.Y = rand.Next(-1, 2);
    //restrict to 2D?
    if (!restrictToXY)
        enemy.RandomVelocity.Z = rand.Next(-1, 2);

    enemy.ChangeDirectionTimer = 0;
}

enemy.Velocity = enemy.RandomVelocity;

enemy.Velocity *= moveUnit;

enemy.Color = Color.Orange;
}
```

Sometimes random movement can appear intelligent. Our method is utilizing the game time to keep track of how long the enemy should keep moving. It is very similar to the code we used for our fading method. This method checks to see if enough time has passed to change directions. Once enough time has elapsed, the enemy velocity vector is populated by random numbers ranging from -1 to 1. We need to add the following random number variable to our code:

```
Random rand = new Random();
```

Random numbers are very important in AI work. We have taken care to not just have our enemies be jittery by changing directions every frame. As a result we can have enemies that look like they are searching or patrolling. None of the code we have seen has been rocket science. All the algorithms are pretty simple but can provide great results.

We can replace our line in Update with:

```
MoveRandomly(enemy, gameTime);
```

Before we can run the code to see the results of our randomly moving enemies, we need to initialize our properties. We do this inside of the enemy for loop in the Initialize method:

```
enemies[i].ChangeDirectionTimer = 0;
enemies[i].RandomVelocity = Vector3.Left;
enemies[i].RandomSeconds = (i + 2) / 2;
```

As we run the code we can see that each enemy is just moving around randomly. They are not moving in synchronization and they definitely appear random.

Creating a Finite State Machine

We have three decent AI algorithms that we can apply to our enemies. However, it is likely that our enemies will want to perform each one of these behaviors at different times throughout their life. This is where we can create an FSM and see how it can work in code. We discussed FSMs in the last chapter and really focused on game state. We can give our enemies a state machine that decides which state the enemy should be in. We will create an enumerated type with three states: Attack, Retreat, and Search. Each state will determine when it should change states. We will hook up the methods we have created to each state. We can start by creating the enumerated type in our Enemy class:

```
public enum AIState { Attack, Retreat, Search }
```

Next, we need to actually create a State property for our enemy by adding this to our Enemy class:

```
public AIState State;
```

To help us know how to change states we are going to add a Health property in which we will store a whole number from 1 to 10. The idea is that if our enemies have a lot of health, they will be more aggressive, but if they are low in health they will run away. Of course, our enemies' personalities could be based on other things, so this is just an example. We can add a Health property to our Enemy class:

```
public int Health;
```

We can initialize these properties inside of the enemy for loop in our Initialize method:

```
enemies[i].State = Enemy.AIState.Search;
//alternate every other enemy to either attack or evade (based on health)
if (i % 2 == 0)
    enemies[i].Health = 1;
else
    enemies[i].Health = 10;
```

We set each enemy to start out in a searching state. We also set every other enemy to have a high health and a low health. This will come into play soon, as it will help decide if they should attack or retreat.

Now we can actually set up our state machine in our Update method. We want to replace our call to the MoveRandomly method with the following switch statement:

```
switch (enemy.State)
{
    case Enemy.AIState.Search:
        {
            MoveRandomly(enemy, gameTime);
            break;
        }
    case Enemy.AIState.Attack:
        {
            TrackPlayer(enemy);
            break;
        }
    case Enemy.AIState.Retreat:
        {
            EvadePlayer(enemy);
            break;
        }
    default:
        {
            throw (new ApplicationException("Unknown State: " +
                enemy.State.ToString()));
        }
}
```

We are simply calling one of the methods we have set up based on the state our enemy is in. We have initialized our enemies to start in the Search state, which we have associated with the MoveRandomly method, but we have not created any way for them to actually change states. Each state will determine if a different state should be called. Our game states did the same thing. While we were in a playing state, it would change to a paused state if the user pressed the Start button. Each state determines the next state. This means we need to modify the three methods that are being called every frame.

We are going to have our enemies continuously checking to see how close they are to the player. If they are close enough they will change their state to either attacking or retreating depending on how much health they have. We need to set up some constants to hold the radius in which we will be looking for the player:

```
private const float SeekRadius = 75.0f;
private const float EvadeRadius = 75.0f;
```

We have set these to the same value but we have the flexibility to modify them independently as we tweak the code. We can start modifying our methods by looking at our MoveRandomly method. This is our search method and as such we need to do something if our search provides results. In other words, if the enemies stumble on the player through their random movements we need to change their state to either attack or retreat depending their health status. We can do that by adding the following code at the end of our MoveRandomly method:

```
float distance = (player.Position - enemy.Position).Length();

if (distance < EvadeRadius)
    if (enemy.Health < 5)
        enemy.State = Enemy.AIState.Retreat;

if (distance < SeekRadius)
    if (enemy.Health >= 5)
        enemy.State = Enemy.AIState.Attack;
```

We are simply getting the distance between our player and our enemy. We are checking to see if the distance is within our radius check. If it is, we check our health and change our state to attack or retreat appropriately.

Next we can modify our `EvadePlayer` method by adding the following condition to the end of the method:

```
if (distance > EvadeRadius * 1.25f)
    enemy.State = Enemy.AIState.Search;
```

We are simply checking to see if we are more than 25 percent further away than our evade radius. If we are, we can go back into our random mode by setting the state to Search. We declare and set our local distance variable right after our first line and before we normalize our vector. We need to add the following line:

```
float distance = tv.Length();
```

`TrackPlayer` and `TrackPlayerStraightLine` can both be updated by adding the following code to the end of the methods:

```
float distance = (enemy.Position - player.Position).Length();
if (distance > SeekRadius * 1.25f)
    enemy.State = Enemy.AIState.Search;
```

All of this code is doing the same thing: It is getting the length of vector between our player and our enemy, and if we are close enough we change our state back into a search mode. We can run our code to see our enemies behaving differently.

We could also make a quick improvement by sending the retreating enemies back to the player's starting point if we touch them. We can also send the player to the origin if an enemy touches us. Now, if an enemy gets the player while at the origin, there is no way to get loose and the game is over.

To make this modification, we need to add the following conditions at the end of our enemy foreach loop in our `Update` method:

```
//reset player or enemy if collided
if ((enemy.Position - player.Position).Length() <
    (sphere.Meshes[0].BoundingSphere.Radius * 2))
```

```
{
    if (enemy.State == Enemy.AIState.Attack)
        player.Position.X = player.Position.Y = 0;
    else
        enemy.Position.X = enemy.Position.Y = 0;
}
```

This simply checks to see if an enemy has collided with the player. Depending on the state of the enemy, either the player is sent to the player's initial starting point or the enemy is. Now we can come up with different algorithms and have a test bed in which to try them out.

Summary

We have touched on only a very few AI algorithms. The field is broad and there are volumes of books written on the subject. This chapter's purpose was to introduce the concept so we could research some more in-depth ways to make our game characters come to life. Many other AI topics include things like path finding, fuzzy logic, minimap trees, and neural networks (having our AI creatures actually remember things). For example, "The last time the player did x and y he did z right after, so let me get ready for that in the next frame."

We discussed how to create an enemy that tracks the player, evades the player, and moves randomly (or searches for the player). We put the concept of the FSM that we learned about in the last chapter into practice in this chapter. We saw how each state could determine which state the enemy should be in next. We even finished up by making a small game with the player trying to catch the fleeing enemies without being caught by the attacking enemies.

The AI we add to our games can be very simplistic or very complex. Certain simplistic algorithms like the ones we saw in this chapter can be very effective in many games. When we are working on core opponents of our player we definitely want to create an FSM with many states. For example, it might be that the enemy attacks in different ways based on the weapon the player has. It might be they appear erratic in their movement even as they are attacking to keep the player on their toes. The sky is the limit with this material.

16

PART VII

3D Effects

IN THIS PART

CHAPTER 17

Advanced Texturing Techniques

In this chapter we are going to light our scene using more realistic lights. We are also going to discuss some ways we can create better texturing effects to provide more realism in our games.

3D Lighting

Before we can really get down to business on some of the ways we can texture our objects to make them appear realistic, we need to discuss lighting in more detail. The only way we can get a realistic effect on our textures is to have lights shining on them appropriately. Some of the common lighting algorithms are ambient lighting, directional lighting, point lights, spot lights, and specular lighting. We discuss the first two types of lights in this chapter.

Creating a Custom Vertex Format

To get started we are going to create a demo that will allow us to texture the rectangle we created in Chapter 4, "Creating 3D Objects." We need to create a new solution called AdvancedTexturingDemo. We are going to be modifying our XELibrary, so we need to add that project to our solution and reference it as a project.

We need to create a new struct for our XELibrary. We can call our new code file VertexPositionNormalTangent.cs. This will hold our vertex declaration. When we created our first rectangle we used the `VertexPositionNormalTexture` struct that XNA has built in. This struct describes the vertex data. It stored the position, texture coordinates, and normal of the vertex. Although we could get by with that for this lighting demo, the next section is going to need tangent information as well, so we are going to spend the time now to set up our own struct to handle all of the data we need for this chapter. The code for our struct is in Listing 17.1.

LISTING 17.1   VertexPositionNormalTexture.cs

```
using System;
using System.Collections.Generic;
using Microsoft.Xna.Framework;
using Microsoft.Xna.Framework.Graphics;

namespace XELibrary
{
    public struct VertexPositionNormalTangentTexture
    {
        public Vector3 Position;
        public Vector3 Normal;
        public Vector3 Tangent;
        public Vector2 TextureCoordinate;

        public VertexPositionNormalTangentTexture(
            Vector3 Position,
            Vector3 Normal,
            Vector3 Tangent,
            Vector2 TextureCoordinate)
        {
            this.Position = Position;
            this.Normal = Normal;
            this.Tangent = Tangent;
            this.TextureCoordinate = TextureCoordinate;
        }

        public static int SizeInBytes = 11 * sizeof(float);

        public static VertexElement[] VertexElements =
            {
                new VertexElement(
                    0, 0, VertexElementFormat.Vector3,
                    VertexElementMethod.Default,
                    VertexElementUsage.Position, 0),
                new VertexElement(0, sizeof(float)*3,
                    VertexElementFormat.Vector3,
                    VertexElementMethod.Default,
                    VertexElementUsage.Normal, 0),
                new VertexElement(0, sizeof(float)*6,
                    VertexElementFormat.Vector3,
```

LISTING 17.1   Continued

```
                    VertexElementMethod.Default,
                    VertexElementUsage.Tangent, 0),
               new VertexElement(0, sizeof(float)*9,
                    VertexElementFormat.Vector2,
                    VertexElementMethod.Default,
                    VertexElementUsage.TextureCoordinate, 0)
          };
     }
}
```

Our struct is going to store our vertex position, normal, tangent, and texture coordinates. The only new piece of data is our tangent. When loading models, the tangent data can be stored with the model and a vertex declaration would not be needed. Most likely the reading of the model data would be done in a custom content processor. An excellent example of this is the NormalMapSample found on the XNA Creator's Web site (http://creators.xna.com/). This sample code uses an .fbx model that includes additional information that is extracted by the custom content processor. This way it can be loaded just like any other asset and the information will automatically be passed to our shaders.

However, we are not loading data from an outside source. Instead, we are using our example rectangle, so we need to specify the type of data we are storing for each of our vertices. Our struct has a public static variable called SizeInBytes. This is to mimic the vertex declaration structs built in by XNA. We need to use this information when we set up our vertex buffer. The struct has three Vector3 types and one Vector2 type. That is a total of 11 floats. So we hard-code the SizeInBytes variable to return 11 times the size of our float value.

We need an array to store the vertex elements. This is what describes the properties we expose in our struct. When we initialize our vertex declaration in our game code, we have to pass in an array of vertex elements. We followed XNA's lead and called it VertexElements. We have four properties and so our array has four elements. The constructor for the VertexElement takes in the stream number to use. We will always use the first data stream. The second parameter is where we set the offset in the stream this element starts. So our first element in our first stream starts with no offset—zero. The next element's offset is at sizeof(float) * 3 because our first element was a Vector3 type (which holds three floats). Likewise, the next element bumps it by another three floats. The next parameter we pass in is the actual type of data. The next parameter we always pass in is VertexElementMethod.Default. This parameter rarely needs to be anything else. The purpose of the parameter is to tell the tessellator how to process the vertex data. We do not want it to do any additional calculations so we leave it set to the default method. The other three options are LookUp, LookUpPresampled, and UV. More information on these methods can be found in the documentation. The next to the last parameter tells XNA how the vertex element data is going to be used. The possible values are Position, BlendWeight, BlendIndices, Normal, PointSize, TextureCoordinate, Tangent, Binormal, TessellateFactor, Color, Fog, Depth, and Sample. We are using Position, Normal,

Tangent, and TextureCoordinate for our vertices. The final parameter is the usage index. This would be used if we wanted to store information in an additional usage type. For example, if we need to store information that did not have a specific usage type predefined, we could reuse the TextureCoordinate and pass in 1 as the usage index.

Creating the Demo

The demo we are creating allows us to easily switch between the different effects we are going to be discussing this chapter. We are going to start with ambient lighting because we discussed it in Chapter 13, "Advanced HLSL." Then we finish this 3D lighting section of the chapter with directional lighting. The next sections we add in different mapping techniques.

To begin with, we need to add the following private member fields to our Game1.cs code:

```
private FirstPersonCamera camera;
private InputHandler input;

private VertexPositionNormalTangentTexture[] vertices;
private VertexBuffer vertexBuffer;
private VertexDeclaration vertexDeclaration;
private short[] indices;

private Effect ambientEffect;
private Effect currentEffect;
private Texture2D colorMap;
```

There is nothing surprising here. We have our favorite game components FirstPersonCamera and InputHandler. In Chapter 4 we used the VertexPositionNormalTexture but now we are using our custom VertexPositionNormalTangentTexture struct. We set up a field to reference our ambient effect and our texture (which we called color map).

Inside of our constructor we need to set up our game components like normal:

```
input = new InputHandler(this, true);
Components.Add(input);
camera = new FirstPersonCamera(this);
Components.Add(camera);
```

Now we need to add in the same methods we created in Chapter 4 to set up the vertices that create our rectangle:

```
private void InitializeVertices()
{
    Vector3 position;
    Vector2 textureCoordinates;

    vertices = new VertexPositionNormalTangentTexture[4];
```

```
    //top left
    position = new Vector3(-1, 1, 0);
    textureCoordinates = new Vector2(0, 0);
    vertices[0] = new VertexPositionNormalTangentTexture(position,
        Vector3.Forward, Vector3.Left, textureCoordinates);


    //bottom right
    position = new Vector3(1, -1, 0);
    textureCoordinates = new Vector2(1, 1);
    vertices[1] = new VertexPositionNormalTangentTexture(position,
        Vector3.Forward, Vector3.Left, textureCoordinates);


    //bottom left
    position = new Vector3(-1, -1, 0);
    textureCoordinates = new Vector2(0, 1);
    vertices[2] = new VertexPositionNormalTangentTexture(position,
        Vector3.Forward, Vector3.Left, textureCoordinates);


    //top right
    position = new Vector3(1, 1, 0);
    textureCoordinates = new Vector2(1, 0);
    vertices[3] = new VertexPositionNormalTangentTexture(position,
        Vector3.Forward, Vector3.Left, textureCoordinates);


    vertexBuffer = new VertexBuffer(graphics.GraphicsDevice,
        VertexPositionNormalTangentTexture.SizeInBytes * vertices.Length,
        ResourceUsage.WriteOnly, ResourceManagementMode.Automatic);
    vertexBuffer.SetData<VertexPositionNormalTangentTexture>(vertices);
}

private void InitializeIndices()
{
    //six vertices make up two triangles, which make up our rectangle
    indices = new short[6];


    //triangle 1 (bottom portion)
    indices[0] = 0; // top left
    indices[1] = 1; // bottom right
    indices[2] = 2; // bottom left


    //triangle 2 (top portion)
    indices[3] = 0; // top left
    indices[4] = 3; // top right
    indices[5] = 1; // bottom right
}
```

17

These methods are identical to how we left them in Chapter 4, but the only difference is that we are now setting the tangent vector. We simply set it to `Vector3.Left` because our normal is set to `Vector3.Up`. Neither the normal nor tangent data is needed for ambient lighting. They are ignored in our current shader. We discuss the normal when we look at directional lighting. We discuss how the tangent vector relates to the normal vector later in this chapter. The `InitializeIndices` method did not change at all and is only listed here to avoid page flipping.

Inside of our `Initialize` method, we need to call those two methods and set up our vertex declaration. The code to do that is as follows:

```
InitializeVertices();
InitializeIndices();

//Initialize our Vertex Declaration
vertexDeclaration = new VertexDeclaration(graphics.GraphicsDevice,
    VertexPositionNormalTangentTexture.VertexElements);
```

The only change is that we are now referencing our newly created custom vertex type.

Inside of the `loadAllContent` condition in the `LoadGraphicsContent` method, we need to load our content by adding the following code:

```
colorMap = content.Load<Texture2D>(@"Content\Textures\rockbump_color");
ambientEffect = content.Load<Effect>(@"Content\Effects\AmbientTexture");
currentEffect = ambientLight;
```

We need to add our color map (texture) so we can apply the correct colors to the correct pixels. We also initialize our ambient effect. Finally, we set our `currentEffect` variable to our ambient light effect (which happens to be our only effect at this point).

Next we need to actually draw our rectangle on the screen with our ambient light effect. The following code should be very familiar:

```
graphics.GraphicsDevice.RenderState.CullMode = CullMode.None;
graphics.GraphicsDevice.VertexDeclaration = vertexDeclaration;

Matrix world = Matrix.CreateScale(100.0f) * Matrix.CreateTranslation(
    new Vector3(0, 0, -450));
currentEffect.Parameters["World"].SetValue(world);
currentEffect.Parameters["View"].SetValue(camera.View);
currentEffect.Parameters["Projection"].SetValue(camera.Projection);

currentEffect.Parameters["AmbientColor"].SetValue(.8f);

currentEffect.Parameters["ColorMap"].SetValue(colorMap);

currentEffect.Begin();
```

```
foreach (EffectPass pass in currentEffect.CurrentTechnique.Passes)
{
    pass.Begin();

    graphics.GraphicsDevice.DrawUserIndexedPrimitives
        <VertexPositionNormalTangentTexture>(
        PrimitiveType.TriangleList, vertices, 0, vertices.Length,
        indices, 0, indices.Length / 3);

    pass.End();
}

currentEffect.End();
```

Because we are just drawing a rectangle, we have turned off culling. This way if we move behind the rectangle we will still be able to see it (although, depending on the effect, it might be black). We scale our rectangle and move it back in our world some, mainly so we can get an interesting lighting effect later on. The code is pretty much the same as it was in Chapter 4, and the only difference is that we are using our new struct.

Ambient Lighting

Now that we have our demo set up, we need to actually create the ambient effect that we referenced earlier. We can add our Content\Effects folder to our solution. We start with our previous AmbientTexture.fx file from Chapter 13. We can find the starting code in Listing 17.2.

LISTING 17.2   AmbientTexture.fx

```
float4x4 World : WORLD;
float4x4 View;
float4x4 Projection;

float4 AmbientColor : COLOR0;

float4x4 WorldViewProjection : WORLDVIEWPROJECTION;
texture ColorMap;
sampler ColorMapSampler = sampler_state
{
    texture = < ColorMap >;
    magfilter = LINEAR;
    minfilter = LINEAR;
    mipfilter = LINEAR;
    addressU = mirror;
    addressV = mirror;
};
```

LISTING 17.2   Continued

```
struct VertexInput
{
    float4 Position : POSITION0;
    float2 TexCoord : TEXCOORD0;
};

struct VertexOutput
{
    float4 Position : POSITION0;
    float2 TexCoord : TEXCOORD0;
};

VertexOutput vertexShader(VertexInput input)
{
    VertexOutput output = (VertexOutput)0;
    WorldViewProjection = mul(mul(World, View), Projection);
    output.Position = mul(input.Position, WorldViewProjection);
    output.TexCoord = input.TexCoord;

    return( output );
}

struct PixelInput
{
    float2 TexCoord : TEXCOORD0;
};

float4 pixelShader(PixelInput input) : COLOR
{
    return( tex2D(ColorMapSampler, input.TexCoord) * AmbientColor);
}

technique Default
{
    pass P0
    {
        VertexShader = compile vs_1_1 vertexShader();
        PixelShader = compile ps_1_1 pixelShader();
    }
}
```

This code is not exactly how we left it, but there are only two small modifications. The first is that we removed the vertex displacement. The second is that we renamed Texture to ColorMap. The purpose of the texture has not changed: It is there to provide the color pixels of our object. In later sections we are going to be adding more textures that have different purposes. They all map onto the 3D object, but do so for different reasons. We are just preparing for that now by calling our texture our color map. We need to put this AmbientTexture.fx file in our Content\Effects folder. We can compile our demo and see our rectangle with our example texture with the same ambient light we saw in Chapter 13.

Directional Lighting

When we first created our 3D rectangle in Chapter 4 we set a normal vector for our vertex. We just briefly glossed over explaining a normal, stating that it was used for lighting. Well, now we can see exactly how a vertex normal can help us light our objects better. This is going to require some vector and matrix math.

The normal is a vector that is perpendicular to the surface of our triangle. We know that every 3D object is made up of a bunch of vertices and that we use triangles that connect those points to create complex objects. Each triangle has a normal, which basically tells us in which direction the triangle is facing. This is very important when trying to calculate how well lit or how dark the triangle is. Triangles facing away (their normal vector is in the opposite direction of the light) will not be lit by that light, whereas triangles facing directly toward the light will be greatly lit. If the light source is close enough, the triangle will be white (or whatever color the light is).

The other piece to this is our light, of course. We know which direction our triangles are facing and now we just need to know where our light source is. Where is it pointing and how far away is it? We can specify both of those values with a vector. This is where the vector math comes in. We are going to take the dot product of both of those vectors to determine the angular relationship between them. This can be seen in Figure 17.1.

17

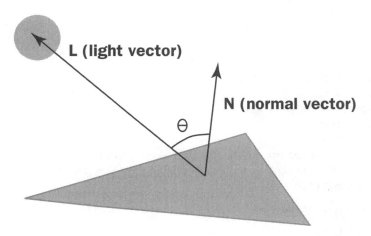

L (light vector)

N (normal vector)

θ

θ
(Theta) Angle between two vectors

FIGURE 17.1   The normal vector is the perpendicular to our triangle. The light vector is the line from our light vector to the origin of the normal vector.

The larger the angle is between the two vectors, the darker the surface will be. The smaller the angle, the more lit the surface will be. We are only going to be talking about directional lighting in this section but other lighting techniques do exist. The common light algorithms are ambient, directional, point, spot, and specular. Point, spot, and specular light algorithms can be found on the Web in many places, so we do not spend time on them in this book. The concepts are the same, but the algorithms change between them to better model the type of light they are mimicking.

Let's take a look at the code needed to create a directional light. We need to make a few changes to our game code. We need to add the following private member fields for our directional light:

```
private Vector3 LightPosition;
private Effect directionalEffect;
```

We can initialize our light position in our `Initialize` method:

```
LightPosition = new Vector3(0, 0, -500);
```

We can initialize our directional light effect in our `LoadGraphicsContent` method:

```
directionalEffect = content.Load<Effect>(@"Content\Effects\DirectionalLight");
```

We want to be able to switch between our different effects easily. We also want to be able to move the light that we set up. We add the following code to our `Update` method:

```
if (input.KeyboardState.IsHoldingKey(Keys.Z))
    LightPosition.Y++;
if (input.KeyboardState.IsHoldingKey(Keys.X))
    LightPosition.Y—;

Window.Title = "LightPosition: " + LightPosition.ToString();

if (input.KeyboardState.WasKeyPressed(Keys.D1))
    currentEffect = ambientEffect;
if (input.KeyboardState.WasKeyPressed(Keys.D2))
    currentEffect = directionalEffect;
```

There is nothing shocking here, as we just update the position of our light if we press the Z or X keys. We update our window title caption with our updated light position. We change our current effect by pressing the 1 and 2 keys.

In the `Draw` method we need to add the light position to our effect's parameters:

```
if (currentEffect.Parameters["LightPosition"] != null)
    currentEffect.Parameters["LightPosition"].SetValue(LightPosition);
```

Now we just need to create our DirectionalLight.fx file. This file needs to be put into our Effects folder. The HLSL code can be found in Listing 17.3.

LISTING 17.3 DirectionalLight.fx

```
float4x4 World : WORLD;
float4x4 View;
float4x4 Projection;

float4 AmbientColor : COLOR0;
float3 LightPosition;

texture ColorMap;

sampler2D ColorMapSampler = sampler_state
{
    texture = <ColorMap>;
    magfilter = LINEAR;
    minfilter = LINEAR;
    mipfilter = LINEAR;
    addressU = mirror;
    addressV = mirror;
};

struct VertexInput
{
    float3 Position : POSITION;
    float3 Normal : NORMAL;
    float2 TexCoord : TEXCOORD0;
};

struct VertexOutput
{
    float4 Position : POSITION;
    float2 TexCoord : TEXCOORD0;
    float3 WorldSpacePosition : TEXCOORD1;
    float3 Normal : TEXCOORD2;
};

VertexOutput vertexShader(VertexInput input)
{
    VertexOutput output;
    output.WorldSpacePosition = mul(float4(input.Position, 1.0f), World);
    float4x4 worldViewProjection = mul(mul(World, View), Projection);
    output.Position = mul(float4(input.Position, 1.0f), worldViewProjection);
    output.TexCoord = input.TexCoord;
    output.Normal = normalize(mul(input.Normal, World));
    return output;
}
```

17

LISTING 17.3   Continued

```
float4 pixelShader(VertexOutput input) : COLOR
{
    float3 LightDirection = normalize(LightPosition - input.WorldSpacePosition);
    float DiffuseLight = dot(LightDirection, input.Normal);

    return( tex2D(ColorMapSampler, input.TexCoord) * DiffuseLight + AmbientColor);
}

technique Default
{
    pass P0
    {
        VertexShader = compile vs_2_0 vertexShader();
        PixelShader = compile ps_2_0 pixelShader();
    }
}
```

Only the code shown in bold type changed from our ambient HLSL code. We added two variables to hold our light position and our diffuse light color. This is the color that is spread across the surfaces that the light hits. Our vertex input struct takes in the normal passed in from our demo. We output the world position of our vertex along with the texture coordinates of our normal map texture and the diffuse color of our light.

Our vertex shader translates our vertex position into world space so our pixel shader can work with the position in world space. We calculate the inverse transpose of our world view projection matrix. This could be done inside of our demo code instead of inside of HLSL.

In our pixel shader we calculate the light direction by normalizing the vector between our vertex position and our light position. Our diffuse light color is then calculated by taking the dot product of our light direction and our normal.

The key to this shader is that our normal is passed in as part of the vertex. It is then passed to the pixel shader so that all of the pixels around the vertex can be shaded appropriately. Each pixel in a triangle surface has the exact same normal—that is the normal of the triangle itself. This might be sufficient in some scenarios, but we can actually set normal data per pixel. We will see how to do that in the next section of this chapter.

Bump Mapping

Bump mapping is a general term used to describe providing some kind of roughness to an object by texturing the object. The object will look complex on the screen with many divots, dimples, and bumps, but the actual 3D object is smooth. The reason it looks "bumpy" is because of mapping our texture(s) onto the object a little differently than we have so far.

Normal Mapping

Not only do we have our color map, but we will also have a normal map. This normal map is a texture that describes a normal for each and every pixel. Instead of using the vertex's normal for all of the pixels on a triangle, we can declare each one individually. This is done with the RGB values of each pixel in the texture.

Normals pointing forward will have the RGB value of 127,127,255. This is a purplish blue color. Normals pointing to the right will have the RGB value of 255,127,255. This is a pink color. Normals pointing up will have an RGB value of 127,255,127. This is a greenish color.

Normal maps can be created by taking a grayscale of a color map (often called a bump map, height map, or depth map) and running it through a processor that converts it. NVIDIA has a plug-in that does this that is available for PhotoShop. There is a free plug-in for Paint.NET as well. Of course, this can also be done through code. We could create a custom content processor to handle this. In fact, the SpriteEffects sample on the Creator's Club Web site (http://creators.xna.com/) contains an example processor that does exactly that.

By having a normal map, our flat object can appear to have much more detail. This is because the light will modify the color of the pixel based on the normal associated with that pixel. Not only do we need to know the normal of our pixel, but we also need to know the tangent of our pixel as well as the binormal (also known as the bitangent) of the pixel. For our example, we are setting them manually because we are creating our vertices by hand. The tangent will be perpendicular to our normal. The binormal can be calculated by taking the cross-product of our tangent vector and our normal vector. These vectors describe to the shader the way that the "up" direction has been mapped onto the geometry. This way, the shader will know how to transform the light direction from world space into the 2D coordinate system used by the normal map texture.

The HLSL code to produce this effect is in Listing 17.4.

LISTING 17.4   NormalMapping.fx

```
float4x4 World  : WORLD;
float4x4 View;
float4x4 Projection;

float4 AmbientColor : COLOR0;
float3 LightPosition;
float4 LightDiffuseColor : COLOR1;

texture ColorMap;

sampler2D ColorMapSampler = sampler_state
{
    texture = <ColorMap>;
    magfilter = LINEAR;
```

LISTING 17.4   Continued

```
    minfilter = LINEAR;
    mipfilter = LINEAR;
    addressU = mirror;
    addressV = mirror;
};

texture2D NormalMap;

sampler2D NormalMapSampler = sampler_state
{
    texture = <NormalMap>;
    minFilter = linear;
    magFilter = linear;
    mipFilter = linear;
};

struct VertexInput
{
    float3 Position : POSITION;
    float3 Normal : NORMAL;
    float3 Tangent : TANGENT;
    float2 TexCoord : TEXCOORD0;
};

struct VertexOutput
{
    float4 Position : POSITION;
    float2 TexCoord : TEXCOORD0;
    float3 LightDirection : TEXCOORD1;
    float2 Normal : TEXCOORD2;
};

VertexOutput vertexShader(VertexInput input)
{
    VertexOutput output;
    output.LightDirection = LightPosition - input.Position;

    float4x4 worldViewProjection = mul(mul(World, View), Projection);
    output.Position = mul(float4(input.Position, 1.0f), worldViewProjection);
    output.TexCoord = input.TexCoord;
    output.Normal = input.TexCoord;

    float3x3 tbnMatrix;
    tbnMatrix[0] = mul(input.Tangent, worldViewProjection);
```

LISTING 17.4   Continued

```
    tbnMatrix[1] = mul(cross(input.Tangent, input.Normal),
        worldViewProjection);
    tbnMatrix[2] = mul(input.Normal, World);
    output.LightDirection = mul(tbnMatrix, output.LightDirection);
    return(output);
}

float4 pixelShader(VertexOutput input) : COLOR
{
    input.LightDirection = normalize(input.LightDirection);

    float3 Normal = 2.0f * (tex2D(NormalMapSampler, input.Normal).rgb - 0.5f);

    return( (LightDiffuseColor * saturate(dot(input.LightDirection, Normal)) +
        AmbientColor) * tex2D(ColorMapSampler, input.TexCoord));
}

technique Default
{
    pass P0
    {
        VertexShader = compile vs_2_0 vertexShader();
        PixelShader = compile ps_2_0 pixelShader();
    }
}
```

We can call this file NormalMapping.fx. We have added a global variable where we can set our light diffuse color. In our vertex input struct we added a tangent vector. Instead of calculating our light direction inside of the pixel shader we are calculating it inside of the vertex shader and passing it in with our new LightDirection vector in our VertexOutput struct.

To start the vertex shader, we calculate our light direction vector. We use this value a little later in the function. Our normal is not calculated like it was in the last effect. Instead it is read in from our normal map. Next we transform our light vector into tangent space (sometimes this is called texture space). We need to do this transformation so that our math is being done in the right coordinate system. To do this, we create a matrix that is called a tangent binormal normal (TBN) matrix. We take the product of our tangent and our inverse transposed world matrix and store that in our first row. The second row gets the cross-product of our tangent and our normal. The third row gets the product of our normal and the inverse transposed world view projection matrix. After creating the TBN matrix, we can multiply that by our light direction vector to transform it into tangent space.

The pixel shader takes in this light direction and normalizes it for each pixel. The normal we have from our normal map has component values in the range of 0 to 1. We need them to be in the range of -1 to 1. To convert them we simply subtract .5 from our color and multiply that by 2. This changes the range like we need. The last thing the pixel shader does is calculate the diffuse color based on the dot product of our light direction vector and our normal. The saturate intrinsic function just clamps the value from 0 to 1. We factor in our light diffuse color along with the ambient color of our scene.

To see this effect in action, we need to modify our demo to load it. We need to add the following private member fields:

```
private Effect normalEffect;
private Texture2D normalMap;
```

Next we need to initialize those variables inside of our LoadGraphicsContent method:

```
normalMap = content.Load<Texture2D>(@"Content\Textures\rockbump_normal");
normalEffect = content.Load<Effect>(@"Content\Effects\NormalMapping");
```

After adding our effect file to our effects folder, we also need to add in our normal map to our textures folder.

The Update method can be modified to allow us to easily switch between this effect and the other two by adding this condition:

```
if (input.KeyboardState.WasKeyPressed(Keys.D3))
    currentEffect = normalEffect;
```

Finally in our Draw method we need to add the two new parameters we added for this effect: our actual normal map and the diffuse color of the light. The code is shown here:

```
if (currentEffect.Parameters["LightDiffuseColor"] != null)
    currentEffect.Parameters["LightDiffuseColor"].SetValue(
        Color.White.ToVector4());

if (currentEffect.Parameters["NormalMap"] != null)
    currentEffect.Parameters["NormalMap"].SetValue(normalMap);
```

When we run the code we can see a much better looking texture. It has a lot more detail, which can easily be seen as we switch between effects by pressing 1, 2, or 3.

There is actually another type of normal mapping as well. We have been discussing tangent space normal mapping. Object space normal mapping is done by 3D modeling programs. We do not discuss it in this book, but the idea behind object space normal mapping is that two identical objects are made, one with a high polygon count with a lot of detail (one that could never make it in a game because of all of the polygons) and another low-polygon-count object (which is what we would use in our game). Inside of the 3D modeling program the two objects are placed at the same point in the world. Then a special normal process is executed that creates normals from the low-polygon-count object to the high-polygon-count object. When used in a game the end result is a 3D object with very little detail looking like it has a lot of detail because of the generated normal map.

Parallax Mapping

Although normal mapping gives us a lot of bang for our buck, there is another form of mapping that produces even nicer results. It takes a little more computation power, but it is worth it. This is the type of texture mapping that can be found in the game Gears of War. It is a variant of normal mapping. It adds another texture called a depth map (sometimes called height map), so not only do we have our color map and our normal map, but we have a third map that specifies how high the pixels should be. Let's see how we implement this.

First we can look at our new ParallaxMapping.fx file:

```
float4x4 World : WORLD;
float4x4 View;
float4x4 Projection;

float4 AmbientColor : COLOR0;
float3 LightPosition;
float4 LightDiffuseColor : COLOR1;

float2 ScaleAmount;
float3 CameraPosition;

texture ColorMap;

sampler2D ColorMapSampler = sampler_state
{
    texture = <ColorMap>;
    magfilter = LINEAR;
    minfilter = LINEAR;
    mipfilter = LINEAR;
    addressU = mirror;
    addressV = mirror;
};

texture2D NormalMap;

sampler2D NormalMapSampler = sampler_state
{
    texture = <NormalMap>;
    minFilter = linear;
    magFilter = linear;
```

17

```
    mipFilter = linear;
};

texture2D DepthMap;

sampler2D DepthMapSampler = sampler_state
{
    texture = <DepthMap>;
    minFilter = linear;
    magFilter = linear;
    mipFilter = linear;
};

struct VertexInput
{
    float3 Position : POSITION;
    float3 Normal : NORMAL;
    float3 Tangent : TANGENT;
    float2 TexCoord : TEXCOORD0;
};

struct VertexOutput
{
    float4 Position : POSITION;
    float2 TexCoord : TEXCOORD0;
    float3 LightDirection : TEXCOORD1;
    float2 Normal : TEXCOORD2;
    float3 ViewDirection : TEXCOORD3;
};


VertexOutput vertexShader(VertexInput input)
{
    VertexOutput output;

    output.LightDirection = LightPosition - input.Position;

    float3 worldPosition = mul(float4(input.Position, 1.0f), World).xyz;
    output.ViewDirection = worldPosition  - CameraPosition;

    float4x4 worldViewProjection = mul(mul(World, View), Projection);
    output.Position = mul(float4(input.Position, 1.0f), worldViewProjection);
    output.TexCoord = input.TexCoord;

    output.Normal = input.TexCoord;
```

```
    // Transform the light vector from object space into tangent space
    float3x3 tbnMatrix;
    tbnMatrix[0] = mul(input.Tangent, worldViewProjection);
    tbnMatrix[1] = mul(cross(input.Tangent, input.Normal),
        worldViewProjection);
    tbnMatrix[2] = mul(input.Normal, World);
    output.LightDirection = mul(tbnMatrix, output.LightDirection);
    output.ViewDirection = mul(tbnMatrix, output.ViewDirection);
    return(output);
}

float4 pixelShader(VertexOutput input) : COLOR
{
    float3 viewDirection = normalize(input.ViewDirection);
    float depth = ScaleAmount.x *
        (float)tex2D(DepthMapSampler, input.TexCoord) + ScaleAmount.y;
    input.TexCoord = depth * viewDirection + input.TexCoord;

    input.LightDirection = normalize(input.LightDirection);

    float3 Normal = 2.0f * (tex2D(NormalMapSampler, input.Normal).rgb - 0.5f);

    return( (LightDiffuseColor * saturate(dot(input.LightDirection, Normal)) +
        AmbientColor) * tex2D(ColorMapSampler, input.TexCoord));
}


technique Default
{
    pass P0
    {
        VertexShader = compile vs_2_0 vertexShader();
        PixelShader = compile ps_2_0 pixelShader();
    }
}
```

We discussed how we need an additional depth map for this effect. Not only did we add this new map, but we also added the camera position and the scale amount, which is simply the bias amount we are going to apply to our depth map.

In our vertex shader we calculate the view direction based on the camera position. We then transform it into tangent space just like we did with our light direction vector.

In our pixel shader we normalize our view direction vector for each pixel. We then read in our depth value from our map and scale it based on the scale amount passed in. The last addition to the code is setting the color map texture coordinate taking into account our view direction and the depth we just calculated. This stretches the color map a little to create a nice 3D effect on a 2D image. The rest of the pixel shader is unchanged from the normal mapping pixel shader.

We need to add the references to the effect and the depth map texture to our game code:

```
private Effect parallaxEffect;
private Texture2D depthMap;
```

We can initialize these variables in our `LoadGraphicsContent` method:

```
depthMap = content.Load<Texture2D>(@"Content\Textures\rockbump_depth");
parallaxEffect = content.Load<Effect>(@"Content\Effects\ParallaxMapping");
```

We need to add our depth map texture to our solution. We also need to be able to switch to this effect in our demo. We just need to add the following condition to our `Update` method:

```
if (input.KeyboardState.WasKeyPressed(Keys.D4))
    currentEffect = parallaxEffect;
```

Finally, we need to set this effect's parameters in our `Draw` method:

```
if (currentEffect.Parameters["DepthMap"] != null)
    currentEffect.Parameters["DepthMap"].SetValue(depthMap);
if (currentEffect.Parameters["ScaleAmount"] != null)
    currentEffect.Parameters["ScaleAmount"].SetValue(
        new Vector2(0.03f, -0.025f));
if (currentEffect.Parameters["CameraPosition"] != null)
    currentEffect.Parameters["CameraPosition"].SetValue(camera.Position);
```

The only value worth mentioning is our 2D vector that contains our scale bias amount. This is simply the amount the effect uses to add more depth by sampling an offset pixel. Parallax mapping can provide nice effects for our objects without having to actually create complex geometry.

Relief Mapping

The next advanced texturing technique we review is relief mapping. Relief mapping is similar to parallax mapping but it does not require the additional depth map. The depth map is included in the normal map. It is in the alpha portion of the color for each pixel. This keeps us from having to maintain and process another texture. We can call this HLSL code ReliefMapping.fx. The code for this shader is in Listing 17.5.

LISTING 17.5   ReliefMapping.fx

```
float4x4 World : WORLD;
float4x4 View;
float4x4 Projection;

float4 AmbientColor : COLOR0;
float3 LightPosition;
```

LISTING 17.5   Continued

```
float4 LightDiffuseColor : COLOR1;

float2 ScaleAmount;
float3 CameraPosition;

texture ColorMap;
sampler2D ColorMapSampler = sampler_state
{
    texture = <ColorMap>;
    magfilter = LINEAR;
    minfilter = LINEAR;
    mipfilter = LINEAR;
    addressU = mirror;
    addressV = mirror;
};

texture2D ReliefMap;
sampler2D ReliefMapSampler = sampler_state
{
    texture = <ReliefMap>;
    minFilter = linear;
    magFilter = linear;
    mipFilter = linear;
};

struct VertexInput
{
    float3 Position : POSITION;
    float3 Normal : NORMAL;
    float3 Tangent : TANGENT;
    float2 TexCoord : TEXCOORD0;
};

struct VertexOutput
{
    float4 Position : POSITION;
    float2 TexCoord : TEXCOORD0;
    float3 LightDirection : TEXCOORD1;
    float3 ViewDirection : TEXCOORD3;
};

VertexOutput vertexShader(VertexInput input)
{
    VertexOutput output;
```

17

LISTING 17.5   Continued

```
    output.LightDirection = LightPosition - input.Position;

    float3 worldPosition = mul(float4(input.Position, 1.0f), World).xyz;
    output.ViewDirection = worldPosition - CameraPosition;

    float4x4 worldViewProjection = mul(mul(World, View), Projection);
    output.Position = mul(float4(input.Position, 1.0f), worldViewProjection);
    output.TexCoord = input.TexCoord;

    float3x3 tbnMatrix;
    tbnMatrix[0] = mul(input.Tangent, worldViewProjection);
    tbnMatrix[1] = mul(cross(input.Tangent, input.Normal),
        worldViewProjection);
    tbnMatrix[2] = mul(input.Normal, World);
    output.LightDirection = mul(tbnMatrix, output.LightDirection);
    output.ViewDirection = mul(tbnMatrix, output.ViewDirection);

    return(output);
}

float4 pixelShader(VertexOutput input) : COLOR
{
    const int numStepsLinear = 15;  //linear search number of steps
    const int numStepsBinary = 6;   //binary search number of steps

    float3 position = float3(input.TexCoord,0);
    float3 viewDirection = normalize(input.ViewDirection);

    float depthBias = 1.0 - viewDirection.z;
    depthBias *= depthBias;
    depthBias *= depthBias;
    depthBias = 1.0 - depthBias * depthBias;
    viewDirection.xy *= depthBias;
    viewDirection.xy *= ScaleAmount;


// ray intersect depth map using linear and binary searches
// depth value stored in alpha channel (black at is object surface)
    viewDirection /= viewDirection.z * numStepsLinear;
    int i;
    for( i=0; i<numStepsLinear; i++ )
    {
        float4 tex = tex2D(ReliefMapSampler, position.xy);
        if (position.z < tex.w)
```

LISTING 17.5   Continued

```
            position += viewDirection;
    }
    for( i=0; i<numStepsBinary; i++ )
    {
        viewDirection *= 0.5;
        float4 tex = tex2D(ReliefMapSampler, position.xy);
        if (position.z < tex.w)
            position += viewDirection;
        else
            position -= viewDirection;
    }

    input.TexCoord = position;
    //transform to tangent space
    viewDirection = normalize(input.ViewDirection);
    input.LightDirection = normalize(input.LightDirection);

    float3 Normal = 2.0f * (tex2D(ReliefMapSampler, input.TexCoord) - 0.5f);
    Normal.y = -Normal.y;
    Normal.z = sqrt(1.0 - Normal.x*Normal.x - Normal.y*Normal.y);

    return( (LightDiffuseColor * saturate(dot(input.LightDirection, Normal)) +
        AmbientColor) * tex2D(ColorMapSampler, input.TexCoord));
}

technique Default
{
    pass P0
    {
        VertexShader = compile vs_2_0 vertexShader();
        PixelShader = compile ps_2_a pixelShader();
    }
}
```

We removed the depth map sampler and renamed our normal map sampler to the relief map sampler. We also removed the normal from our VertexOutput and are no longer setting it in our vertex shader. That is the only thing that changed in that part of the code. The biggest change is inside of our pixel shader.

The pixel shader normalizes the viewing direction just like we do for the parallax mapping pixel shader. After modifying a copy of the view direction vector to account for any additional depth bias we want, relief mapping does a linear search to find the first point inside of the height-field surface that our viewing direction intersects. Once this is done, the binary search is carried out to narrow down the point of intersection. The reason the algorithm starts with a linear search instead of just using a binary search is because if the view ray intersects the height-field in more than one place it could easily return the wrong intersection. By starting in a linear fashion this is avoided. Another variation of this algorithm is called `IntervalMapping`. We do not discuss that variant, but it works the same way, except it uses a secondary linear search instead of a binary search. In some cases it can perform better, as it does not take as long to find the intersection.

After the binary search is completed, we normalize our unmodified view direction from our input as well as our light direction. We then calculate the normal based on the calculate position. We use the same position to retrieve the color from our color map.

In our game code we need to add the following private member fields:

```
private Effect reliefEffect;
private Texture2D reliefMap;
```

As usual, we need to initialize these in the `LoadGraphicsContent` method:

```
reliefMap = content.Load<Texture2D>(@"Content\Textures\rockbump_relief");
reliefEffect = content.Load<Effect>(@"Content\Effects\ReliefMapping");
```

In the `Update` method we allow changing to this effect by pressing the number 5:

```
if (input.KeyboardState.WasKeyPressed(Keys.D5))
    currentEffect = reliefEffect;
```

Finally, we need to set the relief map parameter in our effect:

```
if (currentEffect.Parameters["ReliefMap"] != null)
    currentEffect.Parameters["ReliefMap"].SetValue(reliefMap);
```

We can now run our demo and see the nice effect relief mapping gives us. We now have many different ways to map textures onto our 3D objects. Our relief mapping allows self-shadowing, which provides very nice results without the need for additional geometry.

Texture Animation

In this last section of the chapter we discuss a relatively simple but effective texturing technique. We are going to see how we can animate a texture. In this demo we will be texturing our rectangle, but we could easily do the same thing with a loaded 3D object like our asteroid.

We need to set up a new solution that we can call AnimateTextureDemo. We need to reference our XELibrary, but it is not necessary to actually include the project in the solution. We need to create the Textures and Effects subfolders in the Content folder.

After our solution is created we can create a new effect file called AnimateTexture.fx. This effect will be identical to the DirectionalLight.fx file we used in a previous section of this chapter. We only need to change one line of code and add this variable:

```
Vector2 offset = Vector2.Zero;
```

We are changing our pixel shader's return value to include the offset that our demo will pass in. We need to replace this line:

```
return( tex2D(ColorMapSampler, input.TexCoord) * DiffuseLight + AmbientColor);
```

with this line:

```
return( tex2D(ColorMapSampler, input.TexCoord + Offset) *
    DiffuseLight + AmbientColor);
```

We simply added the offset 2D vector to our 2D texture coordinates.

Our Game1.cs will need the InitializeVertices and InitializeIndices methods from the previous demo. All of the vertex information needs to be added to the code. We will not list it here, as it is listed earlier in this chapter. We need to set up a camera and our input handler. We need to add the following private member fields to our demo:

```
private Effect effect;
private Texture2D colorMap;
private Vector3 LightPosition;
private Vector2 offset = Vector2.Zero;
```

We can initialize our light position inside of the Initialize method:

```
LightPosition = new Vector3(0, 0, -300);
```

We can set up our colorMap and our effect in the LoadGraphicsContent method:

```
colorMap = content.Load<Texture2D>(@"Content\Textures\example");
effect = content.Load<Effect>(@"Content\Effects\AnimateTexture");
effect.Parameters["AmbientColor"].SetValue(.05f);
effect.Parameters["ColorMap"].SetValue(colorMap);
effect.Parameters["LightPosition"].SetValue(LightPosition);
```

Because those values are not going to change per frame, we just set them once when we set up our effect. We are going to animate our texture based on the game's timer. We want it to update every frame, so we can add the following lines to the Update method:

```
offset.X += (float)gameTime.ElapsedGameTime.TotalSeconds * 0.0333f;
offset.Y += (float)gameTime.ElapsedGameTime.TotalSeconds * 0.0033f;
```

We are simply adding a small amount to our offset value that will get passed to our shader. We are going to scroll horizontally faster than we will scroll vertically. Our Draw method will be similar to our previous project. The difference is that we do not need to set all of the different values for the different mapping techniques and that we are adding in our offset parameter. We need to insert the following code into the Draw method:

```
Matrix world = Matrix.CreateScale(100.0f) *
    Matrix.CreateTranslation(new Vector3(0, 0, -250));
effect.Parameters["World"].SetValue(world);
effect.Parameters["View"].SetValue(camera.View);
effect.Parameters["Projection"].SetValue(camera.Projection);
effect.Parameters["Offset"].SetValue(offset);
```

When we run the demo we can see texture scrolling to the left and up. We would just need to subtract our values from the X and Y components of our offset to reverse the direction. Our shader has set up the addressU and addressV values of our texture sampler to mirror. As a result, when our texture scrolls, it is a mirror of itself. If we just wanted it to wrap without mirroring itself we could change those values to wrap instead. Another option is clamp, which would result in our texture just moving off of the rectangle entirely. Of course, addressU and addressV can store different values. For example, we could set addressU to wrap and addressV to mirror.

TIP

A great example of how we could use the addressU and addressV values in a real application would be to gave multiple layers of alpha blended textures scrolling in different directions. By doing this, we could get effects like water, clouds, or even plasma fields.

Summary

In this chapter we discussed how to set up a directional light and reviewed our ambient light. We then discussed different types of bump mapping. We looked at normal mapping, which just uses a normal map (RGB values) to determine the normal of each pixel so that when lights shine on it the object appears to have depth even though there is no extra geometry. Then we discussed parallax mapping, which takes in a depth (height) map in addition to the normal map. This extra data adds depth to objects. The last mapping technique we discussed was relief mapping. This also uses depth information, but it uses it inside of the alpha channel of the normal map. This way there is no need to store and process an additional texture. It also allows self-shadowing, producing much more realistic results.

We finished up the chapter by discussing texture animation. We saw how easy it was to animate a texture on a 3D object by simply adding an offset to our texture coordinates. We updated that offset every frame with our game time. This allowed our texture to scroll left to right and up and down in a slow diagonal movement.

CHAPTER 18

Special Effects

Creating special effects is a great way to polish games. Most of the time it is not absolutely critical to game play, but it really adds the extra special touch our games need to stand out from the crowd. In this chapter we discuss transitions as well as the improved "new school" way of doing a procedural fire effect.

Transitions

We have already touched on one transition in this book— fading. We have faded to black and we have faded to a specified color. This fade is simple and can help give us that polished look. However, we can easily learn a couple more transition techniques. One of these techniques builds on top of the knowledge we gained when we discovered how to do the fade to color transition.

Before we continue in this section, we need create a new project called TransitionsDemo. We only need to reference the XELibrary because we will not be modifying the code in this chapter. There is no need to add the actual XELibrary project to our solution.

We need to add our private member fields:

```
private enum TransitionState { None, CrossFade, Wipe };

private FirstPersonCamera camera;
private InputHandler input;

private Model model;
private Texture2D texture;
private Effect effect;

private SpriteBatch spriteBatch;
private Texture2D splashScreen;
```

```
private RenderTarget2D renderTarget;

private TransitionState state = TransitionState.CrossFade;
```

We are going to be transitioning from a 3D scene into a 2D scene. We are simulating fading into the start menu. We have set up an enumerated type to store the different states in this demo. "None" could really be "playing" as it means there are no transitions taking place. We are going to create the `CrossFade` and `Wipe` transitions after we get the framework set up for this demo.

Because we are transitioning from a 3D scene we are going to need to render our 3D scene into a 2D texture. This is where the render target comes in. Finally, we create our demo state field, which we also initialize to the cross-fade effect.

We do not want to break tradition, so we will look at the code we need to add to our constructor:

```
graphics.PreferredBackBufferWidth = 1280;
graphics.PreferredBackBufferHeight = 720;

input = new InputHandler(this, true);
Components.Add(input);

camera = new FirstPersonCamera(this);
Components.Add(camera);
```

We are going to be using the same splash screen that we used in Chapter 9, "2D Basics." This texture is 1280 x 720, so we are asking our graphics device to use that resolution. We set up our input handler and our camera like usual.

The code in the `LoadGraphicsContent` method is as follows:

```
GraphicsDevice device = graphics.GraphicsDevice;

if (loadAllContent)
{
    model = content.Load<Model>(@"Content\Models\asteroid1");
    texture = content.Load<Texture2D>(@"Content\Textures\asteroid1");
    effect = content.Load<Effect>(@"Content\Effects\AmbientTexture");
    splashScreen = content.Load<Texture2D>(@"Content\Textures\splashscreen");

    spriteBatch = new SpriteBatch(graphics.GraphicsDevice);
}

renderTarget = new RenderTarget2D(device, device.Viewport.Width,
    device.Viewport.Height, 1, device.DisplayMode.Format,
    device.PresentationParameters.MultiSampleType,
    device.PresentationParameters.MultiSampleQuality);
```

This code is simply a review of what we have done many times before. If a refresher is needed on the render target, one can be found back in Chapter 13, "Advanced HLSL." We also want to make sure we dispose of our render target inside of the `UnloadGraphicsContent` method. We need to actually add the files we need for this demo as well. They can be found in the usual places.

Next, we can look at the framework for the `Update` method:

```
UpdateInput();

switch (state)
{
    case TransitionState.CrossFade:
        {
            UpdateFade(gameTime);
            break;
        }
    case TransitionState.Wipe:
        {
            UpdateWipe(gameTime);
            break;
        }
    default:
        {
            break;
        }
}

base.Update(gameTime);
```

Our `UpdateInput` method will simply check to see if the A button or the spacebar has been pressed. If so, it will change the state. We can see that method here, along with `UpdateFade` and `UpdateWipe` stubbed out:

```
private void UpdateInput()
{
    if (input.KeyboardState.WasKeyPressed(Keys.Space) ||
        input.ButtonHandler.WasButtonPressed(0, InputHandler.ButtonType.A))
    {
        state—;

        if (state < TransitionState.None)
            state = TransitionState.Wipe;

        InitializeValues();
    }
}
```

```
private void UpdateFade(GameTime gameTime) { }

private void UpdateWipe(GameTime gameTime) { }
```

Every time we change our state, we also call the `InitializeValues` method, which can be created as an empty method for now. After creating that method, we can dig into the Draw methods:

```
protected override void Draw(GameTime gameTime)
{
    GraphicsDevice device = graphics.GraphicsDevice;

    //Set up our render target
    device.SetRenderTarget(0, renderTarget);
    //Clear out our render target
    device.Clear(Color.Black);

    //Draw Scene
    Matrix world = Matrix.CreateRotationY(
            MathHelper.ToRadians(45.0f *
            (float)gameTime.TotalGameTime.TotalSeconds)) *
            Matrix.CreateTranslation(new Vector3(0, 0, -4000)));
    DrawModel(ref model, ref world, texture);

    //resolve what we just drew to our render target
    device.ResolveRenderTarget(0);
    //clear it out
    device.SetRenderTarget(0, null);

    //now, we can draw it for real ...
    //clear out our buffer
    device.Clear(Color.CornflowerBlue);

    spriteBatch.Begin(SpriteBlendMode.AlphaBlend, SpriteSortMode.Immediate,
        SaveStateMode.SaveState);

    //start transition
    switch (state)
    {
        case TransitionState.CrossFade:
            {
                break;
            }
        case TransitionState.Wipe:
            {
                break;
```

```
            }
        default:
            {
                spriteBatch.Draw(renderTarget.GetTexture(), Vector2.Zero,
                Color.White);
                break;
            }
    }

    //close our batch
    spriteBatch.End();

    base.Draw(gameTime);
}

private void DrawModel(ref Model m, ref Matrix world, Texture2D texture)
{
    Matrix[] transforms = new Matrix[m.Bones.Count];
    m.CopyAbsoluteBoneTransformsTo(transforms);

    foreach (ModelMesh mesh in m.Meshes)
    {
        foreach (ModelMeshPart mp in mesh.MeshParts)
        {
            effect.Parameters["ColorMap"].SetValue(texture);
            effect.Parameters["Projection"].SetValue(camera.Projection);
            effect.Parameters["View"].SetValue(camera.View);
            effect.Parameters["World"].SetValue(world * mesh.ParentBone.Transform);
            mp.Effect = effect;
        }
        mesh.Draw();
    }
}
```

There is nothing new in the way we have set up this code. We have our faithful DrawModel method, which we call from within our default case in our Draw method. The other two cases do not draw anything at this point. We are simply putting the framework in place so the next sections can focus solely on what is needed for the transition.

The first part of our Draw method is where we draw our model like normal, except we are drawing it to our render target. Then we use our sprite batch to draw that texture on the screen. We save our state for this simple demo. Doing this once or twice per frame is not going to be total devastation, but any more and it will really degrade performance. In Chapter 9, "2D Basics," we discussed the states that the sprite batch sets, and for optimal performance, these states should just be set back manually.

At this point we have our transition demo framework created. If we ran the code, we would need to press the spacebar (or the A button) a couple of times to actually get to see our asteroid because the two case statements for the other states do not actually draw anything on the screen. Now we can move to the actual transitions.

Cross-Fade (Dissolve)

The dissolve transition is a lot like the color fade. However, instead of fading to a color, we fade out of one scene and into another. It looks as though the scene dissolves as the next scene appears. Effectively, we will render one scene on top of the other. To start, both scenes will be fully opaque. This means we will need to draw the scene we are transitioning into under the current scene that we are transitioning out of. Then during the transition period we just update the alpha component of our color. We can see this is very similar to how we did the color fade.

To implement this in our demo, we need to add this private member field:

```
private float fadeAmount;
```

We need to set this value to 0 in our `InitializeValues` method. We need to add the following code to the `UpdateFade` method:

```
fadeAmount += (.0005f * gameTime.ElapsedGameTime.Milliseconds);

//reset fade amount after a short time to see the effect again
if (fadeAmount > 2.0f)
    fadeAmount = 0.0f;
```

This method is called from our demo's `Update` method, assuming we are in the `CrossFade` state. This is being calculated just like the other fade to color demos we have done. The only other piece left for us to complete our dissolve (cross-fade) transition effect is to actually draw the effect. We do this inside of the `CrossFade` case in the `Draw` method:

```
//Draw the screen we are transitioning to first
spriteBatch.Draw(splashScreen, Vector2.Zero, Color.White);

//Then draw the screen we are transitioning from
spriteBatch.Draw(renderTarget.GetTexture(), Vector2.Zero,
    new Color(new Vector4(Color.White.ToVector3(), 1.0f - fadeAmount)));
```

We are simply drawing the scene we are transitioning into first so it will be under our current scene. Then we draw our current scene, passing in our fade amount. We are actually subtracting our fade amount from one to start fully opaque and transition into a transparent image.

The update is letting it update for a little bit and then just resetting the fade amount back to zero so the transition can start over again. In a real game, instead of just resetting that value, it would transition to a new state (e.g., StartMenu). We are done with this transition effect. Once we put the framework in place, the actual transition is very simple and straightforward. Now if we run the demo we can see our asteroid fade out as our start menu fades in. Remember, it does not actually do any fading, it just appears because the texture being drawn on top of it is slowly becoming transparent.

Directional Wipes

Directional wipes are a great transitional effect. We see these a lot in movies, where one scene pushes the previous scene out of the way. We will be implementing four directional wipes: left, right, up, and down. A left directional wipe will have the new scene drawn starting on the left side of the screen. We can see the different stages of this in Figures 18.1 through 18.4.

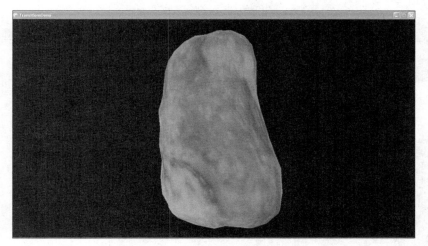

FIGURE 18.1   Our favorite asteroid represents the current playing scene that we will be transitioning from.

FIGURE 18.2   Our start menu and splash page represents the scene that we will be transitioning to.

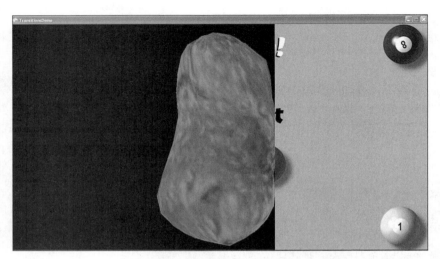

FIGURE 18.3   Using a left directional wipe, the splash screen starts to display on top of the current scene.

FIGURE 18.4   Using a left directional wipe, the splash screen is 50 percent on top of the current scene.

To implement this, we need to set up a few private member fields:

```
private Rectangle wipeInDestinationRectangle;
private Rectangle wipeInSourceRectangle;
private Rectangle wipeOutDestinationRectangle;
private Rectangle wipeOutSourceRectangle;
private enum WipeDirection { Left, Right, Up, Down };
private WipeDirection wipeDirection = WipeDirection.Left;
```

```
private int wipeX, wipeY, wipeWidth, wipeHeight;
private float wipeAmount;
```

We need to have several variables to manage our directional wipes. We are allowing four different wipes and so we have set up an enumeration type to handle that. We have also set up a `wipeDirection` state, which we have initialized to Left. We have a `wipeAmount` variable that we will use much like we did our `fadeAmount`. The four rectangle variables hold our source and destination rectangles of both the scene coming in and the scene going out. We need to initialize the `wipeAmount` variable to 0 inside of the `InitializeValues` method.

Next we are going to look at all of the update methods to handle directional wipes:

```
private void UpdateWipe(GameTime gameTime)
{
    Viewport viewport = graphics.GraphicsDevice.Viewport;

    wipeAmount += (0.5f * (float)gameTime.ElapsedGameTime.Milliseconds);

    switch (wipeDirection)
    {
        case WipeDirection.Left:
            {
                WipeLeft(viewport);
                break;
            }
        case WipeDirection.Right:
            {
                WipeRight(viewport);
                break;
            }
        case WipeDirection.Up:
            {
                WipeUp(viewport);
                break;
            }
        case WipeDirection.Down:
            {
                WipeDown(viewport);
                break;
            }
    }
}

private void WipeDown(Viewport viewport)
{
```

```
    wipeY = 0;
    wipeX = 0;
    wipeWidth = viewport.Width;
    wipeHeight = Convert.ToInt32(wipeAmount);

    wipeInDestinationRectangle = new Rectangle(0, 0, wipeWidth, wipeHeight);
    wipeInSourceRectangle = new Rectangle(0, 0, wipeWidth, wipeHeight);
    wipeOutDestinationRectangle = new Rectangle(wipeX, wipeHeight, wipeWidth,
        viewport.Height - wipeHeight);
    wipeOutSourceRectangle = new Rectangle(wipeX, wipeHeight, wipeWidth,
        viewport.Height - wipeHeight);

    if (wipeAmount > viewport.Height)
        ChangeWipe();
}

private void WipeUp(Viewport viewport)
{
    wipeY = Convert.ToInt32(viewport.Height - wipeAmount);
    wipeX = 0;
    wipeWidth = viewport.Width;
    wipeHeight = Convert.ToInt32(wipeAmount);

    wipeInDestinationRectangle = new Rectangle(wipeX, wipeY, wipeWidth,
        wipeHeight);
    wipeInSourceRectangle = new Rectangle(wipeX, wipeY, wipeWidth, wipeHeight);
    wipeOutDestinationRectangle = new Rectangle(0, 0, wipeWidth, wipeY);
    wipeOutSourceRectangle = new Rectangle(0, 0, wipeWidth, wipeY);

    if (wipeAmount > viewport.Height)
        ChangeWipe();
}

private void WipeRight(Viewport viewport)
{
    wipeY = 0;
    wipeX = 0;
    wipeWidth = Convert.ToInt32(wipeAmount);
    wipeHeight = viewport.Height;

    wipeInDestinationRectangle = new Rectangle(0, 0, wipeWidth, wipeHeight);
    wipeInSourceRectangle = new Rectangle(0, 0, wipeWidth, wipeHeight);
    wipeOutDestinationRectangle = new Rectangle(wipeWidth, wipeY,
        viewport.Width - wipeWidth, wipeHeight);
    wipeOutSourceRectangle = new Rectangle(wipeWidth, wipeY,
```

```
            viewport.Width - wipeWidth, wipeHeight);

    if (wipeAmount > viewport.Width)
        ChangeWipe();
}

private void WipeLeft(Viewport viewport)
{
    wipeY = 0;
    wipeX = Convert.ToInt32 (viewport.Width - wipeAmount);
    wipeWidth = Convert.ToInt32(wipeAmount);
    wipeHeight = viewport.Height;

    wipeInDestinationRectangle = new Rectangle(wipeX, wipeY, wipeWidth,
        wipeHeight);
    wipeInSourceRectangle = new Rectangle(wipeX, wipeY, wipeWidth, wipeHeight);
    wipeOutDestinationRectangle = new Rectangle(0, 0, wipeX, wipeHeight);
    wipeOutSourceRectangle = new Rectangle(0, 0, wipeX, wipeHeight);

    if (wipeAmount > viewport.Width)
        ChangeWipe();
}

private void ChangeWipe()
{
    wipeAmount = 0.0f;
    wipeDirection--;
    if (wipeDirection < WipeDirection.Left)
        wipeDirection = WipeDirection.Down;
}
```

There is quite a bit of code here, but it is basically the same thing repeated four times. The actual UpdateWipe method is very straightforward. We update the wipeAmount and then, depending on the wipe state we are in, we call one of the directional wipes. We next look in detail at the WipeLeft method.

The first thing we do is set our wipeY, wipeX, wipeWidth, and wipeHeight variables. For our left wipe, we are not modifying our y value and setting our x value to our width minus our wipe amount. Our height is simply the same height as our viewport. With these values set, we can set up our four rectangles for this wipe.

We start with the rectangles associated with the scene we are wiping in. The destination rectangle is the rectangle on our screen where we want to put the texture. The source rectangle is the rectangle of the texture we are pulling from. We used the source rectangles when we did cel animation. In this situation, we do not want to squish the entire texture onto the destination rectangle on the screen, so we specify which part of the scene we are transitioning in we are going to display.

The rectangles we use to wipe out the current scene simply take up the other part of the screen, so in the case of this left wipe, they start on the right side of the screen and extend out to the wipeX value, which is being updated with the `wipeAmount`. We can see this in Figure 18.4.

After the rectangle values are set up, a final condition is checked to determine if the wipe amount has exceeded the width or the height of the viewport. Width is checked for the left and right wipes and height is checked for the up and down wipes. If the threshold was exceeded, the `ChangeWipe` method is called, which just resets the `wipeAmount` value and changes the wipe direction state.

We can run our demo and see that not only do we have a nice cross-fade transition, but we have an additional four directional wipe transitions. With these wipes under our belts, it would not be much of a stretch to tackle directional pushes. We do not cover them in this book, but with a left push, the new scene comes in from the left and pushes the old scene out to the right. The only values that would need to change are the `wipeOutDestinationRectangle` and `wipeOutSourceRectangle` variables.

Making Fire

In Chapter 10, "2D Effects," we made a fire demo old school style, but we want to know how to make a fire effect on today's hardware using shaders. We will create a demo in this section that does just that. We need to create a demo called HLSLFireDemo. We will be referencing the XELibrary, but we will not be modifying it, so we do not need to add the actual project to our solution if we do not wish to.

Before we dig into the code, we can briefly describe how we will do the fire effect in this chapter and how it differs from how we did it before. Before, all of the calculations were done in software on the CPU. We modified a texture pixel by pixel and displayed that on the screen. In this demo, we will be using a pixel shader to do some of the heavy work. We will not be using a palette file in this demo. In fact, instead of the 256 colors we used in the earlier fire demo, we are only going to six colors, after which the other color values will be computed inside the pixel shader. We are not going to be modifying a texture directly in our code; instead we are going to render to a couple of render targets to achieve this effect.

In each frame, we are going to animate the fire upward by drawing our previous render target onto the current one. We are going to offset our texture vertically and use a pixel shader to fade our fire. We are going to create our hot spots across the bottom of the screen by using a bunch of 4 x 1 sprites with a sprite batch.

The private member fields we need for this demo are as follows:

```
private InputHandler input;
private FPS fps;

private SpriteBatch spriteBatch;
private Effect fireEffect;
```

```
private Random rand = new Random();

private Texture2D hotSpotTexture;
private Texture2D fire;
private Rectangle tileSafeArea;

private RenderTarget2D renderTarget1;
private RenderTarget2D renderTarget2;

private int offset = -128;
private Color[] colors = {
    Color.Black,
    Color.Yellow,
    Color.White,
    Color.Red,
    Color.Orange,
    new Color(255,255,128) //yellowish white
};
```

We see the usual suspects along with our two render targets, an offset value, and finally an array of six colors. We are going to use the offset to help us animate the fire upward. The color array is what we are going to use to generate the hot spots of the fire at the bottom of the screen.

We need to add the following lines to our constructor:

```
input = new InputHandler(this, true);
Components.Add(input);

fps = new FPS(this, true, true);
Components.Add(fps);
```

Our FPS component is set to draw at a consistent rate. We can check our frame rate when we want, but for the flames to move at a reasonable rate, we need the Draw method to be called at a consistent pace. Next, we can see the code we need to add to the LoadGraphicsContent method:

```
GraphicsDevice device = graphics.GraphicsDevice;

if (loadAllContent)
{
    tileSafeArea = Utility.GetTitleSafeArea(device, .8f);
    hotSpotTexture = CreateTexture(4, 1);
    spriteBatch = new SpriteBatch(device);
    fireEffect = content.Load<Effect>(@"Content\Effects\Fire");
}
```

18

```
renderTarget1 = new RenderTarget2D(device, device.Viewport.Width,
    device.Viewport.Height, 1, device.DisplayMode.Format,
    device.PresentationParameters.MultiSampleType,
    device.PresentationParameters.MultiSampleQuality);

renderTarget2 = new RenderTarget2D(device, device.Viewport.Width,
    device.Viewport.Height, 1, device.DisplayMode.Format,
    device.PresentationParameters.MultiSampleType,
    device.PresentationParameters.MultiSampleQuality);

fire = null;
```

We create our hotSpotTexture with the CreateTexture method, which we will see in a moment. We are telling the method that we want the hot spot to be 4 pixels wide and 1 pixel tall. We load in our fire effect, which we will look at in a moment. Finally, we set up both of our render targets and we set our fire texture to null. We will see why we do this here when we look at the Draw method a little later. For now, we can look at the CreateTexture method:

```
private Texture2D CreateTexture(int width, int height)
{
    Texture2D texture = new Texture2D(graphics.GraphicsDevice, width, height, 1,
        ResourceUsage.None, SurfaceFormat.Color,
        ResourceManagementMode.Automatic);

    int pixelCount = width * height;
    Color[] pixelData = new Color[pixelCount];

    for (int i = 0; i < pixelCount; i++)
        pixelData[i] = Color.White;

    texture.SetData(pixelData);

    return (texture);
}
```

This method is no different than the other textures we have created. A new texture is created, and we loop through all of the pixels, setting them to a particular color—white in this case. We save the pixel information on the texture and return it to the calling method.

It is important that when we create render targets, we dispose of them properly. We do this in the UnloadGraphicsContent method:

```
protected override void UnloadGraphicsContent(bool unloadAllContent)
{
    if (unloadAllContent == true)
```

```
      content.Unload();

    renderTarget1.Dispose();
    renderTarget2.Dispose();
}
```

Our Draw method is as follows:

```
GraphicsDevice device = graphics.GraphicsDevice;

//Draw hotspots on the first Render Target
device.SetRenderTarget(0, renderTarget1);
device.Clear(Color.Black);

spriteBatch.Begin();

//get last drawn screen — if not first time in
//fire is null first time in, and when device is lost (LoadGraphicsContent)
if (fire != null) //render target have valid texture
    spriteBatch.Draw(fire, Vector2.Zero, Color.White);

//draw hotspots
for (int i = 0; i < device.Viewport.Width / hotSpotTexture.Width; i++)
{
    spriteBatch.Draw(hotSpotTexture,
        new Vector2(i * hotSpotTexture.Width,
            device.Viewport.Height - hotSpotTexture.Height),
        colors[rand.Next(colors.Length)]);
}

spriteBatch.End();

//resolve what we just drew to our render target
device.ResolveRenderTarget(0);

//clear it out
device.SetRenderTarget(0, null);

// Transfer from first to second render target
device.SetRenderTarget(0, renderTarget2);

fireEffect.Begin();
spriteBatch.Begin(SpriteBlendMode.None, SpriteSortMode.Immediate,
    SaveStateMode.None);

EffectPass pass = fireEffect.CurrentTechnique.Passes[0];
```

```
pass.Begin();
spriteBatch.Draw(renderTarget1.GetTexture(),
    new Rectangle(0, offset, device.Viewport.Width,
    device.Viewport.Height - offset), Color.White);
spriteBatch.End();
pass.End();
fireEffect.End();

//resolve what we just drew to our render target
device.ResolveRenderTarget(0);

//clear it out
device.SetRenderTarget(0, null);

device.Clear(Color.Black);

//set texture to render
fire = renderTarget2.GetTexture();

// Draw second render target onto the screen (back buffer)
spriteBatch.Begin(SpriteBlendMode.Additive);

//render texture three times (in additive mode) to saturate color
spriteBatch.Draw(fire, tileSafeArea, Color.White);
spriteBatch.Draw(fire, tileSafeArea, Color.White);
spriteBatch.Draw(fire, tileSafeArea, Color.White);

spriteBatch.End();

base.Draw(gameTime);
```

The Draw method is broken down into three sections. The first section draws the hotspots of the fire onto the previous render target. The second section applies the postprocessing effect and animates the texture upward. The third and final section displays the final result on the screen, which is used by the first section in the next frame and starts the process all over again.

If this is the first time in, then only the hotspots will be drawn. The hotspots are drawn all across the bottom of the screen, with each hotspot using one of the six colors in our array. If this is not the first frame of the demo, then the contents that we last displayed on the screen are first drawn.

Once we are done with the first render target, we start drawing to our second render target. We draw the texture from our first render target and send it through a postprocessing pixel shader, which we have not yet discussed. We also use the offset value to animate our texture upward. Once the pixel shader is done, we then start rendering to our back buffer. We store the second render target's texture into our fire texture variable.

In the first section, we check this fire texture variable to make sure it is not null before trying to use it. It would be null on two occasions: when the demo first starts and when the device is lost. When the device is reset after it is lost, the `LoadGraphicsContent` method is called. This is why we set the fire texture variable to null then. Otherwise, when `Draw` is called after the reset, it would not have a valid texture and would crash the demo.

The final section of the `Draw` method takes our final texture that is created after the post-processing, and we use additive blending mode and write the texture to the screen three times. The postprocessing effect dulls the colors by blending them together. This is needed, but we definitely need our fire to be bright, and with additive blending we can easily achieve that effect by just drawing the same texture a few times. The end result is a nice looking fire.

The only thing left is our effect file. We can call this effect Fire.fx and the code is as follows:

```
texture Fire;

sampler FireMapSampler = sampler_state
{
    texture = <Fire>;
    magfilter = LINEAR;
    minfilter = LINEAR;
    mipfilter = LINEAR;
    addressU = wrap;
    addressV = wrap;
};

struct PixelInput
{
    float2 TexCoord : TEXCOORD0;
};

float4 pixelShader(PixelInput input) : COLOR0
{
    float4 color;
    float2 Right, Left, Above, Below;
    Left = Right = Above = Below = input.TexCoord;

    Right.x += .001;
    Left.x -= .001;
    Above.y += .001;
    Below.y -= .001;

    //Sample the four texture positions
    color = tex2D(FireMapSampler, Left);
```

18

```
    color += tex2D(FireMapSampler, Right);
    color += tex2D(FireMapSampler, Above);
    color += tex2D(FireMapSampler, Below);

    //Get the average
    color *= 0.25; // divided by 4

    //Cool down flame
    color.rgb -= .035;

    return(color);
}


technique Default
{
    pass P0
    {
        PixelShader = compile ps_2_0 pixelShader();
    }
}
```

The pixel shader is not that bad. This does the blending of surrounding pixel colors. Just like in Chapter 10, we are grabbing the left, right, above, and below pixels and blending those together to get the final color of the pixel we are on. By doing this, we are dulling the color, though, and that is why we display the texture three times at the end of our Draw method. Just like we had a cool-down value in Chapter 10 (we used 3 there) we also have a cool-down value in our pixel shader of -.035. This allows the flame to fade out.

At this point we can run our demo and get much better frame rates than we did in Chapter 10, especially on the Xbox 360. An interesting challenge would be to make a progress bar that was populated with fire, much like the Burnout racing game series.

Summary

In this chapter, we discussed transitions and the way to handle procedural fire on today's hardware. During our discussion of transitions we talked about the dissolve or cross-fade transition as well as wipes. We saw how to wipe the screen in four different directions. With these transitions we can create some nice effects in our games. We finished up the chapter by creating another fire effect. We were able to create the effect with a lot less code that runs more efficiently. In the next chapter, we will be looking at particle systems and then we will move on to making a full 3D game in the last part of the book.

CHAPTER 19

Particle System

In this chapter we discuss how to create a particle system. Although this will be a modest particle system, it should be a good foundation on which to build. The main goal of this chapter is to provide a good understanding of how to create a particle system. Once the basics have been nailed down, the sky is the limit in what we can do with particles.

Particle System Defined

Before we can dig into implementing a particle system, we need to determine exactly what one is. A particle system is simply a system of particles. Perhaps the better question is "What is a particle?" A particle can be anything: It could be dust, snow, rain, ants, sparks, smoke trails, debris, leaves, and so many more things. A particle is a single object. A particle system contains many particles and controls their properties. Some of the properties could be how long they live, their velocity, acceleration, color, texture, and size.

A particle system controls the behavior of a group of particles. The idea is to have one flexible system that can be used for many different effects just by adjusting some values. It could be that a rain and a snow effect share a lot of the same values: They both start on the same horizontal plane and fall downward, for example. Of course, other values would be different between the two particle systems. Rain would fall straight down and not be affected by the wind that much, whereas snow would fall downward but would be drastically affected by the wind.

The particle system we are creating in this chapter is just one of many ways to create a particle system. It should be a great springboard to get started. Hopefully it will serve our near future needs adequately. If not, we can take these concepts and modify our objects to better fit our needs.

Point Sprite Defined

Before we get into our engine, we need to have a firm understanding of the idea behind a point sprite. We use a point sprite to represent a particle in our 3D world. Prior to point sprites, game developers had to create a rectangle (quad) and apply a texture to it for each particle. This meant that there were four vertices for each and every particle. If we were rendering 5,000 particles that would be 20,000 vertices, just on the special effect we were trying to produce!

Fortunately, when DirectX 8 came out, point sprites were added. With point sprites, the graphics card only needs one vertex (a point) for each particle. We can even tell the graphics card the size of that vertex. It can be as small as one pixel to as large as we want. By using a vertex shader, we can set each particle (vertex) to be a different size if we need to for our effect.

XNA automatically maps our texture to the vertex. It also makes sure that the texture is always facing the camera. A point sprite gets its name from being a point (vertex) and being a sprite (having a texture that is always facing the camera). If we wanted to create a 2D particle system, we could use the same concepts in this chapter, except we would use regular sprites instead of point sprites and keep our vectors to 2D.

Creating the Particle Class

We briefly listed some of the values we needed to store for each particle. We are going to firm up that list and create a class that we can use to represent a particle that our system can use. We will be creating this class in our XELibrary project. Let's create a new solution for this chapter called ParticleSystemDemo. We need to include our XELibrary project to our solution. Once our solution is set up we can add a new code file to our XELibrary project called Particle.cs.

Here we will see the different values we want to store for our particle. These are the member fields of our `Particle` class:

```
private Vector3 velocity;
private Vector3 acceleration;
private float lifetime;
private Vector3 externalForce;

internal float Age;
internal bool IsAlive;
internal VertexPointSprite Vertex;
internal float ColorChangeRate;
internal float CurrentColorTime;
internal int CurrentColorIndex;
```

We are storing the particle's velocity and acceleration, which we have discussed in detail in the past. Next, we store a value to hold the amount of time this particle should live in seconds. The last private field is a vector storing the external force that should be applied to the particle. This is where we model gravity and wind direction. Our wind will be in x and z directions and gravity will be in the y direction.

Next are our internal member fields. Our particle system will need to access each of these directly and there is no need for an outside source (e.g., our game) to access these values. If we decided that our game did need read access to a value (like Age) then we could mark it as private and create a set method. We will see that in just a moment for the private fields that we have set up.

Our age value is what we use to compare against our lifetime value to determine if it is time for us to fade away. The alive boolean flag just lets us easily know if this particle is being updated and drawn on the screen. Once our age is greater than our lifetime, our alive flag is set to false. The last field holds our vertex data of type `VertexPointSprite`. This type is not an XNA type. We need to create that struct, which we do in the next section. For now, the main thing to know is that it stores the particle's position, color, and size.

The last three variables relate to the color of our point sprite (or rather how our texture is actually tinted). We discuss these in detail later when we use it in an example. For now, it is only important to know that we might want to have our particle change its color over time and these variables allow that.

We will create the constructor for our class:

```
public Particle()
{
    Age = 0.0f;
    Vertex = new VertexPointSprite();
    CurrentColorIndex = 0;
    CurrentColorTime = 0;
}
```

Our default constructor simply sets the initial age of our particle and creates a new instance of its vertex. It also initializes the color fields we have created.

Our particle system needs an `Update` method. This will allow the particle to be updated every frame. The `Update` method for our `Particle` class is as follows:

```
internal void Update(float elapsedTime)
{
    Age += elapsedTime;
    CurrentColorTime += elapsedTime;

    if (Age >= lifetime)
        IsAlive = false;
    else
    {
        velocity += acceleration;
        velocity -= externalForce;
```

```
        Vertex.Position += velocity * elapsedTime;
    }
}
```

This method is very simple. Depending on what is needed, this could be complex enough to include some of the physics we saw in previous chapters or even state management so the particle would do different things at different states in its life. For our purposes, we are going to keep it simple and just update our velocity and position.

The first task the method performs is to add the amount of seconds that have passed since the last frame to the total age of our particle. It adds this same value to the total amount of time the particle has been tinted with the current color (Vertex.Color).

Then we check to see if we have lived past our lifetime. If so, we set our IsAlive flag to false. If we are still alive then we update our velocity with our current acceleration. We then subtract any external forces from our velocity. This does not take into account any kind of friction, but that would be trivial to add later if needed. Once the velocity has its final value, we update our position.

We need a way to initialize all of the particle's values. We are going to create an Initialize method. Actually, we are going to create two overloaded methods. These Initialize methods are as follows:

```
internal void Initialize(ParticleSystemSettings settings)
{
    Initialize(settings, true);
}


internal void Initialize(ParticleSystemSettings settings, bool makeAlive)
{
    Age = 0;
    IsAlive = makeAlive;

    Vector3 minPosition = (settings.EmitPosition - (settings.EmitRange * .5f));
    Vector3 maxPosition = (settings.EmitPosition + (settings.EmitRange * .5f));

    Vector3 position = Utility.GetRandomVector3(minPosition, maxPosition);

    Vertex.Position = position;

    if (settings.EmitRadius != Vector2.Zero)
    {
        float angle = Utility.GetRandomFloat(0, MathHelper.TwoPi);

        Vertex.Position = new Vector3(
            position.X + (float)Math.Sin(angle) * settings.EmitRadius.X,
            position.Y,
```

```
            position.Z + (float)Math.Cos(angle) * settings.EmitRadius.Y);
    }

    velocity = Utility.GetRandomVector3(
        settings.MinimumVelocity, settings.MaximumVelocity);

    acceleration = Utility.GetRandomVector3(
        settings.MinimumAcceleration, settings.MaximumAcceleration);

    lifetime = Utility.GetRandomFloat(
        settings.MinimumLifetime, settings.MaximumLifetime);

    if (settings.DisplayColorsInOrder)
    {
        Vertex.Color = settings.Colors[0];
        ColorChangeRate = lifetime / settings.Colors.Length;
    }
    else
    {
        Vertex.Color =
            settings.Colors[Utility.GetRandomInt(0, settings.Colors.Length)];
    }

    Vertex.PointSize = Utility.GetRandomFloat(
        settings.MinimumSize, settings.MaximumSize);

    externalForce = settings.ExternalForce;
}
```

The first overload simply passes true to our `makeAlive` parameter in the second overload along with the values that were passed in. The values are being passed in with the `ParticleSystemSettings` class. We will see this class in a moment, but it really just contains the different values we need to successfully initialize our particle.

The main overload will do all of the heavy lifting. Overall, this method is taking different settings and determining the initial values of our particle. Most settings have a minimum and a maximum value. We then set our particle variable equal to a random value using the minimum and maximum values as the valid range.

Before we dig into the method, let's look at the settings class we are passing in. We need to create another class in our XELibrary project called ParticleSystemSettings.cs. The code for this class is as follows:

```
public class ParticleSystemSettings
{
    public Texture2D Texture;
```

```
    public float RotateAmount;

    public bool RunOnce = false;
    public int Capacity;
    public int EmitPerSecond;

    public Vector3 ExternalForce;

    public Vector3 EmitPosition;
    public Vector2 EmitRadius = Vector2.Zero;
    public Vector3 EmitRange;

    public Vector3 MinimumVelocity;
    public Vector3 MaximumVelocity;

    public Vector3 MinimumAcceleration;
    public Vector3 MaximumAcceleration;

    public float MinimumLifetime;
    public float MaximumLifetime;

    public float MinimumSize;
    public float MaximumSize;

    public Color[] Colors;
    public bool DisplayColorsInOrder;
}
```

Although each particle will have a specific value, our particle system needs randomness.
After all, it would look rather boring if every raindrop fell in the exact same position! To
accommodate the randomness needed, we require the particle system to pass in
minimum and maximum values for many of the particle properties. Our Initialize
method takes these values and determines the initial value of our particle.

We will run through these fields as well as the particle's Initialize method at the same
time. The first field is not actually used in our particle but is used in our particle system,
as we will see later. If needed, the code could be modified to have an array of textures
much like we have an array of colors. Each point sprite can be rotated and that is set with
the RotateAmount setting. The RunOnce field is used to let the particle system know if it
should just run the effect one time or continuously. Capacity lets the particle system
know the maximum number of particles it will have at any one time. EmitPerSecond tells
the system how many particles it should try to emit per second. It will not emit more
than there is capacity for.

ExternalForce is used to apply things like gravity or wind. It is constant for every particle. EmitPosition, EmitRadius, and EmitRange are all used to set the initial position the

particle. Previously in the `Initialize` method, we first set our position to a random vector based on our calculated minimum and maximum position. These values are determined by using the `EmitRange` vector. Next, we check to see if the particle system has specified a radius, which means that our particles should be emitted in a circular (or oval) pattern. We do this check so we do not need to take the hit of calculating the sine and cosine values if it isn't needed. We factor in the calculated angle and radius to determine our real position.

> **TIP**
>
> For a performance boost, we could create a lookup table of common sine and cosine values. A method could then simply return the value from the lookup table when passed in the angle instead of doing the computation in realtime.

We then store minimum and maximum values for our velocity, acceleration, lifetime, and size. In our `Initialize` method we calculate the initial values the particles will be assigned by retrieving random values between the minimum and maximum values.

We have an array of colors that we either pick from randomly or loop through in order and in even intervals for the life span of the particle. If `DisplayColorsInOrder` is true, the `Initialize` method calculates `ColorChangeRate` to determine how often the particle should change colors so that each color will be visible for the same amount of time. This is done by dividing the number of colors in the array by the particle's lifetime. If `DisplayColorsInOrder` is false, we simply pick a random index of our colors array and set the particle to that color for its entire lifetime.

We need to modify the `Utility` class in our XELibrary to add in the helper methods that return a random value based on a minimum and maximum value passed in:

```
private static Random rand = new Random();

public static int GetRandomInt(int min, int max)
{
    return (rand.Next(min, max));
}
public static float GetRandomFloat(float min, float max)
{
    return (((float)rand.NextDouble() * (max - min)) + min);
}
public static Vector2 GetRandomVector2(Vector2 min, Vector2 max)
{
    return (new Vector2(
        GetRandomFloat(min.X, max.X),
        GetRandomFloat(min.Y, max.Y)));
}
public static Vector3 GetRandomVector3(Vector3 min, Vector3 max)
{
```

19

```
    return (new Vector3(
        GetRandomFloat(min.X, max.X),
        GetRandomFloat(min.Y, max.Y),
        GetRandomFloat(min.Z, max.Z)));
}
```

The key to all of these methods (except the random integer wrapper) is the
`GetRandomFloat` method. This uses the `NextDouble` method, which returns a value
between 0 and 1. We then multiply the difference of our maximum and minimum values
passed in. Finally, we add in our minimum value to this total.

Creating the `VertexPointSprite` Struct

In Chapter 17, "Advanced Texturing Techniques," we created the
`VertexPositionNormalTangent` vertex format. Because we are using a point sprite
we need to create another custom vertex format. This could actually be avoided if
we did not want the flexibility to create particles of different sizes. If we only needed one
size for all of our particles, we could just use the `VertexPositionColor` struct already
provided by XNA. We do want the flexibility of different-sized particles, however, so we
will quickly create another custom vertex format. The `Vertex` field in our `Particle` class is
declared as this type.

The code for this struct is as follows:

```
public struct VertexPointSprite
{
    public Vector3 Position;
    public float PointSize;
    public Color Color;

    public VertexPointSprite(
        Vector3 Position,
        Color Color,
        float PointSize)
    {
        this.Position = Position;
        this.Color = Color;
        this.PointSize = PointSize;
    }

    public static int SizeInBytes = 8 * sizeof(float);

    public static VertexElement[] VertexElements =
        {
            new VertexElement(0, 0, VertexElementFormat.Vector3,
                VertexElementMethod.Default, VertexElementUsage.Position, 0),
            new VertexElement(0, sizeof(float)*3, VertexElementFormat.Single,
                VertexElementMethod.Default, VertexElementUsage.PointSize, 0),
```

```
    new VertexElement(0, sizeof(float)*4, VertexElementFormat.Color,
        VertexElementMethod.Default, VertexElementUsage.Color, 0)
};
}
```

There should not be anything that surprises us with this code. We have three properties that we need to set: `Position`, `PointSize`, and `Color`. We set up our vertex elements just like we did in Chapter 17, "Advanced Texturing Techniques."

Creating the Particle System Engine

Now that we have our particle created along with the required custom vertex format struct, we can look into how we can implement our particle system. We can think of our particle system class like one of the other manager classes we have created in the past. It is simply a means to manage multiple objects of the same type. This class will be an abstract class that will inherit from the `DrawableGameComponent` class. Each individual particle system we make (rain, bubbles, gas, etc.) will inherit from this base `ParticleSystem` class. We need to create the file for this class in our XELibrary project. We can declare our class as follows:

```
public abstract class ParticleSystem : DrawableGameComponent { }
```

As usual, we will start by declaring our private member fields:

```
private Particle[] particles;
private int lastParticleIndex = 0;
private int totalParticlesEmitted = 0;
private int numberOfActiveParticles;
private float rotateAngle = 0;

private Effect effect;
private VertexDeclaration vertexDeclaration;
private VertexPointSprite[] vertices;

private SpriteFont font;
private SpriteBatch sb;
private Rectangle titleSafeArea;
```

We have an array of particles that we are managing. We keep track of the number of particles we have emitted along with the number of active particles. We initialize our rotation angle to 0. This value will rotate the texture around our point sprite. We will see this in detail when we look at our effect file. Because our particles are point sprites, we need to create our vertices. Finally, we declare fields to hold our sprite batch, our sprite font, and the title safe area of the screen we can draw on. We are going to allow drawing some debug information and this is why we need these variables.

Next, we can see the protected and public member fields:

```
protected ParticleSystemSettings settings;
protected ContentManager content;
```

```
public Matrix View;
public Matrix Projection;
public bool DebugInfo = false;
```

Our specific particle system objects that inherit this class will need to initialize the settings that will get passed to the particle's Initialize method. They might also need to load content so we made both the settings and content protected variables. Our game needs to set these fields we have marked as public. The game will set the View and Projection fields during the Draw method so the particles will be displayed correctly. The game can set the debug information flag to display some particle information that can prove helpful while debugging a particular particle system effect.

Our constructor is very straightforward. We are just initializing our settings and content variables:

```
public ParticleSystem(Game game)
    : base(game)
{
    content = new ContentManager(game.Services);
    settings = new ParticleSystemSettings();
}
```

Next, we can initialize our particle system with the following methods:

```
protected abstract ParticleSystemSettings InitializeSettings();

public override void Initialize()
{
    settings = InitializeSettings();

    particles = new Particle[settings.Capacity];

    vertices = new VertexPointSprite[settings.Capacity];

    for (int i = 0; i < settings.Capacity; i++)
    {
        particles[i] = new Particle();
        particles[i].Initialize(settings, false);
    }

    numberOfActiveParticles = 0;

    base.Initialize();
}
```

We populate our settings with a call to our abstract InitializeSettings method. When that is done, we will have all of our settings populated, including the capacity value. We use the value to determine how big our particle array needs to be. We also create a vertex array of the same size. We loop through all of the particles and initialize each one by calling the Initialize method on the particle itself. This is the method that created the values by getting random values based on the minimum and maximum values populated in the settings class. The makeAlive parameter is false because we do not actually want all of the particles to be generated at once and show up on the screen. We want to ease into the effect.

Before we get to our Update method, let's look at the LoadGraphicsContent method we need:

```
protected override void LoadGraphicsContent(bool loadAllContent)
{
    if (loadAllContent)
    {
        titleSafeArea = Utility.GetTitleSafeArea(GraphicsDevice, .80f);

        effect = content.Load<Effect>(@"Content\Effects\PointSprites");
        font = content.Load<SpriteFont>(@"Content\Fonts\Arial");

        sb = new SpriteBatch(GraphicsDevice);

        vertexDeclaration = new VertexDeclaration(GraphicsDevice,
            VertexPointSprite.VertexElements);
    }


    base.LoadGraphicsContent(loadAllContent);
}
```

There is nothing too surprising here. We calculate our title safe area. We load our effect (which we talk about a little later) and our font. We create a new sprite batch and initialize our vertex declaration. These are all straightforward tasks.

Now we are ready to jump into our Update method. The purpose of this method is to make sure our particles that are alive continue to move as needed and to create any new particles that should be created based on the emit rate. The following is the contents of our Update method:

```
float elapsedTime = (float)gameTime.ElapsedGameTime.TotalSeconds;

int particlesToEmitThisFrame =
    (int)(settings.EmitPerSecond * elapsedTime + .99);
int particlesEmitted = 0;
bool canCreateParticle;

for (int i = 0; i < particles.Length; i++)
{
    if (particles[i].IsAlive)
    {
```

```
        particles[i].Update(elapsedTime);
        if (!particles[i].IsAlive)
        {
            numberOfActiveParticles—;
            particles[i].CurrentColorTime = 0;
            particles[i].CurrentColorIndex = 0;

            canCreateParticle = ShouldCreateParticle(
                              particlesEmitted, particlesToEmitThisFrame);
        }
        else
        {
            if (settings.DisplayColorsInOrder)
            {
                if (particles[i].CurrentColorTime >
                    particles[i].ColorChangeRate)
                {
                    //due to rounding errors with floats we need to make sure
                    //we actually have another color
                    if (particles[i].CurrentColorIndex <
                        settings.Colors.Length - 1)
                    {
                        particles[i].CurrentColorIndex++;
                        particles[i].SetColor(
                            settings.Colors[particles[i].CurrentColorIndex]);
                        particles[i].CurrentColorTime = 0;
                    }
                }
            }
        }
    }
    else
    {
        canCreateParticle = ShouldCreateParticle(
                          particlesEmitted, particlesToEmitThisFrame);
    }

if (canCreateParticle)
    {
        particles[i] = CreateParticle();
        particlesEmitted++;
        numberOfActiveParticles++;
        totalParticlesEmitted++;
    }
}
```

```
if (settings.RotateAmount > 0)
{
    rotateAngle += settings.RotateAmount;
    if (rotateAngle > MathHelper.TwoPi)
        rotateAngle = 0;
}

base.Update(gameTime);
```

The first thing we do in this method is calculate the number of particles we should emit this frame. The calculation emits the same amount of particles every frame. We add the .99 at the end of the formula because we are truncating the value from a double to an integer. As a result we would not emit enough particles that frame. We should emit one more particle than we can than not emit enough particles. We then loop through each particle and check to determine if the particle is alive or not.

If our particle is alive we call the particle's Update method. Remember, this method actually determines if the particle has lived its entire life and if so, it sets the IsAlive flag to false. So after calling the Update method, we check that flag. If the particle died during that update cycle we update our number of active particles counter as well as reset our color time and index. This is important for when we loop through our colors in order. We also check to see if we should immediately replace that particle with a new one. We will look at the condition inside of the ShouldCreateParticle method in a moment.

If our particle is still alive even after calling the particle's Update method, we need to have our particle system manage which color our particle should be. This is only done if we are actually displaying our colors in order. Otherwise, there is nothing to do because the initial color of the particle will remain the same until the particle dies.

When we first came into our for loop checking each particle, we asked if the particle was alive or not. We just discussed what happens when the particle is alive when we come into this Update method. Now we will see what we do with our particle if it is not alive.

If our particle is not alive, we need to determine if we want to create another particle. We are using the ShouldCreateParticle method again so now is a good time to see exactly what that method is doing:

```
private bool ShouldCreateParticle(
    int particlesEmitted, int particlesToEmitThisFrame)
{
```

19

```
    if (!settings.RunOnce || totalParticlesEmitted < settings.Capacity)
        return (particlesEmitted < particlesToEmitThisFrame);
    else
        return (false);
}
```

We determine if we should create a new particle by looking at a few variables. As long as we are not running the particle system effect once or if we are running the effect once but we have not reached our capacity yet, then we continue to our next check; otherwise we return false that we should not create another particle. The next check we do is to see if we can still emit particles in this frame. We return that value.

This brings us to the canCreateParticle condition back in our Update method. If the preceding method told us we can create a particle, then we do by calling CreateParticle and we update our counters. We will see that method in just a moment.

The last task we perform in our Update method is that we update our rotation angle with the rotation amount supplied in the settings. If the rotation amount is set to zero, we do not actually update our rotation angle. Not setting the rotation amount, or setting it to zero, tells our particle system that we do not want our point sprite (or more accurately, our texture applied to our point sprite) to rotate. We will see how this value is used in our effect file in the next section.

The CreateParticle method is listed here:

```
private Particle CreateParticle()
{
    int index = lastParticleIndex;
    for (int i = 0; i < particles.Length; i++)
    {
        if (!particles[index].IsAlive)
            break;
        else
        {
            index++;
            if (index >= particles.Length)
                index = 0;
        }
    }

    //at this point index is the one we want ...
    particles[index].Initialize(settings);
    lastParticleIndex = index;

    return (particles[index]);
}
```

In this method we loop through our particles to find an empty slot (a particle that is not alive). Once we find this slot, we call the particle's `Initialize` method to set all of the random values for this particle. We then update our index stating where the last particle we created was located. This is done for performance reasons. The idea is that the particles are created in order and that if the lifetimes are relatively close then we might find an empty slot close to the last place we found the empty slot. In a worst-case scenario, we would loop through the entire list but by doing it this way. However, that should not happen anywhere near the amount of times it would if we always started with the first index.

Now that we have updated our particles, we need to actually draw them. We are going to be creating an effect file to draw our point sprites. We are also going to allow drawing debugging information on the screen. We need to load the effect and the font in our `LoadGraphicsContent` method:

```
protected override void LoadGraphicsContent(bool loadAllContent)
{
    if (loadAllContent)
    {
        titleSafeArea = Utility.GetTitleSafeArea(GraphicsDevice, .80f);

        effect = content.Load<Effect>(@"Content\Effects\PointSprites");
        font = content.Load<SpriteFont>(@"Content\Fonts\Arial");

        sb = new SpriteBatch(GraphicsDevice);

        vertexDeclaration = new VertexDeclaration(GraphicsDevice,
            VertexPointSprite.VertexElements);
    }

    base.LoadGraphicsContent(loadAllContent);
}
```

Besides loading the content and creating our sprite batch, we also set up our vertex declaration using the `VertexPointSprite` we created earlier.

Now, we can get to our actual `Draw` method. The content of our `Draw` method is as follows:

```
if (DebugInfo)
{
    sb.Begin(SpriteBlendMode.AlphaBlend, SpriteSortMode.Immediate,
        SaveStateMode.SaveState);
    sb.DrawString(font, "Particles Capacity: " + settings.Capacity.ToString(),
        new Vector2(titleSafeArea.Left, titleSafeArea.Top), Color.Black);
    sb.DrawString(font, "Active Particles: " +
        numberOfActiveParticles.ToString(),
```

19

```
        new Vector2(titleSafeArea.Left, titleSafeArea.Top + 20), Color.Black);
    sb.DrawString(font, "Free Particles: " +
        (particles.Length - numberOfActiveParticles).ToString(),
        new Vector2(titleSafeArea.Left, titleSafeArea.Top + 40), Color.Black);
    sb.End();
}

GraphicsDevice.RenderState.PointSpriteEnable = true;
GraphicsDevice.RenderState.DepthBufferWriteEnable = false;

SetBlendModes();

GraphicsDevice.VertexDeclaration = vertexDeclaration;

PopulatePointSprites();

if (numberOfActiveParticles > 0)
{

    effect.Parameters["View"].SetValue(View);
    effect.Parameters["Projection"].SetValue(Projection);
    effect.Parameters["ColorMap"].SetValue(settings.Texture);
    effect.Parameters["World"].SetValue(Matrix.Identity);

    effect.Parameters["RotateAngle"].SetValue(rotateAngle);

    effect.Begin();
    effect.CurrentTechnique.Passes[0].Begin();

    GraphicsDevice.DrawUserPrimitives(
        PrimitiveType.PointList, vertices, 0, numberOfActiveParticles);

    effect.CurrentTechnique.Passes[0].End();
    effect.End();
}

base.Draw(gameTime);
```

If we need to write out our debugging information, then we display the counter information for our particles. Obviously, we could display anything we find helpful. We are taking a performance hit here by having our sprite batch save the state, but we will not be displaying the text in the game itself so this is no problem.

The next task we complete is to set our render state to handle our point sprites. We tell our graphics device that we are going to be rendering point sprites. We then have a method that will set our blend modes. This is done as a method so our derived particle systems can override it if they would like. This could be useful, for example, if we ever had a particle system that needed to appear to glow, as we could set the blend modes to an additive blend mode. The code for the `SetBlendModes` method is as follows:

```
protected virtual void SetBlendModes()
{
    GraphicsDevice.RenderState.AlphaBlendEnable = true;
    GraphicsDevice.RenderState.SourceBlend = Blend.SourceAlpha;
    GraphicsDevice.RenderState.DestinationBlend = Blend.InverseSourceAlpha;
}
```

By default our particle system will use alpha blending. Our derived particle systems can override this method to change the blend mode.

Back in our `Draw` method, we set our graphics device vertex declaration so it will draw the point sprites correctly. We then actually populate our point sprites. The `PopulatePointSprites` method is shown here:

```
private void PopulatePointSprites()
{
    if (numberOfActiveParticles == 0)
        return;

    int currVertex = 0;
    for (int i = 0; i < particles.Length; i++)
    {
        if (particles[i].IsAlive)
        {
            vertices[currVertex] = particles[i].Vertex;
            currVertex++;
        }

        if (currVertex >= numberOfActiveParticles)
            break; //stop looping, we have found all active particles
    }
}
```

In this method we are setting each of our vertices that will be piped to the graphics card. We do this by looping through all of our particles and if the particle is active, we set that vertex value to our particle's vertex value. We do not change the size of our vertices array. Instead, we just keep track of the number of active particles and make sure that the first part of our array contains all of the valid values.

We can see back in our `Draw` method we pass in this list of vertices along with the primitive count (the number of active particles). This tells the `DrawUserPrimitives` method to use the vertices from offset 0 to the number of active particles. By doing it this way, we are not constantly allocating and deallocating memory.

19

Before we actually call the `DrawUserPrimitives` method, we make sure we actually have active particles to draw. Assuming we have particles (vertices) to draw, we set the view, projection, world, texture, and rotation angle parameters of our effect file.

Before we look at our effect file, we need to round out our `ParticleSystem` class by adding in these methods that either our derived particle systems or our game will need:

```
protected void SetTexture(Texture2D texture)
{
    settings.Texture = texture;
}

public void SetPosition(Vector3 position)
{
    settings.EmitPosition = position;
}

public void ResetSystem()
{
    if (settings.RunOnce)
    {
        totalParticlesEmitted = 0;
    }
}
```

These methods are very straightforward. We allow our derived particle systems to set our texture. We could make this public if we also wanted our game to actually set the texture for the particle system. We do allow the game to set the initial emit position of our particle system. The last method we have here actually resets our system. Our game code can reset a particle system that only runs once. A good use for this would be for a fireworks particle system effect. Each time the game wanted to kick off the fireworks, it could call this reset system. The caveat exists that the particle system would have to be completed as it only resets the total particles emitted counter. Of course, this could be modified to be more robust if needed.

Point Sprite Effect File

Finally we can look at the effect file we need to create to process our point sprites. We can see the global variables here, which should familiar by now:

```
float4x4 World  : WORLD;
float4x4 View;
float4x4 Projection;

float RotateAngle = 0;

texture ColorMap;
```

```
sampler2D ColorMapSampler = sampler_state
{
    Texture = <ColorMap>;
    magfilter = LINEAR;
    minfilter = LINEAR;
    mipfilter = LINEAR;
    addressU = mirror;
    addressV = mirror;
};
```

Next, we have our vertex input and output structs:

```
struct VertexInput
{
    float4 Position    : POSITION0;
    float Size         : PSIZE0;
    float4 Color       : COLOR0;
};

struct VertexOutput
{
    float4 Position    : POSITION0;
    float Size         : PSIZE0;
    float4 Color       : COLOR0;
};
```

These are actually identical and we could have used the same struct for both the input and the output. To avoid confusion we left it as two different structs. Just like our VertexPointSprite custom vertex struct, we are expecting the Position, Size, and Color values from our application.

Our vertex shader is simple:

```
VertexOutput vertexShader (VertexInput input)
{
    VertexOutput output;
    float4x4 worldViewProjection = mul(mul(World, View), Projection);
    output.Position = mul(input.Position, worldViewProjection);
    output.Color = input.Color;
    output.Size = input.Size;

    return output;
}
```

We transform our position like normal, then we just set our output size and color to what we received as input.

Our pixel shader is not complex either, but the Xbox 360 has a different semantic for handling point sprite texture coordinates. Because of this, we need to declare our texture coordinates differently. We also need to extract those coordinates differently based on our platform. Let's take a look at the code before we get into the explanation:

```
struct PixelInput
{
    float3 Position : POSITION0;

    #ifdef XBOX360
        float4 TexCoords : SPRITETEXCOORD0;
    #else
        float2 TexCoords : TEXCOORD0;
    #endif
    float4 Color : COLOR0;
};

float4 pixelShader(PixelInput input) : COLOR0
{
    float2 texCoords;

    #ifdef XBOX360
        texCoords = abs(input.TexCoords.zw);
    #else
        texCoords = input.TexCoords.xy;
    #endif

    return ( saturate(tex2D(ColorMapSampler, texCoords) * input.Color) );
}
```

Our pixel input gets the position, texture coordinates, and the color. We have the XBOX360 preprocessor directive condition in place so that we use the appropriate semantic for the different platforms. In the actual pixel shader we need to take the absolute value of the last two components of the texture coordinates for the Xbox 360. It is possible for the values to be negative, so it is very important for us to take the absolute value. For Windows, we take the typical x and y components of our 2D vector.

We actually have another section of code we need to add right before the `return` statement in our `pixelShader` function:

```
//only take the rotation penalty if we need to
if (RotateAngle > 0)
{
    texCoords -= .5f;

    float ca = cos(RotateAngle);
    float sa = sin(RotateAngle);
```

```
    float2 tempCoords;
    tempCoords.x = texCoords.x * ca - texCoords.y * sa;
    tempCoords.y = texCoords.x * sa + texCoords.y * ca;
    texCoords = tempCoords;
    texCoords *= 1.4142135623730951; //sqrt(2);

    texCoords += .5f;
}
```

Instead of cluttering the core of the pixel shader just given with our rotation code, it is listed here. The great thing about this code is that we can simply ignore if our particles should not rotate. If they do rotate, then we need to rotate our texture coordinates to simulate that the point sprite is actually rotating. We use the rotation angle that our game passes in to calculate the new texture coordinates that our pixel shader should sample. This is done with a little bit of trigonometry. When we complete this calculation, our texture coordinates have been changed based on the rotation angle.

Finally, we set up our default technique with the only pass that includes our pixel and vertex shaders:

```
technique Default
{
    pass P0
    {
        VertexShader = compile vs_1_1 vertexShader();
        PixelShader  = compile ps_1_1 pixelShader();
    }
}
```

We need to create the Effects subfolder under our Contents folder in our XELibrary project. We need to add this file to that folder.

Particle System Demo

Now that we have created our particle, custom point sprite vertex format, particle system, and our effect file, we can finally create our demo to use our new particle system. We are actually setting up the framework, as we do not actually have any particle effects created yet. We will create several particle system effects in the next section.

As usual, we will begin with setting up our private member fields. We have all the usual suspects:

```
private FirstPersonCamera camera;
private InputHandler input;
private FPS fps;

private Model model;
private Texture2D texture;
```

```
private Effect effect;
private Skybox skybox;

private ParticleSystem ps;
```

We are going to using our FPS game component as the number of particles we have will directly affect performance. We will be using our skybox and we can add the skybox2.tga file to the Content\Skyboxes folder.

There are no surprises in our constructor:

```
public Game1()
{
    graphics = new GraphicsDeviceManager(this);
    content = new ContentManager(Services);

    input = new InputHandler(this, true);
    Components.Add(input);

    camera = new FirstPersonCamera(this);
    Components.Add(camera);

    fps = new FPS(this, false, true);
    Components.Add(fps);
}
```

When we set up our input handler, we let it know that we can exit out of this game by just pressing the Back button or Escape. This is done by passing in true as the second parameter. We tell our FPS game component that we do not want to synchronize with our monitor's retrace but we do want our update method to run at a given rate.

TIP

An enhancement to our library would be to change the FPS and InputHandler game component's boolean values to enumerated types. This way, it would not be so cumbersome to read as we look back over the code. It does not add that much clutter, but in order to keep it a little cleaner we left it out. It is usually not considered good design to simply have boolean values that signify if something is supposed to happen or not. It requires memorization, extra documentation, or reliance on intellisense of the IDE. Having a well-described enumerated type avoids confusion. Code is read a lot more than it is written, so it makes a lot of sense to create enumerated types for readability.

After our constructor, the next thing we typically do is set up our LoadGraphicsContent method:

```
protected override void LoadGraphicsContent(bool loadAllContent)
{
    if (loadAllContent)
```

```
    {
        model = content.Load<Model>(@"Content\Models\asteroid1");
        texture = content.Load<Texture2D>(@"Content\Textures\asteroid1");
        effect = content.Load<Effect>(@"Content\Effects\AmbientTexture");
        effect.Parameters["AmbientColor"].SetValue(
            Color.WhiteSmoke.ToVector4());

        skybox = content.Load<Skybox>(@"Content\Skyboxes\skybox2");
    }
}
```

We are going to display an asteroid model that will be surrounded by our particles. This is
not required, but it helps us know that we are setting our render states properly. We will
discuss that some more in a moment. For now, we are going load our content like
normal. We load our model and its texture. Those can be added to our project as usual.
We are using the ambient texture effect file. We set the ambient color to XNA's
WhiteSmoke color. Our skybox is loaded next. We need to make sure that our skybox
processor is set up in our solution. Now that we have our content loaded we can take a
look at the Draw method. Most of the code is actually drawing our asteroid:

```
protected override void Draw(GameTime gameTime)
{
    graphics.GraphicsDevice.Clear(Color.Black);

    graphics.GraphicsDevice.RenderState.AlphaBlendEnable = false;
    graphics.GraphicsDevice.RenderState.PointSpriteEnable = false;
    graphics.GraphicsDevice.RenderState.DepthBufferWriteEnable = true;

    skybox.Draw(camera.View, camera.Projection, Matrix.CreateScale(5000.0f));

    Matrix world = Matrix.CreateRotationY(
        MathHelper.ToRadians(45.0f * (float)gameTime.TotalGameTime.TotalSeconds)) *
        Matrix.CreateTranslation(new Vector3(0, 0, -4000));
    DrawModel(ref model, ref world, texture);

    base.Draw(gameTime);
}

private void DrawModel(ref Model m, ref Matrix world, Texture2D texture)
{
    Matrix[] transforms = new Matrix[m.Bones.Count];
    m.CopyAbsoluteBoneTransformsTo(transforms);

    foreach (ModelMesh mesh in m.Meshes)
    {
        foreach (ModelMeshPart mp in mesh.MeshParts)
```

```
        {
            if (texture != null)
                effect.Parameters["ColorMap"].SetValue(texture);

            effect.Parameters["Projection"].SetValue(camera.Projection);
            effect.Parameters["View"].SetValue(camera.View);
            effect.Parameters["World"].SetValue(world * mesh.ParentBone.Transform);
            mp.Effect = effect;
        }
        mesh.Draw();
    }
}
```

We clear our device and then set our render state before drawing our asteroid. Remember that we enable alpha blending and enable our point sprites as well as disabling our depth buffer when we draw our particles. So we need to make sure we set the render state to the state we want it before we actually render our world. We then draw our skybox as we have in the past, as well as our loaded model.

We have not completed the code for our demo, but we have the framework in place. We could run the demo now, but we would only see our spinning asteroid in a room. In the next section we will dig into our specific particle system effects and incorporate them into our demo.

Creating Particle Effects

We are going to create actual particle systems that derive from our abstract particle system class. We will also add these to our demo so we can see them in action. Even with the basic particle system infrastructure we have set up we can create a number of different effects. This section lists a few of them that show off some of the features. Because we will have a few particle systems, it might be beneficial to create a subfolder in our game solution called ParticleSystems.

Rain

To get started, we are going to create a rain effect. We can create our first code file inside of the ParticleSystems folder called Rain.cs.

Because this is the first particle system we are creating, we will list the code in its entirety in Listing 19.1.

LISTING 19.1   Rain.cs

```
using System;
using System.Collections.Generic;
using System.Text;
using Microsoft.Xna.Framework;
using Microsoft.Xna.Framework.Graphics;
```

LISTING 19.1   Continued

```
using XELibrary;

namespace ParticleSystemDemo
{
    public class Rain : XELibrary.ParticleSystem
    {
        public Rain(Game game, int capacity, Vector3 externalForce)
            : base(game)
        {
            settings.Capacity = capacity;
            settings.ExternalForce = externalForce;
        }

        public Rain(Game game, int capacity)
            : this(game, capacity, new Vector3(0, 0, 0)) { }

        public Rain(Game game) : this(game, 5000) { }

        protected override ParticleSystemSettings InitializeSettings()
        {
            settings.EmitPerSecond = 1100;

            settings.EmitPosition = new Vector3(0, 4000, 0);
            settings.EmitRange = new Vector3(4000, 0, 4000);

            settings.MinimumVelocity = new Vector3(0, -10, 0);
            settings.MaximumVelocity = new Vector3(0, -50, 0);

            settings.MinimumAcceleration = new Vector3(0, -10, 0);
            settings.MaximumAcceleration = new Vector3(0, -10, 0);

            settings.MinimumLifetime = 5.0f;
            settings.MaximumLifetime = 5.0f;

            settings.MinimumSize = 5.0f;
            settings.MaximumSize = 15.0f;

            settings.Colors = new Color[] {
                Color.CornflowerBlue,
                Color.LightBlue
            };

            settings.DisplayColorsInOrder = false;
```

LISTING 19.1   Continued

```
        return (settings);
    }

    protected override void  LoadGraphicsContent(bool loadAllContent)
    {
        if (loadAllContent)
        {
            SetTexture(
                content.Load<Texture2D>(@"Content\Textures\raindrop"));
        }

        base.LoadGraphicsContent(loadAllContent);
    }

}
}
```

All of the effects will have three constructors. The default constructor for our rain effect will set the capacity to 5,000 particles that we need to allocate memory for as well as an external force of 0 in all directions. We allow overriding any of those values with the main constructor. Remember, our abstract particle system class initializes our settings variable. In our main constructor we set the capacity and external forces. A particle system does not need to have three constructors. If it is needed we could just have one constructor and not allow (or force) our game to set the different values. This provides a lot of flexibility.

The core of our particle system effect is in the InitializeSettings method. This is where we actually specify the minimum and maximum values of our particles. Specifically for our rain effect, we are saying we want to emit about 1,000 particles every second. This number was chosen because we are setting the minimum and maximum life value to five seconds and we will only have a total of 5,000 particles available to us. So we can basically emit 1,000 particles every second so there is no lull in the amount of particles we are creating.

We set the position and the range around the position where we will create the particles. In this case we are creating them 4,000 units above the origin. We are letting the particle system pick random positions within 4,000 units to the left or right (EmitRange.X) or 4,000 units ahead or behind (EmitRange.Z). We are not letting it pick random spots on the y axis as we want them to all start from the same plane above us.

We set the initial velocity of our raindrops to be between 10 and 100. They are supposed to fall downward so we have negated those values. We have forced the acceleration to be 10 by setting both the minimum and maximum values to the same value. We allow the size of our raindrops to vary in size from 5 to 10.

Finally, we set up the colors that our raindrops should be tinted. We have set it to light blue and our favorite color, cornflower blue. We want each raindrop to pick a random color and not change colors over time, so we set the `DisplayColorsInOrder` flag to false.

The last thing we do with this effect is set our raindrop texture. We do this in our `LoadGraphicsContent` method, of course. There should not be any surprises with the code as we are just loading the content like normal. We do need to add the raindrop.png file to the Textures subfolder in our solution.

To see this particle system, we need to actually create it in our demo. We need to declare a private member field to hold our particle system in our game code:

```
private Rain rain;
```

Next, in our game's constructor we need to initialize the game component:

```
rain = new Rain(this);
Components.Add(rain);
```

If we want to display the debugging info on this particle system we just need to set the `DebugInfo` property to `true`. Because this is a game component, if we did not want this to be displayed or updated we could set the `Visible` and `Enabled` properties to false.

In our game's `Draw` method we need to set the particle system's `View` and `Projection` properties. We do this by assigning them our camera's `View` and `Projection` properties:

```
rain.View = camera.View;
rain.Projection = camera.Projection;
```

That is it. It is very painless to plug in an effect to our demo. We can run our demo and see rain falling from the sky.

Bubbles

The next effect we create is one that looks like bubbles. We can copy our Rain.cs file and rename it Bubbles.cs. We will rename the class to `Bubbles`. We need to change one of the constructors as we want our default external force to be different:

```
public Bubbles(Game game, int capacity)
    : this(game, capacity, new Vector3(0, .05f, 0)) { }
```

The texture we will be using is called bubble, so we can replace raindrop with bubble. We can add bubble.png to our Textures subfolder. This leaves the `InitializeSettings` method. Our new method is listed here:

```
protected override ParticleSystemSettings InitializeSettings()
{
    settings.EmitPerSecond = 1000;

    settings.EmitPosition = new Vector3(0, 0, -500);
```

```
    settings.EmitRange = new Vector3(50, 60, 50);

    settings.MinimumVelocity = new Vector3(-1, -1, -1);
    settings.MaximumVelocity = new Vector3(1, 20, 1);

    settings.MinimumAcceleration = new Vector3(-0.1f, -0.1f, -0.1f);
    settings.MaximumAcceleration = new Vector3(.1f, .1f, .1f);

    settings.MinimumLifetime = 1.0f;
    settings.MaximumLifetime = 25.0f;

    settings.MinimumSize = 5.0f;
    settings.MaximumSize = 15.0f;

    settings.Colors = new Color[] {
        Color.WhiteSmoke,
        Color.White,
        Color.NavajoWhite,
        Color.Khaki};

    settings.DisplayColorsInOrder = false;

    return (settings);
}
```

We just modified our settings, but the concept is the same. We set our range so that it would find a random position somewhere within 50 units in front or behind or left or right of the position. It can place the particle within 60 units above or below the position as well. This is the same concept as our rain effect, except that we are allowing it to pick random Y values as well to plot our points. The lifetime of our particles is no longer a constant 5 seconds. We now have a minimum life span of 5 seconds with a maximum life span of 25 seconds. We are using four colors instead of two now, but are still just setting them initially to random values.

We would add this effect to our game the same way we did our rain effect. We need to set up a variable and the initialize the variable in our game's constructor. We need to add the particle system to our game components and finally we need to set its View and Projection properties in our Draw method.

Laser Shield

This effect produces a cylinder around our asteroid simulating a laser shield of sorts. We can copy our Rain.cs file and rename it LaserShield.cs and rename the class to LaserShield. We start by replacing two of the constructors we had in our rain class:

```
public LaserShield(Game game, int capacity)
    : this(game, capacity, new Vector3(0, 0, 0)) { }
public LaserShield(Game game) : this(game, 2500) { }
```

We have no external force and we are only creating 2,500 particles in this system. We need to add the texture 3dtubegray.png to the Textures subfolder in our solution and replace raindrop with 3dtubegray in our `LoadGraphicsContent` method.

The heart of this particle system effect is in the `InitializeSettings` method:

```
protected override ParticleSystemSettings InitializeSettings()
{
    settings.EmitPosition = new Vector3(0, -1500, -4000);
    settings.EmitPerSecond = settings.Capacity;

    settings.EmitRadius = new Vector2(1200, 1200);

    settings.MinimumVelocity = new Vector3(0, 0, 0);
    settings.MaximumVelocity = new Vector3(0, 0, 0);

    settings.MinimumAcceleration = new Vector3(0, 100, 0);
    settings.MaximumAcceleration = new Vector3(0, 100, 0);

    settings.MinimumLifetime = 1.0f;
    settings.MaximumLifetime = 1.0f;

    settings.MinimumSize = 50.0f;
    settings.MaximumSize = 50.0f;

    settings.Colors = new Color[] {
        new Color(new Vector4(Color.SteelBlue.ToVector3(), .1f)),
        new Color(new Vector4(Color.Silver.ToVector3(), .1f))
    };
    settings.DisplayColorsInOrder = false;

    return (settings);
}
```

We set the lifetime of the particles to be one second. As a result we set our `EmitPerSecond` value to match our capacity (2,500). We are positioning our particle system at the same place as our asteroid: 4,000 units in front of us. However, we are starting the particle system under the asteroid so we set the y value to -1,500. Our acceleration (both minimum and maximum values) is set to 100 units upward. In the one-second life span of our particle, it allows it to travel to the top of our asteroid.

What makes this effect unique from the previous two is the fact that we are using the `EmitRadius` setting. Remember way back at the beginning of this chapter when we set up the `Initialize` method of our `Particle` class? We had a condition where we check to see if the `EmitRadius` value was set to zero or not. If it was set to something other than its initial value then we calculated a random angle and used that angle in a calculation with our random position and the `EmitRadius`. That code is listed here for quick reference:

19

```
if (settings.EmitRadius != Vector2.Zero)
{
    float angle = Utility.GetRandomFloat(0, MathHelper.TwoPi);

    Vertex.Position = new Vector3(
        position.X + (float)Math.Sin(angle) * settings.EmitRadius.X,
        position.Y,
        position.Z + (float)Math.Cos(angle) * settings.EmitRadius.Y);
}
```

An enhancement to this particle system could be to actually have a minimum and a maximum emit radius. This way instead of having a constant circular or oval pattern it could be all over the place.

After we set up the effect in our demo, we can run our demo and see a shield surround our asteroid.

Laser Scanner

Our laser scanner effect will actually inherit from the laser shield class in the previous section. Because of this, it is given in its entirety in Listing 19.2.

LISTING 19.2   LaserScanner.cs

```
using System;
using System.Collections.Generic;
using System.Text;
using Microsoft.Xna.Framework;
using Microsoft.Xna.Framework.Graphics;
using XELibrary;

namespace ParticleSystemDemo
{
    public class LaserScanner : LaserShield
    {
        public LaserScanner(Game game, int capacity, Vector3 externalForce)
            : base(game, capacity, externalForce) { }

        public LaserScanner(Game game, int capacity)
            : base(game, capacity) { }

        public LaserScanner(Game game) : base(game) { }

        protected override ParticleSystemSettings InitializeSettings()
        {
            base.InitializeSettings();
```

LISTING 19.2   Continued

```
            settings.EmitPerSecond = (int)(settings.Capacity * 4);

            settings.Colors = new Color[] {
                new Color(new Vector4(Color.Red.ToVector3(), .025f))
            };

            return (settings);
        }
    }
}
```

We can see that each constructor is simply passing the values to the base `LaserShield` class. If we wanted to change the capacity or external force we could, but we just left the majority of the code alone. In our `InitializeSettings` method, the first thing we do is call our base class `InitializeSettings`. By doing this, we only need to modify the settings that are truly unique in this scanner effect we are making.

We have changed our `EmitPerSecond` setting to be four times the capacity of our particle system. Because we cannot emit more particles than is within the capacity of the system, we can make the particles we want to emit do so faster. The result is an effect where the particles are more dense than normal but there is a lull in the action as there are no more particles to create at the origin. In this effect the four determines how wide the band is that is scanning the asteroid. The smaller the number, the more continuous the scanning will be. The higher the number, the smaller the band, causing a greater distance between the particles.

We can add the effect to our demo like normal by creating a variable and initializing it in our constructor and adding it to our collection of game components. Running more than two of these effects at once can make most systems crawl, so be careful how many vertices you try to process at once.

TIP

An enhancement could be made to the particle system. There is a bottleneck in passing the data from our application to the graphics card. The graphics card is sitting idle while we generate our vertices to pass to it. Instead of building them all and sending them to the graphics card all at once, we could build them in chunks. A couple of options that come to mind are 10 chunks of 10 percent or 3 chunks of 33 percent. There is no hard and fast rule as to the best way to do this. However, the current code definitely produces a bottleneck when the particle count is very high. We will not be modifying the call in our `Draw` method but it would be a good exercise to do if performance is suffering.

Poisonous Gas

The next effect we create is one that simulates a thick gas. The same effect could be used for smoke if we wanted. We will be using the Rain class as a starting point. We can call this class PoisonGas. The constructors we replace are as follows:

```
public PoisonGas(Game game, int capacity)
    : this(game, capacity, new Vector3(0, 0, 0)) { }

public PoisonGas(Game game) : this(game, 5000) { }
```

We need to add the smoke.png file to our Textures subfolder. In our LoadGraphicsContent method, we can replace raindrop with smoke. Finally, our InitializeSettings method is as follows:

```
protected override ParticleSystemSettings InitializeSettings()
{
    settings.EmitPosition = new Vector3(0, -2500, -4000);
    settings.EmitPerSecond = 500;

    settings.EmitRadius = new Vector2(10, 10);

    settings.MinimumVelocity = new Vector3(-.1f, 0, -.1f);
    settings.MaximumVelocity = new Vector3(.1f, 0, .1f);

    settings.MinimumAcceleration = new Vector3(-.5f, .6f, -.5f);
    settings.MaximumAcceleration = new Vector3(.5f, .6f, .5f);

    settings.MinimumLifetime = 5.0f;
    settings.MaximumLifetime = 20.0f;

    settings.MinimumSize = 50.0f;
    settings.MaximumSize = 50.0f;

    settings.Colors = new Color[] {
        new Color(new Vector4(Color.Green.ToVector3(), .05f))
    };

    settings.DisplayColorsInOrder = false;

    settings.RotateAmount = 0.025f;

    settings.RunOnce = true;

    return (settings);
}
```

The only thing new about this effect is the fact that we have told it to only run once. We also set the rotation amount so that each particle's texture will rotate. We can add the following code to our particle system demo's Update method so we can kick off the effect again:

```
if (input.ButtonHandler.WasButtonPressed(0, InputHandler.ButtonType.A) ¦¦
    input.KeyboardState.WasKeyPressed(Keys.Space))
{
    gas.ResetSystem();
}
```

We simply check to see if we have pressed the spacebar or the A button on the game pad. If we have, we call the ResetSystem method on our gas particle system effect. This simply sets the totalParticlesEmitted variable to 0. Remember, this is checked when determining if we should create particles. So effectively, even if our particle system is only supposed to run one time, resetting this counter lets it continue to emit particles. The method does not actually kill off any existing particles; it just resets the counter for any particles that are being emitted.

The Colorful Effect

The last particle system effect we make is one that shows off the displaying the colors in order feature. We can actually start this effect by copying the bubble effect. We can call this new effect Colorful. That is creativity at its best. As usual, we start by replacing two of our constructors:

```
public Colorful(Game game, int capacity)
    : this(game, capacity, new Vector3(0, .05f, 0)) { }

public Colorful(Game game) : this(game, 2500) { }
```

We will be leaving the bubble texture for this effect, so nothing needs to change there. The following is our InitializeSettings method:

```
protected override ParticleSystemSettings InitializeSettings()
{
    settings.EmitPerSecond = 2500;

    settings.EmitPosition = new Vector3(0, 0, -1000);
    settings.EmitRange = new Vector3(50, 160, 50);
    settings.EmitRadius = new Vector2(100,100);

    settings.MinimumVelocity = new Vector3(-1, -1, -1);
    settings.MaximumVelocity = new Vector3(1, 20, 1);

    settings.MinimumAcceleration = new Vector3(-5, -10, -5);
    settings.MaximumAcceleration = new Vector3(5, 10, 5);
```

```
    settings.MinimumLifetime = 1.0f;
    settings.MaximumLifetime = 1.0f;

    settings.MinimumSize = 15.0f;
    settings.MaximumSize = 15.0f;

    settings.Colors = new Color[] {
        Color.Green,
        Color.Yellow,
        Color.Red,
        Color.Blue,
        Color.Purple};

    settings.DisplayColorsInOrder = true;

    settings.RunOnce = true;

    return (settings);
}
```

The main thing to notice in this effect is the fact that we set our `DisplayColorsInOrder` flag to true. This means for each particle, it will change its color as often as it needs to. It will display each color for the same amount of time starting with the first color in the array.

We have also set this effect to only run once, so we will want to hook this up in our demo's `Update` class after we declare the variable and initialize it and add it to our game component collection.

Summary

This was a rather long chapter, but hopefully a good grasp of particle systems has been gained. This implementation is not extremely robust, but we were able to see just a couple of examples of totally different effects by just modifying a few settings. The foundation is laid so that more complex particle systems can be created if needed. The main thing to keep in mind is that a particle system should only be as complex as needed.

We have covered a lot of ground in this book so far. We have a decent library we have been adding to and several neat tricks under our belt. In the next part of the book we will actually take what we have learned and put it into practice by creating a 3D game.

PART VIII

Putting It Into Practice

IN THIS PART

Creating a 3D Game

We have covered a lot of ground in this book. There will be some new material in these next two chapters, but most of it will be review as we take what we learned and put it into practice. We are going to be creating a full 3D game, complete with sound effects, music, artificial intelligence, physics, a head's up display (HUD), and scoring.

Creating the Tunnel Vision Game

The game is set in outer space. The tunnel to our space station is being attacked, so we need to defend our tunnel and not let the enemies breach the opening. We have missiles that we can fire. Fortunately, the enemy does not have any. They simply attack in swarms, which mean we need to take swift action to destroy them.

Creating the Game States

To get started, we need to make a copy of our GameStateDemo from Chapter 15, "Finite State Machines and Game State Management." We want to use the latest XELibrary from the last chapter. We need to add the project to our solution, as we will be making a modification to it a little later.

Rename Game1.cs to TunnelVision.cs. We can also change the name of this class and our namespace to TunnelVision. Figure 20.1 shows how we can rename our namespace through the IDE. This will modify all of our source files for us. This will also have to be done in the GameState folder. The IDE assumes that each subfolder is a different namespace and does not automatically replace them. We also need to rename our Game1 class to TunnelVision. The easiest way to do this is through the Replace in Files dialog box, which can be opened by pressing Ctrl+Shift+H. It can also be browsed to from the Edit menu. It can be found under Search and Replace. We can also rename the actual code file to TunnelVision.cs.

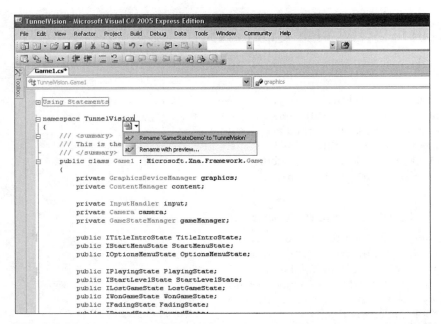

FIGURE 20.1   Visual C# Express allows renaming the namespace through the IDE.

Adding a Skybox to Our Game

Let's add a skybox to our world. We can find the skybox.tga file and add it to our Content\Skyboxes solution folder. We need to add a skybox content processor to our solution, and select SkyboxProcessor as the content processor for the skybox texture. Then we can add the following private member field to our game:

```
private Skybox skybox;
```

Next we can load the skybox in our LoadGraphicsContent method:

```
skybox = Content.Load<Skybox>(@"Content\Skyboxes\skybox");
```

The private member field content needs to changed to a public member field that can be called Content. To finish up our skybox, we only need to draw it. We can add the following statement to the Draw method:

```
skybox.Draw(Camera.View, Camera.Projection, Matrix.CreateScale(1000));
```

Compiling the Game

While we are in our `Draw` method, we can remove the `SpriteBatch Begin` and `End` methods, as each game component will need to call its own. We need to leave the `base.Draw` method, of course.

We need to add a camera to our game. We are going to change this camera to one that is more suitable for our game, but for now we can just reference the normal `Camera` class. We need to change our private member field camera to a public member field `Camera`:

```
public Camera Camera;
```

To get our game to run successfully, we need to modify our game states that utilize the sprite batch to actually call `Begin` and `End` because we removed it from the main `TunnelVision` game class. Once those methods are modified, we can compile and run our game.

Creating the Game Logic

After we successfully compile and run our game, we can start working on our game logic. Fortunately, we have the framework in place where we can easily put in our game code. We will first work on our game play by modifying the playing state code file.

We need to remove the font from our private member fields and add in the following fields:

```
private MissileManager missileManager;
private EnemyManager enemyManager;
private List<Level> Levels;
private int currentLevel;

private float totalCreatedEnemies;
public int TotalCollisions;

private BoundingSphere playerSphere;
```

We are going to manage our enemies and our missiles so we have set up some variables for those. We also created a list to store our levels. Before we dig into our playing state any further, we can build out these classes. The code for our `Level` class is as follows:

```
public class Level
{
    public int Missiles;
    public int Enemies;
    public int Time;
    public float EnemySpeed;

    public Level(int missiles, int enemies, int time, float enemySpeed)
    {
```

20

```
        Missiles = missiles;
        Enemies = enemies;
        Time = time + 1;
        EnemySpeed = enemySpeed;
        }
    }
```

The class is pretty straightforward, as we are providing a way to store the number of missiles that we are allowing on the screen at one time. One of the challenges of the game is to not expend too many bullets at one time. The next is how many enemies this level needs to generate before the level is over. We also have a timer that we will be using to award bonus points if all of the enemies are killed before the timer runs out. Finally, we store the speed at which the enemy is moving in this level.

The enemy and missile managers manage missiles and enemies. We need to create these objects first, but they share a lot of the same properties. Therefore, we are going to introduce a `SceneObject` and then have a `PhysicalObject` that inherits from our `SceneObject`. Although everything in this game will really be a physical object, it might be that we have a trigger that, if someone reaches it, would kick off some animation; it would need to be a scene object, but not a physical object. This will make more sense as we look at the code, starting with the `SceneObject`:

```
public abstract class SceneObject
{
    public Matrix World;
    public BoundingSphere BoundingSphere;
}
```

This is a very simplistic abstract class that stores our world matrix for the object as well as a bounding sphere. This allows us to place the object in the world and assign it a sphere so that if something collides with it we could kick off something like spawning enemies, opening doors, doing a cut scene, and really anything else we wanted. In our game, we will not be using an object that is purely a scene object, but it is good to have it here for future projects. Our physical object inherits from this and has more properties for an actual drawable object. The code for the `PhysicalObject` class is as follows:

```
public abstract class PhysicalObject : SceneObject
{
    public Vector3 Position;
    public Vector3 Velocity;
    public Vector3 Acceleration;
    public float Mass;
    public float Scale = 1.0f;
    public float Radius = 1.0f;
    public Color Color;
    public Matrix Rotation = Matrix.Identity;
```

```
public virtual void Move(float elapsed)
{
//adjust velocity with our acceleration
Velocity += Acceleration;

//adjust position with our velocity
Position += elapsed * Velocity;

World = Matrix.CreateScale(Scale) * Rotation *
    Matrix.CreateTranslation(Position);

BoundingSphere = new BoundingSphere(Position, Radius);
    }
}
```

We inherit from SceneObject so we get the bounding sphere and the world matrix, but we also add position, velocity, acceleration, mass, scale, radius, color, and rotation. This allows us to assign physical properties to our objects. We have a Move method that applies the physical forces we talked about in Chapter 14, "Physics Basics." This method adds the acceleration to our velocity and adds our velocity (taking the time delta into account) to our position. It then uses the scale, rotation, and position to update the world matrix for the object. Finally, it recalculates the bounding sphere based on the position and radius of the object.

Now we are ready to look at our EnemyManager and MissileManager, which manage objects that inherit from our PhysicalObject. We will start with our MissileManager and our Missile class in particular:

```
class Missile : PhysicalObject
{
    public DateTime StartTime;
    public bool IsActive;
}
```

The missile object inherits all of the properties from our physical object class and also includes the start time and a flag that states if the missile is active. We will be treating this much like we did for our particle system. We can jump right into our MissileManager to see how to manage these objects. Our MissileManager object will inherit from the DrawableGameComponent. As usual, we can start with our member fields and constructor:

```
public const int MISSILE_LIFE = 5; //5 seconds
private Model missile;
private Effect effect;

public Matrix View;
public Matrix Projection;
```

```
private Missile[] missiles;
private Texture2D missileTexture;

private int lastMissileIndex;
private float timer = 0;

private TunnelVision ourGame;

public MissileManager(Game game)
    : base(game)
{
    ourGame = (TunnelVision)game;
}
```

We have a constant that determines how long our missile should stay on the screen if it does not hit any enemies. One of the challenges we are presenting gamers is that there are only a certain number of missiles that can be on the screen at any given time for each level. The more accurate the players are, the more frequently they can fire a missile. If they miss, then the missile is active for five seconds and if they have fired their allotment, players need to wait until the five seconds is up before they can fire another missile.

We also have fields that store the missile model and the effect we will be using for that model. We set our View and Projection properties (which our effect needs) inside of the game, so we set those fields with the public modifier. We have an array where we store and manage our actual missile objects and the texture we apply to the object. Much like we did for our particle system, we are going to keep track of the last index in our array to which we added a missile so we know where to start when a new request is created to add a missile to our list.

Our constructor is empty and only passes the game object to the base DrawableGameComponent class. Next, we can look at the Load method that our game will call every time we start a new level. Each time a new level is started, we reset our array of missiles to only handle the maximum amount that the level allows us to fire at one time. The code for the Load method is as follows:

```
public void Load(int capacity)
{
    missiles = new Missile[capacity];
    lastMissileIndex = 0;

    for (int i = 0; i < missiles.Length; i++)
    missiles[i] = new Missile();
}
```

At the beginning of the level, we reallocate our array and reset our last missile index. Finally, we loop through all of the missiles and store an instance of each. Our LoadGraphicsContent and UnloadGraphicsContent methods are next:

```
protected override void LoadGraphicsContent(bool loadAllContent)
{
    if (loadAllContent)
    {
        missileTexture = ourGame.Content.Load<Texture2D>(
            @"Content\Textures\FireGrade");
        missile = ourGame.Content.Load<Model>(@"Content\Models\sphere");
        effect = ourGame.Content.Load<Effect>(
            @"Content\Effects\VertexDisplacement");
        effect.Parameters["ColorMap"].SetValue(missileTexture);
        effect.Parameters["AmbientColor"].SetValue(0.8f);
    }

    base.LoadGraphicsContent(loadAllContent);
}

protected override void UnloadGraphicsContent(bool unloadAllContent)
{
    if (unloadAllContent)
    {
        missiles = null;
    }

    base.UnloadGraphicsContent(unloadAllContent);
}
```

In our `LoadGraphicsContent` method we retrieve the texture from our `TextureManager` and the effect from our `EffectManager`. We then set the parameters on the effect. Our `UnloadGraphicsContent` method is setting our missiles array to null. We need to add the FireGrade texture to our project. We also need to add the sphere model to our project. Both of these assets can be found on the accompanying CD in this chapter's code folder.

When the player fires a missile, it needs to tell our `MissileManager` to add a missile to its array. We provide a public method called `AddMissile`:

```
public bool AddMissile(Vector3 position, Vector3 direction, DateTime startTime)
{
    int index = lastMissileIndex;
    for (int i = 0; i < missiles.Length; i++)
    {
        if (!missiles[index].IsActive)
            break;
        else
        {
            index++;
            if (index >= missiles.Length)
```

20

```
                index = 0;
        }

    if (index == lastMissileIndex)
        return (false);
}

//at this point index is the one we want ...
InitializeMissile(index, position, direction, startTime);

missiles[index].IsActive = true;

lastMissileIndex = index;

return (true);
}
```

The AddMissile method loops through the entire array, finding the first empty slot it can initialize a missile into. If there are no free slots, the user has fired all of the missiles allowed and the method returns false. The details of the InitializeMissile method are as follows:

```
private void InitializeMissile(int index, Vector3 position, Vector3 direction,
    DateTime startTime)
{
    missiles[index] = new Missile();
    missiles[index].Position = position;
    missiles[index].Acceleration = direction * 10f;
    missiles[index].Velocity = Vector3.Zero;
    missiles[index].StartTime = startTime;
}
```

The InitializeMissile method sets the values passed in from AddMissile, which gets the values from the game. Our MissileManager class also has a collision detection method. CheckCollision is used to determine if any of the missiles have collided with the bounding sphere passed in:

```
public bool CheckCollision(BoundingSphere check)
{
    for (int i = 0; i < missiles.Length; i++)
    {
        if ((missiles[i].IsActive) &&
            (missiles[i].BoundingSphere.Intersects(check)))
        {
            RemoveMissile(i);
            return (true);
```

```
        }
    }

    return (false);
}
```

If a collision is detected, we remove the missile from the list by setting its active flag to false. This is done in the RemoveMissile method:

```
private void RemoveMissile(int index)
{
    missiles[index].IsActive = false;
}
```

This leaves just the Update and Draw methods. The Update method simply loops through all of the active missiles and checks to see how long they have lived. If they have lived too long, they are removed from the array. If they are still alive, they are moved by calling the Move method on the Missile object, which ultimately calls the Move method on the PhysicalObject class:

```
public override void Update(GameTime gameTime)
{
    float elapsed = (float)gameTime.ElapsedGameTime.TotalSeconds;

    timer += 0.655f;

    for (int mi = 0; mi < missiles.Length; mi++)
    {
        if (!missiles[mi].IsActive)
            continue;

        if ((DateTime.Now - missiles[mi].StartTime) >
                TimeSpan.FromSeconds(MissileManager.MISSILE_LIFE))
            RemoveMissile(mi);
        else
            missiles[mi].Move(elapsed);
    }

    base.Update(gameTime);
}
```

The Update method also adds a fixed amount to a timer, which is used for the effect of the missile. The Draw method is as follows:

```
public override void Draw(GameTime gameTime)
{
    GraphicsDevice.RenderState.DepthBufferEnable = true;
```

```
GraphicsDevice.RenderState.AlphaBlendEnable = true;

effect.Parameters["Timer"].SetValue(timer);

effect.Parameters["View"].SetValue(View);
effect.Parameters["Projection"].SetValue(Projection);

for (int mi = 0; mi < missiles.Length; mi++)
{
    if (!missiles[mi].IsActive)
        continue;

    effect.Parameters["World"].SetValue(missiles[mi].World);

    Matrix[] transforms = new Matrix[missile.Bones.Count];
    missile.CopyAbsoluteBoneTransformsTo(transforms);

    foreach (ModelMesh mesh in missile.Meshes)
    {
        for (int i = 0; i < mesh.MeshParts.Count; i++)
        {
            // Set this MeshParts effect to our RedWire effect
            mesh.MeshParts[i].Effect = effect;
        }

        mesh.Draw();

        missiles[mi].BoundingSphere = mesh.BoundingSphere;
        missiles[mi].BoundingSphere.Center += missiles[mi].World.Translation;
    }
}

base.Draw(gameTime);
}
```

The Draw method makes sure that the render state is in the right state before drawing anything. It sets the appropriate effect parameters, then it loops through all of the missiles and applies the effect to them. It alsorecalculates the bounding sphere of the missile.

Before we get back to the PlayingState, we need to add the enemy manager. The concept is the same as our missile manager: There are a certain number of enemies that can be displayed at one time. This is determined by each level. The enemy object has tracking AI built into it as well. We start by creating the Enemy class, which inherits from PhysicalObject:

```
public class Enemy : PhysicalObject
{
    Random random = new Random(DateTime.Now.Millisecond);

    public Vector3 Target = Vector3.Zero;
    public Texture2D Texture;
    private float moveSpeed;
    private Vector3 Up, Forward;

    public Enemy(Texture2D texture, float moveSpeed)
    {
        Texture = texture;
        this.moveSpeed = moveSpeed;
        Scale = 0.01f;
        Radius = 5f;
        Position = XELibrary.Utility.GetRandomVector3(
            new Vector3(-300, -100, -100), new Vector3(300, 100, -100));

        Up = Vector3.Up;
        Forward = Vector3.Forward;
    }

    public override void Move(float elapsed)
    {
        Vector3 tv = Target - Position;
        tv.Normalize();

        Velocity = tv * moveSpeed;

        Forward = tv;

        Vector3 Right = Vector3.Normalize(Vector3.Cross(Forward, Vector3.Up));

        Up = Vector3.Normalize(Vector3.Cross(Right, Forward));

        Rotation = Matrix.Identity;
        Rotation.Forward = Forward;
        Rotation.Up = Up;
        Rotation.Right = Right;

        base.Move(elapsed);
    }
}
```

20

moveSpeed is the speed at which the enemies are moving toward the player. The Up and
Forward vectors are stored so we can calculate the rotation. The position in which an

enemy is generated is random. The Move method handles the AI for tracking the player as well as setting the rotation so the enemy is always facing the player. We define two vectors: Up and Forward. Then we calculate our Right vector by normalizing the cross-product of the Forward and Up vectors. Then we recalculate the Up vector again to make sure they are truly perpendicular. Once we have all three vectors perfectly perpendicular to each other we just set our rotation matrix's vectors so we could use it inside of our base class. After setting all of the properties for our enemy, the base class is called to finish the move process.

Our EnemyManager class inherits from the DrawableGameComponent class just like our MissileManager class. The member fields we need for this class are as follows:

```
public const int MAX_ENEMIES = 10;
private Texture2D[] enemyTextures;
private Model enemy;
private Effect effect;
private Random rand = new Random();

public Matrix View;
public Matrix Projection;

public List<Enemy> Enemies = new List<Enemy>(MAX_ENEMIES);

private TunnelVision ourGame;
```

In our constructor we need to store a reference to our game object:

```
public EnemyManager(Game game) : base(game)
{
    ourGame = (TunnelVision)game;
}
```

The LoadGraphicsContent method of EnemyManager is as follows:

```
protected override void LoadGraphicsContent(bool loadAllContent)
{
    if (loadAllContent)
    {
        enemyTextures = new Texture2D[3];
        enemyTextures[0] = ourGame.Content.Load<Texture2D>(
            @"Content\Textures\wedge_p2_diff_v1");
        enemyTextures[1] = ourGame.Content.Load<Texture2D>(
            @"Content\Textures\wedge_p2_diff_v2");
        enemyTextures[2] = ourGame.Content.Load<Texture2D>(
            @"Content\Textures\wedge_p2_diff_v3");
        enemy = ourGame.Content.Load<Model>(@"Content\Models\p2_wedge");
        effect = ourGame.Content.Load<Effect>(
            @"Content\Effects\AmbientTexture");
```

```
        effect.Parameters["AmbientColor"].SetValue(.8f);
    }


    base.LoadGraphicsContent(loadAllContent);
}
```

We are loading three different textures that the model we are loading can use. This model and these textures are taken from the Spacewar starter kit. They can also be found on the accompanying CD in this chapter's code folder. The assets should be added to the appropriate folders in which the code is expecting to find them.

The UnloadGraphicsContent simply clears out the list of enemies:

```
protected override void UnloadGraphicsContent(bool unloadAllContent)
{
    if (unloadAllContent)
    {
        Enemies.Clear();
        Enemies = null;
    }


    base.UnloadGraphicsContent(unloadAllContent);
}
```

The last method in our enemy manager class is the Draw method:

```
public override void Draw(GameTime gameTime)
{
    GraphicsDevice.RenderState.AlphaTestEnable = false;
    GraphicsDevice.RenderState.AlphaBlendEnable = false;
    GraphicsDevice.RenderState.PointSpriteEnable = false;
    GraphicsDevice.RenderState.DepthBufferWriteEnable = true;
    GraphicsDevice.RenderState.DepthBufferEnable = true;

    effect.Parameters["View"].SetValue(View);
    effect.Parameters["Projection"].SetValue(Projection);

    for (int ei = 0; ei < Enemies.Count; ei++)
    {
        effect.Parameters["World"].SetValue(Enemies[ei].World);
        effect.Parameters["ColorMap"].SetValue(Enemies[ei].Texture);

        Matrix[] transforms = new Matrix[enemy.Bones.Count];
        enemy.CopyAbsoluteBoneTransformsTo(transforms);

        foreach (ModelMesh mesh in enemy.Meshes)
        {
            foreach (ModelMeshPart mp in mesh.MeshParts)
```

```
        {
            mp.Effect = effect;
        }

        mesh.Draw();
    }
}

base.Draw(gameTime);
}
```

First, we set our render state properties to the values we require. Then we set our effect's view and projection properties. Finally, we loop through all of our enemies and draw each one with the appropriate texture and world matrix being passed into the effect.

The last method we need to add in our `EnemyManager` class is the `AddEnemy` method:

```
public void AddEnemy(float moveSpeed)
{
    Enemies.Add(new Enemy(enemyTextures[rand.Next(0, 3)], moveSpeed));
}
```

This is a public method the playing state code will use to tell the manager to add another enemy to the list. The enemy will be assigned one of the three textures we have specified along with the movement speed for the enemy.

Let's return to the playing state code and add the following to the constructor:

```
playerSphere = new BoundingSphere(OurGame.Camera.Position, 1.5f);

missileManager = new MissileManager(Game);
Game.Components.Add(missileManager);
missileManager.Enabled = false;
missileManager.Visible = false;

enemyManager = new EnemyManager(Game);
Game.Components.Add(enemyManager);
enemyManager.Enabled = false;
enemyManager.Visible = false;

Levels = new List<Level>(10);
Levels.Add(new Level(50, 10, 60, 9.0f));
Levels.Add(new Level(25, 10, 60, 9.0f));
Levels.Add(new Level(15, 15, 60, 9.0f));
Levels.Add(new Level(10, 15, 60, 9.0f));
Levels.Add(new Level(5, 15, 60, 9.0f));
Levels.Add(new Level(5, 20, 60, 9.0f));
Levels.Add(new Level(5, 25, 60, 9.0f));
```

```
Levels.Add(new Level(5, 30, 60, 10.0f));
Levels.Add(new Level(5, 40, 90, 10.0f));
Levels.Add(new Level(3, 50, 90, 10.0f));

currentLevel = 0;
enemyManager.Enemies = new List<Enemy>(Levels[CurrentLevel].Enemies);
```

In this game, we are using a stationary camera, so we are not going to continually update the player's bounding sphere. Instead, it is set once in the constructor. We add the missile manager and enemy manager game components and create all of our levels.

Our StartMenuState will start the game. The exposed method calls two private methods to prepare for the game and then to actually start the level. These three methods are as follows:

```
public void StartGame()
{
    SetupGame();
    StartLevel();
}

private void SetupGame()
{
    TotalCollisions = 0;
    currentLevel = 0;
}

public void StartLevel()
{
    GamePad.SetVibration(0, 0, 0);
    enemyManager.Enemies.Clear();
    totalCreatedEnemies = 0;

    missileManager.Load(Levels[CurrentLevel].Missiles);

    GameManager.PushState(OurGame.StartLevelState.Value);
}
```

The only thing to point out in this code is that we push the StartLevelState onto the stack inside the StartLevel method.

Next, we can look at the Update method in our PlayingGameState. We can replace the contents of the existing Update method with the following:

```
float elapsed = (float)gameTime.ElapsedGameTime.TotalSeconds;

if (Input.WasPressed(0, InputHandler.ButtonType.Back, Keys.Escape))
```

20

```
        GameManager.PushState(OurGame.StartMenuState.Value);

if (Input.WasPressed(0, InputHandler.ButtonType.Start, Keys.Enter))
{
    // push our paused state onto the stack
    GameManager.PushState(OurGame.PausedState.Value);
}

if ((Input.WasPressed(0, InputHandler.ButtonType.A, Keys.Space)) ¦¦
    (Input.WasPressed(0, InputHandler.ButtonType.RightShoulder,
        Keys.LeftControl)) ¦¦
    Input.GamePads[0].Triggers.Right > 0
    )
{
    if (missileManager.AddMissile(new Vector3(
            OurGame.Camera.Position.X,
            OurGame.Camera.Position.Y - 1,
            OurGame.Camera.Position.Z + 1
        ), OurGame.Camera.Target - OurGame.Camera.Position,
        DateTime.Now))
    {
        //play sound
    }
}

if (enemyManager.Enabled)
{
    UpdateEnemies(elapsed);

    while (CheckCollisions())
    {
        //increase score if enemy was hit
    }

    //Are we finished with this level?
    if (TotalCollisions == Levels[CurrentLevel].Enemies)
    {
        TotalCollisions = 0;
        currentLevel++;

        //Are we finished with the game?
        if (CurrentLevel == Levels.Count)
        {
            //You won the game!!!
            GameManager.PushState(OurGame.WonGameState.Value);
            currentLevel—; //reset count back
```

```
            }
            else
            {
                StartLevel();
            }
        }
    }

base.Update(gameTime);
```

We check our input and push on the start menu state or the paused state if it is appropriate. We check to see if the player has fired a missile and have a placeholder for playing a sound.

We update all of the enemies that are on the screen and then check to see if any of the missiles have collided with them. We will see the CheckCollisions method next. If a collision did occur, we have a placeholder to increase our score. Now we check to see if there are any more enemies left. If not, we check to see if there are any more levels left. If all of the levels have been finished, the game is won. Otherwise, we move on to the next level. The CheckCollisions method is as follows:

```
private bool CheckCollisions()
{
    for (int ei = 0; ei < enemyManager.Enemies.Count; ei++)
    {
        //See if an enemy is too close first
        if (enemyManager.Enemies[ei].BoundingSphere.Intersects(playerSphere))
        {
            GameManager.PushState(OurGame.LostGameState.Value);
            return (false);
        }

        //if not, then we can check our missiles
        if (missileManager.CheckCollision(enemyManager.Enemies[ei].BoundingSphere))
        {
            enemyManager.Enemies.RemoveAt(ei);

            TotalCollisions++;

            return (true);
        }
    }

    return (false);
}
```

First, we check to see if an enemy has collided with the camera. If that happens, the game is over. Otherwise, we check to see if any of the missiles have collided with the enemies. Our `Update` method also called the `UpdateEnemies` method, which we can see here:

```
private void UpdateEnemies(float elapsed)
{
    if (totalCreatedEnemies < Levels[CurrentLevel].Enemies)
    {
        if (enemyManager.Enemies.Count < EnemyManager.MAX_ENEMIES)
        {
            enemyManager.AddEnemy(Levels[CurrentLevel].EnemySpeed);
            totalCreatedEnemies++;
        }
    }

    for (int ei = 0; ei < enemyManager.Enemies.Count; ei++)
    {
        enemyManager.Enemies[ei].Target = OurGame.Camera.Position;
        enemyManager.Enemies[ei].Move(elapsed);
    }
}
```

The `UpdateEnemies` method checks to see if there are still enemies to be generated. We only allow `MAX_ENEMIES` on the screen at one time, so if a level has more than that, when an enemy is destroyed another one is spawned. The method then loops through all of the enemies and updates their target based on the camera's position. For this game, it really is not needed because we have a stationary camera. We then move each enemy.

For now our `Draw` method is very lightweight, as it is only setting the view and projection properties for the missile manager and the enemy manager. We can replace the current contents of the `Draw` method with the following:

```
missileManager.View = OurGame.Camera.View;
missileManager.Projection = OurGame.Camera.Projection;

enemyManager.View = OurGame.Camera.View;
enemyManager.Projection = OurGame.Camera.Projection;

base.Draw(gameTime);
```

We need to clear out the contents of the `LoadGraphicsContent` method. We will be adding code to that method a little later, but for now we just need to remove the old font we used in the previous demo.

We need to know which level we are on outside of our playing state, so we need to make a public property to expose it:

```
public int CurrentLevel
{
    get { return (currentLevel); }
}
```

We also need to modify our `GameStateInterfaces` code. Specifically, we need to modify the `IPlayingState` interface to include our `StartGame` method and this `CurrentLevel` property:

```
void StartGame();
int CurrentLevel { get; }
```

The final method we need to add to our `PlayingState` class is the `StateChanged` method. We override this method so we can turn on and off the appropriate game components:

```
protected override void StateChanged(object sender, EventArgs e)
{
    base.StateChanged(sender, e);

    if (GameManager.State != this.Value)
    {
        Visible = true;
        Enabled = false;
        missileManager.Enabled = false;
        missileManager.Visible = false;
        enemyManager.Enabled = false;
        enemyManager.Visible = false;
    }
    else
    {
        missileManager.Enabled = true;
        missileManager.Visible = true;
        enemyManager.Enabled = true;
        enemyManager.Visible = true;

    }
}
```

We specified an effect file for both the missile manager and the enemy manager. The enemy manager is using the AmbientTexture effect file we used in the last chapter. The file needs to be added to our projects. The missile manager, however, is using a new effect file. The basis of the effect is the vertex deformation effect we made in Chapter 13, "Advanced HLSL." The code for VertexDisplacement.fx is as follows:

```
float4x4 World  : WORLD;
float4x4 View;
float4x4 Projection;
```

```
float4 AmbientColor : COLOR0;
float Timer : TIME;
float Offset = 1.0f;

texture ColorMap;
sampler ColorMapSampler = sampler_state
{
    texture = <ColorMap>;
    magfilter = LINEAR;
    minfilter = LINEAR;
    mipfilter = LINEAR;
    AddressU = Wrap;
    AddressV = Wrap;
};

struct VertexInput
{
    float4 Position : POSITION0;
    float2 TexCoord : TEXCOORD0;
};

struct VertexOutput
{
    float4 Position : POSITION0;
    float2 TexCoord : TEXCOORD0;
};

VertexOutput vertexShader(VertexInput input)
{
    VertexOutput output = (VertexOutput)0;
    float4x4 WorldViewProjection = mul(mul(World, View), Projection);
    output.TexCoord = input.TexCoord  + Timer * .005;

    float4 Pos = input.Position;
    float y = Pos.y * Offset + Timer
    float x = sin(y) * Offset;
    Pos.x += x;

    output.Position = mul(Pos, WorldViewProjection);

    return( output );
}

struct PixelInput
{
```

```
    float2 TexCoord : TEXCOORD0;
};

float4 pixelShader(PixelInput input) : COLOR
{
    float4 color;
    color = tex2D(ColorMapSampler, input.TexCoord);
    return(color);
}

technique Default
{
    pass P0
    {
        VertexShader = compile vs_1_1 vertexShader();
        PixelShader = compile ps_1_4 pixelShader();
    }
}
```

The effect code is identical to the code we used in Chapter 13. The only difference is inside of the vertex shader. Besides modifying the vertex position, we also modify the texture coordinates. When we shoot our missiles, they will wobble.

The next state we need to modify is our StartLevelState. We need to clear out the code inside of the class and add the following private member fields:

```
private bool demoMode = true;
private bool displayedDemoDialog = false;

private DateTime levelLoadTime;
private readonly int loadSoundTime = 2500;

private string levelText = "LEVEL";
private string currentLevel;

private Vector2 levelTextPosition;
private Vector2 levelTextShadowPosition;
private Vector2 levelNumberPosition;
private Vector2 levelNumberShadowPosition;
```

We are going to play a sound as we are loading the level. We want the actual game play to start as soon as the sound is over. There is no way to get notified of a sound being completed, so we put in our own timer. We will add the sound later, but put the code into place now to handle the timing. The start level state will also display the level number we are starting. We store the level text once so we can use it multiple times. We also set up two sets of vectors to hold the locations of the level text (i.e., LEVEL) as well as the level number (i.e., 1) and their drop shadow locations.

The constructor did not change, but is listed for completeness:

```
public StartLevelState(Game game)
    : base(game)
{
    game.Services.AddService(typeof(IStartLevelState), this);
}
```

The StateChanged method allows us to start the logic when we enter our start level state:

```
protected override void StateChanged(object sender, EventArgs e)
{
    base.StateChanged(sender, e);

    bool startingLevel = true;

    if (GameManager.State == this.Value)
    {
        if (demoMode && !displayedDemoDialog)
        {
            //We could set properties on our YesNoDialog
            //so it could have a custom message and custom
            //Yes / No buttons ...
            //YesNoDialogState.YesCaption = "Of course!";
            GameManager.PushState(OurGame.YesNoDialogState.Value);
            this.Visible = true;
            displayedDemoDialog = true;
            startingLevel = false;
        }
    }

    if (startingLevel)
    {
        //play sound

        levelLoadTime = DateTime.Now;

        currentLevel = (OurGame.PlayingState.CurrentLevel + 1).ToString();

        Vector2 viewport = new Vector2(GraphicsDevice.Viewport.Width,
            GraphicsDevice.Viewport.Height);
        Vector2 levelTextLength = OurGame.Font.MeasureString(levelText);
        Vector2 levelNumberLength = OurGame.Font.MeasureString(currentLevel);
        levelTextShadowPosition = (viewport - levelTextLength * 3) / 2;
        levelNumberShadowPosition = (viewport - levelNumberLength * 3) / 2;
        levelNumberShadowPosition.Y += OurGame.Font.LineSpacing * 3;
```

```
        levelTextPosition.X = levelTextShadowPosition.X + 2;
        levelTextPosition.Y = levelTextShadowPosition.Y + 2;
        levelNumberPosition.X = levelNumberShadowPosition.X + 2;
        levelNumberPosition.Y = levelNumberShadowPosition.Y + 2;
    }
}
```

The first part of the method is the same as it was in our previous game state demo. However, we also create a startingLevel flag with the initial value of true. We modify the demo condition to set the startingLevel flag to false. Assuming we are really starting the level, which will occur the first time if we are not in demo mode, or after the dialog box is closed if we are in demo mode, we actually start playing our starting level sound. We have put a placeholder in to play that sound for now. We also initialize our level load time and set our current level variable. Finally, we initialize the vectors that store the position of the text we want to display when the level starts. The text will be centered on the screen.

The Update method for this state is as follows:

```
public override void Update(GameTime gameTime)
{
    if (DateTime.Now > levelLoadTime + new TimeSpan(0, 0, 0, 0, loadSoundTime))
    {
        //stop sound

        // change state to playing
        GameManager.ChangeState(OurGame.PlayingState.Value);
    }

    base.Update(gameTime);
}
```

Inside of the Update method, we change to the PlayingState and stop the sound if enough time has passed for the sound to stop. For now, we just have a placeholder where we will eventually stop the sound. The last method in this state is the Draw method:

```
public override void Draw(GameTime gameTime)
{
    OurGame.SpriteBatch.Begin();
    OurGame.SpriteBatch.DrawString(OurGame.Font, levelText,
        levelTextShadowPosition, Color.Yellow, 0, Vector2.Zero, 3.0f,
        SpriteEffects.None, 0);
    OurGame.SpriteBatch.DrawString(OurGame.Font, levelText,
        levelTextPosition, Color.Red, 0, Vector2.Zero, 3.0f,
        SpriteEffects.None, 0);
    OurGame.SpriteBatch.DrawString(OurGame.Font, currentLevel,
        levelNumberShadowPosition, Color.Yellow, 0, Vector2.Zero, 3.0f,
```

```
        SpriteEffects.None, 0);
    OurGame.SpriteBatch.DrawString(OurGame.Font, currentLevel,
        levelNumberPosition, Color.Red, 0, Vector2.Zero, 3.0f,
        SpriteEffects.None, 0);
    OurGame.SpriteBatch.End();

    base.Draw(gameTime);
}
```

The `Draw` method simply draws the level text and the level number in the right position, complete with a drop shadow effect.

We need to declare a font variable in our `TunnelVision` game class:

```
public SpriteFont Font;
```

Inside of the `LoadGraphicsContent` method we need to load our font:

```
Font = content.Load<SpriteFont>(@"Content\Fonts\Arial");
```

Before we compile and run our changes we need to modify the `StartMenuState` class. Inside of the `Update` method, we need to replace the contents of the condition where we check if either `Start` or `Enter` was pressed with the following code:

```
if (GameManager.ContainsState(OurGame.PlayingState.Value))
    GameManager.PopState(); //got here from our playing state, just pop myself off
the stack
else
{
    //starting game, queue first level
    GameManager.ChangeState(OurGame.PlayingState.Value);
    OurGame.PlayingState.StartGame();
}
```

We are still popping off our start menu state if our stack contains a playing state. However, instead of changing the state to the `StartLevelState` like the previous demo did, we are changing the state to `PlayingState` and calling its `StartGame` method.

At this point we can compile and run the game. The game logic is in place, but it is rather rough around the edges.

Creating the Crosshair

To allow better aiming, we need to add a crosshair to our screen. To start we need to add the following texture to our member field list of the `PlayingState` class:

```
private Texture2D crossHair;
```

Inside of our Draw method we need to add the following code:

```
OurGame.SpriteBatch.Begin();
if (OurGame.DisplayCrosshair)
{
    OurGame.SpriteBatch.Draw(crossHair, new Rectangle(
        (GraphicsDevice.Viewport.Width - crossHair.Width) / 2,
        (GraphicsDevice.Viewport.Height - crossHair.Height) / 2,
        crossHair.Width, crossHair.Height), Color.White);
}
OurGame.SpriteBatch.End();
```

We actually populate the crosshair texture inside of our LoadGraphicsContent method:

```
protected override void LoadGraphicsContent(bool loadAllContent)
{
    if (loadAllContent)
    {
        crossHair = Content.Load<Texture2D>(@"Content\Textures\crosshair");
    }
    base.LoadGraphicsContent(loadAllContent);
}
```

The texture can be found in the usual place. Later, we are going to provide an option to turn the crosshair on or off so we need to create the public boolean DisplayCrosshair field in our TunnelVision game code. It should be initialized to true. Now, we can more easily see where we are aiming!

Creating the Game-Specific Camera

Now, we are going to add a new camera directly to our game. We are not going to add this to the XELibrary because it is a special camera that most likely will not be reused. The purpose of this new camera is to handle input a little differently and to restrict movement. The code for the new TunnelVisionCamera.cs file is as follows:

```
using System;
using System.Collections.Generic;
using Microsoft.Xna.Framework;
using Microsoft.Xna.Framework.Input;

namespace XELibrary
{
    public partial class TunnelVisionCamera : Camera
    {
    private float spinLeft = 0;
    private float spinRight = 0;
    private float spinDown = 0;
```

```csharp
private float spinUp = 0;

private float spinLeftChange = 0;
private float spinRightChange = 0;
private float spinDownChange = 0;
private float spinUpChange = 0;

public TunnelVisionCamera(Game game) : base(game) {}

public override void Update(GameTime gameTime)
{
    if (!UpdateInput)
    return;

    float timeDelta = (float)gameTime.ElapsedGameTime.TotalSeconds;

    if (input.KeyboardState.IsKeyDown(Keys.Left))
        spinLeftChange += .1f;
    else
        spinLeftChange -= .1f;
    spinLeftChange = MathHelper.Clamp(spinLeftChange, 0, 1);
    spinLeft = spinLeftChange;
    if (input.GamePads[playerIndex].ThumbSticks.Left.X < 0)
        spinLeft = -input.GamePads[playerIndex].ThumbSticks.Left.X;
    if (spinLeft > 0)
        cameraYaw += (Utility.PowerCurve(spinLeft) * SpinRate *
            timeDelta);

    if (input.KeyboardState.IsKeyDown(Keys.Right))
        spinRightChange += .1f;
    else
        spinRightChange -= .1f;
    spinRightChange = MathHelper.Clamp(spinRightChange, 0, 1);
    spinRight = spinRightChange;
    if (input.GamePads[playerIndex].ThumbSticks.Left.X > 0)
        spinRight = input.GamePads[playerIndex].ThumbSticks.Left.X;
    if (spinRight > 0)
        cameraYaw -= (Utility.PowerCurve(spinRight) * SpinRate *
            timeDelta);

    if (input.KeyboardState.IsKeyDown(Keys.Down))
        spinDownChange += .1f;
    else
        spinDownChange -= .1f;
    spinDownChange = MathHelper.Clamp(spinDownChange, 0, 1);
```

```
spinDown = spinDownChange;
if (input.GamePads[playerIndex].ThumbSticks.Left.Y < 0)
    spinDown = -input.GamePads[playerIndex].ThumbSticks.Left.Y;
if (spinDown > 0)
    cameraPitch -= (Utility.PowerCurve(spinDown) * SpinRate *
        timeDelta);

if (input.KeyboardState.IsKeyDown(Keys.Up))
    spinUpChange += .1f;
else
    spinUpChange -= .1f;
spinUpChange = MathHelper.Clamp(spinUpChange, 0, 1);
spinUp = spinUpChange;
if (input.GamePads[playerIndex].ThumbSticks.Left.Y > 0)
    spinUp = input.GamePads[playerIndex].ThumbSticks.Left.Y;
if (spinUp > 0)
    cameraPitch += (Utility.PowerCurve(spinUp) * SpinRate *
        timeDelta);

//reset camera angle if needed
if (cameraYaw > 80)
    cameraYaw = 80;
else if (cameraYaw < -80)
    cameraYaw = -80;

//keep camera from rotating a full 90 degrees in either direction
if (cameraPitch > 89)
    cameraPitch = 89;
if (cameraPitch < -89)
    cameraPitch = -89;

Matrix rotationMatrix;
Vector3 transformedReference;

Matrix.CreateRotationY(MathHelper.ToRadians(cameraYaw),
    out rotationMatrix);

//add in pitch to the rotation
rotationMatrix = Matrix.CreateRotationX(
    MathHelper.ToRadians(cameraPitch)) * rotationMatrix;

// Create a vector pointing the direction the camera is facing.
Vector3.Transform(ref cameraReference, ref rotationMatrix,
    out transformedReference);
// Calculate the position the camera is looking at.
```

20

```
        Vector3.Add(ref cameraPosition, ref transformedReference,
            out cameraTarget);

        Matrix.CreateLookAt(ref cameraPosition, ref cameraTarget,
            ref cameraUpVector, out view);
        }
    }
}
```

This is very similar to the base object's Update method, except that we are restricting movement. We only allow the camera to move 80 degrees left or right. The pitch did not change. Instead of going through the entire class line by line we can look at the section of code that handles if the user rotated to the left and infer how the rest of the movements work:

```
if (input.KeyboardState.IsKeyDown(Keys.Left))
    spinLeftChange += .1f;
else
    spinLeftChange -= .1f;
spinLeftChange = MathHelper.Clamp(spinLeftChange, 0, 1);
spinLeft = spinLeftChange;
if (input.GamePads[playerIndex].ThumbSticks.Left.X < 0)
    spinLeft = -input.GamePads[playerIndex].ThumbSticks.Left.X;
if (spinLeft > 0)
    cameraYaw += (Utility.PowerCurve(spinLeft) * SpinRate *
        timeDelta);
```

When playing the game, the keyboard movement was too fast and too jerky. To solve this, we build up our spin left value. In the base class, it simply gets set to 1. Here, we are adding 10 percent each frame and clamping the results to 1. Now we can tap the keyboard to have more precise control over targeting our enemies. If the game pad is used to rotate the camera, then we use a new helper method to produce a curve in the movement. In the Utility.cs file in the XELibrary we can add the following code:

```
const float power = 3;
public static float PowerCurve(float value)
{
    return ((float)Math.Pow(Math.Abs(value), power) * Math.Sign(value));
}
```

The PowerCurve helper method provides a curve we can apply to the values our thumbstick produces. Instead of strictly using the value of the thumbstick, we are making the low values lower, which gives us more control. Now as we barely move the thumbstick, the camera will barely move. Now when we move the controller to target our enemies we can have more precise control.

We need to modify our `Camera` object in the XELibrary. The following public member field needs to be created:

```
public bool UpdateInput = true;
```

Inside of the `Update` method the following condition needs to be added at the very top of the method:

```
if (!UpdateInput)
{
    base.Update(gameTime);
    return;
}
```

We also want to change the modifier for the `playerIndex`, `cameraReference`, `cameraTarget`, `cameraUpVector`, `view`, `cameraYaw`, and `cameraPitch` fields to be protected instead of private. The private const `spinRate` and `moveRate` should be changed to public and no longer be a const because we need to be able to set them anywhere.

To use this new camera, we need to change our `TunnelVision` game class to use the `TunnelVisionCamera` instead of `Camera`. We also need to modify our `PlayingState` class to use the new `UpdateMethod` boolean property. Inside of the `StateChanged` method we need to add the following code to the first branch of our condition:

```
OurGame.Camera.UpdateInput = false;
```

We need to do the opposite in the else of our if condition:

```
OurGame.Camera.UpdateInput = true;
```

Inside of the constructor of the `PlayingState` we need to add the following code that sets the move rate and spin rate of our camera:

```
OurGame.Camera.MoveRate = 10;
OurGame.Camera.SpinRate = 60;
```

We have improved our input handling and have restricted movement on our camera so we only rotate 80 degrees to the left or right instead of the full 360 degrees.

Summary

In this chapter we have laid the foundation for creating our game. We have put into place all of the game logic. There were not really any new concepts in this chapter, but by putting what we learned in previous chapters into practice we should be well on our way to creating our own masterpieces. The next two chapters are spent updating our game states and UI enhancements.

20

Improving the Game

In this chapter the game is enhanced by adding a 2D radar of the enemies. A level timer and scoring is also created and displayed on the screen. Finally, high scores are stored and saved to a storage device.

Creating the Radar

As we play the game, it becomes difficult to know where the enemies are. We need to spin around often to see where they are. Although some prefer to play games this way, it makes it much more difficult and many gamers will get frustrated and not play the game if we do not give them a bird's-eye view of what is going on. We are going to create a radar in this section that does just that.

Inside of our playing state's Draw method we need to add the following condition before we call SpriteBatch.End:

```
if (OurGame.DisplayRadar)
{
    if (enemyManager.Radar != null)
        OurGame.SpriteBatch.Draw(enemyManager.Radar,
            new Rectangle(
                TitleSafeArea.Left,
                TitleSafeArea.Bottom - 200,
                200, 200),
            new Color(new Vector4(1, 1, 1, .5f)));
}
```

We are checking to see if the Radar texture our enemy manager exposes is null. If it is not null, we display it on the bottom left of our screen. We can add the public boolean DisplayRadar field to our TunnelVision game initialized to true. Later, we provide an option where gamers can turn this feature on or off as they play.

We need to actually create this radar texture inside of our enemy manager. To start, we need to add the following fields to our EnemyManager class:

```
private RenderTarget2D radarRenderTarget;
private Texture2D radarPlayerDot;
public Texture2D Radar;
```

Inside of the LoadGraphicsContent method we need to add the following code inside of the loadAllContent condition:

```
radarPlayerDot = new Texture2D(GraphicsDevice, 1, 1, 1, ResourceUsage.None,
    SurfaceFormat.Color, ResourceManagementMode.Automatic);
radarPlayerDot.SetData(new Color[] { Color.White } );
```

In the center of our radar we are going to place a white dot that represents the player. This code simply creates the 1 x 1 white pixel. While we are inside of this method, we can add the following code outside of the condition:

```
radarRenderTarget = new RenderTarget2D(GraphicsDevice, 200,
    200, 1, GraphicsDevice.DisplayMode.Format,
    GraphicsDevice.PresentationParameters.MultiSampleType,
    GraphicsDevice.PresentationParameters.MultiSampleQuality);
```

Because we are creating a texture that our game can use to display on the screen, we need to create a render target that we can render our enemies onto. We need to make sure to dispose of the render target in our UnloadGraphicsContent method. This should also be done outside of the unloadAllContent condition.

The final piece we need to complete to have a radar in our game is to actually draw our enemies on our texture. Inside of the Draw method, before the base.Draw method we need to add the following code:

```
GraphicsDevice.SetRenderTarget(0, radarRenderTarget);
GraphicsDevice.Clear(Color.Green);

Matrix birdsEyeView = Matrix.CreateLookAt(new Vector3(ourGame.Camera.Position.X,
    250, ourGame.Camera.Position.Z), ourGame.Camera.Position, Vector3.Forward);

effect.Parameters["View"].SetValue(birdsEyeView);
effect.Parameters["Projection"].SetValue(ourGame.Camera.Projection);
```

We set our render target like we have done in the past and clear the device to green. This will make our radar a nice shade of green. We need to view our world (or at least the enemies in our world) from a bird's-eye view. To do this, we set up a new view. Instead of using our normal camera view, which is looking straight at the enemies, we create a bird's-eye view by positioning our camera 250 units above our player (camera). Finally, we set the effect's view and projection parameters.

Next, we need to actually draw our enemies. We are already doing this in our `Draw` method, so we should refactor the for loop code that draws our enemies and make another method called `DrawEnemies`. We then need to actually call this newly created method:

```
DrawEnemies();
```

After drawing our enemies on the render target, we can draw the player dot texture we created earlier:

```
ourGame.SpriteBatch.Begin();
ourGame.SpriteBatch.Draw(radarPlayerDot, new Vector2(100, 100), Color.White);
ourGame.SpriteBatch.End();
```

Next, we need to resolve our render target and set our Radar texture:

```
//resolve what we just drew to our render target
GraphicsDevice.ResolveRenderTarget(0);

//clear it out
GraphicsDevice.SetRenderTarget(0, null);

Radar = radarRenderTarget.GetTexture();
```

Now we can see our enemies when they come into range!

Creating the Tunnel

With a name like tunnel vision, it would be wise to actually add a tunnel to the game. We need to create a code file named Tunnel.cs for our projects. This file will have all of the normal using statements. The class will inherit from the `DrawableGameComponent`. The member fields we will need for the `Tunnel` class are as follows:

```
private VertexPositionNormalTangentTexture[] vertices;
private short[] indices;
private VertexDeclaration vertexDeclaration;

private Effect effect;
private Texture2D colorMap;
private Texture2D normalMap;

public Matrix View;
public Matrix Projection;

private TunnelVision ourGame;
```

We will be creating the four tunnel walls manually. We created the rectangle in the early chapters of this book. We will be using the same code and transforming it to make up our tunnel. We will be using the normal mapping technique to texture our tunnel walls. We also expose two public fields the playing state can set for the view and projection matrices.

Now, we can look at the constructor and initialize methods of our Tunnel class:

```
public Tunnel(Game game) : base(game)
{
    ourGame = (TunnelVision)ourGame;
}

public override void Initialize()
{
    base.Initialize();

    InitializeVertices();
    InitializeIndices();
}
```

The InitializeVertices and InitializeIndices methods are not new, but are listed here for completeness:

```
private void InitializeVertices()
{
    Vector3 position;
    Vector2 textureCoordinates;

    vertices = new VertexPositionNormalTangentTexture[4];

    //top left
    position = new Vector3(-100, 100, 0);
    textureCoordinates = new Vector2(0, 0);
    vertices[0] = new VertexPositionNormalTangentTexture(
        position, Vector3.Forward, Vector3.Left, textureCoordinates);

    //bottom right
    position = new Vector3(100, -100, 0);
    textureCoordinates = new Vector2(1, 1);
    vertices[1] = new VertexPositionNormalTangentTexture(
        position, Vector3.Forward, Vector3.Left, textureCoordinates);

    //bottom left
    position = new Vector3(-100, -100, 0);
    textureCoordinates = new Vector2(0, 1);
    vertices[2] = new VertexPositionNormalTangentTexture(
        position, Vector3.Forward, Vector3.Left, textureCoordinates);

    //top right
```

```
    position = new Vector3(100, 100, 0);
    textureCoordinates = new Vector2(1, 0);
    vertices[3] = new VertexPositionNormalTangentTexture(
        position, Vector3.Forward, Vector3.Left, textureCoordinates);
}

private void InitializeIndices()
{
    //6 vertices make up 2 triangles which make up our rectangle
    indices = new short[6];

    //triangle 1 (bottom portion)
    indices[0] = 0; // top left
    indices[1] = 1; // bottom right
    indices[2] = 2; // bottom left

    //triangle 2 (top portion)
    indices[3] = 0; // top left
    indices[4] = 3; // top right
    indices[5] = 1; // bottom right
}
```

Next, we can look at the LoadGraphicsContent method. We are simply setting up our vertex declaration as well as our effect and maps for the tunnel:

```
protected override void LoadGraphicsContent(bool loadAllContent)
{
    //Initialize our Vertex Declaration
    vertexDeclaration = new VertexDeclaration(GraphicsDevice,
        VertexPositionNormalTangentTexture.VertexElements);

    if (loadAllContent)
    {
        effect = ourGame.Content.Load<Effect>(
            @"Content\Effects\NormalMapping");
        colorMap = ourGame.Content.Load<Texture2D>(
            @"Content\Textures\rockbump_color");
        normalMap = ourGame.Content.Load<Texture2D>(
            @"Content\Textures\rockbump_normal");
    }

    base.LoadGraphicsContent(loadAllContent);
}
```

The NormalMapping effect file we used in Chapter 17, "Advanced Texturing Techniques," needs to be added to our project. The rockbump_color and rockbump_normal texture files also need to be added. The files can be found in this chapter's code folder on the accompanying CD.

The code for our `Draw` method is as follows:

```
public override void Draw(GameTime gameTime)
{
    GraphicsDevice.RenderState.AlphaTestEnable = false;
    GraphicsDevice.RenderState.AlphaBlendEnable = false;
    GraphicsDevice.RenderState.PointSpriteEnable = false;
    GraphicsDevice.RenderState.DepthBufferWriteEnable = true;
    GraphicsDevice.RenderState.DepthBufferEnable = true;

    GraphicsDevice.VertexDeclaration = vertexDeclaration;

    Matrix world = Matrix.Identity;
    effect.Parameters["World"].SetValue(world);
    effect.Parameters["View"].SetValue(View);
    effect.Parameters["Projection"].SetValue(Projection);
    effect.Parameters["AmbientColor"].SetValue(.05f);
    effect.Parameters["ColorMap"].SetValue(colorMap);
    effect.Parameters["NormalMap"].SetValue(normalMap);
    effect.Parameters["LightPosition"].SetValue(Vector3.Zero);
    effect.Parameters["LightDiffuseColor"].SetValue(Color.White.ToVector4());

    DrawRectangle(world * Matrix.CreateRotationY(
        MathHelper.ToRadians(-90)) *
        Matrix.CreateTranslation(60, 0, 100), effect); //right
    DrawRectangle(world * Matrix.CreateRotationY(
        MathHelper.ToRadians(90)) *
        Matrix.CreateTranslation(-60, 0, 100), effect); //left
    DrawRectangle(world * Matrix.CreateRotationX(
        MathHelper.ToRadians(90)) *
        Matrix.CreateTranslation(0, 60, 100), effect); //top
    DrawRectangle(world * Matrix.CreateRotationX(
        MathHelper.ToRadians(-90)) *
        Matrix.CreateTranslation(0, -60, 100), effect); //bottom

    base.Draw(gameTime);
}
```

We make sure the render state is set up the way we need it to be to render our tunnel. Then we set our vertex declaration and populate our effect. We then create four rectangles passing in the transformation to position and rotate those rectangles to make a tunnel. We also pass in the effect to the method that creates the rectangle. The code for the `DrawRectangle` method is as follows:

```
private void DrawRectangle(Matrix world, Effect effect)
{
    effect.Parameters["World"].SetValue(world);
    effect.Begin();
    foreach (EffectPass pass in effect.CurrentTechnique.Passes)
    {
        pass.Begin();

        GraphicsDevice.DrawUserIndexedPrimitives(
            PrimitiveType.TriangleList, vertices, 0, vertices.Length,
            indices, 0, indices.Length / 3);

        pass.End();
    }
    effect.End();
}
```

The DrawRectangle method uses the DrawUserIndexedPrimitives method to create the rectangle. The world transformation that is passed in is applied to the effect that is used.

We need to modify our playing state to load the tunnel. The following private member field needs to be added:

```
private Tunnel tunnel;
```

In the constructor we need to add the following code:

```
tunnel = new Tunnel(Game);
Game.Components.Add(tunnel);
```

We need to set the tunnel's View and Projection properties to inside of the Draw method:

```
tunnel.View = OurGame.Camera.View;
tunnel.Projection = OurGame.Camera.Projection;
```

We can compile and run the code and see our tunnel on the edges of our screen.

Creating the Level Timer

Our game itself is looking better, but we need a sense of urgency added to the game play. Our levels each have a timer associated with it, but we have not implemented it yet. To start, we can add the following private member fields to PlayingState:

```
private TimeSpan? storedTime;
private TimeSpan currentLevelTime;
private DateTime currentLevelStopTime = DateTime.Now;
```

The `storedTime` field is a private field that allows a null value and will be used to handle us pausing the game. We do not want our timer to continue to count down while we are paused. We also store our current time and the stop time of our level.

In the `SetupGame` method we need to add this statement:

```
currentLevelTime = TimeSpan.Zero;
```

In our `StartLevel` method we need to add this statement:

```
storedTime = null;
```

In our `Update` method, we need to add the following code:

```
currentLevelTime = currentLevelStopTime.Subtract(DateTime.Now);
if (currentLevelTime.Seconds < 0)
    currentLevelTime = TimeSpan.Zero;
```

We continually update our current level time, making sure our level time does not go negative. Next we need to store our current time if we pause the game. The following conditions need to be modified inside of the `Update` method:

```
if (Input.WasPressed(0, InputHandler.ButtonType.Back, Keys.Escape))
{
    storedTime = currentLevelTime;
    GameManager.PushState(OurGame.StartMenuState.Value);
}

if (Input.WasPressed(0, InputHandler.ButtonType.Start, Keys.Enter))
{
    storedTime = currentLevelTime;
    GameManager.PushState(OurGame.PausedState.Value);
}
```

At the bottom of the else condition inside the `StateChanged` method, we need to add the following code:

```
if (storedTime != null)
    currentLevelStopTime = DateTime.Now + (TimeSpan)storedTime;
else
    currentLevelStopTime = DateTime.Now +
        new TimeSpan(0, 0, Levels[CurrentLevel].Time);
```

When we come into our playing state, we set our current level stop time to either the stored time (from where we paused the game) or if this is the first time in the playing state, we use the current time, adding in the length of time we have for this level. We will create a HUD where we can display the remaining time next.

Creating the HUD

We have created some variables to store the level time, but we do not display it anywhere to the gamer. In this section we are going o display the current level, the number of enemies that remain, and the remaining amount of time. We will add the score in the next section. For now, we need to add in the following private member fields in our PlayingState class:

```
private string levelText = string.Empty;
private Vector2 levelTextShadowPosition;
private Vector2 levelTextPosition;

private string enemiesText = string.Empty;
private Vector2 enemiesTextShadowPosition;
private Vector2 enemiesTextPosition;

private string timeText = string.Empty;
private Vector2 timeTextShadowPosition;
private Vector2 timeTextPosition;
```

We are storing the actual text we will be displaying as well as the position of the text and the offset shadow position of the text. The text can be set inside of our Update method:

```
levelText = "Level: " + ((int)(CurrentLevel + 1)).ToString();
timeText = "Time: " + ((int)currentLevelTime.TotalSeconds).ToString();
enemiesText = "Enemies: " +
    ((int)(Levels[CurrentLevel].Enemies - TotalCollisions)).ToString();
```

We calculate the number of enemies by subtracting the total number of collisions we have had by the number of enemies inside of the current level.

Inside of the Draw method we can actually draw our text on the screen. We need to add the following code to our Draw method:

```
OurGame.SpriteBatch.DrawString(OurGame.Font, levelText,
    levelTextShadowPosition, Color.Black);
OurGame.SpriteBatch.DrawString(OurGame.Font, levelText,
    levelTextPosition, Color.WhiteSmoke);

OurGame.SpriteBatch.DrawString(OurGame.Font, enemiesText,
    enemiesTextShadowPosition, Color.Black);
OurGame.SpriteBatch.DrawString(OurGame.Font, enemiesText,
    enemiesTextPosition, Color.Firebrick);

OurGame.SpriteBatch.DrawString(OurGame.Font, timeText,
    timeTextShadowPosition, Color.Black);
OurGame.SpriteBatch.DrawString(OurGame.Font, timeText,
    timeTextPosition, Color.Firebrick);
```

Finally, we need to actually initialize the positions of the text and their drop shadow counterparts. This is done inside of the LoadGraphicsContent method inside of the loadAllContent condition:

```
levelTextShadowPosition = new Vector2(TitleSafeArea.X, TitleSafeArea.Y);
levelTextPosition = new Vector2(TitleSafeArea.X + 2.0f,TitleSafeArea.Y + 2.0f);

enemiesTextShadowPosition = new Vector2(TitleSafeArea.X, TitleSafeArea.Y +
    OurGame.Font.LineSpacing);
enemiesTextPosition = new Vector2(TitleSafeArea.X + 2.0f, TitleSafeArea.Y +
    OurGame.Font.LineSpacing + 2.0f);

timeTextShadowPosition = new Vector2(TitleSafeArea.X, TitleSafeArea.Y +
    OurGame.Font.LineSpacing * 2);
timeTextPosition = new Vector2(TitleSafeArea.X + 2.0f, TitleSafeArea.Y +
    OurGame.Font.LineSpacing * 2 + 2.0f);
```

The lines of text are positioned in the top left part of the screen with the drop shadow having a two-pixel offset.

Adding Scoring

Our game play is shaping up, but it would be nice to actually be gaining points when we destroy the enemy ships. We will award points every time an enemy is destroyed and we will give bonus points for every second that remains after all of the enemy ships have been eliminated.

We start by listing the private member fields that need to be added to the PlayingState class:

```
private string scoreText = string.Empty;
private Vector2 scoreTextShadowPosition;
private Vector2 scoreTextPosition;
public int score;
```

We have created variables to store the text that will display our score as well as a variable to store the score itself. We want to initialize the score to zero when the game starts, so we need to add the following statement inside of the SetupGame method:

```
score = 0;
```

We will award a point each time a missile collides with an enemy ship, so inside of the CheckConditions while loop in the Update method we can add this statement:

```
score += 100; //100 points for each enemy
```

Immediately following this while loop is a condition that checks to see if the level is over. To award the points when the level is over and time still remains we need to add the following code to the top of that condition:

```
if (currentLevelTime.Seconds > 0)
    score += ((int)currentLevelTime.TotalSeconds * 500);
```

We can store the score text at the end of our Update method:

```
scoreText = "Score: " + score.ToString();
```

We will draw the score on the screen by adding the following code to the Draw method right after we draw the level time remaining:

```
OurGame.SpriteBatch.DrawString(OurGame.Font, scoreText,
    scoreTextShadowPosition, Color.Black);
OurGame.SpriteBatch.DrawString(OurGame.Font, scoreText,
    scoreTextPosition, Color.Firebrick);
```

We will initialize the position vectors for the text and the drop shadow text just in the LoadGraphicsContent method's loadAllContent condition:

```
scoreTextShadowPosition = new Vector2(TitleSafeArea.X, TitleSafeArea.Y +
    OurGame.Font.LineSpacing * 3);
scoreTextPosition = new Vector2(TitleSafeArea.X + 2.0f, TitleSafeArea.Y +
    OurGame.Font.LineSpacing * 3 + 2.0f);
```

We make sure that the score shows up under the remaining time in the top left corner of our screen. We can compile and run the game and see all of our new additions. A screenshot of the game in its current state can be seen in Figure 21.1.

FIGURE 21.1   TunnelVision screenshot with crosshair, HUD, and scoring.

Keeping Track of High Scores

After playing the game and seeing the score, the next logical step is to create a way to store our high score list. Currently, the XNA Framework does not expose the gamer tag's profile name. It also does not expose the built-in display keyboard. To keep the code simple, we are going to hard-code the name "Player1" when a high score is reached. There are a couple of community projects where developers have created keyboard game components. If desired, they could be plugged into the code to allow entering the player's name when he or she reaches a high score.

This section is going to describe what is needed to create an initial high score file as well as what is needed to save new names to the file. This is one of the few sections in this part of the book that has new material.

Because saving high score data is something we will do in many games, we should create the core pieces in our XELibrary's Utility file. We can add the struct we will use to actually hold the high score data:

```
[Serializable]
public struct HighScoreData
{
    public string[] PlayerName;
    public int[] Score;
    public int[] Level;

    public int Count;

    public HighScoreData(int count)
    {
        PlayerName = new string[count];
        Score = new int[count];
        Level = new int[count];

        Count = count;
    }
}
```

We mark this struct as serializable so we can save the data to a file. We are simply storing a list of player names, their scores, and the levels they reached. The constructor requires a count parameter that determines how many player names will be stored in the high score list. We need to add the System.Xml.Serialization namespace to our using statements.

We need to add two helper methods to our Utility class. One will save the high scores and the other will load them. The code for the SaveHighScores method is as follows:

```
public static void SaveHighScores(HighScoreData data, string filename)
{
    // Get the path of the saved game
```

```
    string fullpath = Path.Combine(StorageContainer.TitleLocation, filename);

    // Open the file, creating it if necessary
    FileStream stream = File.Open(fullpath, FileMode.OpenOrCreate);
    try
    {
        // Convert the object to XML data and put it in the stream
        XmlSerializer serializer = new XmlSerializer(typeof(HighScoreData));
        serializer.Serialize(stream, data);
    }
    finally
    {
        // Close the file
        stream.Close();
    }
}
```

We need to add the System.IO and Microsoft.Xna.Framework.Storage namespaces to our using statements in the Utility.cs file. Regardless if we are using the Xbox 360 or Windows, we use normal .NET Framework methods to load and save files. We use the Combine method from the Path class to combine the TitleLocation path we retrieved from XNA's StorageContainer class with the filename passed into the method. We wrap the serialization code around a try/finally block in case something goes wrong. We do not want to leave the file stream open. Serializing data in the .NET Framework is extremely easy.

Next, we can see how we load the high scores in the LoadHighScores method:

```
public static HighScoreData LoadHighScores(string filename)
{
    HighScoreData data;

    // Get the path of the saved game
    string fullpath = Path.Combine(StorageContainer.TitleLocation, filename);

    // Open the file
    FileStream stream = File.Open(fullpath, FileMode.OpenOrCreate,
        FileAccess.Read);
    try
    {

        // Read the data from the file
        XmlSerializer serializer = new XmlSerializer(typeof(HighScoreData));
        data = (HighScoreData)serializer.Deserialize(stream);
    }
    finally
```

```
    {
        // Close the file
        stream.Close();
    }

    return (data);
}
```

The code is very similar to how we saved the data. The filename is passed into the method and we obtain the full path the same way. We open the file for read-only access and then deserialize the high score data inside of a try/finally block. We then return the high score data.

When our game starts we want to check to see if the high score file exists on the system. If it does not, we need to create it with some default high scores. We do this inside of the TunnelVision game code's Initialize method:

```
// Get the path of the saved game
string fullpath = Path.Combine(StorageContainer.TitleLocation, HighScoresFilename);

// Check to see if the save exists
if (!File.Exists(fullpath))
{
    //If the file doesn't exist, make a fake one...
    // Create the data to save
    HighScoreData data = new HighScoreData(5);
    data.PlayerName[0] = "Neil";
    data.Level[0] = 10;
    data.Score[0] = 200500;

    data.PlayerName[1] = "Shawn";
    data.Level[1] = 10;
    data.Score[1] = 187000;

    data.PlayerName[2] = "Mark";
    data.Level[2] = 9;
    data.Score[2] = 113300;

    data.PlayerName[3] = "Cindy";
    data.Level[3] = 7;
    data.Score[3] = 95100;

    data.PlayerName[4] = "Sam";
    data.Level[4] = 1;
    data.Score[4] = 1000;

    Utility.SaveHighScores(data, HighScoresFilename);
}
```

The code simply populates some default high score values and saves them to a file. We need to add the System.IO namespace to our game's using statements. The HighScoresFilename field needs to be added to our code:

```
public readonly string HighScoresFilename = "highscores.lst";
```

The last thing we need to do is actually save the score when a game is over if it belongs in the list. Regardless if the gamer wins or loses, the FadingState is pushed onto the stack. We can modify this state to determine if the player's score should be stored in the high score list. We can create the SaveHighScore method inside of our FadingState class:

```
private void SaveHighScore()
{
    // Create the data to save
    HighScoreData data = Utility.LoadHighScores(OurGame.HighScoresFilename);

    int scoreIndex = -1;
    for (int i = 0; i < data.Count; i++)
    {
        if (OurGame.PlayingState.Score > data.Score[i])
        {
            scoreIndex = i;
            break;
        }
    }

    if (scoreIndex > -1)
    {
        //New high score found ... do swaps
        for (int i = data.Count-1; i > scoreIndex; i—)
        {
            data.PlayerName[i] = data.PlayerName[i - 1];
            data.Score[i] = data.Score[i - 1];
            data.Level[i] = data.Level[i - 1];
        }

        data.PlayerName[scoreIndex] = "Player1"; //Retrieve User Name Here
        data.Score[scoreIndex] = OurGame.PlayingState.Score;
        data.Level[scoreIndex] = OurGame.PlayingState.CurrentLevel + 1;

        Utility.SaveHighScores(data, OurGame.HighScoresFilename);
    }
}
```

We start the method by loading our high score file. We then loop through each high score checking to see if the score we ended the game with is higher than the one we are checking. We loop through the scores in order. They are saved highest to lowest and if we find that the game score is greater than the stored score, we store the index.

If a new high score should be added, then we loop through current high scores and swap out as many as needed. We push the other scores down the list and then save our high score in the newly available spot. Finally, we save the high score list again. We actually call this method inside of the Update method right after we change our state:

```
SaveHighScore();
```

The last task we need to complete is to expose the Score we have been using in the code. PlayingState does not currently expose that field. We need to create a property in both the class and in the IPlayingState interface.

After running the game on Windows we can see the highscore.lst file in the bin folder. We are not displaying the values yet, but will create a game state just for that purpose in the next chapter.

Summary

In this chapter, we improved the game by adding a radar to more easily see the enemies. We actually created the tunnel and added it to our world. We added a level timer and displayed the time along with the number of enemies we had left to clear the level on the screen. We added scoring to our game. Finally, we learned how to serialize high score data to save it to a file on Windows and the Xbox 360. We also saw how to deserialize the same data.

CHAPTER 22

Finishing Touches

In this last chapter we are going to finish our 3D game. We are going to update the title screen, the start menu, and option menu. We are also going to create the high score screen. We are going to add a particle system that will be executed when an enemy is destroyed. We are going to create a sound project in XACT and add it to our game.

Updating the Title Screen

We are going to spice up the title screen some by adding in the same fire effect we used in Chapter 18, "Special Effects." We need to add the following private member fields to our `TitleIntroState` class:

```
private Effect fireEffect;
private Random rand = new Random();
private Texture2D hotSpotTexture;
private Texture2D fire; //gets render target's texture

private RenderTarget2D renderTarget1;
private RenderTarget2D renderTarget2;

private int offset = -128;
private Color[] colors = {
    Color.Black,
    Color.Yellow,
    Color.White,
    Color.Red,
    Color.Orange,
    new Color(255,255,128) //yellowish white
};
```

The code is listed for completeness, but there is not much description, as it was discussed in detail in Chapter 18. The current position of our texture in the Draw method needs to be changed to the following so it will be centered on the screen:

```
Vector2 pos = new Vector2((GraphicsDevice.Viewport.Width - texture.Width) / 2,
    (GraphicsDevice.Viewport.Height - texture.Height) / 2);
```

After setting that variable and before calling Begin on the SpriteBatch, the following code needs to be added:

```
GraphicsDevice device = GraphicsDevice;

//Draw hotspots on the first Render Target
device.SetRenderTarget(0, renderTarget1);
device.Clear(Color.Black);
```

After the call to Begin and before the call to SpriteBatch.Draw we need to add the following code:

```
//get last drawn screen — if not first time in
//fire is null first time in, and when device is lost (LoadGraphicsContent)
if (fire != null) //render target has valid texture
    OurGame.SpriteBatch.Draw(fire, Vector2.Zero, Color.White);

//draw hotspots
for (int i = 0; i < device.Viewport.Width / hotSpotTexture.Width; i++)
    OurGame.SpriteBatch.Draw(hotSpotTexture,
        new Vector2(i * hotSpotTexture.Width,
        device.Viewport.Height - hotSpotTexture.Height),
        colors[rand.Next(colors.Length)]);

OurGame.SpriteBatch.End();

//resolve what we just drew to our render target
device.ResolveRenderTarget(0);

//clear it out
device.SetRenderTarget(0, null);

// Transfer from first to second render target
device.SetRenderTarget(0, renderTarget2);

fireEffect.Begin();
OurGame.SpriteBatch.Begin(SpriteBlendMode.None, SpriteSortMode.Immediate,
    SaveStateMode.None);

EffectPass pass = fireEffect.CurrentTechnique.Passes[0];
pass.Begin();
```

```
OurGame.SpriteBatch.Draw(renderTarget1.GetTexture(), new Rectangle(0, offset,
    device.Viewport.Width, device.Viewport.Height - offset), Color.White);
OurGame.SpriteBatch.End();
pass.End();
fireEffect.End();

//resolve what we just drew to our render target
device.ResolveRenderTarget(0);

//clear it out
device.SetRenderTarget(0, null);

device.Clear(Color.Black);

//set texture to render
fire = renderTarget2.GetTexture();

// Draw second render target onto the screen (back buffer)
OurGame.SpriteBatch.Begin(SpriteBlendMode.Additive);
```

None of the code changed from how this was accomplished in Chapter 18. After creating the fire and setting the texture, we set up our sprite batch in additive blending mode so we can add our texture. That code is already in the state. After the sprite batch call to draw the texture, we need to actually draw our fire texture:

```
OurGame.SpriteBatch.Draw(fire, Vector2.Zero, Color.White);
OurGame.SpriteBatch.Draw(fire, Vector2.Zero, Color.White);
OurGame.SpriteBatch.Draw(fire, Vector2.Zero, Color.White);

OurGame.SpriteBatch.Draw(fire, Vector2.Zero, null, Color.White, 0,
    Vector2.Zero, 1.0f, SpriteEffects.FlipVertically, 0);
OurGame.SpriteBatch.Draw(fire, Vector2.Zero, null, Color.White, 0,
    Vector2.Zero, 1.0f, SpriteEffects.FlipVertically, 0);
OurGame.SpriteBatch.Draw(fire, Vector2.Zero, null, Color.White, 0,
    Vector2.Zero, 1.0f, SpriteEffects.FlipVertically, 0);
```

The first three lines are identical to Chapter 18. We are drawing the fire texture three times to keep the color intensity we lost from the averaging of colors. The second set of three lines does the same thing, except it flips the texture vertically so the fire is coming from the top of the screen as well.

We need to add the CreateTexture method to our class:

```
private Texture2D CreateTexture(int width, int height)
{
    Texture2D texture = new Texture2D(GraphicsDevice, width, height, 1,
        ResourceUsage.None, SurfaceFormat.Color,
```

```
        ResourceManagementMode.Automatic);

    int pixelCount = width * height;
    Color[] pixelData = new Color[pixelCount];

    for (int i = 0; i < pixelCount; i++)
        pixelData[i] = Color.White;

    texture.SetData(pixelData);

    return (texture);
}
```

Next, we can replace the entire contents of the LoadGraphicsContent method with the following code:

```
GraphicsDevice device = GraphicsDevice;
if (loadAllContent)
{
    hotSpotTexture = CreateTexture(4, 1);
    OurGame.SpriteBatch = new SpriteBatch(device);
    fireEffect = Content.Load<Effect>(@"Content\Effects\Fire");
    texture = Content.Load<Texture2D>(@"Content\Textures\titleIntro");
}
renderTarget1 = new RenderTarget2D(device, device.Viewport.Width,
    device.Viewport.Height, 1, device.DisplayMode.Format,
    device.PresentationParameters.MultiSampleType,
    device.PresentationParameters.MultiSampleQuality);

renderTarget2 = new RenderTarget2D(device, device.Viewport.Width,
    device.Viewport.Height, 1, device.DisplayMode.Format,
    device.PresentationParameters.MultiSampleType,
    device.PresentationParameters.MultiSampleQuality);

fire = null;
base.LoadGraphicsContent(loadAllContent);
```

The titleIntro.png file has changed since the game state demo. The new titleIntro.png file can be found in this chapter's code folder on the accompanying CD. The Fire.fx file can be found in the same location. It did not change from Chapter 18. Most of this code should be reviewed. We incorporated the demo we made in the Special Effects chapter into our game. The title screen can be seen in Figure 22.1.

FIGURE 22.1   The title screen consists of a texture and the fire effect.

Updating the Start Menu

Our start menu is going to have a major overhaul. We create actual items that can be selected instead of the fake texture we have in place currently. Some of the code in this section is taken from Microsoft's GameStateManagementDemo, which can be found on the Creator's Club Web site (http://creators.xna.com/). To get started, we need to add the following private member fields to our `StartMenuState` class:

```
private SpriteFont font;
private GamePadState currentGamePadState;
private GamePadState previousGamePadState;
private int selected;

private string[] entries =
    {
        "Play",
        "Options",
        "High Scores",
        "Exit Game"
    };
```

We keep track of our game pad state so the selection between the menu items can be done effectively. The actual menu items are stored in an array.

In our `Update` method we can leave the condition that checks for the Escape key or the Back button alone. However, we need to replace the next condition that checks for starting the game with the following:

```
if (Input.KeyboardState.WasKeyPressed(Keys.Up) ||
    (currentGamePadState.DPad.Up == ButtonState.Pressed &&
     previousGamePadState.DPad.Up == ButtonState.Released) ||
    (currentGamePadState.ThumbSticks.Left.Y > 0 &&
     previousGamePadState.ThumbSticks.Left.Y <= 0))
{
    selected--;
}
if (Input.KeyboardState.WasKeyPressed(Keys.Down) ||
    (currentGamePadState.DPad.Down == ButtonState.Pressed &&
     previousGamePadState.DPad.Down == ButtonState.Released) ||
    (currentGamePadState.ThumbSticks.Left.Y < 0 &&
     previousGamePadState.ThumbSticks.Left.Y >= 0))
{
    selected++;
}

if (selected < 0)
    selected = entries.Length - 1;
if (selected == entries.Length)
    selected = 0;

if (Input.WasPressed(0, InputHandler.ButtonType.Start, Keys.Enter) ||
    (Input.WasPressed(0, InputHandler.ButtonType.A, Keys.Space)))
{
    switch (selected)
    {
        case 0: //Start Game
            {
                if (GameManager.ContainsState(OurGame.PlayingState.Value))
                    GameManager.PopState();
                else
                {
                    GameManager.ChangeState(OurGame.PlayingState.Value);
                    OurGame.PlayingState.StartGame();
                }
                break;
            }
        case 1: //Options Menu
            {
                GameManager.PushState(OurGame.OptionsMenuState.Value);
                break;
```

```
            }
        case 2: //High Scores
            {    ʼ
                break;
            }
        case 3: //Exit
            {
                GameManager.ChangeState(OurGame.TitleIntroState.Value);
                break;
            }
    }
}

previousGamePadState = currentGamePadState;
currentGamePadState = Input.GamePads[0];
```

The code checks to see if the player is pressing up or down and changes the selected index appropriately. The index is kept within the bounds of the array of menu items. Now, when the Enter key or the Start button is pressed the case statement checks to see which menu item is selected and changes the state accordingly. We have put in a place-holder for the high score screen but will be adding that screen in the next section. The final condition in the Update method can be removed, as it was bringing up the option menu before we had a way to select it from the menu.

The contents of the Draw method can be replaced with the following:

```
Vector2 pos = new Vector2((GraphicsDevice.Viewport.Width - texture.Width) / 2,
    (GraphicsDevice.Viewport.Height - texture.Height) / 2);
Vector2 position = new Vector2(pos.X + 140, pos.Y + texture.Height / 2);

OurGame.SpriteBatch.Begin();
OurGame.SpriteBatch.Draw(texture, pos, Color.White);

for (int i = 0; i < entries.Length; i++)
{
    Color color;
    float scale;

    if (i == selected)
    {
        // The selected entry is yellow, and has an animating size.
        double time = gameTime.TotalGameTime.TotalSeconds;

        float pulsate = (float)Math.Sin(time * 12) + 1;

        color = Color.White;
```

```
        scale = 1 + pulsate * 0.05f;
    }
    else
    {
        // Other entries are white.
        color = Color.Blue;
        scale = 1;
    }
    // Draw text, centered on the middle of each line.
    Vector2 origin = new Vector2(0, font.LineSpacing / 2);
    Vector2 shadowPosition = new Vector2(position.X - 2, position.Y - 2);

    //Draw Shadow
    OurGame.SpriteBatch.DrawString(font, entries[i],
        shadowPosition, Color.Black, 0, origin, scale, SpriteEffects.None, 0);
    //Draw Text
    OurGame.SpriteBatch.DrawString(font, entries[i],
        position, color, 0, origin, scale, SpriteEffects.None, 0);

    position.Y += font.LineSpacing;
}
OurGame.SpriteBatch.End();

base.Draw(gameTime);
```

The code calculates the center of the screen as well as the position to print the title on top of the texture. After beginning our sprite batch, we draw our screen texture. Next is the part of the code that used techniques from the GameStateManagementSample demo from Microsoft. The code loops through all of the menu items and when it finds the menu item that is selected, it sets its color to white and starts scaling the text in and out. The rest of the menu items are displayed in blue with no animation. The last section of the code in the for loop actually displays the menu items, spacing them vertically so they do not draw on top of each other.

The final piece is to update our LoadGraphicsContent method. We need to replace the entire contents of the method with the following code:

```
if (loadAllContent)
{
    texture = Content.Load<Texture2D>(@"Content\Textures\startMenu");
    font = Content.Load<SpriteFont>(@"Content\Fonts\menu");
}
base.LoadGraphicsContent(loadAllContent);
```

The startMenu.png texture has changed from the game state demo we created. The file can be found on the accompanying CD in this chapter's code folder. We also use a new font to display these menu items. We can create a new font file inside of the solution called menu.spritefont. We need to change the font name to Comic Sans MS and the size to 32. We can also set the demo flag at the top of our code to false so the demo message is not displayed.

Before we compile and run the code, we need to make a small modification to our TunnelVision game code. When we add the camera game component in the constructor we need to add the following statement to keep the camera from accepting input:

```
Camera.UpdateInput = false;
```

Turning off the input to our camera keeps the background from moving when we select our menu items. We can now compile and run the code and see our improved start menu screen. The start menu screen can be seen in Figure 22.2.

FIGURE 22.2   The TunnelVision start menu screen.

Creating the High Score Screen

In the last chapter, we saved and loaded high scores but we did not have a way to display them. In this section, we are going to create a high score screen that displays the high score list. This screen can be entered from the main start menu or after the game is over if the player had a high enough score to be entered into the high score list.

Because we are creating another game state, we need to add an IHighScoresState interface to our GameStateInterfaces.cs file:

```
public interface IHighScoresState : IGameState { }
```

Next, we can add a HighScoresState.cs file to our GameStates folder. We need to make sure the namespace is simply TunnelVision. The sealed class needs to inherit from BaseGameState and IHighScoresState. The following private member fields need to be added to the HighScoresState class:

```
private Texture2D texture;
private SpriteFont font;
private HighScoreData entries = new HighScoreData(5);
```

As with the rest of our game states, our constructor method needs to add itself to the game's services:

```
public HighScoresState(Game game)
    : base(game)
{
    game.Services.AddService(typeof(IHighScoresState), this);
}
```

The LoadGraphicsContent method will load a new texture that can be found in this chapter's code folder on the accompanying CD and the menu font we added in the previous section:

```
protected override void LoadGraphicsContent(bool loadAllContent)
{
    if (loadAllContent)
    {
        texture = Content.Load<Texture2D>(@"Content\Textures\highscores");
        font = Content.Load<SpriteFont>(@"Content\Fonts\menu");
    }

    base.LoadGraphicsContent(loadAllContent);
}
```

The highscores.png file, located on the accompanying CD, needs to be added to our projects. The UnloadGraphicsContent also needs to be added to the class:

```
protected override void UnloadGraphicsContent(bool unloadAllContent)
{
    if (unloadAllContent)
    {
        texture = null;
    }
    base.UnloadGraphicsContent(unloadAllContent);
}
```

We need to override the StateChanged method to actually load the high scores into our entries array:

```
protected override void StateChanged(object sender, EventArgs e)
{
    base.StateChanged(sender, e);

    if (GameManager.State == this.Value)
    {
        //Load high scores
        entries = Utility.LoadHighScores(OurGame.HighScoresFilename);
    }
}
```

Next, we can create our Update method, which simply exits the state when the appropriate input values are true:

```
public override void Update(GameTime gameTime)
{
    if (Input.WasPressed(0, InputHandler.ButtonType.Back, Keys.Escape) ||
        (Input.WasPressed(0, InputHandler.ButtonType.Start, Keys.Enter) ||
        (Input.WasPressed(0, InputHandler.ButtonType.A, Keys.Space))))
    {
        GameManager.PopState();
    }

    base.Update(gameTime);
}
```

The last section of code we need in this class is the Draw method:

```
public override void Draw(GameTime gameTime)
{
    Vector2 pos = new Vector2(
        (GraphicsDevice.Viewport.Width - texture.Width) / 2,
        (GraphicsDevice.Viewport.Height - texture.Height) / 2);

    Vector2 position =
        new Vector2(pos.X + 90, pos.Y + texture.Height / 2 - 50);

    OurGame.SpriteBatch.Begin();
    OurGame.SpriteBatch.Draw(texture, pos, Color.White);
    if (entries.PlayerName != null)
    {
        for (int i = 0; i < entries.Count; i++)
        {
            // Draw text, centered on the middle of each line.
            Vector2 origin = new Vector2(0, font.LineSpacing / 2);
            Vector2 scorePosition = new Vector2(position.X + 150, position.Y);
```

22

```
            Vector2 levelPosition =
                new Vector2(scorePosition.X + 150, scorePosition.Y);

            Vector2 shadowPosition =
                new Vector2(position.X - 1, position.Y - 1);
            Vector2 shadowScorePosition =
                new Vector2(scorePosition.X - 1, scorePosition.Y - 1);
            Vector2 shadowLevelPosition =
                new Vector2(levelPosition.X - 1, levelPosition.Y - 1);

            //Draw Name Shadow
            OurGame.SpriteBatch.DrawString(font, entries.PlayerName[i],
                shadowPosition, Color.Black, 0, origin, .5f,
                SpriteEffects.None, 0);
            //Draw Name
            OurGame.SpriteBatch.DrawString(font, entries.PlayerName[i],
                position, Color.Blue, 0, origin, 0.5f, SpriteEffects.None, 0);

            //Draw Score Shadow
            OurGame.SpriteBatch.DrawString(font, entries.Score[i].ToString(),
                shadowScorePosition, Color.Black, 0, origin, .5f,
                SpriteEffects.None, 0);
            //Draw Score
            OurGame.SpriteBatch.DrawString(font, entries.Score[i].ToString(),
                scorePosition, Color.Blue, 0, origin, 0.5f,
                SpriteEffects.None, 0);

            //Draw Level Shadow
            OurGame.SpriteBatch.DrawString(font, entries.Level[i].ToString(),
                shadowLevelPosition, Color.Black, 0, origin, .5f,
                SpriteEffects.None, 0);
            //Draw Level
            OurGame.SpriteBatch.DrawString(font, entries.Level[i].ToString(),
                levelPosition, Color.Blue, 0, origin, 0.5f,
                SpriteEffects.None, 0);

            position.Y += font.LineSpacing;
        }
    }
    OurGame.SpriteBatch.End();
    base.Draw(gameTime);
}
```

We calculate the position we need to place our high score texture in the center of the screen. Next we calculate position of the first high score we will be displaying on the screen. Then we display the texture and loop through all of the high scores, displaying them on the screen with exact spacing between the name, the score, and the level. We also increment the y position for each line having the text drawn down the screen.

Now that we have the high score state created, we can modify our `StartMenuState` code to execute this state when the player selects the high score list from the menu. Inside of the switch statement in the `Update` method under the high score case we can add the following statement:

```
GameManager.PushState(OurGame.HighScoresState.Value);
```

We also need to kick off the high score state at the end of the game if the player's score was added to the high score list. We need to add the following statement to the end of the fading state's `SaveHighScore` method:

```
GameManager.PushState(OurGame.HighScoresState.Value);
```

We have not actually added the `HighScoresState` to our game yet. We need to open up our `TunnelVision` game class and add the following public member field:

```
public IHighScoresState HighScoresState;
```

We also need to add the following statement to the constructor of our game:

```
HighScoresState = new HighScoresState(this);
```

Now, we can compile and run the code and see the high scores displayed in the appropriate places. The high score screen can be seen in Figure 22.3.

FIGURE 22.3   The TunnelVision high score screen.

Updating the Options Menu

The options menu is currently just a placeholder. We are going to add functionality that allows the player to turn the radar on or off as well as the crosshair. To begin, we need to add the following private member fields to our `OptionsMenuState` class:

```
private GamePadState currentGamePadState;
private GamePadState previousGamePadState;
private Texture2D select;
private Texture2D check;
private int selected;
```

For both options we have two check boxes that signify if the option is turned on or not. Instead of using the menu entry like we did for the start menu state, the options are embedded directly in the texture. We only need to display which option is selected and then display an X when an option is turned on.

The `Update` method can be replaced with the following code:

```
public override void Update(GameTime gameTime)
{
    if (Input.WasPressed(0, InputHandler.ButtonType.Back, Keys.Escape))
        GameManager.PopState();

    if (Input.KeyboardState.WasKeyPressed(Keys.Up) ¦¦
        (currentGamePadState.DPad.Up == ButtonState.Pressed &&
         previousGamePadState.DPad.Up == ButtonState.Released) ¦¦
        (currentGamePadState.ThumbSticks.Left.Y > 0 &&
         previousGamePadState.ThumbSticks.Left.Y <= 0))
    {
        selected--;
    }
    if (Input.KeyboardState.WasKeyPressed(Keys.Down) ¦¦
        (currentGamePadState.DPad.Down == ButtonState.Pressed &&
         previousGamePadState.DPad.Down == ButtonState.Released) ¦¦
        (currentGamePadState.ThumbSticks.Left.Y < 0 &&
         previousGamePadState.ThumbSticks.Left.Y >= 0))
    {
        selected++;
    }
    if (selected < 0)
        selected = 1;
    if (selected == 2)
        selected = 0;

    if ((Input.WasPressed(0, InputHandler.ButtonType.Start, Keys.Enter)) ¦¦
        (Input.WasPressed(0, InputHandler.ButtonType.A, Keys.Space)))
    {
```

```
    switch (selected)
    {
        case 0: //Display Crosshairs
            {
                OurGame.DisplayCrosshair = !OurGame.DisplayCrosshair;
                break;
            }
        case 1: //Display Radar
            {
                OurGame.DisplayRadar = !OurGame.DisplayRadar;
                break;
            }
    }
}

    previousGamePadState = currentGamePadState;
    currentGamePadState = Input.GamePads[0];

    base.Update(gameTime);
}
```

The code simply allows the player to move up and down the options menu and it stores the selected index. If the player presses the Start or A button or presses the Enter key or spacebar, then the option that is selected is toggled.

In the Draw method we can replace the first statement that calculates the position of the options menu texture with the following code:

```
Vector2 pos = new Vector2((GraphicsDevice.Viewport.Width - texture.Width) / 2,
    (GraphicsDevice.Viewport.Height - texture.Height) / 2);
Vector2 crosshairCheckPos = new Vector2(pos.X + 142, pos.Y + 44);
Vector2 radarCheckPos = new Vector2(pos.X + 142, pos.Y + 136);
Vector2 crosshairSelectPos = new Vector2(pos.X + 145, pos.Y + 81);
Vector2 radarSelectPos = new Vector2(pos.X + 145, pos.Y + 173);
```

The previous code also sets the position of the option texture to be centered on the screen. The code also calculates the position of the selected texture and the checked texture for both options.

The rest of the Draw code, which simply draws the option menu texture, can remain. However, we do need to add the following code before we call the End method on the sprite batch:

```
if (OurGame.DisplayCrosshair)
    OurGame.SpriteBatch.Draw(check, crosshairCheckPos, Color.White);

if (OurGame.DisplayRadar)
    OurGame.SpriteBatch.Draw(check, radarCheckPos, Color.White);
```

22

```
switch (selected)
{
    case 0: //Display Crosshairs
        {
            OurGame.SpriteBatch.Draw(select, crosshairSelectPos, Color.White);
            break;
        }
    case 1: //Display Radar
        {
            OurGame.SpriteBatch.Draw(select, radarSelectPos, Color.White);
            break;
        }
}
```

The code determines if the check should be displayed for either option. It then draws the selected texture for whichever option is currently selected. The last piece of code we need to add to our OptionsMenuState is actually loading the select and check textures inside of our LoadGraphicsContent method:

```
check = Content.Load<Texture2D>(@"Content\Textures\x");
select = Content.Load<Texture2D>(@"Content\Textures\select");
```

The x.png, select.png, and the new optionsMenu.png files can be found on the accompanying CD under this chapter's code folder. Compiling and running the code allows us to turn on and off the radar and crosshair. The options menu can be seen in Figure 22.4.

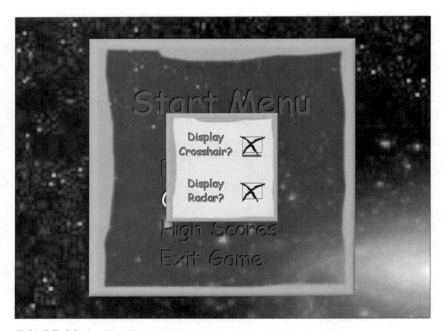

FIGURE 22.4   The TunnelVision options menu screen.

Updating the Remaining States

We need to tweak some of the game states a little more to make the game a little nicer. We will be modifying the won and lost game states . We can remove the `LoadingGraphicsContent` and the `UnloadGraphicsContent` methods from the `WonGameState`, `LostGameState`, `YesNoDialogState`, and `PausedState` classes. We can also remove the font member field from all four classes. We need to add the following code to our won game state's `Draw` method:

```
Vector2 viewport = new Vector2(GraphicsDevice.Viewport.Width,
    GraphicsDevice.Viewport.Height);
Vector2 fontLength = OurGame.Font.MeasureString("You Won!!!");
Vector2 pos = (viewport - fontLength * 3) / 2;
```

We are calculating the position to center the text on the screen. Similarly, we need to add the following code to the lost game state's `Draw` method:

```
Vector2 viewport = new Vector2(GraphicsDevice.Viewport.Width,
    GraphicsDevice.Viewport.Height);
Vector2 fontLength = OurGame.Font.MeasureString("You Lost!");
Vector2 pos = (viewport - fontLength * 3) / 2;
```

We need to do the same task for the `PausedState`:

```
Vector2 viewport = new Vector2(GraphicsDevice.Viewport.Width,
    GraphicsDevice.Viewport.Height);
Vector2 fontLength = OurGame.Font.MeasureString("PAUSED");
Vector2 pos = (viewport - fontLength) / 2;
```

We need do the exact same task for the `YesNoDialogState`:

```
Vector2 viewport = new Vector2(GraphicsDevice.Viewport.Width,
    GraphicsDevice.Viewport.Height);
Vector2 fontLength = OurGame.Font.MeasureString("PAUSED");
Vector2 pos = (viewport - fontLength) / 2;
```

On all four states we need to replace the old private font the `Draw` method was using with the `OurGame.Font`. We also need to use the pos vector to position the text.

Using the Particle System

In this section we are going to add some particles when an enemy ship is destroyed. We need to copy the Colorful.cs particle system file from Chapter 19, "Particle System." We need to add the private member field that holds a reference to our particle system inside of our `PlayingState`:

```
private Colorful colorful;
```

We can also remove the color field that was left over from the previous game state demo. We need to add the particle system to our game components by adding the following to the constructor:

```
colorful = new Colorful(Game);
Game.Components.Add(colorful);
```

Inside of the Draw method we need to set the particle system's View and Projection properties:

```
colorful.View = OurGame.Camera.View;
colorful.Projection = OurGame.Camera.Projection;
```

Finally, when a collision occurs, we need to set the position of the particle system and call its ResetSystem method. The following code needs to be added to the missileManager.CheckCollision condition inside of the CheckCollisions method:

```
colorful.SetPosition(enemyManager.Enemies[ei].Position);
colorful.ResetSystem();
```

We need to add the bubble.png texture that the Colorful particle system uses to our projects. The texture can be found in this chapter's code folder on the accompanying CD. The colorful particle system needs to be modified slightly to work well in the game. We can replace the last constructor and the InitializeSettings method of the Colorful particle system with the following code:

```
public Colorful(Game game) : this(game, 250) { }

protected override ParticleSystemSettings InitializeSettings()
{
    settings.EmitPerSecond = 250;

    settings.EmitPosition = new Vector3(0, 0, -1000);
    settings.EmitRange = new Vector3(2, 2, 2);
    settings.EmitRadius = new Vector2(3, 3);

    settings.MinimumVelocity = new Vector3(-1, -1, -1);
    settings.MaximumVelocity = new Vector3(1, 20, 1);

    settings.MinimumAcceleration = new Vector3(-5, -10, -5);
    settings.MaximumAcceleration = new Vector3(5, 10, 5);

    settings.MinimumLifetime = 0.2f;
    settings.MaximumLifetime = 0.2f;

    settings.MinimumSize = 3.0f;
    settings.MaximumSize = 3.0f;
```

```
settings.Colors = new Color[] {
    Color.White,
    Color.Yellow,
    Color.Orange,
    Color.Red,
    Color.Black};

settings.DisplayColorsInOrder = true;

settings.RunOnce = true;

return (settings);
}
```

After making those changes we can run our game and see the particle effect when an enemy is destroyed.

Adding Sound

The last piece of the puzzle we need to put into place before completing the game is to add some sound effects and music. The wave files we need to add to our TunnelVision.xap project can be found on the accompanying CD in this chapter's code folder. We need to add the following wave files to the XACT project:

Robotic 4321

Doh

Death

Explosion

TunnelVisionMusic

TunnelVisionMenu

TunnelVisionTheme

If a refresher is needed on working with XACT, take time to look over Chapter 7, "Sounds and Music." After adding the wave files to the wave bank, a sound bank needs to be created. The three music files—TunnelVisionMusic, TunnelVisionMenu, and TunnelVisionTheme—need to be dragged over to the music category. Robotic 4321, Explosion, TunnelVisionMusic, TunnelVisionMenu, and TunnelVisionTheme can all be dragged into the cue pane as is. In the sound pane, we need to make a copy of Explosion for our gunshot. We can call this copy Explosion 2. We need to add a pitch event to this new explosion and set the equation type to constant and the value to 50. We did this in Chapter 7 as well. This is the sound we will play when we fire our missile. The regular explosion is what we will play when an enemy ship is destroyed. We also need to turn down the volume of the Explosion 2 sound. A good value is -16.36. After Explosion 2 is completely set up, we can drag it down to our cue pane and rename the cue to gunshot.

In the Death sound we need to add an additional track and add a play event to that track. We then need to play the Doh wave inside of the additional track's play event. We need to offset when it starts by changing the play event's TimeStamp to 1.25. This will make it wait 1.25 seconds before playing the second track. Finally, we can drag the Death sound to the cue folder and leave the cue name as Death. The detail of setting up the project was covered, but it was very lightweight. For reference, open the XACT project in this chapter's code folder on the accompanying CD.

We need to save the XACT project with the name TunnelVision, then we need to add the XACT project to our game projects. We also need to make sure the wave files are in the same Sounds folder, but they do not need to be included in the project. In our TunnelVision game code we need to add a reference to our sound manager:

```
public SoundManager Sound;
```

Inside of the constructor of our `TunnelVision` game class we need to initialize our sound manager:

```
Sound = new SoundManager(this, "TunnelVision");
```

Then, inside of our `Initialize` method, we can create and start playing the playlist:

```
string[] playList =
    { "TunnelVisionMenu", "TunnelVisionMusic", "TunnelVisionTheme" };
Sound.StartPlayList(playList);
```

Finally, we need to make sure we call the sound manager's `Update` method inside of our `Update` method:

```
Sound.Update(gameTime);
```

Inside of our `PlayingState` class is where we will store most of our sound effects. Inside of the `Update` method, where we add a missile, we have a placeholder. We need to add this line of code there:

```
OurGame.Sound.Play("gunshot");
```

When a collision occurs, we need to play the explosion sound. The following statement needs to be added to the `missileManager.CheckCollision` condition inside of the `CheckCollisions` method:

```
OurGame.Sound.Play("explosion");
```

The next file we need to modify is our lost game state file. When we enter this state we need to play the death sound because the gamer has lost the game. We need to add the following statement at the end of the condition inside of the StateChanged method:

```
OurGame.Sound.Play("Death");
```

Now when the state is changed to the LostGameState, the death sound will be played. The last file we need to modify is the start level state file. When the level loads we are going to play the Robotic 4321 countdown file. Inside of the StateChanged method at the very beginning of the startingLevel condition we can add the following statement:

```
OurGame.Sound.Play("Robotic4321");
```

We have finished adding all of the sound effects and music to our game. We can compile and run our finished game. Have fun playing!

Suggested Improvements

We have completed a lot in these last three chapters. We have created a full game that we can play and share with others. However, some improvements could be made to make this game much better. To start with, better artwork would really add to the game. A more consistent look and feel throughout the game would also be beneficial. The fire on the title screen is cool, but does not really fit with the whole space theme. The options menu could be modified to have a submenu for sound. On that menu, there could be two slider bars: One would specify the level of the sound and the other would specify the level of music. There could be two more check boxes that would turn off one or the other. Because the music is in its own category and the sound effects are all in its default category, this can be done easily.

Another way to improve the game is to have a transition between levels. It would be beneficial to improve the radar by creating a texture that actually looks like a radar screen, with circles surrounding the center. In fact, the texture could have an alpha channel to only appear circular on the screen instead of the green square it is now. With very little effort, a postprocessing effect could be applied to the radar texture that could make it appear to fade in or out or even add static to it.

We currently only allow one particle system at a time and when more than one enemy explodes the particle system is abruptly ended and started again with the newly destroyed enemy. It might be beneficial to allow multiple particle systems. There was no provision to keep the enemies from jumbling up on each other. Another improvement would be to add AI logic that would keep them from occupying the same space.

A modification that could be made to the game is to remove the tunnel and the corresponding camera restriction. The player could move around freely in space and the radar could rotate with the user. In fact, that could be another option. Gamers could decide if they wanted to radar to be static or to rotate with them. There are many more modifications that could make this game better. Have fun with it, or better yet, create your very own masterpiece!

Summary

In this chapter we added a full-function menu system. We added some detail to our title screen. We saw how to use sprite fonts in our menu system as well as using a premade texture in our option menu. We cleaned up the rest of the game states to fit better in our game framework and created a particle system. We created a sound project to bring our game to life. We also created a high score screen to display our high scores. Finally, we listed some improvements that could make the game even better.

Index

Numbers

M

How can we make this index more useful? Email us at indexes@samspublishing.com

W

X-Y-Z

THIS BOOK IS SAFARI ENABLED

INCLUDES FREE 45-DAY ACCESS TO THE ONLINE EDITION

The Safari® Enabled icon on the cover of your favorite technology book means the book is available through Safari Bookshelf. When you buy this book, you get free access to the online edition for 45 days.

Safari Bookshelf is an electronic reference library that lets you easily search thousands of technical books, find code samples, download chapters, and access technical information whenever and wherever you need it.

TO GAIN 45-DAY SAFARI ENABLED ACCESS TO THIS BOOK:

- Go to **http://www.samspublishing.com/safarienabled**
- Complete the brief registration form
- Enter the coupon code found in the front of this book on the "Copyright" page

If you have difficulty registering on Safari Bookshelf or accessing the online edition, please e-mail customer-service@safaribooksonline.com.

UNLEASHED

Unleashed takes you beyond the basics, providing an exhaustive, technically sophisticated reference for professionals who need to exploit a technology to its fullest potential. It's the best resource for practical advice from the experts, and the most in-depth coverage of the latest technologies.

Microsoft Visual C# 2005 Unleashed
ISBN: 0672327767

OTHER UNLEASHED TITLES

Microsoft BizTalk Server 2006 Unleashed
ISBN: 0672329255

Microsoft Exchange Server 2007 Unleashed
ISBN: 0672329204

Microsoft Expression Blend Unleashed
ISBN: 067232931X

Microsoft ISA Server 2006 Unleashed
ISBN: 0672329190

Microsoft Office Project Server 2007 Unleashed
ISBN: 0672329212

Microsoft Operations Manager 2005 Unleashed
ISBN: 067232928X

Microsoft Small Business Server 2003 Unleashed
ISBN: 0672328054

Microsoft Visual Studio 2005 Unleashed
ISBN: 0672328194

VBScript, WMI and ADSI Unleashed
ISBN: 0321501713

Windows Communication Foundation Unleashed
ISBN: 0672329484

Microsoft SharePoint 2007 Development Unleashed
ISBN: 0672329034

Windows PowerShell Unleashed
ISBN 0672329530

Microsoft SharePoint 2007 Unleashed
ISBN: 0672329476

Windows Presentation Foundation Unleashed
ISBN: 0672328917

ASP.NET 2.0 Unleashed
ISBN: 0672328232

SAMS